W9-BPP-727

The Drawing Handbook

Comprehensive, Easy-to-Master Lessons on Composition and Techniques Using Pencil and Pen & Ink

FRANK J. LOHAN

CB

CONTEMPORARY BOOKS
CHICAGO

Library of Congress Cataloging-in-Publication

Lohan, Frank.
The drawing handbook: comprehensive, easy-to-master lessons on composition and techniques using pencil and pen & ink / Frank J. Lohan.
p. cm.
Includes bibliographical references and index.
ISBN 0-8092-3786-5
1. Pencil drawing—Technique. 2. Pen drawing—Technique.
I. Title.
NC890.L598 1993
741.2′4—dc20 93-28380
CIP

Published by Contemporary Books, Inc.
Two Prudential Plaza, Chicago, Illinois 60601-6790
Manufactured in the United States of America
International Standard Book Number: 0-8092-3786-5
10 9 8 7 6 5 4 3 2

To Katie . . . a real charmer

Contents

PART 2. DRAWING EXERCISES

Introduction

Drawings are simply two-dimensional arrangements of lines and tones, flat surfaces containing marks and toned areas that represent the essence of what you are trying to "say" to the viewer. When you produce a drawing or a painting, you create a *composition* to help convey your impression to others. It does not matter whether your approach is realistic, stylized, or nonrepresentational. The key to all good drawing is a pleasing disposition of lines and tones in your picture area; that is, the key is good composition. Only after your composition is resolved do you consider accuracy of rendition and drawing technique.

This book provides some insight into the basics of composition, shows you some ways to see the geometry of objects, and introduces you to the tools of drawing and shows you how to use them. Then it provides you with practice exercises you can use to try different drawing techniques to create form and dimension with many kinds of subject matter. With proper application of these basics, your work will be better, both in the placement of your picture elements (composition) and in the technical execution of their form and texture.

The camera is considered to be quite "literal," showing in a picture just what is actually there. Sometimes, however, it does this with severe distortions. On the other hand, you as an artist can depict the essence of your subject by careful selection and considered arrangement of what you see. These are options not completely available to a photographer. In this sense, *arranging* does not mean changing what is there as much as it does *emphasizing* the significant and subordinating the trivial. This is accomplished sometimes through subtle treatment of perspective, interesting division of space, innovative tonal arrangements, and variety of contour. Only after these compositional problems are resolved do you consider the more mechanical factors, such as techniques, which you use to develop the forms by showing the tones and textures of the subject and its setting.

When you see an artist pick up a pen, pencil, or brush and get right to work with little or no apparent forethought, you can be certain he or she has already considered all the compositional and geometric alternatives. To a working artist, this is accomplished almost unconsciously. Only the less-experienced or beginning artist must make these considerations in a more obvious and deliberate manner each time . . . until doing so becomes second nature.

This handbook contains two parts. Part 1 introduces you to many of the basics of good composition and shows you how some of the old masters applied these basics in their well-known works. You will learn about the tools of drawing—pens, pencils, paper, and erasers—and the fundamentals of drawing—enlarging and reducing composition drawings, the basics of perspective, and other drawing hints. Then the matter of perceiving the geometry of things—the foundation of realistic drawing—is considered. Finally, the techniques for creating form and texture with the pen and with the pencil are discussed and illustrated.

Part 2 provides you with more specific hints on seeing the geometry of different natural things and with the techniques of drawing them with the pencil and with the pen. Step-by-step suggestions are provided for drawing subjects, ranging from landscapes, architecture, and artifacts to the human form, animals, birds, and flowers. I will show you some of the approaches I have learned in forty years of sketching and twenty years of teaching sketching techniques. The drawing exercises present approaches that will help you create more interesting drawings by using variety in your rendition of texture.

Gridded outline compositions are provided with each exercise in Part 2 to help those of you who are just beginning to develop your drawing ability. You may use my gridded compositions (following the instructions in Chapter 3) to assist you in making your own working drawing for each exercise. I believe that this kind of practice allows you to rapidly do more actual drawing. This way you gain more confidence than if you have to first consider the selection of subject matter and then struggle with getting a reasonable composition on paper, all before you can start using the drawing instruments to create form and texture. By copying my drawings for practice, you can quickly gain some dexterity with the pen and with the pencil. You can also begin to stock your mental toolbox with the techniques you will use later in the creation of your own original works.

Technique is the flesh of art, composition is its bones, and vitality is its marrow. This book will help you develop your approach to the flesh and bones. Only *you* can provide the marrow for your art as you continue your development through frequent practice with subjects of your own choosing.

PART 1
BASICS

Composition
Basic Drawing Tools and Materials
Some Fundamentals
Seeing the Geometry of Things
Drawing Techniques

This part of the handbook shows you some of the principle considerations of good composition; introduces you to the tools of drawing; shows you how to copy, reduce, enlarge, and transfer a composition to your final paper; gives you some simplified perspective hints and other things to consider when completing a drawing; explains how you can turn your works into notepaper easily and inexpensively; shows you how to see the geometric basis for natural forms (an essential capability if you want to do realistic drawings on your own); and illustrates some of the techniques of drawing with both the pen and with the pencil. Part 1 ends with two exercises that will give you practice in creating form and texture with the pen and with the pencil. You should try these exercises before you go on to Part 2, which covers actual drawing exercises.

1
Composition

About Composition
Unity and Variety in Composition
Drawing Orientation
Dividing the Drawing Space
Triangular Division
The Golden Section Division
Examples from Master Artists
Balance
Eye Movement and S Curves

About Composition

There is no single formula for creating well-composed drawings, just as there is no one technique for drawing realistic-looking trees, rocks, or other landscape elements. Awareness of the principles that are covered in this chapter, however, will make you more sensitive to the ways the space on your sheet or canvas can be divided. The application of some of the methods discussed will contribute to *better* composition in your work. Technique improvement will continue to come as you draw more and more.

Among other things, composition concerns the divisions of space on your pad or canvas and where in these divisions you place your key forms, your center of interest, and the more significant compositional elements. Placement is not everything, however; the tonal relationship among these elements is of equal importance and is part of what makes a composition "work."

Any subject matter contains essential, subordinate (less important), and irrelevant features. As an artist you must be concerned with the way placement and tone are used to emphasize the essential and subordinate elements in your rendition of the subject. Irrelevant elements should be eliminated so as not to distract the viewer from the true message of your rendering. Your artistic judgment is called upon when you're deciding whether an element is relevant to your message. For instance, do you keep or eliminate the television antenna on a farmhouse in a landscape? The answer depends on what you are trying to say. Of course, if your message is about the spoiling by careless persons of the rustic beauty of the land, then you include the television antennas, burger wrappers, used tires, and pop cans. If your message is about the *beauty* of the scene, then you eliminate those elements. With regard to your picture, you are God! You represent your little universe as you want it to be.

Unity and Variety in Composition

In order to please most critical eyes, a picture (drawing or painting) should have both unity and variety. If a picture is without unity, the viewer gets the impression of a disorganized muddle. If a picture is without variety, the viewer can quickly become bored as his or her eyes scan the picture.

If it has unity, a work's elements all just seem to "hang together," related, yet with appropriate significance or subordination of particular elements. Unity is achieved by proper choice of tone, subtle use of line (edges of forms), and overlap of picture elements, among other devices.

Variety is necessary to minimize boredom as the work is being viewed. A pleasing distribution of shapes on the canvas is essential to variety.

Drawing Orientation

Your paper or canvas may be *oriented*, or positioned, in many different ways. If it is square, it may be oriented upright, or it may be placed in a diamond orientation with opposite corners at the top and the bottom. It may be round or oval; if it is oval, it may be oriented with the long axis vertical or horizontal. Most drawings and paintings are rectangular or square. A vertically oriented rectangle is called a *portrait* orientation, and a horizontal rectangle is called a *landscape* orientation (see figure 1-1). Obviously, portrait orientation is not limited to portraits, nor is landscape orientation only for use with landscapes. These are simply names to differentiate between the two orientations of the paper or canvas.

There are some standard sizes used for paper, canvases, and frames, although any size or proportion can be used. (The use of a nonstandard size, however, generally means making or buying a custom-size frame.) The relative proportions of some of the smaller standard sizes are shown in figure 1-2: 3″ × 5″, 5″ × 7″, 8″ × 10″, 9″ × 12″, 11″ × 14″.

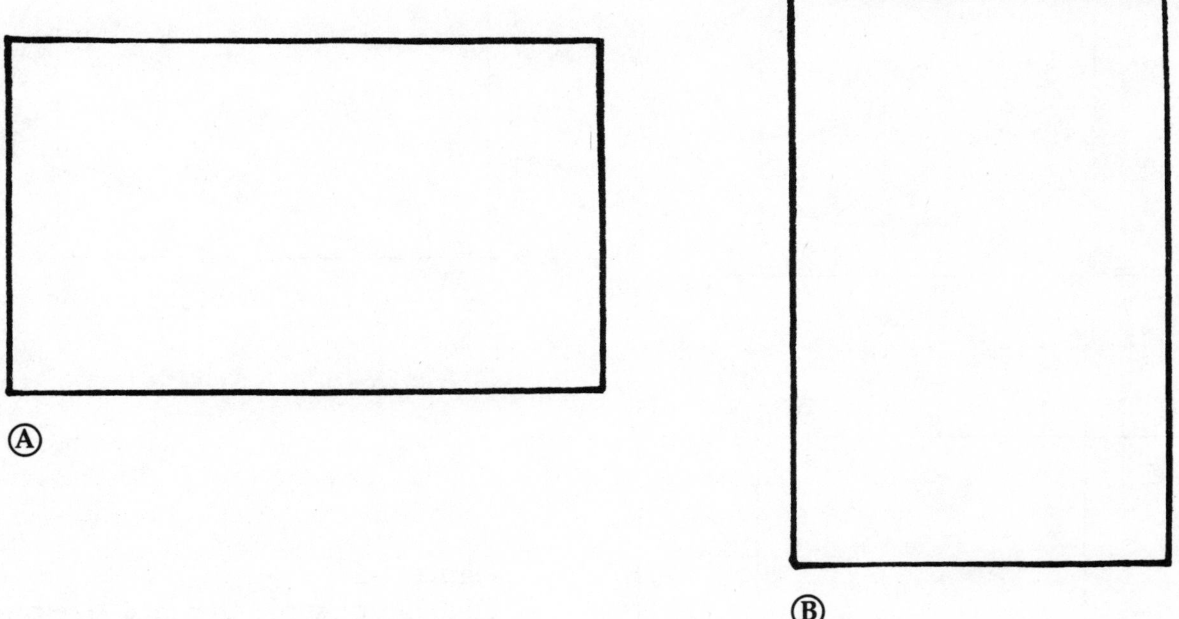
Ⓐ
Ⓑ

Figure 1-1
A Landscape orientation.
B Portrait orientation.

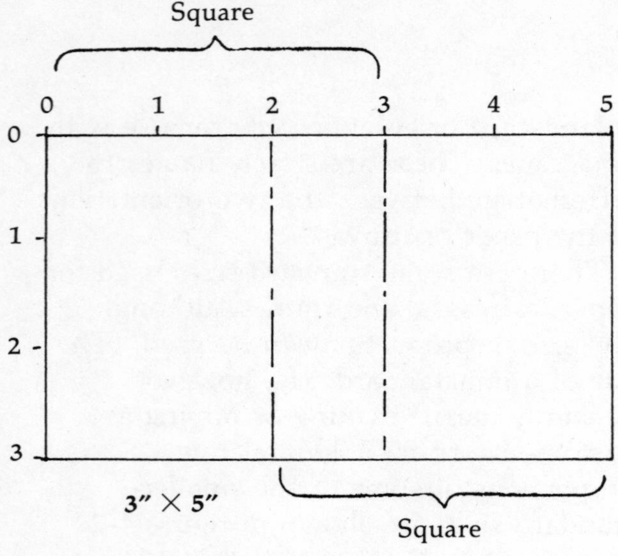
Square
0
1
2
3
4
5
0
1
2
3
Square
3″ × 5″

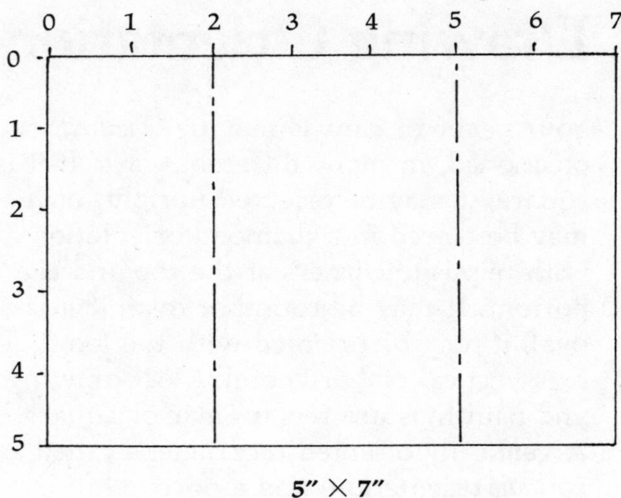
0
1
2
3
4
5
6
7
0
1
2
3
4
5
5″ × 7″

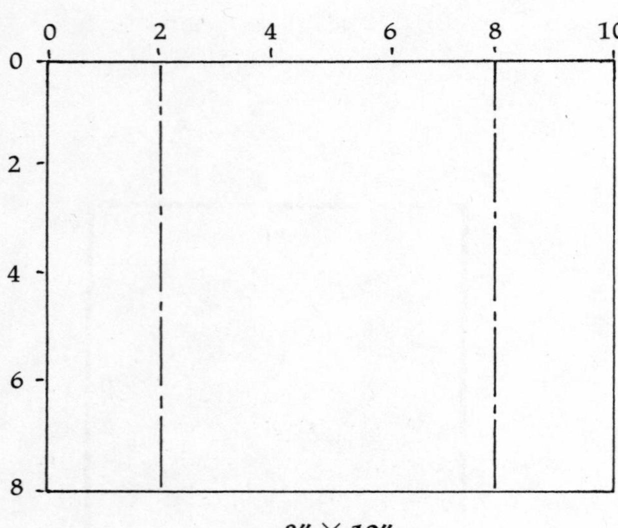
0
2
4
6
8
10
0
2
4
6
8
8″ × 10″

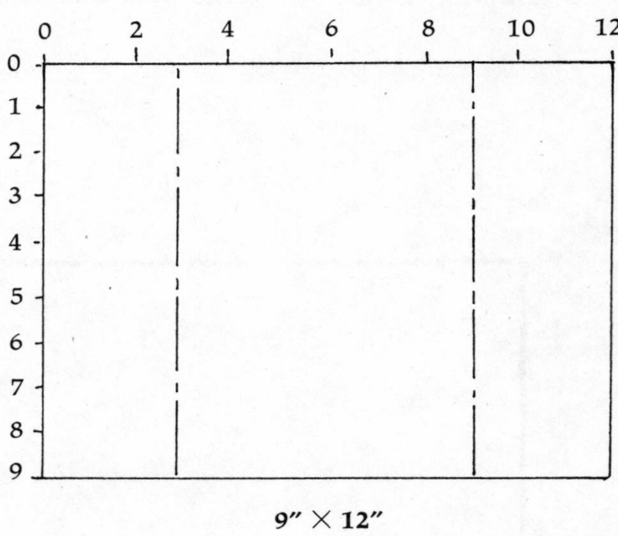
0
2
4
6
8
10
12
0
1
2
3
4
5
6
7
8
9
9″ × 12″

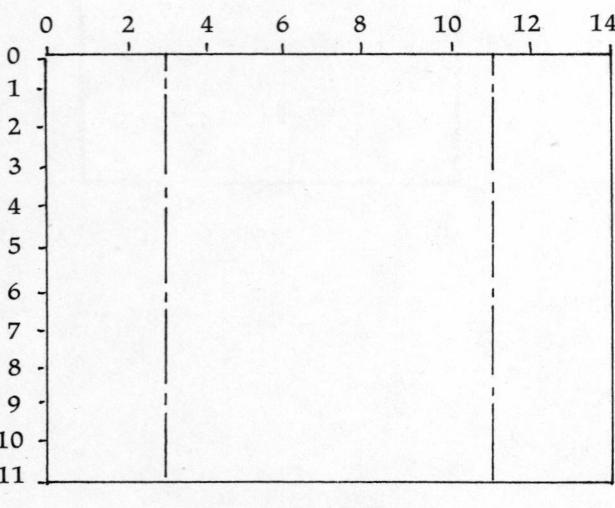
0
2
4
6
8
10
12
14
0
1
2
3
4
5
6
7
8
9
10
11
11″ × 14″

Figure 1-2
Division of some standard-size canvases into two overlapping squares, one from each short end.

Dividing the Drawing Space

There are many mechanisms you can use to divide your picture area. The primary goal is to get variety into the arrangement of the space and thereby create interest for the viewer. Any mechanism or scheme that does this for you is valid. There is no one way that is "proper." In fact, there are several ways to pleasingly divide the drawing space and determine key locations for important elements in your composition.

Also shown in figure 1-2 is one of the possible ways to divide the surface of a rectangular space—by the use of a square. Although these illustrations show landscape orientations, the same ideas apply to the portrait orientation. The square that starts the space division can be based on either of the two shorter sides of the paper. Use of either the left-hand square or the right-hand one gives an unequal division of the picture space, and unequal areas in your picture enhance interest. For example, if your landscape contains a prominent tree or other key figure, a good placement for it (although by no means the *only* good placement for it) is somewhere on the vertical line formed by one of the squares. This would put the figure off center, which is generally a good idea. The use of the squares is just one of several ways of locating appropriate off-center places, key locations for key elements in your composition.

Triangular Division

The off-center placement of the key element of a picture was not always considered the only proper placement. In the thirteenth and fourteenth centuries, it was frequently considered appropriate to place the central figure in a key location along the vertical centerline of the canvas. Often the central figure was placed more toward the top of the canvas with less important figures below in a triangular arrangement, sometimes in conjunction with a circle, square, or both (see figures 1-3 and 1-4). The triangular key location is often used today in advertising layouts since its strong emphasis on the central object gives it a powerful impact. The use of a single triangle as a compositional basis tends to create a quite formal division of the space, and is very successfully demonstrated by a Renoir painting from the late nineteenth century (figure 1-5).

Figure 1-3
A triangular composition within a rectangle. (Titian, *Madonna and Child*, National Gallery, London)

Figure 1-4
A triangular composition within a circle within a square. (Raphael, *The Alba Madonna*, National Gallery, Washington, D.C.)

Figure 1-5
A triangular composition within a rectangle. The key figure is located above the geometric center of the picture area. (Renoir, *Mme Charpentier and Children*, Metropolitan Museum of Art, New York)

The Golden Section Division

A *golden section* is a ratio in which the smaller amount to the larger is the same as that of the larger to the sum of both. The use of some algebra to solve this as a quadratic equation shows that if the smaller amount is five units, the larger will be very close to eight units; the total, therefore, will be thirteen units.[1]

Any line, such as one of the edges of a canvas, can be divided into short and long segments using the golden section so that the short one is five-thirteenths of the total length of the line and the longer one is eight-thirteenths of the total length. The short segment is said to have a length of five units; the longer, eight units. (It is important to remember that a *unit* is not an actual, fixed measurement as is, say, an inch or a meter. It's simply a mathematical indication—a tool used to calculate the proportions of the golden section.)

One of the properties of the golden section proportion that attracted the attention of artists centuries ago was that it provided the ability to continually divide the edges of a golden section rectangle (a rectangle having the proportions of eight units in length and five units in width) by the same five-to-eight proportion, creating an unlimited number of key locations within the canvas, with no two space divisions the same. This is demonstrated in figure 1-6.

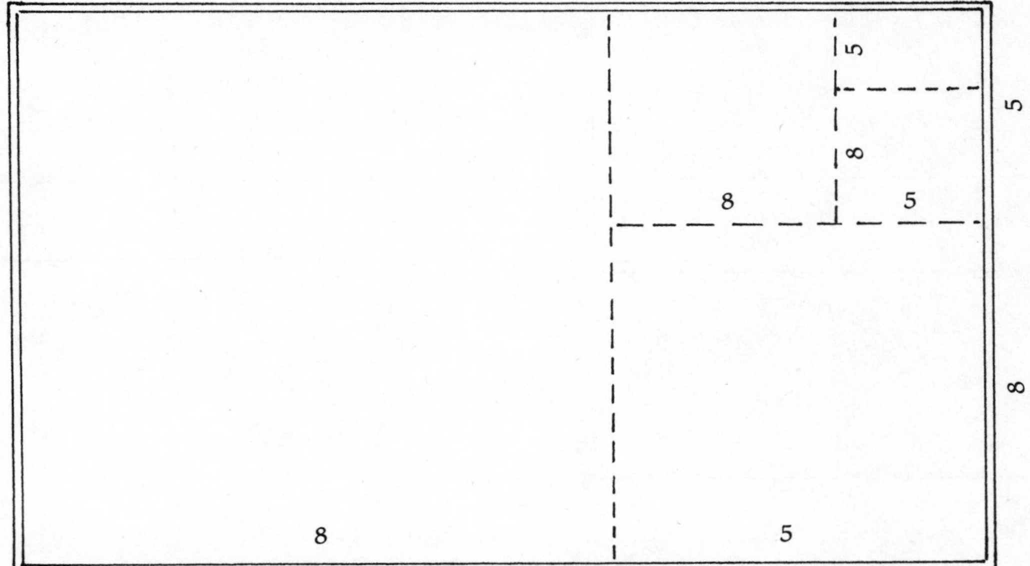
5
8
8
5
5
8
8
5

1. If the shorter side is 5 units, and the longer is x units, the ratio of the shorter side to the longer is $5/x$. This must equal the ratio of the longer side, x, to the total, $5 + x$, or $x/(5 + x)$. The equation then becomes $5 / x = x/(5 + x)$. Simplifying gives $25 + 5x = x^2$. When solved for x, the longer side has a value of 8.1. The 5-to-8 relationship is easy to remember and apply, regardless of the actual length of any line.

Figure 1-6
Successive division of the space of a golden section rectangle into golden sections. First the bottom edge is divided. Then, of the smaller of the resulting rectangles, the longer side is divided by the golden section, and so on. This gives an array of nonduplicating key locations and areas on the canvas.

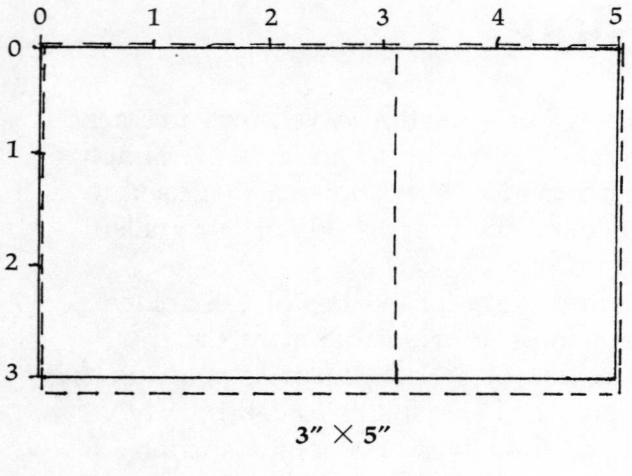
0
1
2
3
4
5
0
1
2
3
3″ × 5″

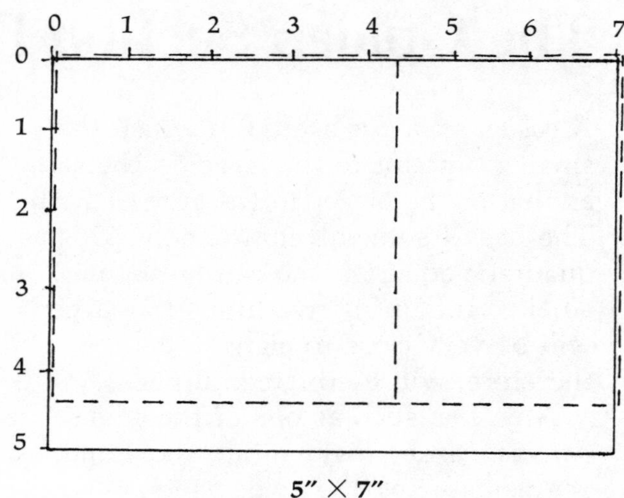
0
1
2
3
4
5
6
7
0
1
2
3
4
5
5″ × 7″

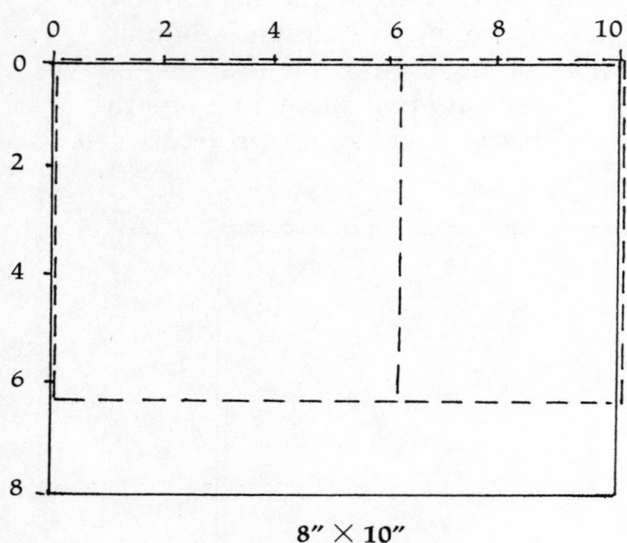
0
2
4
6
8
10
0
2
4
6
8
8″ × 10″

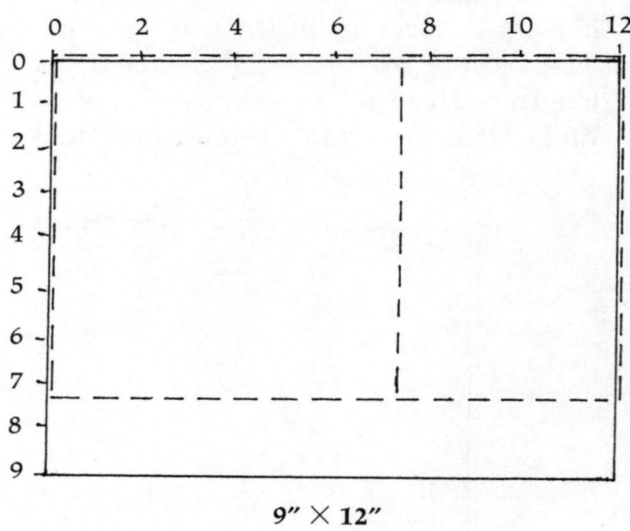
0
2
4
6
8
10
12
0
1
2
3
4
5
6
7
8
9
9″ × 12″

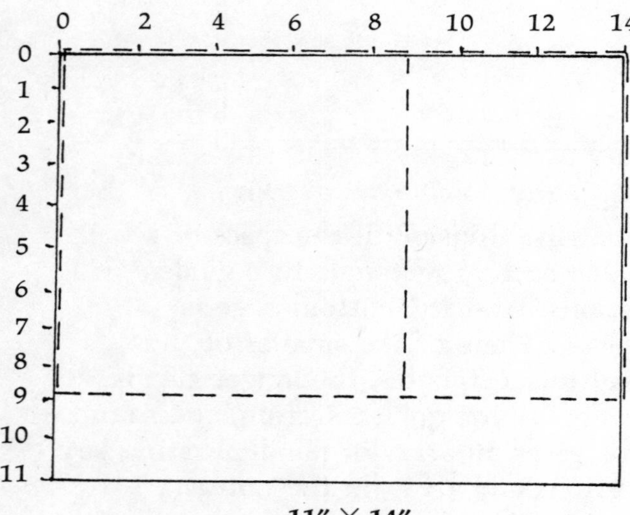
0
2
4
6
8
10
12
14
0
1
2
3
4
5
6
7
8
9
10
11
11″ × 14″

Figure 1-7
Standard canvases and frame sizes (solid lines) compared to the five-to-eight golden section rectangle proportions (broken lines). The horizontal edge of each golden section rectangle is divided by the golden section as shown by the vertical broken line.

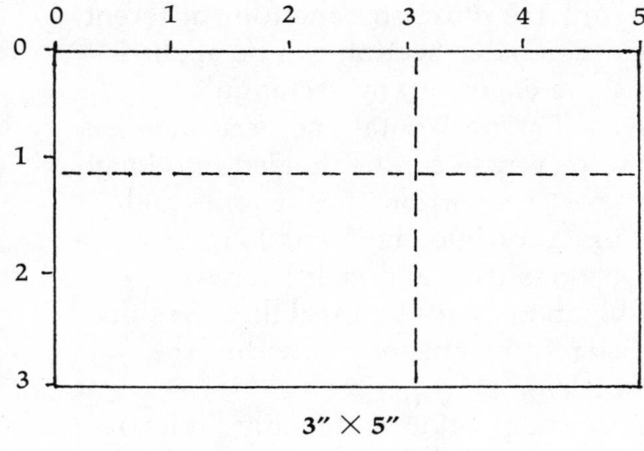
0
1
2
3
4
5
0
1
2
3
3″ × 5″

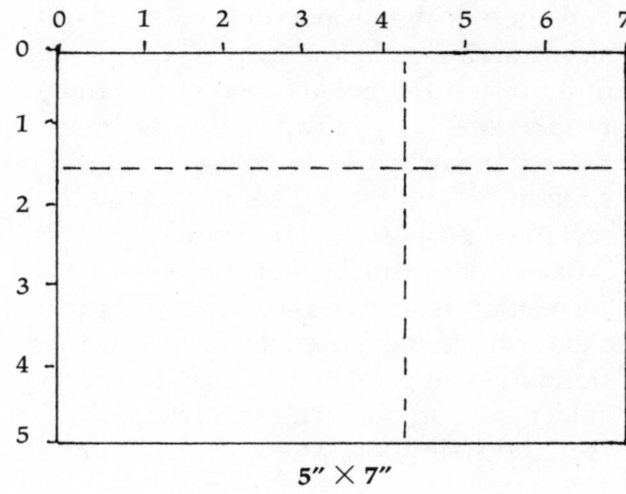
0
1
2
3
4
5
6
7
0
1
2
3
4
5
5″ × 7″

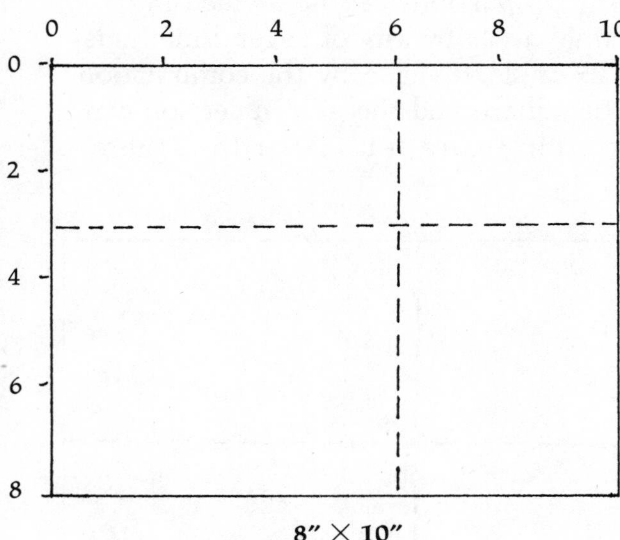
0
2
4
6
8
10
0
2
4
6
8
8″ × 10″

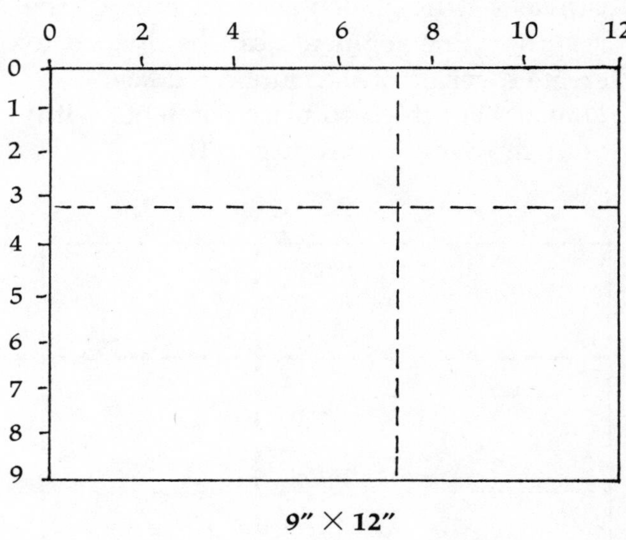
0
2
4
6
8
10
12
0
1
2
3
4
5
6
7
8
9
9″ × 12″

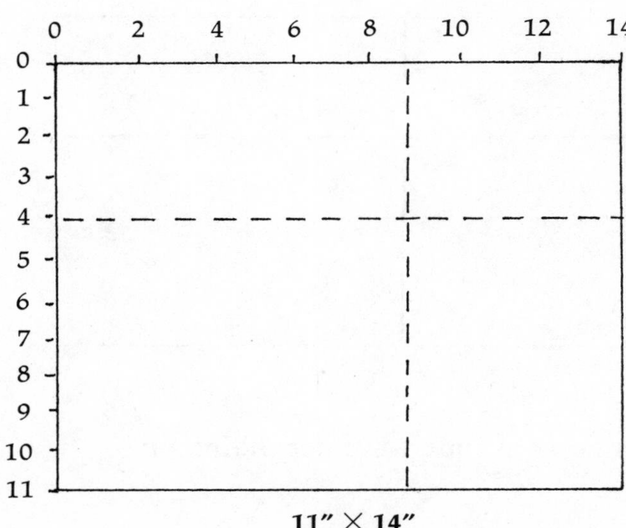
0
2
4
6
8
10
12
14
0
1
2
3
4
5
6
7
8
9
10
11
11″ × 14″

Figure 1-8
Standard canvas sizes with both horizontal and vertical edges divided by golden section proportions. Each of these divisions can be made in four different ways. See figure 1-10.

Although the proportions of standard-size drawing pads and canvases do not quite match the golden section rectangle proportions (as you can see in figure 1-7—standard paper sizes are shown in solid lines, and the golden section rectangle proportions are shown in broken lines), this lack of direct correlation is immaterial, since you can choose to divide the edges of any of these standard-size pads or canvases by the golden section and achieve variety of spatial distribution, as shown in figure 1-8.

As well as dividing the edge of a canvas by the golden section, each of the resulting line segments can be divided to create a series of nonduplicated *key locations* at which to place elements within your drawing (see figure 1-10.)

Figure 1-9 illustrates the four different ways the golden section can be applied using the edges of any rectangular canvas. The horizontal and vertical edges of the rectangle can be divided into long and short proportions (eight units and five units) or into short and long proportions (five and eight). The combination of these possibilities results in different arrangements within the rectangle.

Your imagination is the only limit to the application of the golden section to obtain variety in space division on your drawing surface. In fact, a drawing area of any proportions can be divided into unequal areas by any of several methods. For example, division by the combination of the square and the golden section can be seen in figure 1-11. After the square

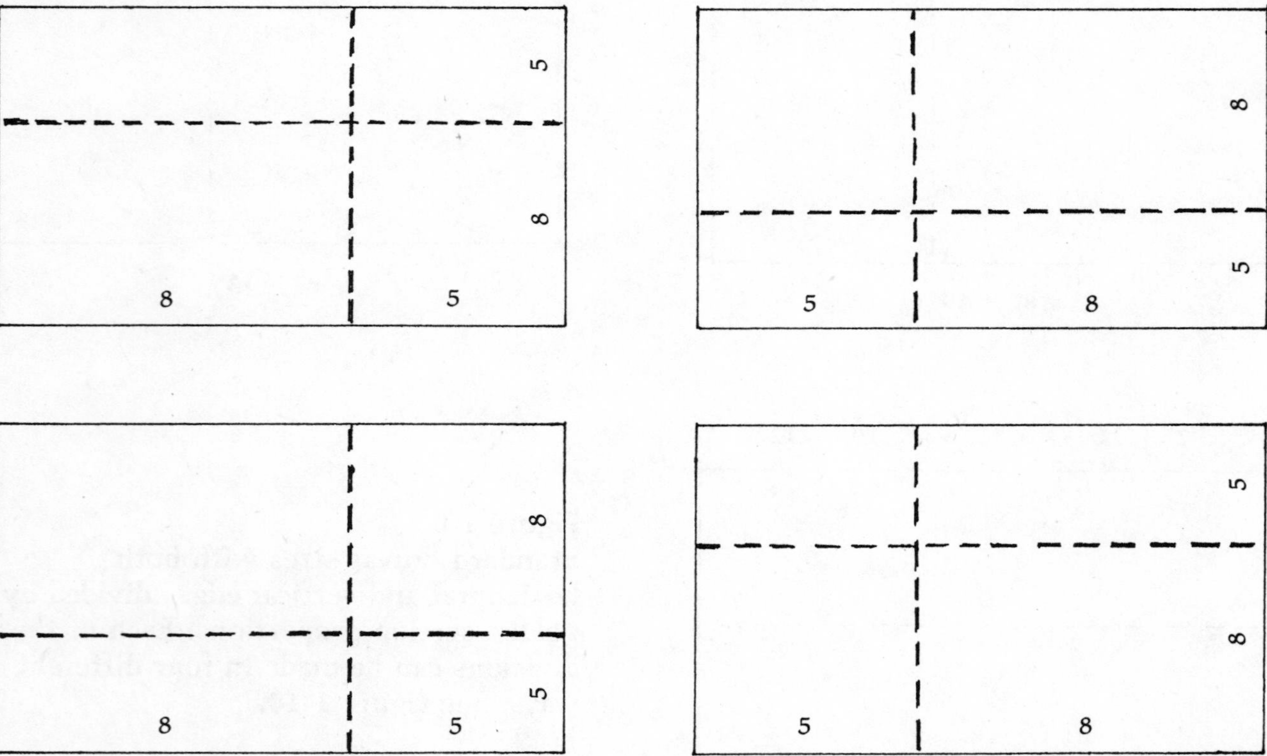
5
8
8
5
8
5
5
8
8
5
8
5
5
8
5
8

Figure 1-9
A golden section division of any rectangle can be done in four ways depending on which edge is used to start.

is drawn, the horizontal edge of the remaining portion is divided by the golden section.

Other examples of space division are shown in figure 1-12. In A, both edges of the square are divided by the golden section. In B, a square is first constructed from the left vertical edge, then the remaining rectangle is divided by the golden section—first on the horizontal edge, then on the vertical. The vertical edge of the square is also divided by the golden section. In C, I divided the rectangle by a diagonal and then drew an arbitrary vertical line. Where the vertical crossed the diagonal, I drew a horizontal line. In D, I divided the rectangle in half vertically, then applied the golden section to the horizontal edge on the right half. Next, I divided the portion from that line to the left edge by the golden section. I applied the golden section to the vertical edge as well.

Remember, there is no *one way* to achieve variety of space division. The important thing is to consciously strive to avoid the monotony of equally spaced key features and equally sized areas on your drawing space *before* you start to draw your subject matter.

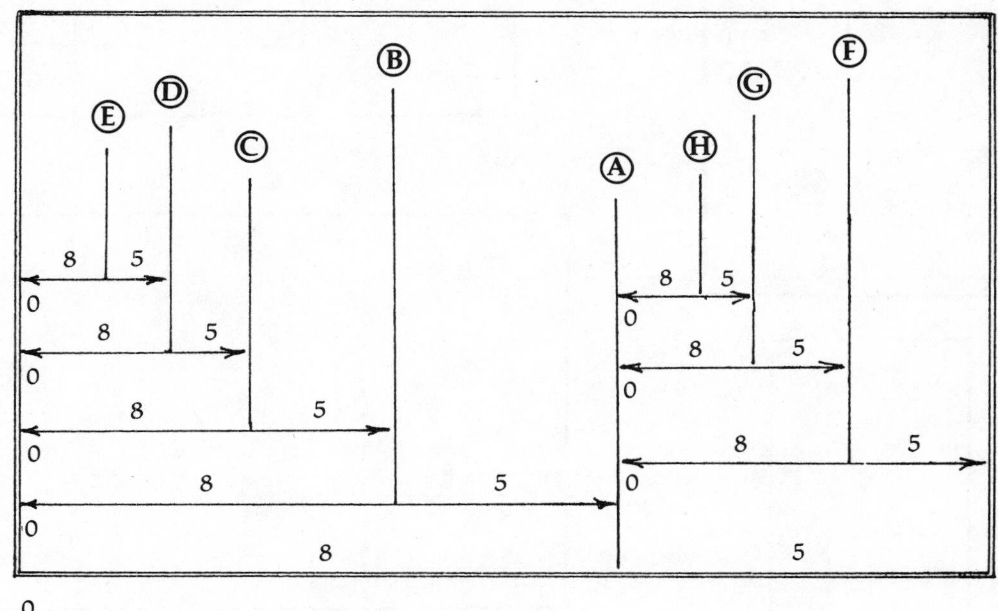
B
F
D
G
E
C
H
A
8 5
0
8 5
0
8 5
0
8 5
0
8 5
0
8 5
0
8 5
0
8 5
0

Figure 1-10
Successive division of the horizontal edge by the golden section to obtain a variety of key locations. The vertical lines A, B, C, D, etc., provide locations for significant compositional elements.

A The first division.
B Division between left-hand edge and A.
C Division of space between left-hand edge and B.
D Division between left-hand edge and C.
E Division between left-hand edge and D.
F Division between right-hand edge and A.
G Division between A and F.
H Division between A and G.

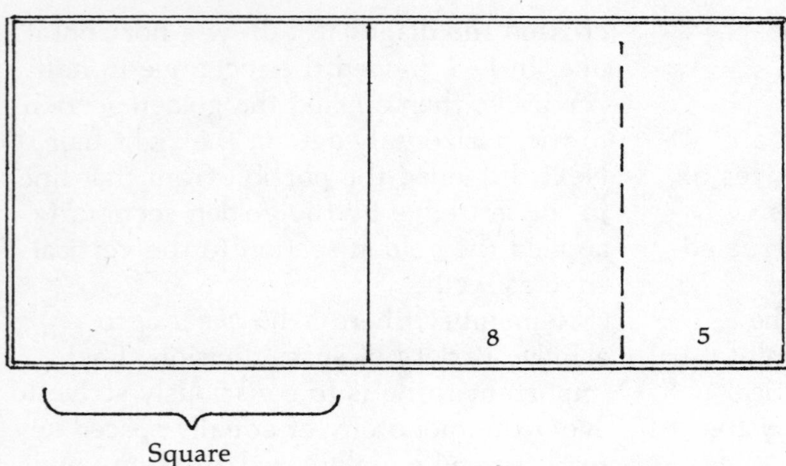
8
5
Square

Figure 1-11
Division into one square and division by golden section to obtain two key locations.

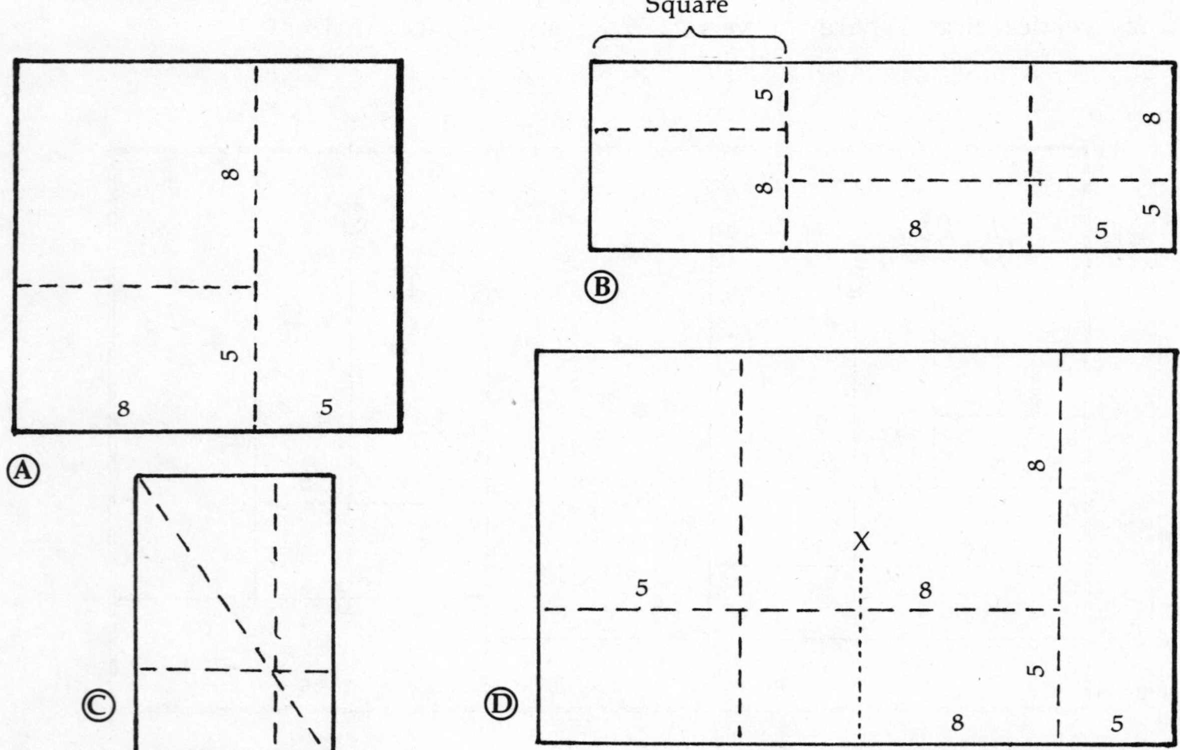
Square
5
8
8
5
8
5
B
8
5
5
8
A
C
X
5
8
5
D
8
5

Figure 1-12
Picture areas of any proportions can be divided into unequal spaces by any of several methods.

A **Golden section division of both horizontal and vertical edges.**

B **Use of a square at the left, then a golden section for the remaining rectangle and golden sections on each vertical edge.**

C **Use of a diagonal line, an arbitrary vertical line, and a horizontal line at the intersection of the diagonal and the vertical.**

D **A golden section division of the right half of the rectangle (from the center vertical line), then a golden section division from that vertical line to the left edge, and a golden section division of the vertical edge.**

Examples from Master Artists

Examination of some applications of the space division principles as used by master artists will show you how the golden section division is effectively applied in landscape pictures. The main elements of the compositions are shown schematically. (For comparison with the original paintings, see any of the more comprehensive art books in your library or books on the individual artists mentioned.) These examples are by no means the only applications of the golden section division. Constable, for instance, more times than not, used the golden section proportion to locate his horizon. Check this out for yourself by measuring the distance from the bottom of one of his scenes to the horizon, then dividing this number by the distance from the bottom to the top of the scene; it will give you a number very close to .38, which is five-thirteenths. The remaining distance, from the horizon to the top of the scene, is then eight-thirteenths of the total height. This can be seen in figure 1-13, where the composition of Constable's *The Leaping Horse* is shown in schematic form. The horizon location is based on the golden section proportion. In this composition, the picture area is also divided by a square, along one side of which the main tree trunks and foreground pilings are located. Other examples of Constable's use of the golden section are indicated in the schematics of figures 1-14, 1-15, and 1-16.

8
5
Square

Figure 1-13
Picture area divided into a square and a remaining rectangle. The horizon divides the vertical space into golden section proportions. (Constable, *The Leaping Horse*, Royal Academy of Arts, London)

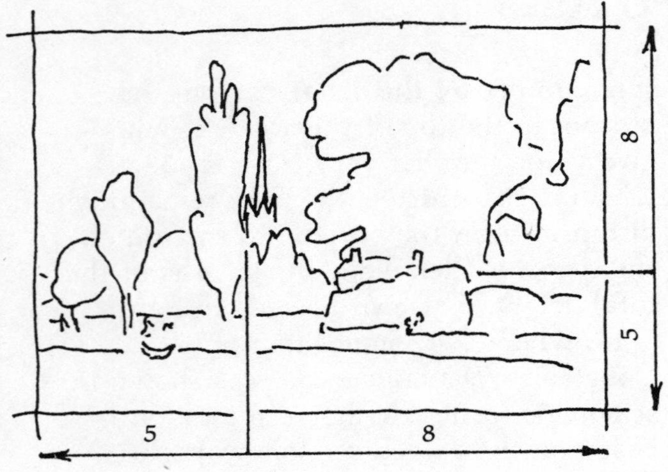
8
5
5
8

Figure 1-14
A landscape with the key figure, the cathedral spire, located at a golden section division. The horizon is also very close to a golden section division. (Constable, *Salisbury Cathedral from the River*, National Gallery, London)

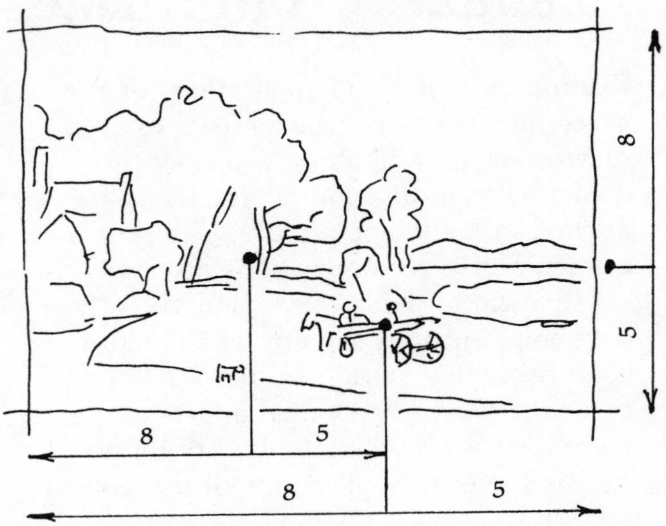

Figure 1-15
A landscape composed on golden section division of both horizontal and vertical edges. (Constable, *The Hay Wain*, National Gallery, London)

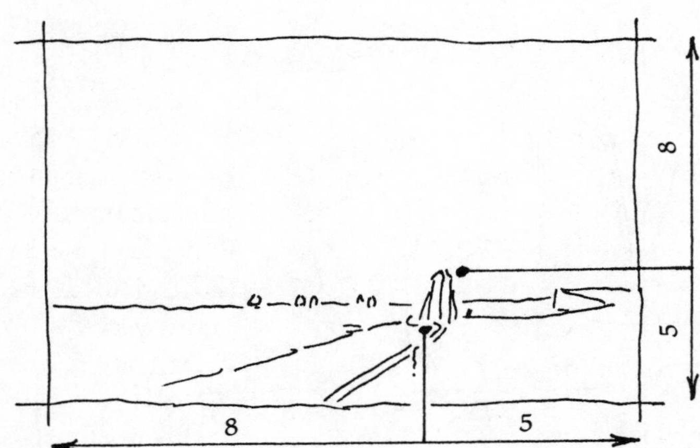
8
5
8
5

Figure 1-16
A seascape with the key structure located near a golden section intersection of each side of the canvas. (Constable, *Harwich, the Low Lighthouse*, National Gallery, London)

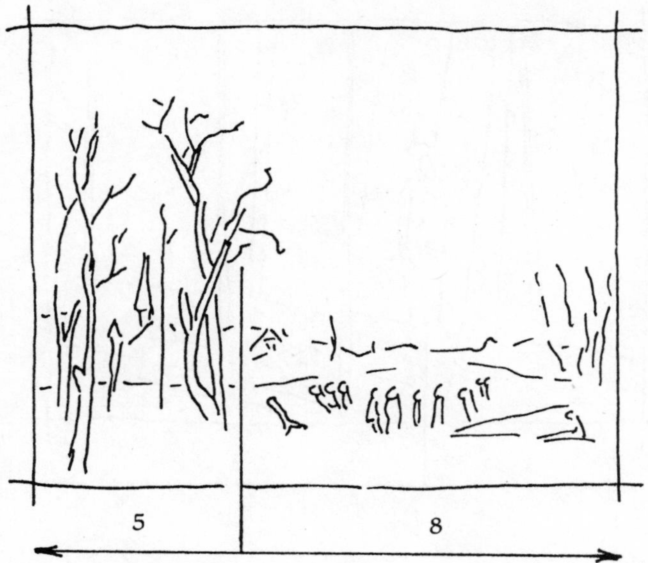
5
8

Figure 1-17
A landscape divided by golden section into two separate subject areas. All the figures are in the larger section and the trees are in the smaller. (Van der Neer, *A Winter Scene,* Rijksmuseum, Amsterdam)

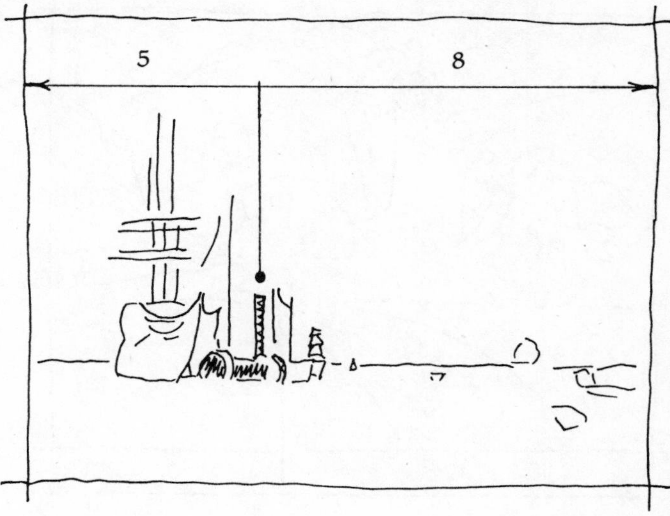
5
8

Figure 1-18
A seascape with the darkest feature, the smokestack, located at a golden section division. (Turner, *The Fighting Temeraire,* Tate Gallery, London)

Van der Neer divided the picture area of his *A Winter Scene* using the five-to-eight proportion. The skaters are in the larger portion, and all the near trees are in the smaller portion, as you see in figure 1-17.

Figure 1-18 shows how Turner placed the darkest element of his *Fighting Temeraire,* a black smokestack, at the five-eighths division. Gauguin and Homer also used that proportion in their landscapes, as shown in figures 1-19 and 1-20. A multiple use of the golden section proportion can be seen in Millet's *The Gleaners,* outlined in figure 1-21.

Every rule has its exceptions, and every convention of art can be successfully ignored if done so in a knowledgeable way. For instance, it is often said that the canvas should not be divided in half by a prominent picture element—Cézanne, however, divided his *Landscape with Viaduct* (shown schematically in figure 1-22) in half with a tree, then divided the right half of the picture in half horizontally with the viaduct. This produced three principal picture areas within one work. So, experimentation certainly is not ruled out by the conventions used to get variety into compositions.

8
5
5
8

Figure 1-19
A landscape with the figure located at a golden section division of the horizontal edge. (Gauguin, *Tahitian Landscape*, Minneapolis Institute of Arts)

Figure 1-20
A landscape with the figure located at a golden section division. (Homer, *Adirondacks*, Fogg Museum, Harvard University)

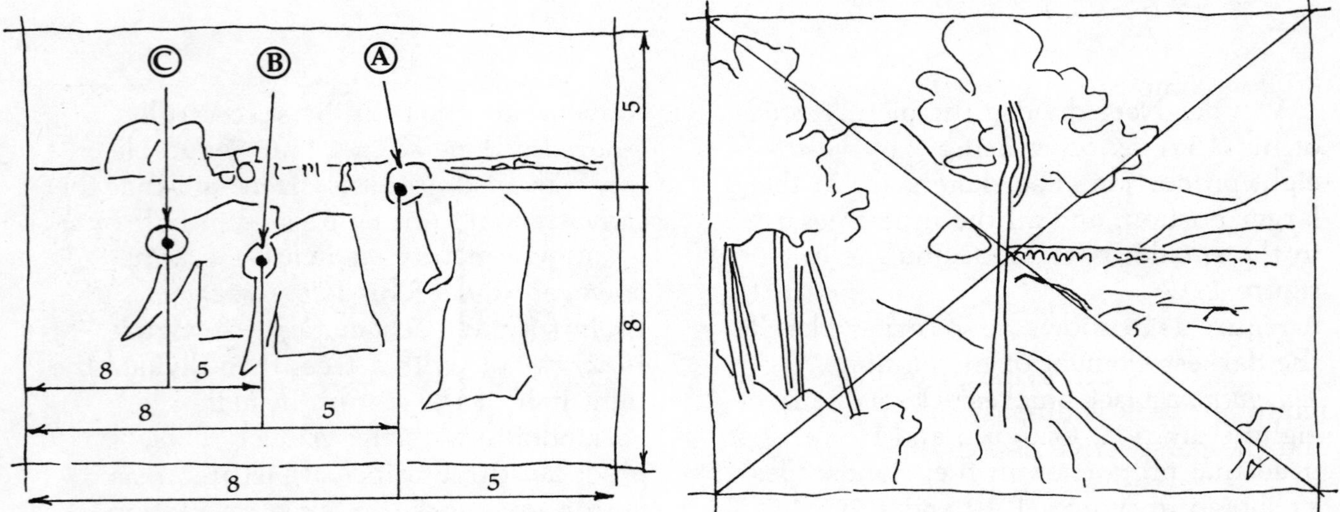
Ⓒ
Ⓑ
Ⓐ
5
8
8
5
8
5
8
5

Figure 1-21
A composition based on golden section division of both horizontal and vertical edges. (Millet, *The Gleaners*, The Louvre, Paris)

Figure 1-22
A landscape divided in half by a tree and the right half divided in half horizontally by the viaduct. (Cézanne, *Landscape with Viaduct*, Metropolitan Museum of Art, New York)

Figure 1-23
The dog's head in the Renoir composition of figure 1-5 acts as a fulcrum to balance the heavier figures on the left with the lighter elements farther out toward the right edge.

Balance

Visual balance in a composition depends on both spatial distribution and tonal distribution. Darker tones seem heavier. A large dark tone in a composition can be balanced by a smaller dark tone, much as a small weight on one side of a balance beam can overcome a much heavier weight on the other side as long as the smaller one has a longer lever arm. I will not get into physics here except to illustrate in figure 1-23 what I mean about balancing. The dog's head in the Renoir composition (as shown in figure 1-5) acts as a fulcrum over which the smaller figures near the right edge balance the heavier figures of the children to the left of the fulcrum.

Eye Movement and S Curves

A good composition provides a primary path for the viewer's eyes to follow through the picture and has variety in the size and shape of the picture elements that the eye encounters. The disposition of lines helps to direct the eye. Figure 1-23, a mountain scene viewed from a road, is an example of *poor* composition. There is too much symmetry. The mountain peak is directly in the center, and the perspective of the straight road leads the eye from the bottom of the picture to the mountain peak, then out of the picture at the top. There is nothing to induce the eye to wander around the picture for a while. The leaning tree at the left also directs the eye out of the scene toward the top. The trees in the picture are all shown the same size. Everything adds up to monotony.

Figure 1-24
A poor composition. The mountain peak is in the center, the road leads directly to the vanishing point, the main trees are all the same height, the dead tree at the left leads the eye out of the picture. The eye tends to travel up the road to the mountain peak and then out of the picture.

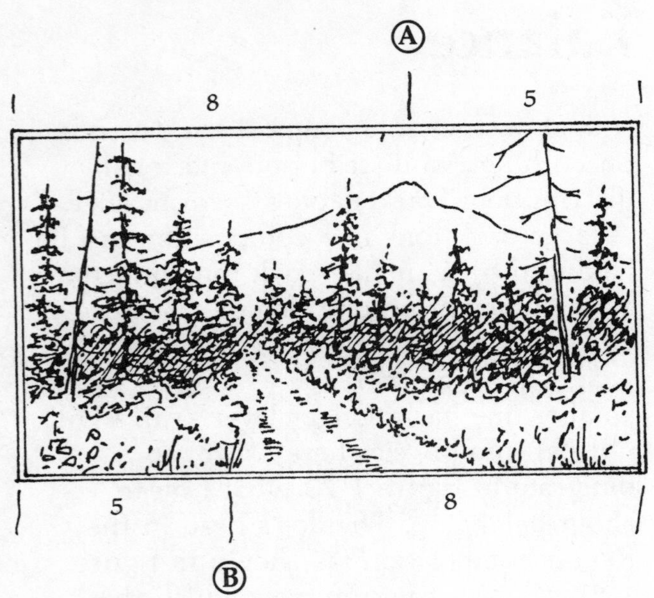
A
8
5
5
8
B

Figure 1-25
A better composition. The mountain peak is moved to the right on the golden section division A, and just one edge of the straight road is viewed head-on at golden section division B. The trees are each a different height, and those that lean a little, near the edges of the picture, lean *into* rather than *out of* the scene. The eye tends to travel along the road, up to the edge of the mountain, then upward to the right along the mountain, and back into the picture again by coming down the dead tree on the right side.

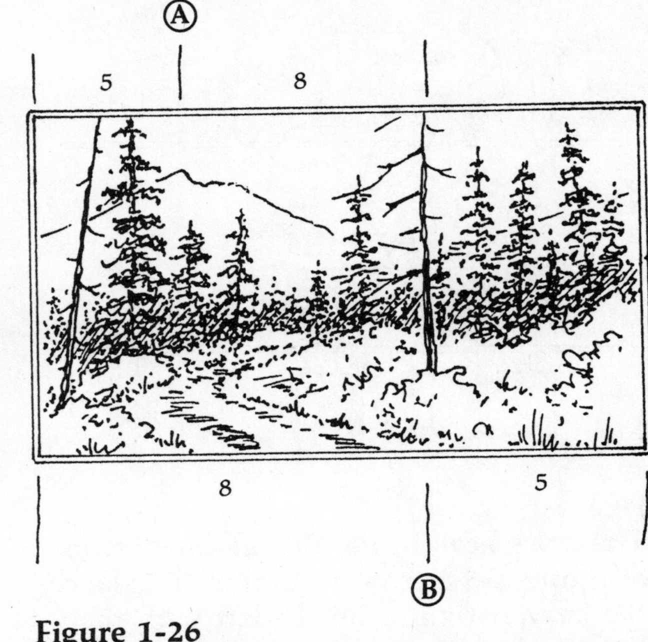
A
5
8
8
5
B

Figure 1-26
A still better composition. The mountain peak is off center on a golden section division (A), the road curves to the left and then to the right around a bend, the big dead tree is located at a golden section division (B), the dead tree at the left "pushes" the viewer's eye back into the picture, the trees are all of different heights. The eye tends to travel up the road and around the bend, up the tree to the mountain and along it to the tree on the left, which directs the eye back into the picture.

Figure 1-25 shows improvement on the composition. The mountain peak is placed off center at a golden section division toward the right (A). Instead of straight up the middle, the road is viewed along one side because it is placed off center toward the left on another golden section division (B). The trees are all different heights, and those that lean near the edges do so to lead the eye *into* rather that *out of* the picture. The eye tends to travel along the road to the mountain, and across the line of the peak to the right until it encounters the large, dead tree, which leads it back down and into the right-hand part of the picture.

Another improved composition, in figure 1-26, includes all the off-center features of figure 1-25 in addition to an S curve in the road. In this version also, the eye follows the road to the mountain peak, up and to the left to the trees that cross the mountain line, and down again into the picture.

The inclusion of the S curve to roads, streams, paths, and other features in landscapes is perhaps the most popular means of adding interest to them. The viewer cannot help wondering, perhaps unconsciously, what might lie around the bend. This gets the viewer mentally involved in the picture, which is what you want.

This has been a brief and incomplete treatment of the subject of composition. It is intended as an introduction for the novice artist. If you are interested in other means of creating variety in compositions, refer to some of the books listed in the bibliography, especially *Creative Illustration* by Andrew Loomis, a book for the commercial artist but one with a wealth of compositional considerations that apply equally well to fine art works.

2
Basic Drawing Tools and Materials

Sketching Pens

Paper for Pen and Ink Drawing

Sketching Pencils

Erasers

Paper for Pencil Drawing

Sketching Pens

There are three basic types of pen used for serious ink sketching: the crowquill, the artist's fountain pen, and the technical pen. Although there are some fine-point ballpoint pens and other disposable pens of various types with points that are quite sharp, they tend not to retain the sharp point for any length of time. Part of the charm of pen-and-ink sketching is the delicate linework that is possible. This is consistently achieved only with a good, sharp, metal point. You *can* start out with a very fine point ballpoint pen or a good, sharp fiber-tip pen to try your hand and assess your interest in sketching, but a crowquill point, holder, and ink will cost hardly more than a good ballpoint pen or fiber-tip pen.

Figure 2-1 shows what crowquill points look like, how to apply the ink to them, and the kind of lines they produce. Years of good sketching are possible with a handful of crowquill points and a holder or two. They have the advantages of being inexpensive and suitable for use with any kind of dark ink. Their primary disadvantage is that you must keep cleaning the point and dipping it or putting a drop of ink on the point as you work. Points of various stiffness and line width are available at most art supply stores. As you work, you must keep the point clean, as the dried ink will quickly impede the ink flow and make the linework erratic.

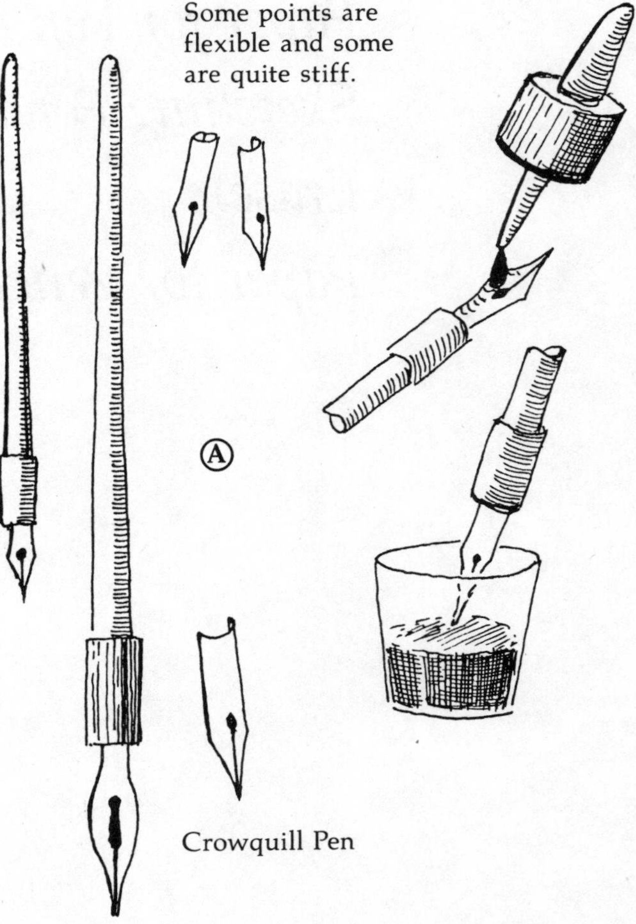
Some points are flexible and some are quite stiff.
A
Crowquill Pen

Figure 2-1
A Typical crowquill, or replaceable-nib, pens. How to apply the ink to the point by dropper or by dipping the point in a wide-mouth container.

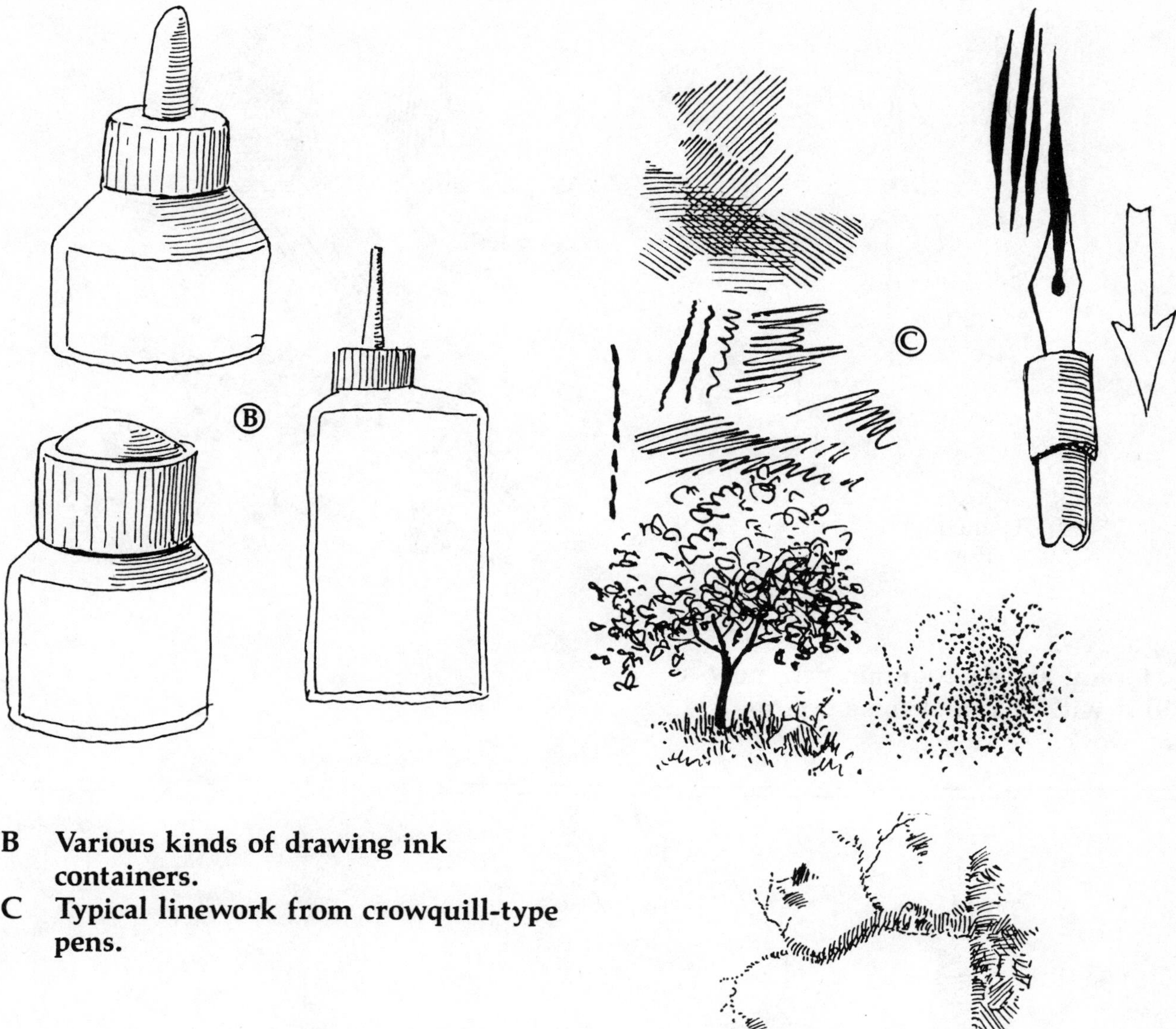
B
C

B Various kinds of drawing ink containers.
C Typical linework from crowquill-type pens.

Figure 2-2 shows a typical artist's fountain pen, how to fill it with ink, and some of the linework possible. Generally, these pens produce a somewhat wider line than the crowquill or technical pens, even when the point is called "fine" or "extra fine." This is not necessarily a disadvantage, however, and it is overshadowed by the tremendous advantage of not having to dip the point of the artist's fountain pen as you work! One more real disadvantage of these fountain pens is that most of the inks available for them are not waterproof. Moisture, as from your hand, can smear your work even after the ink has dried.

Figure 2-3 shows a typical technical pen, the kind used by most draftsmen in engineering offices. This instrument has a tubular point and must be held in a more upright position than the other pens, and each point size produces only one line width. It is a fountain pen, however, and can be filled with waterproof ink—two distinct advantages.

Artists'
Fountain
Pen
Vary pressure
to vary the
line width.

Figure 2-2
A typical artist's fountain pen, how to fill it with ink, and some typical linework.

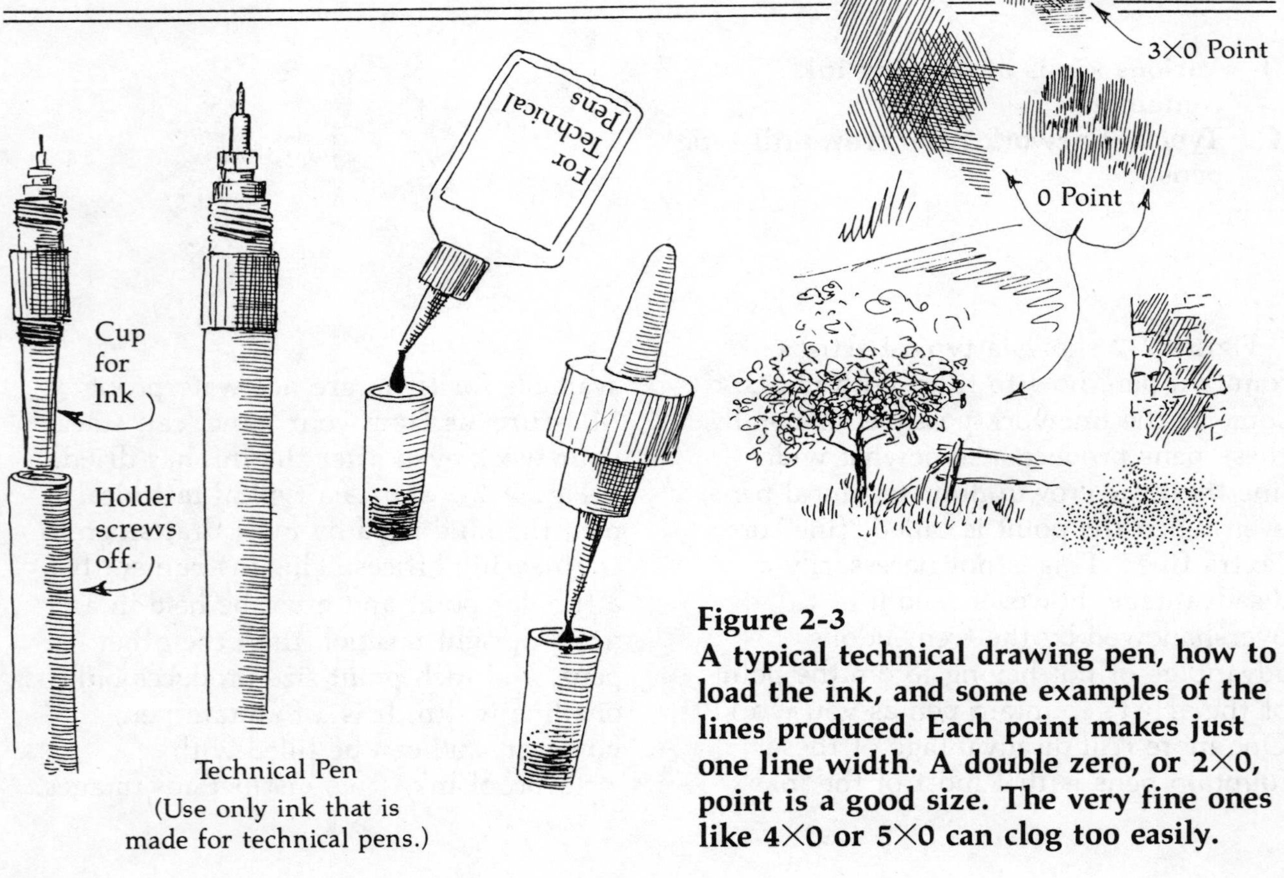
3×0 Point
For
Technical
Pens
0 Point
Cup
for
Ink
Holder
screws
off.
Technical Pen
(Use only ink that is
made for technical pens.)

Figure 2-3
A typical technical drawing pen, how to load the ink, and some examples of the lines produced. Each point makes just one line width. A double zero, or 2×0, point is a good size. The very fine ones like 4×0 or 5×0 can clog too easily.

Paper for Pen and Ink Drawing

Figure 2-4 illustrates some of the many kinds of paper that are suitable for pen work. Ordinary copier paper will do well for your practice, but it is too flimsy for your serious work. My advice is to try any paper you get your hands on. As long as it is not too porous, the way newsprint is, it will probably work fairly well. When you get serious about sketching with the pen, you will want to use heavier paper—60 pound or heavier, as it handles so much better and provides more protection for your work. It can also be great fun to try clear acetate or clear mylar placed directly over a photograph. You must use ink that is made to be used with drafting film, however, since the film is not porous and regular inks will just ball up on its surface. Tracing vellum and watercolor papers are usually made of rag and are permanent; that is, they will not deteriorate rapidly with age. They both take ink well. Bristol board is a standard for ink work. It is sold in art supply stores and is available in pads of different sizes.

Ordinary
Copier Paper

Good for practice drawings.

Bond, Typing,
or Writing
Paper

70 Pound
Copier Paper or
Printing Paper

This is nice, sturdy paper.

Bristol Board
Bristol Board

Good for your permanent work.

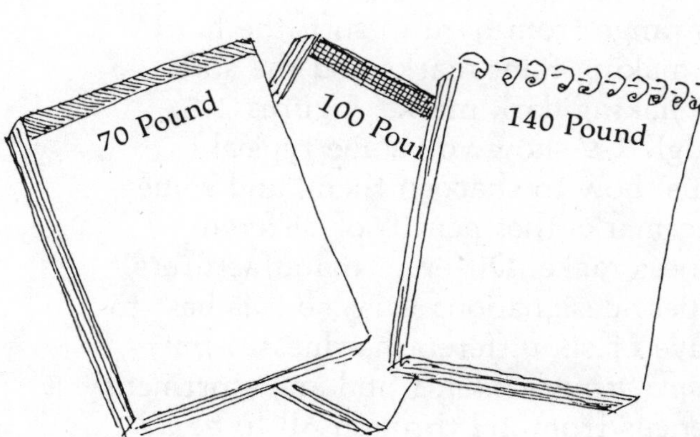
70 Pound
140 Pound

Watercolor Paper

Tracing Vellum

This takes ink very well and is a good-quality, permanent paper. It is great for tracing your subject.

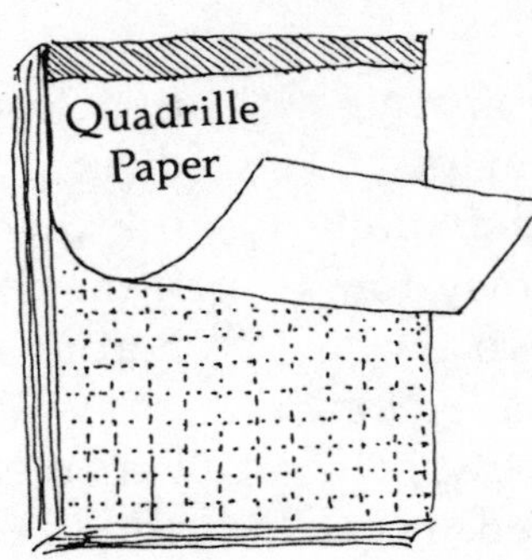
Quadrille Paper

Good for making your composition drawings. The blue lines help keep your verticals and horizontals from drifting. When done, you transfer your composition to good paper for inking.

Clear Acetate or Clear Mylar

You must use ink whose container states "For Film."

Figure 2-4
There are many kinds of paper that take ink quite well. Try different ones when you can, and you will find the kind you like best. The heavier papers, 60 pound and heavier, will be better than the thinner ones (like copier paper) for your permanent work.

Sketching Pencils

Pencils for sketching are usually of the wooden variety, although the use of a couple of mechanical pencils with soft leads is invaluable to my work. Pencil leads range from hard to soft, the hard ones making faint marks and the soft ones making dark marks. Figures 2-5 through 2-9 show you some typical pencils, how to sharpen them, and some of the marks that pencils of different hardness make. Different manufacturers' hardness designations vary, so it is best to get five or six different hardnesses *from the same manufacturer.* I find an assortment of pencils from 2H through 6B to be all I need. The leads for the mechanical pencils also come in a variety of

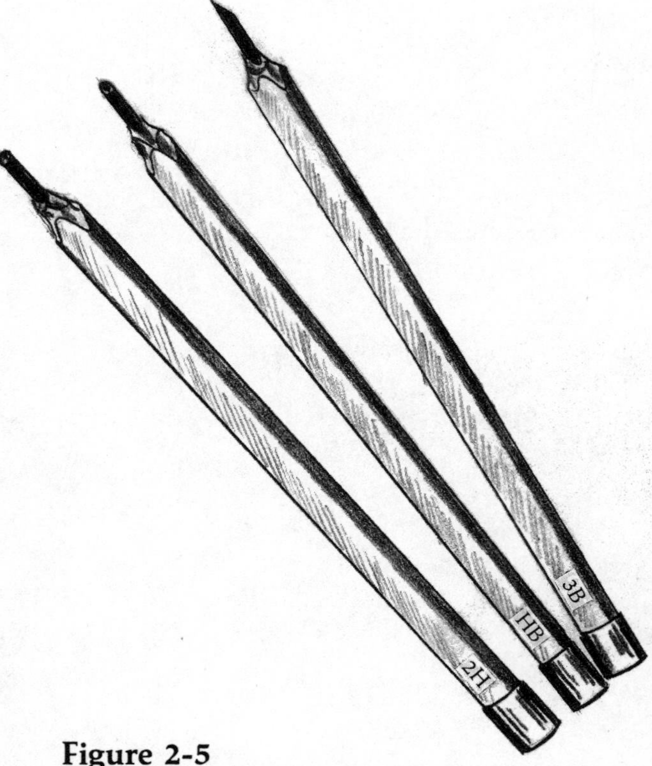
3B
HB
2H

Figure 2-5
Typical wooden sketching pencils.

Figure 2-6
Sharpening a pencil point on sandpaper. Keep the angle constant to produce a flat surface.

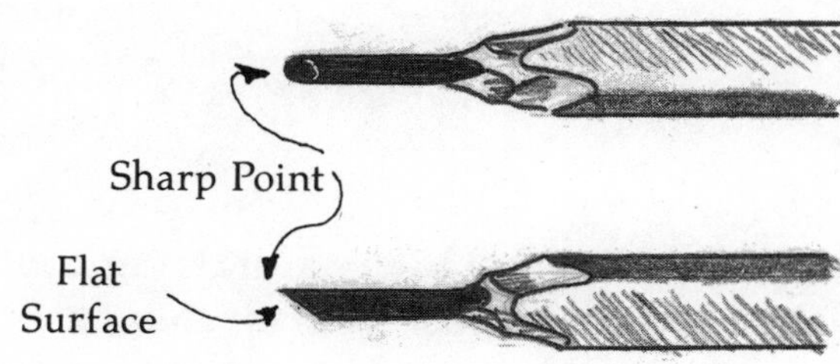
Sharp Point
Flat
Surface

Figure 2-7
A properly sharpened pencil has both a flat area and a sharp point.

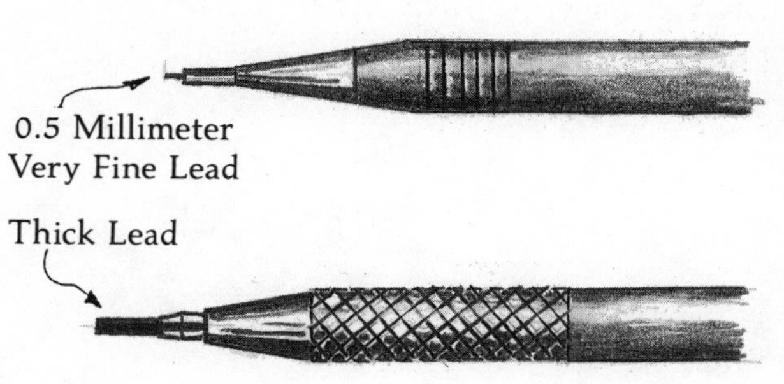
0.5 Millimeter
Very Fine Lead
Thick Lead

Figure 2-8
Two mechanical pencils useful for sketching.

A A 0.5 millimeter lead pencil uses a very fine lead.
B A drafting lead holder uses a thick lead that can be sharpened on sandpaper the way wooden pencils are.

hardnesses, although it will not be as wide a variety as with the wooden pencils. Different papers take the graphite differently also. I make a chart, as in figure 2-9, with all my pencils on each of the papers I use. This gives me a good reference so I know what to expect when I start a sketch. You should do the same and keep the charts with your pencils.

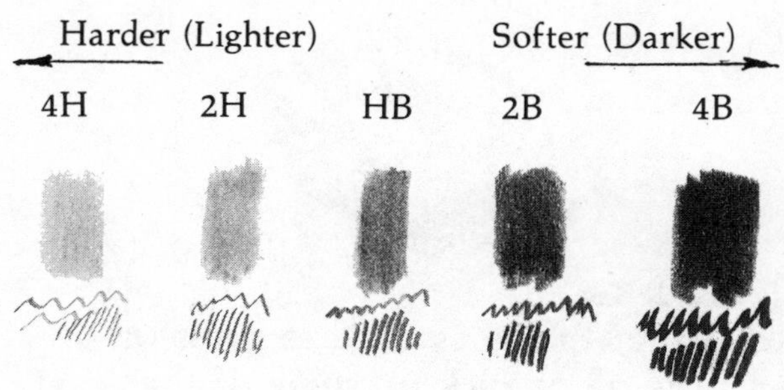
Harder (Lighter)
Softer (Darker)
4H
2H
HB
2B
4B

Figure 2-9
Pencil marks. The higher the H number, the harder the graphite and the lighter the mark. The higher the B number, the softer and therefore darker the mark.

Erasers

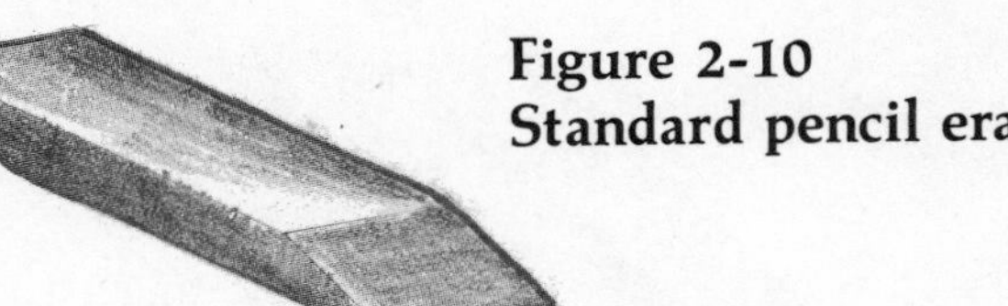

Figure 2-10
Standard pencil eraser.

The eraser is as important to pencil sketching as the pencil itself. Figure 2-10 shows a standard pencil eraser. This is good for cleaning up the white areas of your sketch, since it is impossible to do pencil drawing without smearing some graphite around on the paper. Spray fixatives, such as clear enamel or lacquer sprays, will protect a pencil drawing when it is finished (but they will also make the drawing appear somewhat darker).

Figure 2-11 shows a stainless steel erasing shield. This is used to protect parts of your drawing while you trim other parts with the eraser. As shown in figure 2-12, you can selectively erase delicate parts of the drawing by exposing them through the openings and erasing through them.

Figure 2-13 shows a kneaded eraser. This is a soft, kneadable material that is used by pressing and lifting it, *not* by rubbing it. Figure 2-14 shows how this action lightens dark areas. This eraser greatly extends your ability to create delicate tonal ranges and variations with pencils.

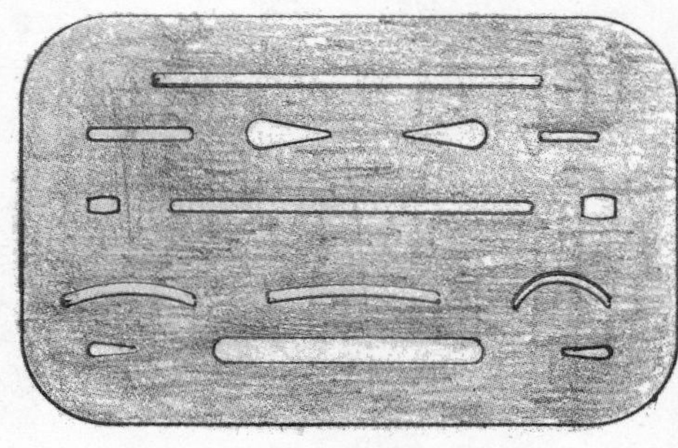

Figure 2-11
Erasing shield. This is a drafting tool that you place over your drawing, exposing the part you want to erase in one of the openings, with the shield protecting the adjacent parts of the drawing as you erase through the opening.

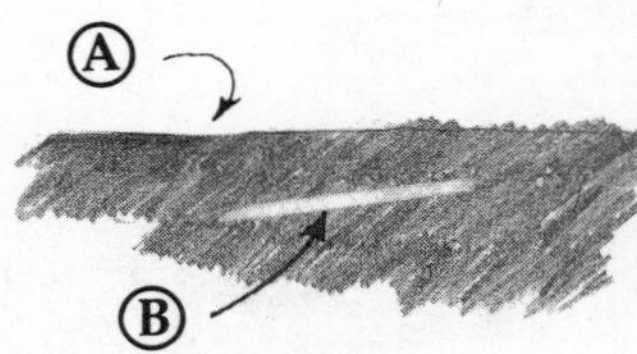
A
B

Figure 2-12

A **An erasing shield can help you to trim up a sharp edge.**

B **It can help you create sharply defined light areas in your pencil tones.**

Figure 2-13
A kneaded eraser is used to press on pencil work to pick up some of the graphite and lighten the tone. The dirty part of the eraser is kneaded into the inside of the eraser so it doesn't print dirty marks on your paper when you use it.

Lightened Features

Figure 2-14
The kneaded eraser is pressed on the drawing to lighten selected areas by lifting the graphite. You do not rub back and forth as with a standard pencil eraser.

Paper for Pencil Drawing

Paper for pencil work should have a *tooth,* a slight roughness that lets the graphite adhere to the paper. Any paper that has this roughness is suitable. Art supply stores have several kinds of padded drawing paper, almost all of which is suitable for pencil drawing. *Linen paper,* a paper with an embossed linen pattern, makes especially attractive pencil drawings because the linen pattern shows through in the darker pencil passages. Heavier papers are best for your good work, as they will not wrinkle as easily as the thinner papers. Figure 2-15 shows some of the kinds of paper that are available.

Newsprint

Takes pencil but is not very durable.

Bond, Typing, or Writing Paper

Good for practice.

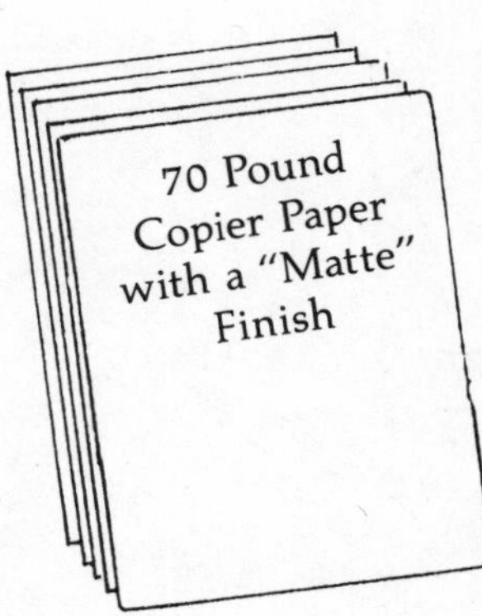
70 Pound Copier Paper with a "Matte" Finish

This is very good as long as it is not too smooth.

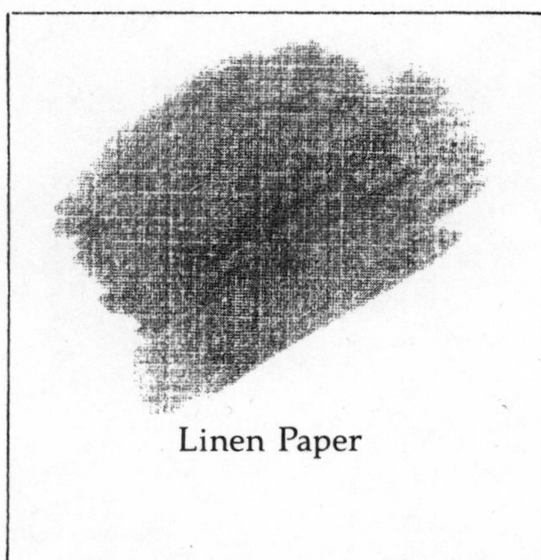
Linen Paper

The embossed linen pattern shows through the darker pencil patches.

Bristol Board

Very good paper, but get a kid or matte finish, so it is not too smooth.

g Paper
Drawing Paper

Any art supply store will have padded drawing paper that is made for pencil drawing.

Figure 2-15
Almost any paper that has a tooth (slight roughness) will take pencil very well. Heavier papers, 60 pound and heavier, are better than the light copier papers for your permanent work.

3
Some Fundamentals

Copying, Reducing, Enlarging, and Transferring

Gridding an Image Area

Frame and Drawing Sizes

Single-Point Perspective

Two-Point Perspective

Things in Front of Other Things

Alternating Lights and Darks

Details—Distant and Close

Making Your Own Notepaper

Copying, Reducing, Enlarging, and Transferring

Sometimes you will want to use a photograph or some other reference as a subject. Other times you will have completed a rough composition of your own that you want to use as the basis of a drawing. In either case, you may want to change the size of the subject before transferring it to your good paper for final work with ink or pencil. To do this, you should draw the subject on composition paper to get everything worked out correctly before you start the pen or pencil work. It is always best to do this preliminary work on a separate piece of paper, because erasing damages the fibers of the paper surface and can change the way ink or pencil "takes" in the erased areas. To make it easy to draw the outline of your subject and retain the perspective and relationship of subject elements, you should use the grid system outlined in figure 3-1 as you copy the outline to your composition paper.

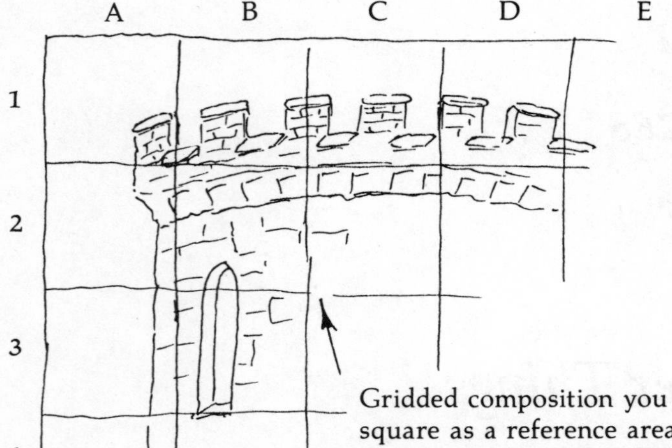
A B C D E
1
2
3
4

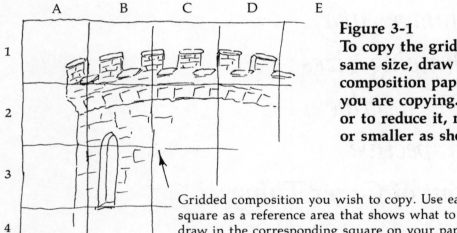

Figure 3-1
To copy the gridded composition the same size, draw the squares on your composition paper the same size as those you are copying. To enlarge the subject or to reduce it, make your squares larger or smaller as shown.

Gridded composition you wish to copy. Use each square as a reference area that shows what to draw in the corresponding square on your paper.

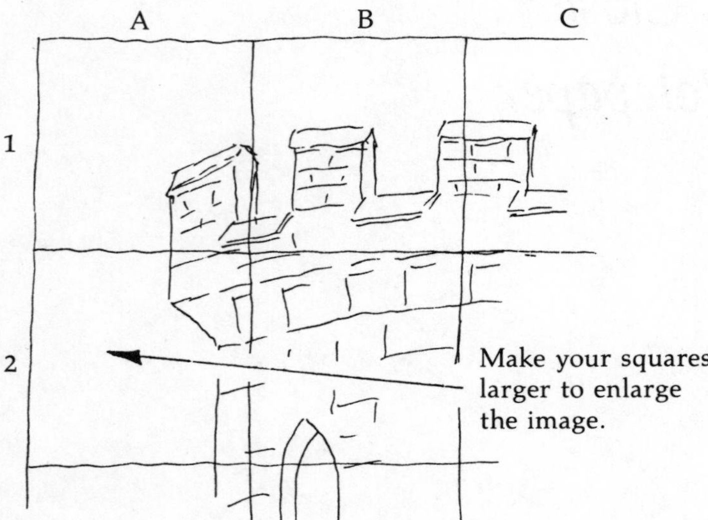
A B C
1
2

Make your squares larger to enlarge the image.

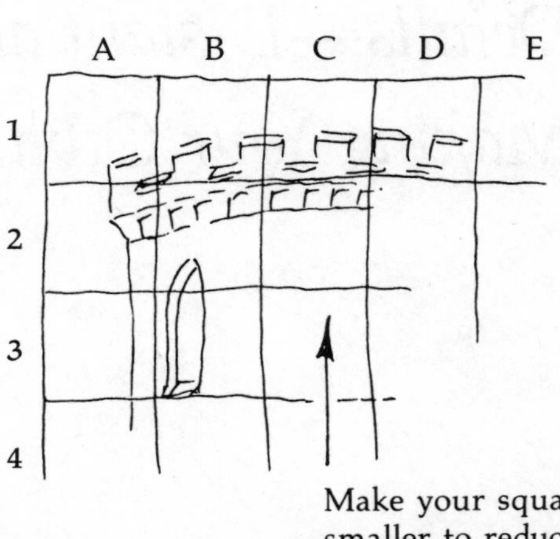
A B C D E
1
2
3
4

Make your squares smaller to reduce the image.

Blacken the back
of your composition
drawing with a
soft pencil.
Paper on
which you
will do
final inking.
Faint image
transferred.
Blackened back
of composition
drawing.
Draw over your
composition drawing
with paper you will
ink on lying under it.

Figure 3-2
How to transfer a faint image of your composition drawing to the paper on which you will do your drawing.

To start, you can draw a grid of squares on your subject photograph or place an already-drawn grid of squares on tracing paper over the photograph (to eliminate ruining the photo by drawing directly on it). These squares give you small areas of reference for redrawing the outlines. Now (you should already have decided how large your drawing is going to be), across the top on your picture area, lightly draw the number of squares that lie across the top of your gridded subject. Continue these squares down to the bottom of your picture area. If your drawn squares are smaller than those on your subject, your drawing will be smaller than the subject. Conversely, if your drawn squares are larger than those on the subject, your drawing will be larger (as shown in figure 3-1). The next section shows you how to divide an image area into any number of squares.

To transfer a composition that you want to draw to your good paper (the paper on which you will do the final drawing), blacken the back of the composition paper with the side of a soft pencil. Then place the composition paper on top of your good paper (as in figure 3-2). Next, draw over the lines of your composition with a sharp pencil. This will place a light graphite image on your good paper that you can use to guide completion of your final drawing. What you have done is to make some graphite carbon paper with which to transfer the drawing. *Never* use ordinary carbon paper to do this. It provides a greasy image that you cannot erase; you can only smear it around the paper and ruin it for sketching.

Gridding an Image Area

When you have decided how large your sketch is to be, you will want to divide that area into the same number of squares across and down as your gridded reference, as in figure 3-3. Most of the time, the distances will not exactly align with the units on a ruler. See A for a case in which a side is to be divided into five equal parts, but the ruler's units do not match. Just line up the beginning of the ruler with the left side and turn it until the 5 lies on the right side, as at B. Now put light pencil dots by each unit (inch) mark (C) and use these to draw vertical lines, as at D. The area now is divided into five equal parts. To make squares on the image area, take the straight edge of another piece of paper and mark it as in figure 3-4A. This is now a gauge to show you just where to mark the horizontal lines to produce squares on your image area. This is illustrated in figure 3-4B, C, and D.

Or, to divide a side into nine parts, for instance, you could line up the four-and-one-half-inch mark with the right side and put your pencil dots at each half-inch mark on the ruler. Using this process, you can easily divide a line into any number of parts.

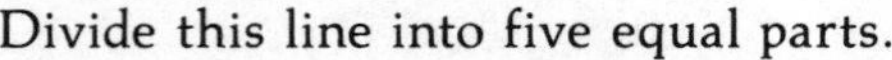
Divide this line into five equal parts.

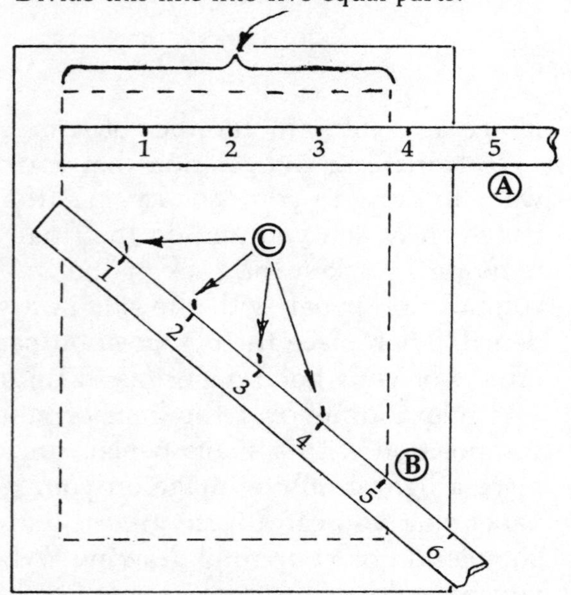
1
2
3
4
5
A
C
1
2
3
4
B
5
6

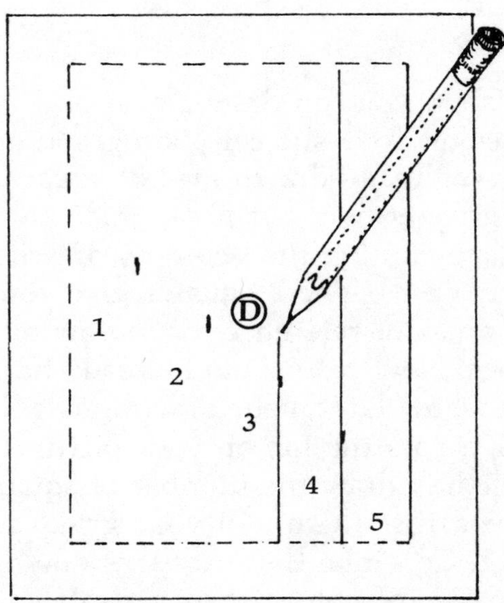
D
1
2
3
4
5

Figure 3-3
To transfer, enlarge, or reduce a subject you must divide your image area into squares. Many times, the length of your image area will not be an even number of inches. In order to divide the image area above into five equal vertical segments, for example, when the divisions on your ruler do not coincide with your image area's length, as at A, simply turn the ruler with the end on the left line until the 5 lies on the right line, as at B, then put a pencil dot at each inch mark, as at C. Run vertical lines through each dot, as at D, and the space will be divided into five parts. See figure 3-4 for the next step.

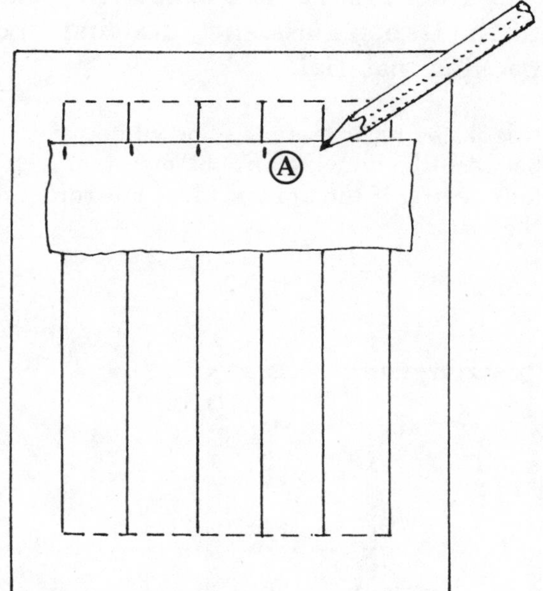
A

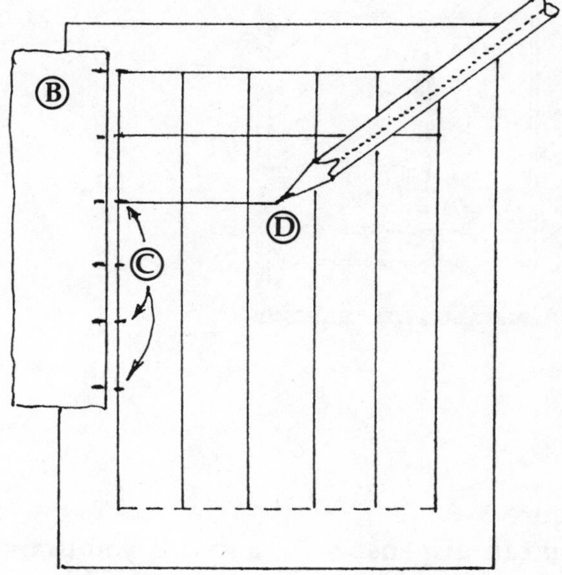
B
C
D

Figure 3-4
To complete the construction of squares, make a gauge on the edge of a piece of paper as at A by marking the distance between the vertical lines. Then place the gauge along a vertical edge as at B. Put pencil dots by the marks as at C. Then draw horizontal lines through the dots as at D.

Frame and Drawing Sizes

A drawing looks best when it is mounted in a mat before it is framed. A matted drawing always looks better if it does not run under the mat; that is, there should be a slight white space showing around the drawing when it is matted. Figure 3-5 represents a matted sketch that has a mat that is a different tint than the drawing paper.

It is not always necessary to have an actual mat, as the effect can often be obtained by drawing a line around the sketch where the edge of a mat would be, as shown in figure 3-6. I frequently use a freehand line like the one you see, but I lightly draw pencil guidelines with a ruler before I ink the line around the drawing. Of course, if you draw the mat, you cannot use a contrasting shade for the mat as you can if the mat is separate.

A few of the standard frame sizes are shown in figure 3-7, along with some reasonable mat openings for each and the maximum image size recommended to prevent the drawing from running under the mat. None of these dimensions are sacred; if you have frames and mats with other dimensions, by all means use them to frame your drawings.

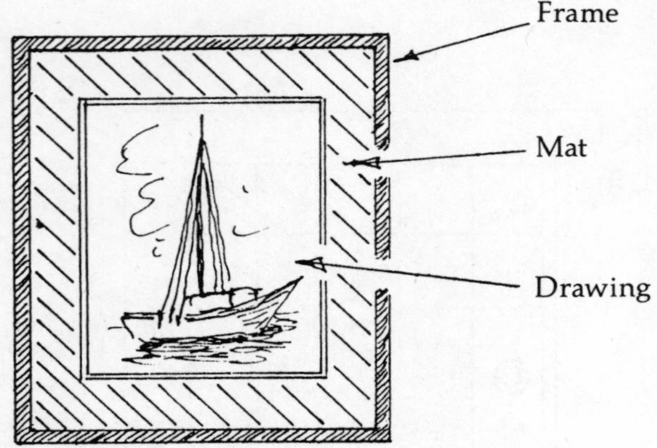
Frame
Mat
Drawing

Figure 3-5
The final product is a sandwich made up of the frame, glass, mat, drawing, and backing material.

It looks better if there is some white paper between the drawing and the mat; that is, it looks better if the drawing does not run under the mat.

Figure 3-6
You can dispense with a mat if you draw lines where the mat opening would be.

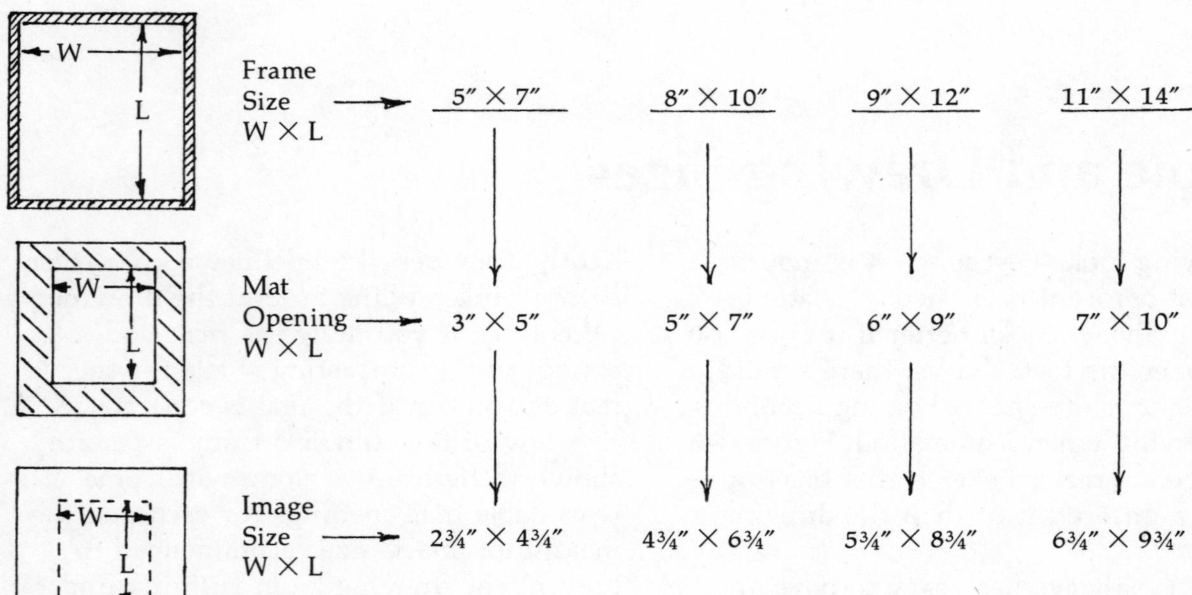
W
L
Frame Size W × L
5″ × 7″
8″ × 10″
9″ × 12″
11″ × 14″
Mat Opening W × L
3″ × 5″
5″ × 7″
6″ × 9″
7″ × 10″
Image Size W × L
2¾″ × 4¾″
4¾″ × 6¾″
5¾″ × 8¾″
6¾″ × 9¾″

Figure 3-7
Suggested mat openings and image sizes for some standard frames. The image size should be slightly smaller than the mat opening so the drawing does not run under the mat.

Single-Point Perspective

Perspective is a subject that by itself could fill a larger book than this one. Knowing just a few perspective principles, however, can make your drawings much better, by eliminating many of the most common perspective mistakes.

The most important thing to remember is that the horizon is always at eye level. Even if your scene contains mountains in the background, there is a horizon on the other side, and you can indicate that horizon by a light line on your drawing. The second most important thing is that all receding horizontal lines converge toward a vanishing point that *lies on the horizon*. With these two things in mind, look at the three sketches in figure 3-8. These sketches demonstrate single-point perspective. In A, railroad tracks and telegraph lines all converge to the vanishing point. Putting the nearest telegraph pole in place and drawing lines from its top and bottom to the vanishing point lets you more easily place the remaining poles and have them look "right." Drawing in one edge of the nearest buildings in B and lightly putting in lines to the vanishing point makes it very easy to correctly locate the remaining doors, windows, and other buildings.

If your drawing contains figures, it is easy to determine how tall middle-distance figures should be and just where they should be if you remember that the horizon is at eye level. If the ground is flat, then for average-size people, all the heads will be on the horizon. Shorter people's heads will be below the horizon,

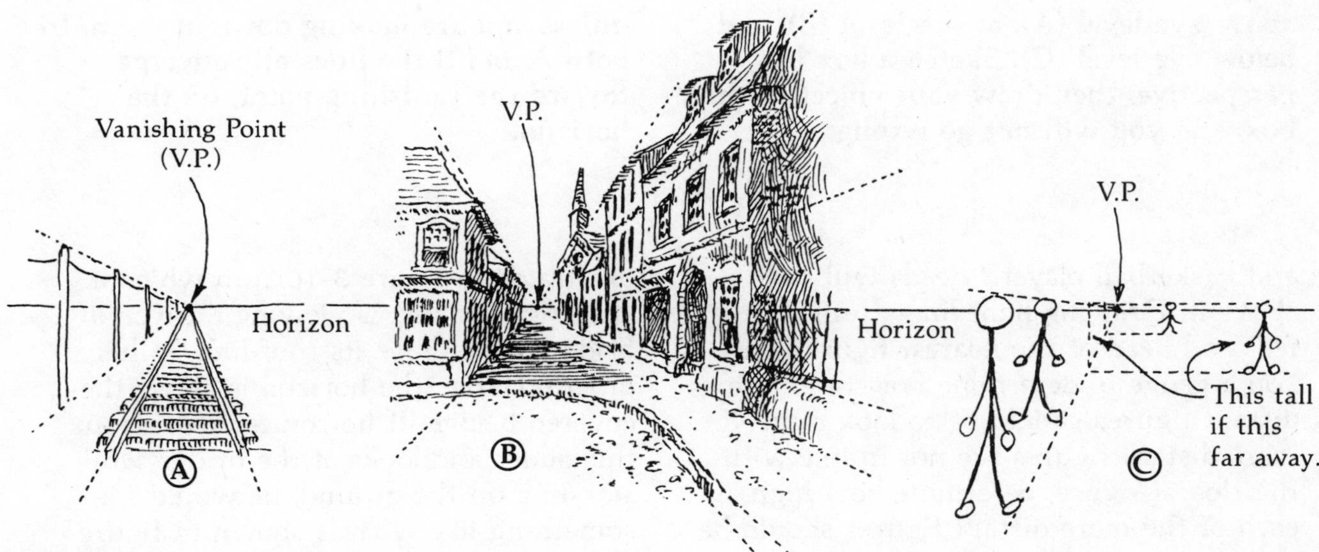
Vanishing Point
(V.P.)
Horizon
A
V.P.
B
V.P.
Horizon
This tall
if this
far away.
C

Figure 3-8
In single-point perspective, receding lines all converge at the vanishing point (V.P.), which lies on the horizon. A shows telegraph lines and railroad tracks, B shows a street, and C shows stick figures. Note that in C the heads lie on the horizon regardless of how far away they are. This is because the horizon is always at eye level, unless the view is upward or downward or the figures are shorter or taller than the average person. C shows how easy it is to determine how tall distant figures should be drawn when they are on level ground.

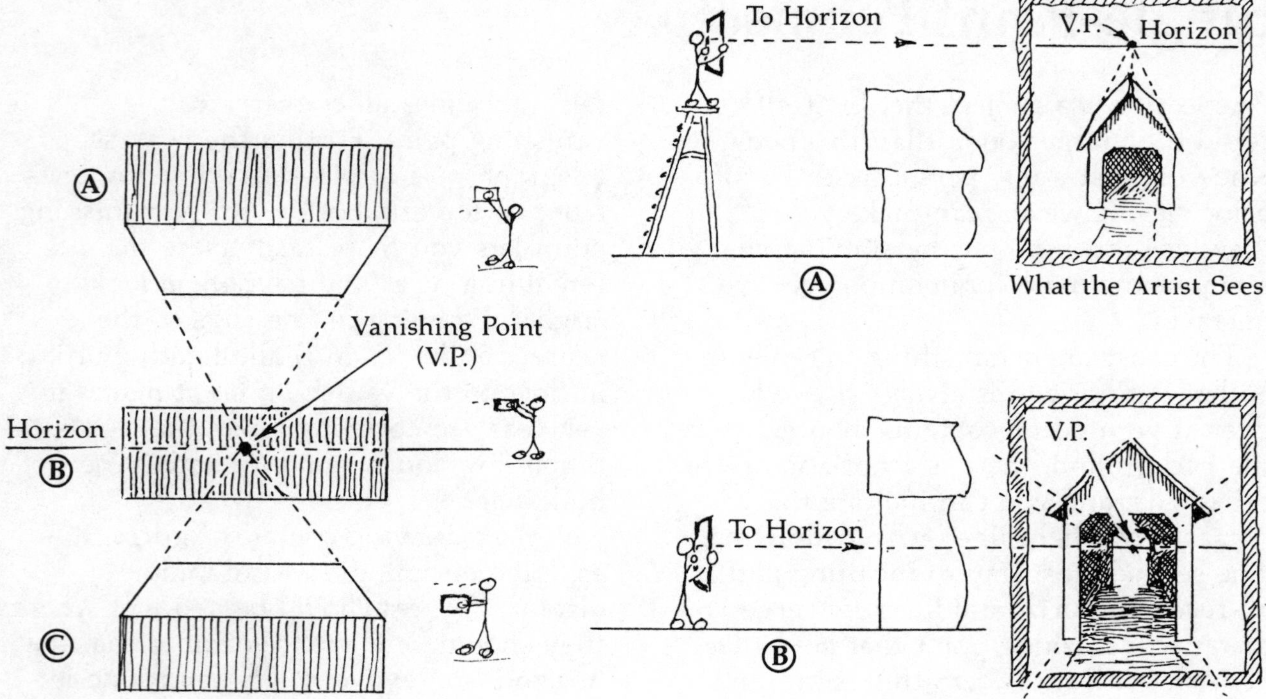
To Horizon
V.P.
Horizon
Ⓐ
What the Artist Sees
Ⓐ
Vanishing Point
(V.P.)
Horizon
Ⓑ
Ⓒ
V.P.
To Horizon
Ⓑ

Figure 3-9
This shows how single-point perspective helps construct objects when they are above eye level (A), at eye level (B), and below eye level (C). Sketch a box in perspective, then draw your object in the box, and you will not go wrong.

Figure 3-10
Objects that are below your eye level will lie below the horizon (as at A) unless you are looking down at them. In both A and B the lines all converge toward the vanishing point, on the horizon.

and basketball players' heads will be above it. Drawing light lines from the feet and head of the nearest figure gives you a gauge to determine how tall more distant figures should be to look right. If more distant figures are not in line with the closest figure, determine how high each of the more distant figures should be and then just move them to the right or left, as shown with the two most distant stick figures in C.

When an object is above eye level, you may see part of its bottom, as in figure 3-9A. From below eye level you see part of the top, as in C, and at eye level you see neither, as in B. This is further illustrated in figure 3-10A, in which a stick figure artist is viewing a covered bridge from above its roof line. In his picture frame, the horizon is above the covered bridge. If he comes down from the ladder and looks at the bridge while standing on the ground, he would see something like what is shown in figure 3-10B. In this case the horizon is near the center of the picture. In all cases note how the lines all converge to the vanishing point. A few minutes spent with the pencil considering these principles during your composition stage will often produce better, more convincing drawings.

Two-Point Perspective

One-point perspective principles apply only when your subject matter will be viewed head-on. In most situations, however, there are two vanishing points instead of just one. These situations will require two-point perspective considerations. In figure 3-11 a box is viewed from below, straight on, and from above in two-point perspective. Compare this illustration with figure 3-9, the corresponding one-point perspective illustration. In both cases edges converge to a vanishing point on the horizon. Instead of a box, figure 3-12 shows a sketch of a barn. You can see how the sides of the barn and those of the box correspond. Since this view is straight on, the horizon is near the center of the picture, and the figure's head is located on the horizon.

If you look up at a subject, as in figure 3-13, the horizon will be at the bottom of the picture or below the picture. Both vanishing points still lie on the horizon, and lines will converge toward them as shown. It is the proper slope of the edges

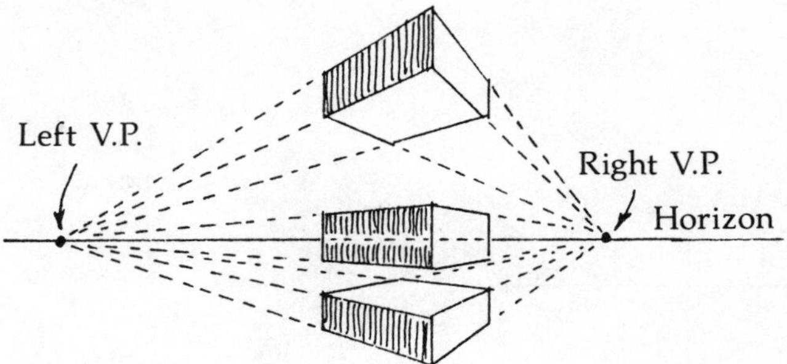
Left V.P.
Right V.P.
Horizon

Figure 3-11
This shows a box in two-point perspective viewed above eye level, at eye level, and below eye level. Note how all horizontal lines converge toward one or the other vanishing point.

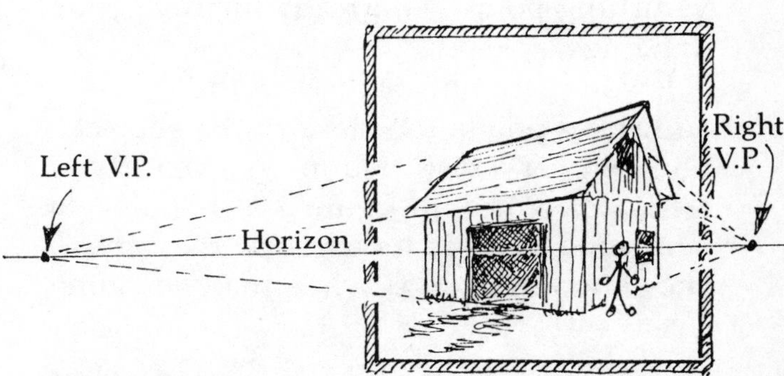
Left V.P.
Horizon
Right
V.P.

Figure 3-12
When looking straight on at a subject, the horizon is within the picture area.

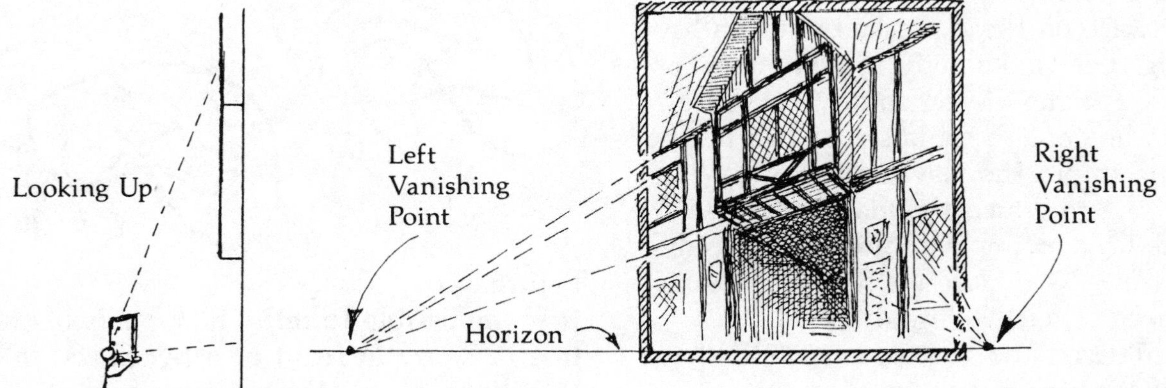
Looking Up
Left
Vanishing
Point
Horizon
Right
Vanishing
Point

Figure 3-13
When you look up at your subject, the horizon is low in the picture area or below it.

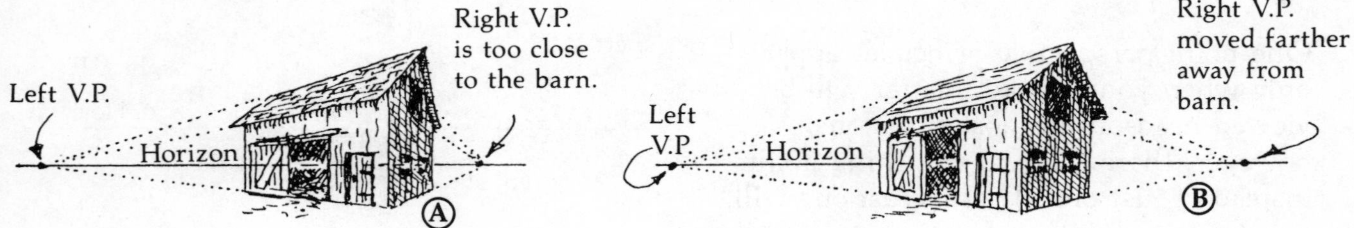
Left V.P.
Horizon
Right V.P. is too close to the barn.
A
Left V.P.
Horizon
Right V.P. moved farther away from barn.
B

Figure 3-14
If your vanishing points are too close to the object, you can get a distorted appearance. In A the right vanishing point is too close to the barn. In B it has been moved to the right, and the barn appears more normal.

of your subject matter that makes your composition look right. Spending a few moments at the composition stage sketching in roughly placed vanishing points and using a ruler or yardstick to connect the edges with the proper vanishing point will greatly improve your drawings.

If you place one or both of the vanishing points too close to the subject, you will get a distorted image even if you follow the rules. In figure 3-14A the right vanishing point is too close to the barn. B shows what happens when that vanishing point is moved farther to the right: the barn looks "righter." It would look "righter" still if I moved the left vanishing point somewhat farther to the left.

Things in Front of Other Things

Drawings are literally nothing more than dark marks on paper. The viewer puts significance on these marks by mentally relating them to something seen in his or her life. For the viewer to do this, there have to be enough signals provided by the drawing to put the viewer on the track of something to which the marks can be related. One example of this idea is found in figure 3-15A. Here we have a drawing of a piece of dark string dropped on paper. There is no way you can tell what part of the string is in front of other parts. A third dimension can be suggested to the viewer, however, so that he or she can quickly get the impression that parts of the string are in front of or in back of

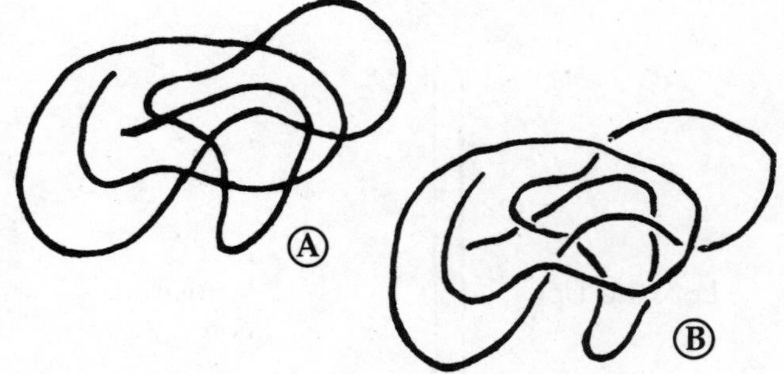
A
B

Figure 3-15
It is impossible to tell which parts of the line in A are in front of other parts. In B the slight breaks in the line where it goes under other segments give an immediate visual signal that allows the viewer to perceive the segments' relationship without thinking about it.

other parts, as you see in B. The device or signal in this case consists of simply leaving a little white space where each segment of string goes under another. This principle of stopping a line that goes behind another line just short so that it does not touch the other line can be used to an artist's advantage in many ways.

Figure 3-16 shows the principle applied to a sketch of a barbed wire fence with weeds growing in front of and behind the fence. It is immediately obvious that the weeds on the right of the fence post are in front of the wire and that those on the left of the post are behind the wire. Figure 3-17 shows part of the rigging on a sailboat. Note that nothing is drawn behind the rigging so it appears to be in front of the cabin. If the cabin lines were drawn crossing the rigging lines, there would be just an incomprehensible jumble there. The same principle is applied to the drawing of a grassy weed in figure 3-18. The lowest leaf shown is obviously in front of the florettes; the upper leaves, behind them.

Figure 3-16
The weeds to the left of the post are obviously behind the barbed wire, because there is a break in the weeds where they go behind the wire. To the right of the post, the breaks in the wire show that the wire goes behind the weeds.

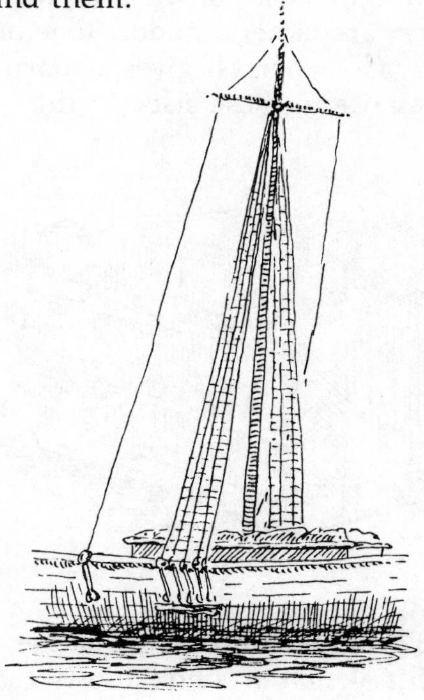

Figure 3-17
The break in the lines that are behind the ratlines let the ratlines appear to be on this side of the boat. If the boat structure were drawn right across the ratlines it would cause the viewer visual confusion.

Figure 3-18
It is easy to see that the two upper leaves are behind the florettes and that the lower one is in front of them. Such slight breaks in lines where they go behind other lines give a three-dimensional feeling to a drawing.

Alternating Lights and Darks

Another quite necessary visual signal in drawings is the alternation of lights and darks to insure distinction between sketch elements. If all sketch elements are in middle tones, it is difficult for a viewer to perceive something definite in the drawing. Figure 3-19 shows a drawing of a box. Note that the upper edges of the slats that form the sides of the box are white, while the sides of the slats that touch them are either a middle tone or a dark tone. This contrast gives a sharp visual presence to these slats. In this figure the ink lines are drawn in different directions where they tone the various parts of the box. Line direction does help to differentiate between different but similar surfaces, but use of this device is not always necessary. Figure 3-20 shows the same drawing done using only slanted lines for the toning of surfaces on the box. The important thing to note here is that different tones were created—dark, intermediate, and light—just as in figure 3-19.

Wider space between
the lines for lighter tone.
Closely spaced lines
for darker tone.
Crosshatch for yet
darker tone.

Figure 3-19
Alternating lighter tones with darker ones in this sketch of a box allows each part of the box to be clearly visible. Note that the top edge of each board is shown by white paper while the surrounding wood is darker.

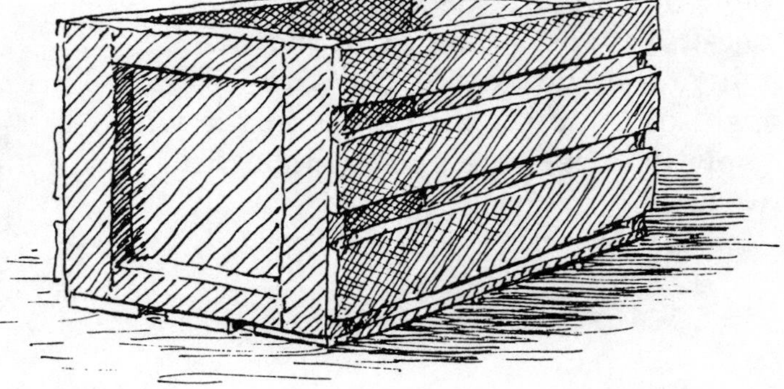

Figure 3-20
The line direction you use to show toned surfaces usually does not matter. Here the box from the previous figure is toned only with diagonal lines, but the spacing of these lines is varied to create the alternating lights and darks that differentiate the various surfaces.

The same light/dark-alternation principle can be seen in figure 3-21, a small portion of a landscape. The light tones between the dark ones help give the impression of succeeding layers of foliage.

Figure 3-22 is a drawing of a portion of a barn. The roof shingles and the horizontal boards are given distinction by the narrow strips of light paper between the darks that tone the surfaces. Sometimes artistic license is required, and you will have to distort some of the tones you see in a subject in order to give them the distinctness you want them to have in your drawing.

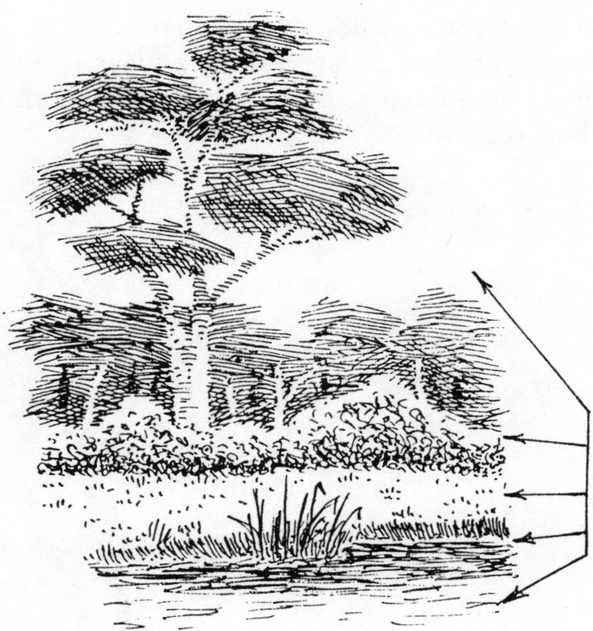
Light tones
between the
dark tones.

Figure 3-21
Each of the more distant features of this landscape is given form by the alternation of light and dark tones. The arrows point to the light areas that separate the darker tones. Note that some of the background tree trunks are shown lighter and some are shown darker than the middle-tone background.

Figure 3-22
Alternating light with dark helps to define the edges of all the roof shingles as well as the horizontal rails enclosing the lower part of the shed.

Details—Distant and Close

Obviously, you can observe detail in an object only when it is reasonably close to you. Distance obscures detail. When you draw some distant flying birds, as in figure 3-23, a short line or two or perhaps some dots are all that you should use to indicate the form. You cannot indicate eyes or feet at such a scale. However, as the subject moves closer to the foreground in your drawing, you must show more and more detail. This is part of your signal to the viewer that the object is closer. Note that in the closeup drawing of the mottled duck, virtually every feather is drawn separately. In the closeup rendition of the twig, every little bump and irregularity is shown. In the distant view of the stone lantern, just a few short lines and two dots are all that can be drawn. In the closer views of the lantern, the irregularities in the stone must be shown.

When drawing a really closeup view of something, you have to show considerable detail—all the detail that would be visible at that distance. To do this you need good reference material—that is, photos, drawings, or the real thing—so you can see yourself what is actually there. You cannot draw what you cannot see. If you are really familiar with a subject, perhaps you could draw a reasonable sketch of it using just your mind's eye, what you remember. But artists almost always use some sort of reference to be sure of detail when they want realistic drawings.

Figure 3-23
It can be difficult to draw some subjects as if they were a great distance from the viewer. Just a few short lines and a few dots define the most distant items in this figure. A dot or two too many and the items' identities would be lost.

As the object comes closer to the foreground, more and more detail must be shown to make the drawing realistic. Note that virtually every feather is drawn in the sketch of the flying duck, while the more distant birds are indicated just by two lines that represent the wings.

You need good reference material to see just what detail does exist in your subject.

Making Your Own Notepaper

It is both fun and easy to use a copier machine to make your own notepaper from pen-and-ink sketches. It can be done from pencil work but you would need to have a printer do it, as pencil drawings have to be screened in order to print properly.

Figure 3-24 shows you how to prepare to make two different standard-size notepapers. The first size (A) is simply an eight-and-one-half-by-eleven-inch standard-size sheet of paper folded twice. Printers carry envelopes that fit such notes.

A less expensive way to make your own notepaper is by using a seven-by-six-and-three-eighths-inch piece of paper folded once. This too fits a standard envelope that is inexpensive and available at office supply stores. D shows how to lay out such a sheet on a standard eight-and-one-half-by-eleven-inch sheet so you can run off your notepaper on a copier; then you must cut each sheet out. I use a metal straightedge and a sharp blade when I do it this way, as scissors do not make a straight enough edge.

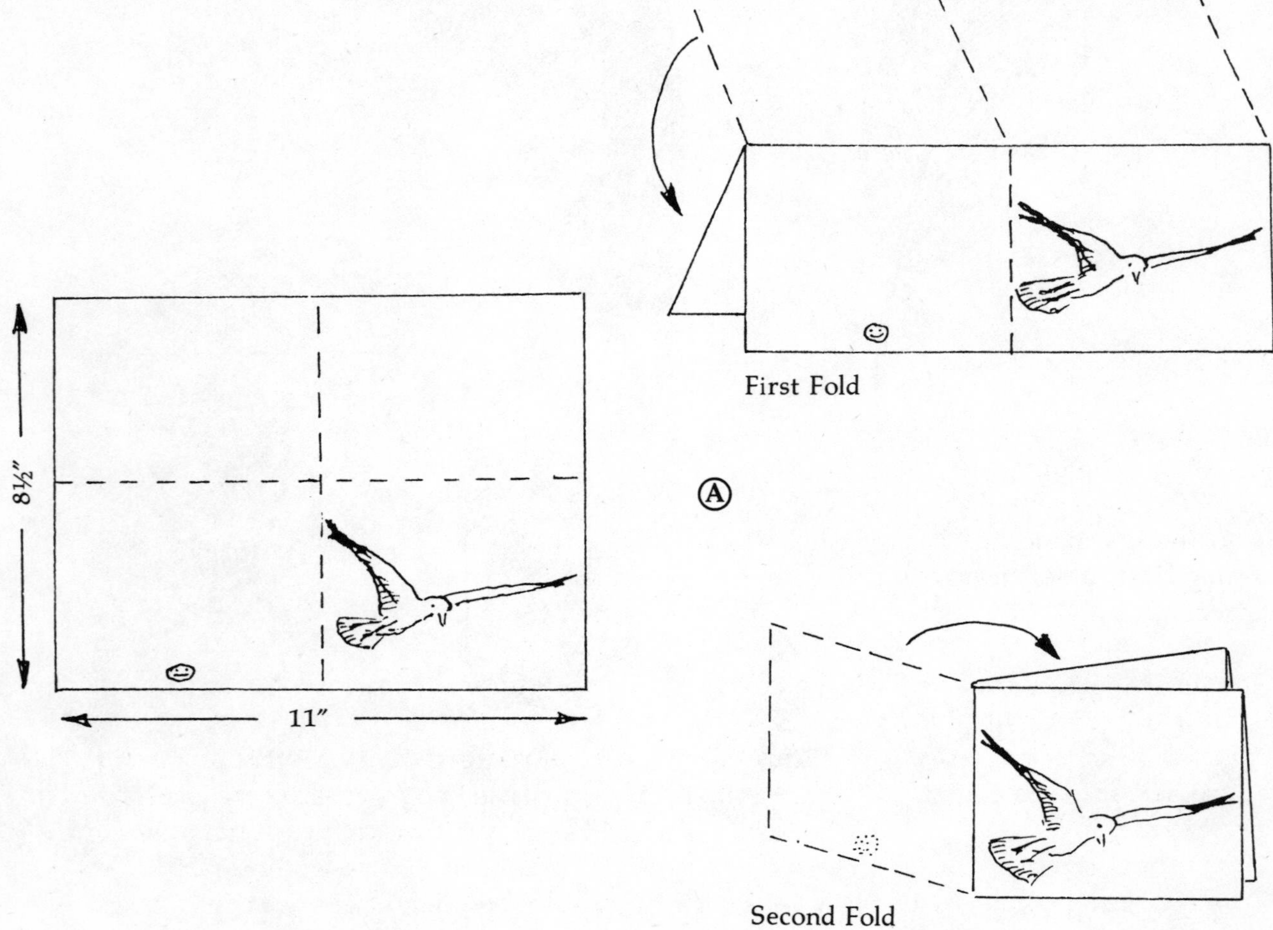
8½″
11″
First Fold
Ⓐ
Second Fold

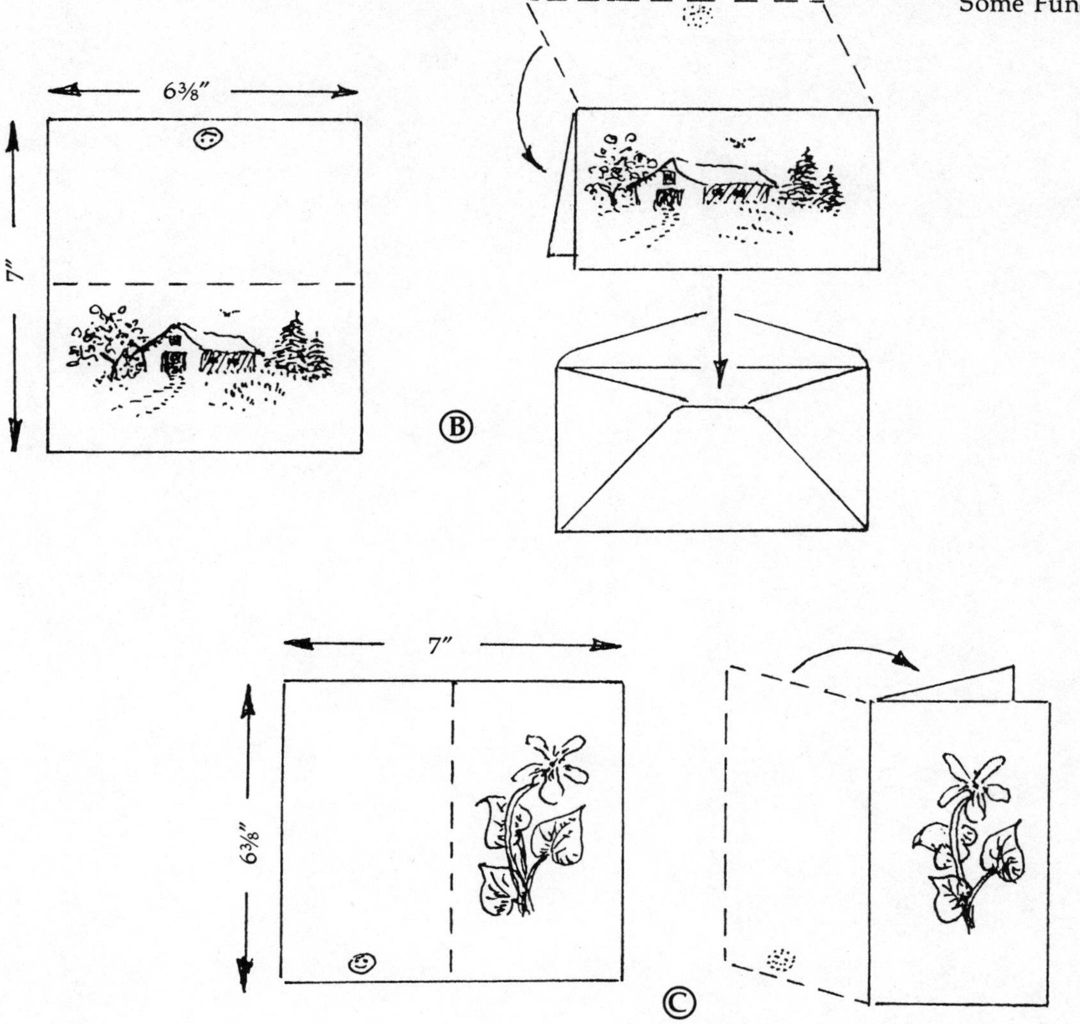
6⅜″
7″
Ⓑ
7″
6⅜″
Ⓒ

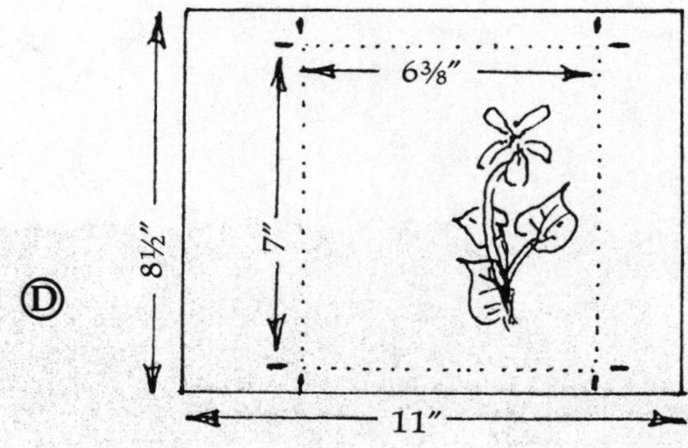
Ⓓ
6⅜″
7″
8½″
11″

Figure 3-24
You can make your own notepaper on a copier directly from your own pen-and-ink drawings. Pencil drawings require *screening* first, a service provided by a printer.

A One way of making notepaper from an ordinary eight-and-one-half-by-eleven-inch sheet of paper. Printers can sell you envelopes for notepaper this size.

B Another notepaper size. These envelopes are standard at any office supply store, usually five hundred to a box for a few dollars.

C An alternative orientation for the smaller notepaper.

D Lay out the smaller notepaper on a standard eight-and-one-half-by-eleven-inch sheet for copying. Each note must then be cut out with a straightedge and a sharp blade.

4
Seeing the Geometry of Things

Basic Geometric Shapes
Circles in Perspective
Peaked Roof in Perspective
Geometry of Architecture
Geometry of Birds
Geometry of Animals
Geometry of Flowers
Geometry of Trees
Geometry of Faces
- *Basic Facial Proportions*
- *Facial Shapes*
- *Facial Variations*

Human Figures
- *Proportions, Female*
- *Proportions, Male*
- *Proportions Versus Age*

Basic Geometric Shapes

For many drawing subjects, it will always be easier for you to first sketch a light framework of some kind representing the general shape and proportions of the object, then develop and place the details of your subject on and around this framework. This approach settles the problems of proportion and perspective before you start to draw the details that will individualize the particular subject. This framework *does not* have to bear a structural relationship with the subject; for example, if your subject is a building, the framework does not have to show the timbers that actually support the building. If your subject is a dog, the framework does not have to show the bone structure of the dog. It is not bad if the bone structure is used (if you are that familiar with the anatomy of dogs), but my point is that it is not essential to know dogs' anatomy in order to draw a credible dog. All you have to do is briefly study the subject and decide, maybe, that it looks something like a square and a circle . . . or whatever might come to your mind. The important thing is to look for some geometric relationship.

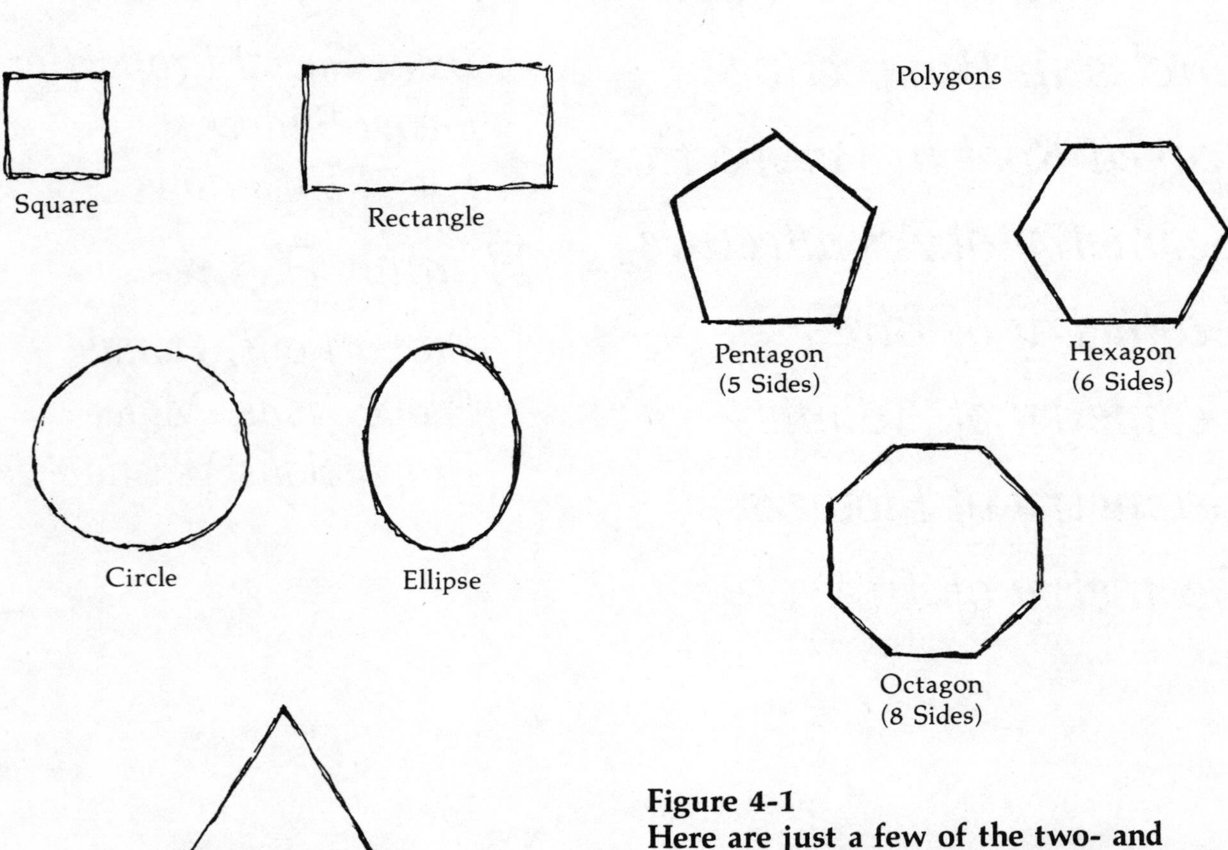
TWO-DIMENSIONAL
Square
Rectangle
Polygons
Pentagon
(5 Sides)
Hexagon
(6 Sides)
Circle
Ellipse
Octagon
(8 Sides)
Triangle

Figure 4-1
Here are just a few of the two- and three-dimensional figures that you can use to rough in the geometric aspects of your subjects.

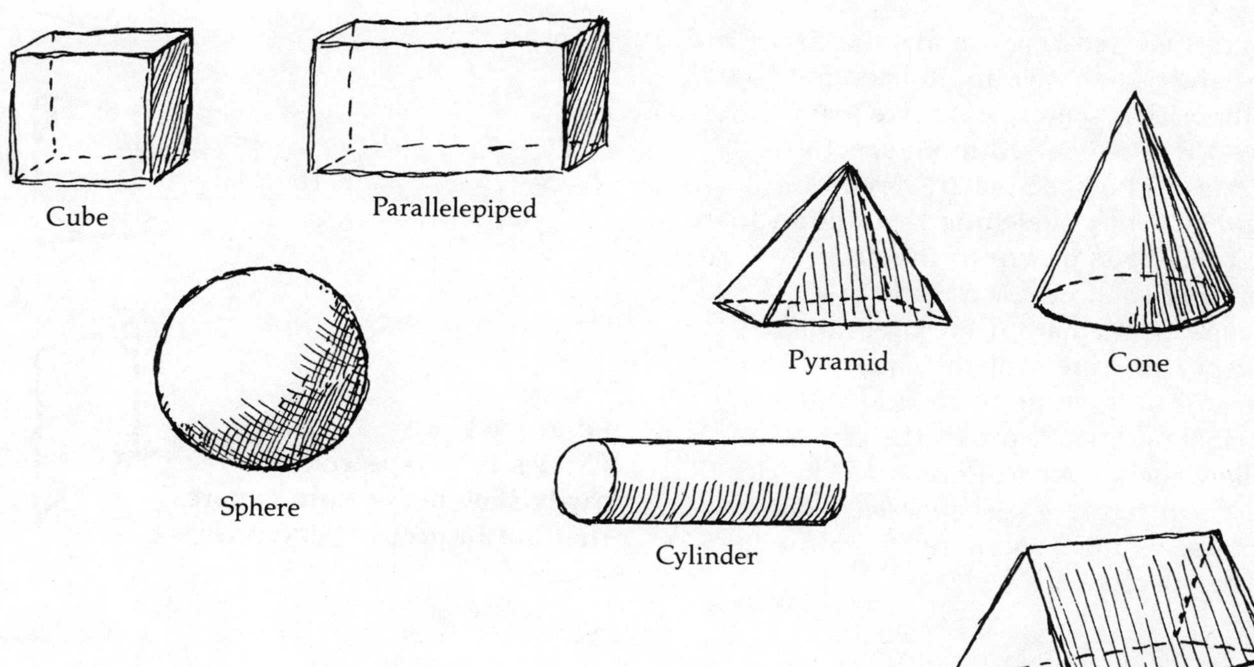
THREE-DIMENSIONAL
Cube
Parallelepiped
Pyramid
Cone
Sphere
Cylinder
Wedge

Observing the geometry of a subject is easy once you learn a few things to look for. This ability to visualize a structure in your subject will prove to be one of the most useful things in your mental toolbox.

Some two-dimensional and three-dimensional geometric figures are shown in figure 4-1. It will be helpful to you to use these shapes when sketching the framework of your subjects. Sometimes it will suffice to see the subject as including a circle, a two-dimensional figure; other times it will be better to visualize it as a sphere, a three-dimensional figure. Yet the circle and the sphere look the same on paper until you put a little shading on the sphere to give it dimension.

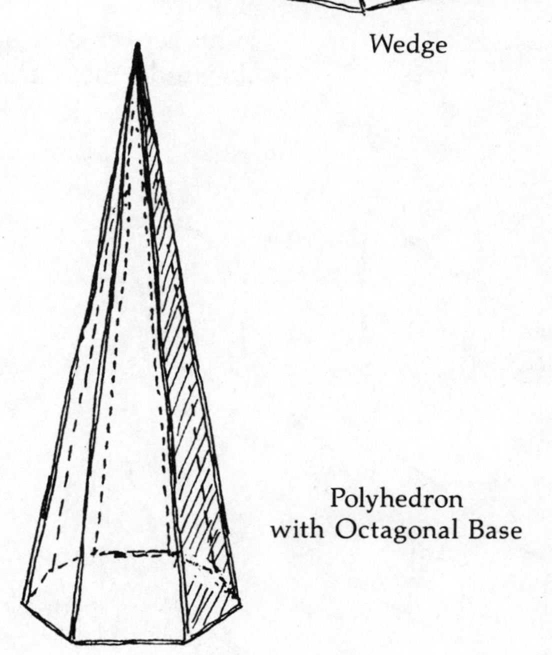
Polyhedron
with Octagonal Base

The use of these geometric shapes should be limited to your composition drawing, the one on which you develop your composition for later transfer to the final paper (as shown in Chapter 3).

Circles in Perspective

Circles viewed head-on as true circles are not always what you will need for your composition sketch. Most frequently, the circle will be viewed in perspective. Circles in perspective are developed (as in figure 4-2) by sketching them in a square that has been drawn in the proper perspective. To draw a circle in a perspective square, first locate the perspective center of the square, as in figure 4-3, then draw vertical and horizontal lines through the center, and follow the steps in figure 4-4. The clock tower in figure 4-4 shows one example of the use of this procedure to draw a circle in perspective.

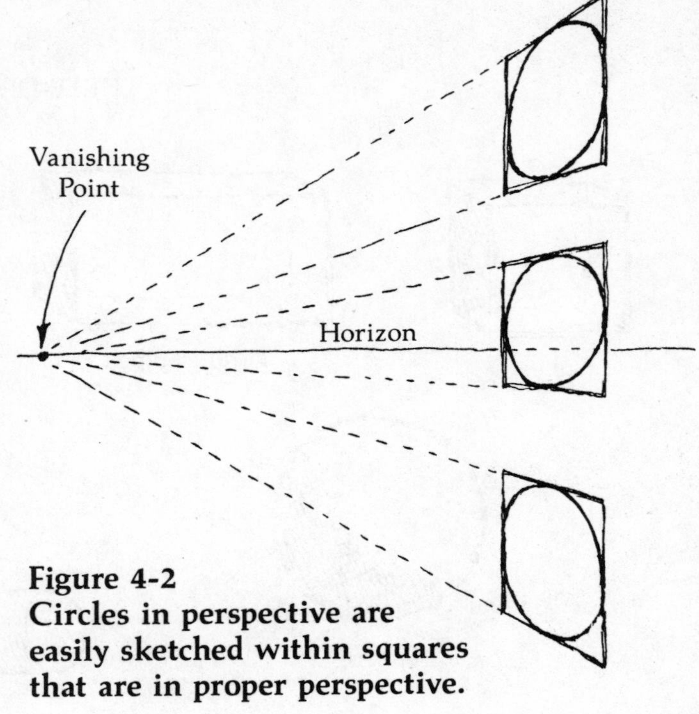
Vanishing Point
Horizon

Figure 4-2
Circles in perspective are easily sketched within squares that are in proper perspective.

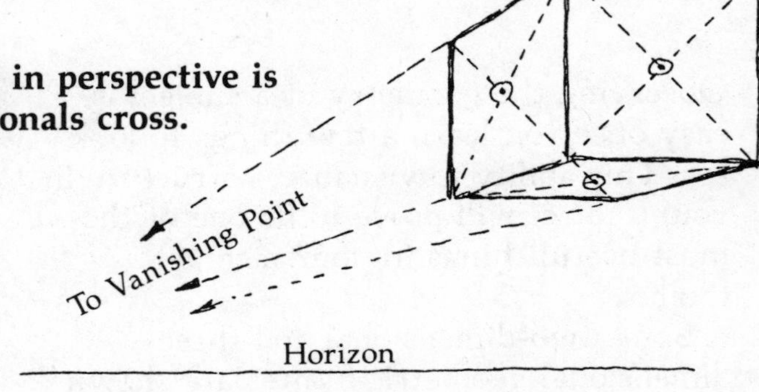
To Vanishing Point
Horizon

Figure 4-3
The center of a square in perspective is located where the diagonals cross.

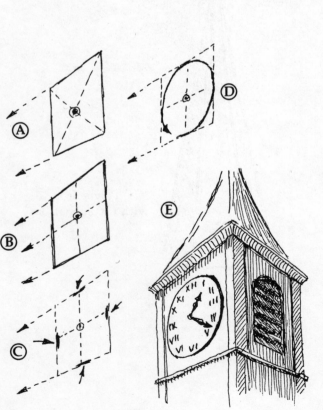

Figure 4-4
Perform steps A through D to sketch a circle in perspective.

- **A Locate the center of the square.**
- **B Draw vertical and horizontal lines through the center.**
- **C Draw short, straight lines along the vertical and horizontal bounding lines where the circle will touch.**
- **D Connect the short, straight lines with smooth curves to complete the circle.**
- **E A practical example of a circle in perspective.**

Peaked Roof in Perspective

When you sketch houses or barns, you will have to get the slope of all parts of the roof looking right. Some of this is done by eye, lightly sketching a line or two or three until you say to yourself, That looks about right! But most of getting the slopes to look right is done by using perspective drawing principles. A few constructions will establish vanishing points toward which your roof lines will trend. Figure 4-5 illustrates the six steps necessary to get the peaked roof of a barn or house looking right. Note that the starting point in figure 4-5A is the location of the perspective center of the wall, as we just covered.

Figure 4-5
Perform steps A through F to complete a peaked-roof structure in perspective.

A Determine the center of the barn side and draw a vertical line upward. The peak of the roof will lie somewhere on this vertical line.

B Estimate the pitch of the roof. Make several tries and choose the one that looks right.

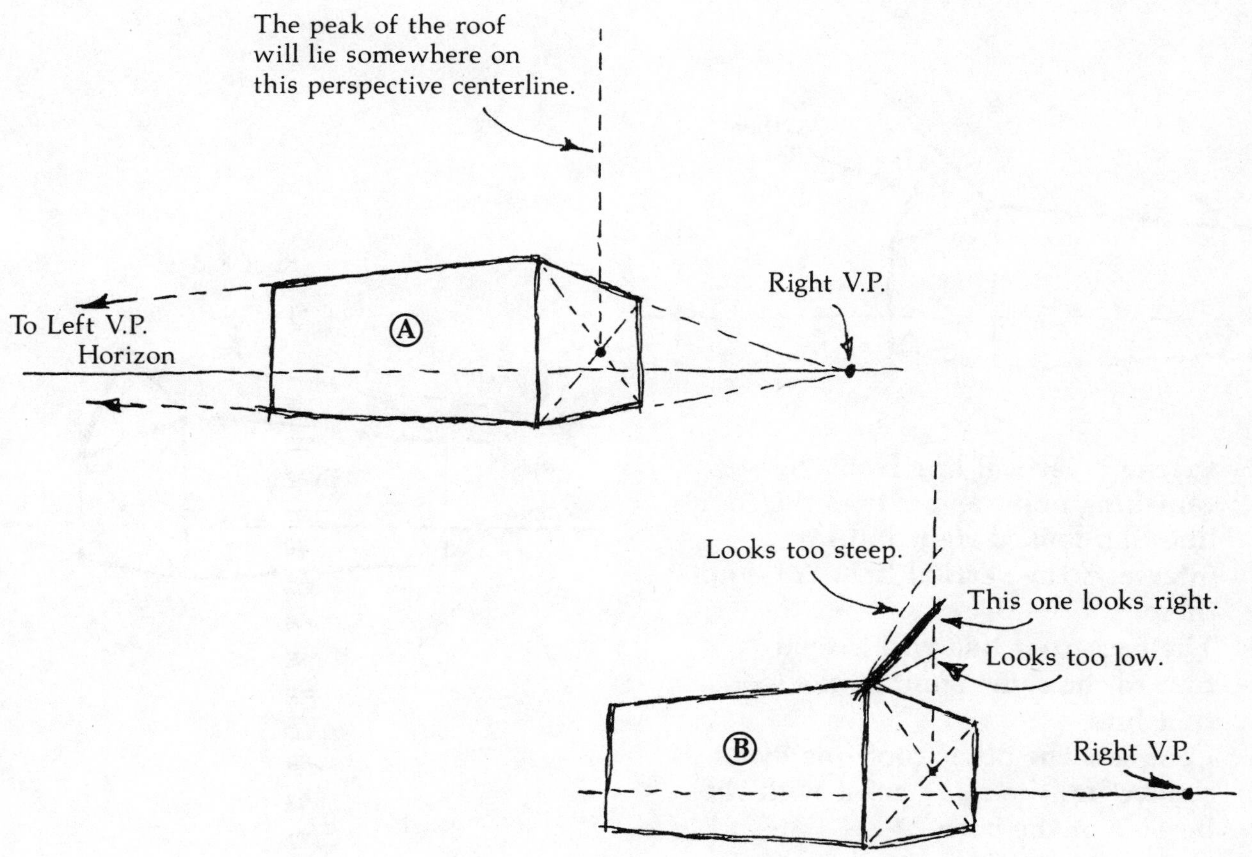
The peak of the roof will lie somewhere on this perspective centerline.
To Left V.P.
Horizon
Ⓐ
Right V.P.
Looks too steep.
This one looks right.
Looks too low.
Ⓑ
Right V.P.

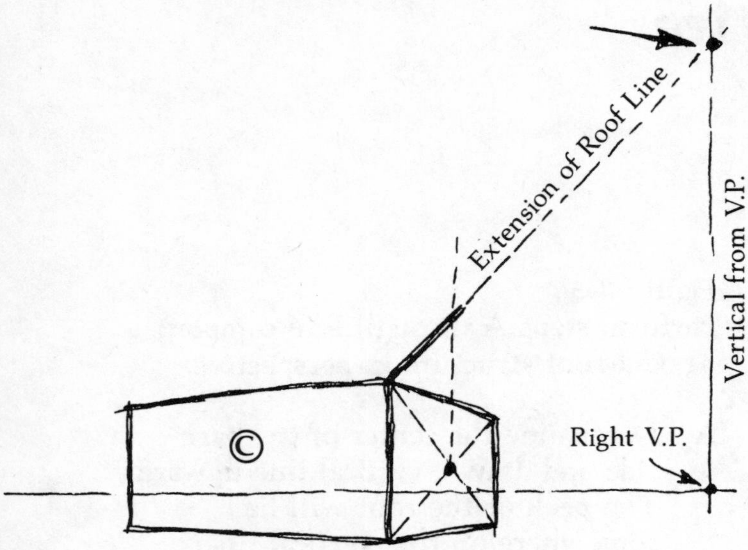

Extension of Roof Line
Vertical from V.P.
Right V.P.
C

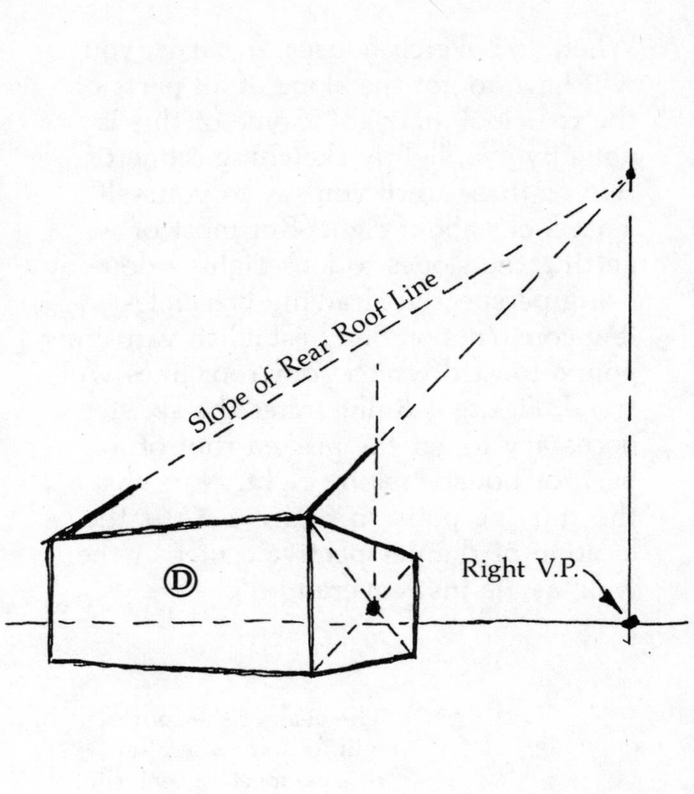
Slope of Rear Roof Line
Right V.P.
D

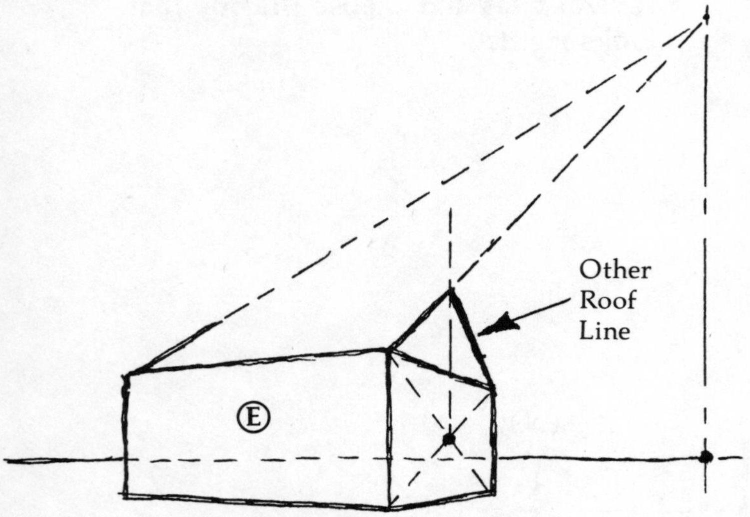

Other
Roof
Line
E

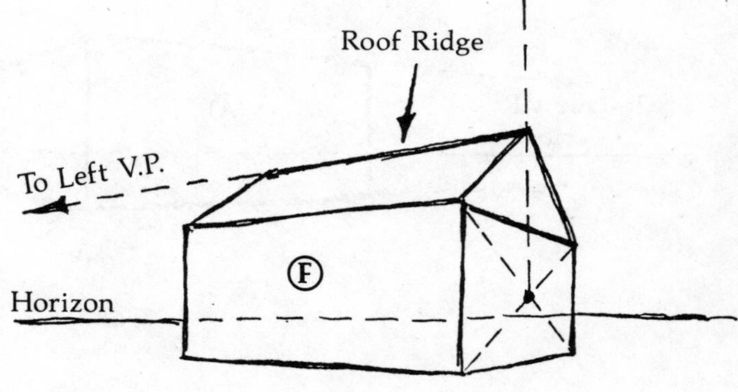
Roof Ridge
To Left V.P.
F
Horizon

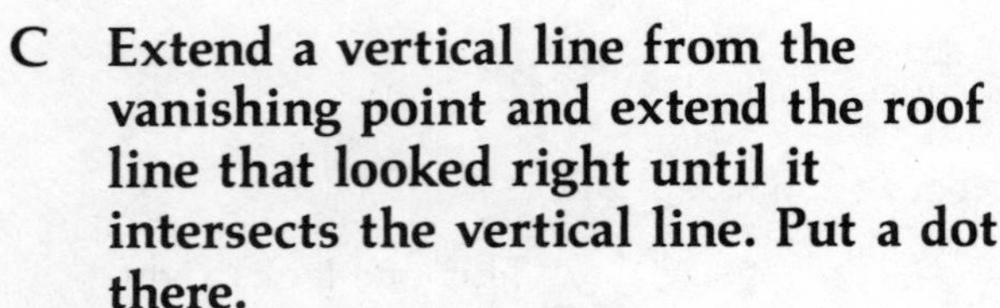

C Extend a vertical line from the vanishing point and extend the roof line that looked right until it intersects the vertical line. Put a dot there.

D The back roof line will extend toward the same point as the front roof line.

E Complete the other roof line by connecting the ridge point with the far side of the barn.

F Complete the roof ridge by drawing it to extend to the left vanishing point.

Geometry of Architecture

The procedure for using some geometric shapes in developing a composition drawing of an architectural subject is shown in figure 4-6. Here, I wanted to draw an eight-sided spire on a stone church tower. First, using right and left vanishing points on my horizon, I roughed in the stone tower. Being above eye level, the roof of the tower is not visible, but I had to imagine the tower is made of glass so I could see through it to the underside of the roof. In A, I established the center of the roof (that I cannot see)—it is where the diagonals cross. The tip of the church spire will lie somewhere on the vertical drawn from this center. Next, I estimated the points where the corners of an eight-sided figure, an octagon, would lie on the flat roof. These are the little Xs in B. I estimated how high the spire is relative to the height of the tower and put a dot on the vertical I drew in the first step (A). The other lines of the spire converge at this dot, as in C. Now, on this framework I started to develop the other details of my subject, knowing that the proportions and the geometry of my tower and spire will look reasonably correct. Eliminating all the construction lines not necessary to the final sketch, I brought the top of the tower to completion, as in D.

Figure 4-6
An eight-sided spire layout is constructed as shown.

A Locate the perspective center of the roof.
B Indicate the eight-sided base (Xs).
C Draw the spire so the lines meet on the center vertical.
D Add other details to the framework as needed.

Perspective Center of the Top Surface
Vertical from Center
To Left V.P.
To Right V.P.
Ⓐ
Ⓑ
Eight-sided (octagonal) layout of the steeple spire base.

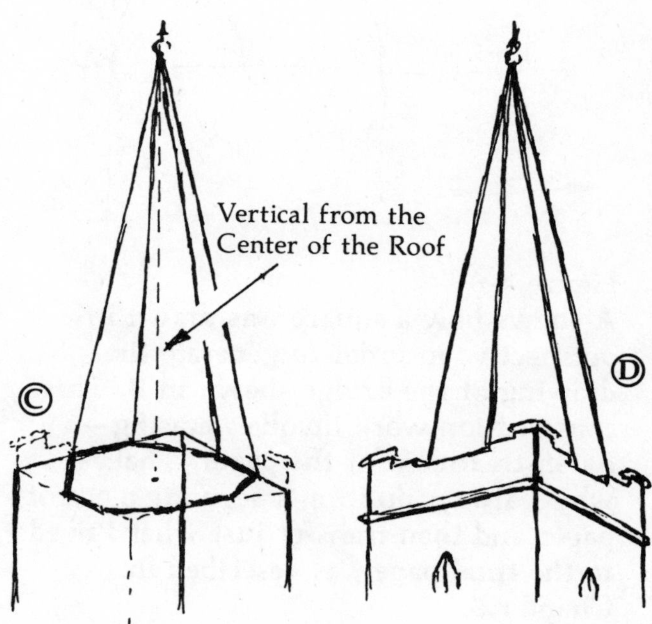
Vertical from the Center of the Roof
Ⓒ
Ⓓ

A summary of the procedure to develop an architectural composition drawing is shown in figure 4-7A, B, and C. This figure shows a very simple barn with the structure geometry developed in A and the actual structural details placed on and over this structure in B. It is only these details that are transferred to your final paper for the finishing touches with ink or pencil, as in C.

One use of a circle seen in perspective is shown in figure 4-8, a sketch of a little bridge. In order to have the arch of the bridge look right, I developed it from the perspective circle you see in A. Note how the lower half of the circle shows where to put the reflected dark underside of the bridge.

A
B
C

Figure 4-7

A Part of a composition sketch based on the elementary geometric shapes in a peaked-roof barn.

B The development on the basic sketch of some of the specific details of the barn.

C The final sketch after transfer of the details to the final paper, as outlined in Chapter 3.

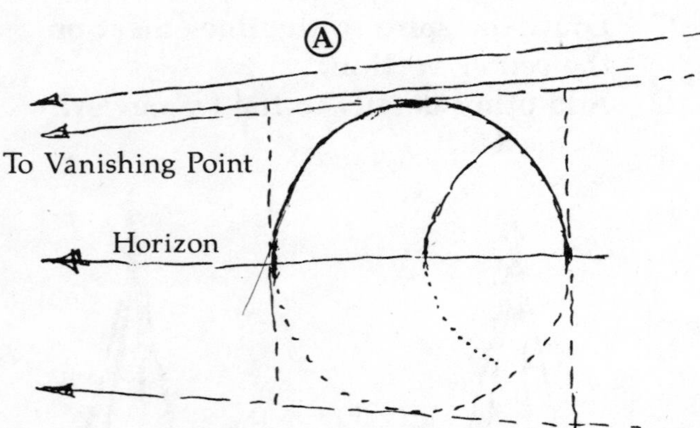
A
To Vanishing Point
Horizon

B

Figure 4-8

A shows how a square was drawn in perspective in order to generate the drawing of the bridge shown in B. This construction work involves erasing—harsh treatment of the paper. That is why I always do it on a separate piece of paper and then transfer just what I need to the final paper, as described in Chapter 3.

Ⓐ
Ⓑ

Six solid geometric shapes are shown in figure 4-9A; they fit together to form the basis for the somewhat complicated structure of the country church in B. The steps in developing the composition drawing that I transferred to good paper are shown in figures 4-10A and B (next page). The outline in A gave me all I needed to develop the composition drawing in B.

Figure 4-9
A shows the basic geometric shapes I used to construct the composition sketch for the drawing at B.

You should learn to visualize the geometry of your subject in this kind of detail at the composition stage to insure that your structure will look right when you complete your drawing.

A
B

Figure 4-10

A My rough composition sketch for the country church in the previous figure.

B Development of the details on this framework before transferring to my final paper.

Geometry of Birds

Drawing birds, or any animals for that matter, requires good reference material. You will not draw a really credible bird from memory unless you have drawn many, many birds before and have the proportions well in mind. Most of us are not in that situation. Most of us need to refer to photographs, often many of them, to do one bird sketch, and the larger the photograph, the better. Your library is a good source of reference material in the form of both books and nature magazines.

When drawing most birds, I have found it very convenient to think of the basic structure as being three circles: one for the head, a larger one for the body, and a smaller one for the rump area. This structure has no real relationship to the anatomy of a bird; it is just a very convenient aid to getting a right-looking rough sketch done quickly. On this I can draw the details that individualize that particular bird. Figure 4-11 shows five bird subjects developed with this scheme. By using tracing paper placed on your reference photograph and playing with some circles, you can see just how three circles should lie and estimate their relative sizes. Then draw that pattern of circles on your composition paper, and you will be well on your way to completing a reasonably good composition sketch of your subject. An alternative to this approach is to use the grid system explained in Chapter 3 to copy the outline of your reference photograph. This circle system applies primarily to freehand drawing.

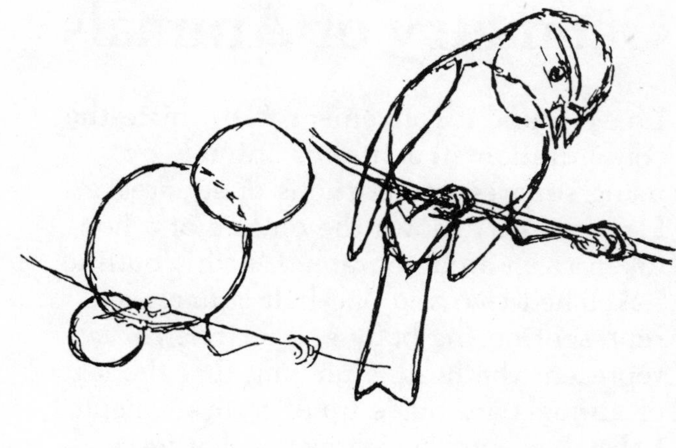

Figure 4-11
When I sketch birds freehand I find it helpful to base the sketch on three circles: one each for the head, the body, and the rump.

If your subject is to be based on a photograph or other picture, place a sheet of tracing paper on the reference and use a soft pencil to see how three circles represent the bird's structure. Then lightly sketch three similar circles on your composition paper and begin to develop the bird's form over this framework. When you are satisfied with the shape and proportions, transfer what you need to your final paper (as suggested in Chapter 3) and complete the drawing.

Geometry of Animals

I have found it convenient to estimate the configuration structure of animals by using squares and portions of squares. Figure 4-12A shows the outline of a lion taken from a photograph. On this outline I sketched two and one-half squares as representing the body and a circle to represent the head. Knowing that the legs of animals are made up of four segments, I sketched four leg segments that were visible in my photograph, as you see in figure 4-12B. These lines now approximate the generic proportions of a lion. I can simply straighten them out, as in figure 4-13A, to represent a standing lion, even though I do not have a photograph showing such a pose. Sketching some details around this framework, as in figure 4-13B, gives me a reasonable drawing of a standing lion. I know that lions are three-dimensional beasts, so I can estimate a three-quarter view of a standing lion by drawing boxes and lines, using the same proportions I determined from the photograph of figure 4-12A, to make a composition drawing as in figure 4-13C. Using the circle for the head allows me to more easily keep the head in proper proportion to the rest of the body as I try to turn my framework into a lion.

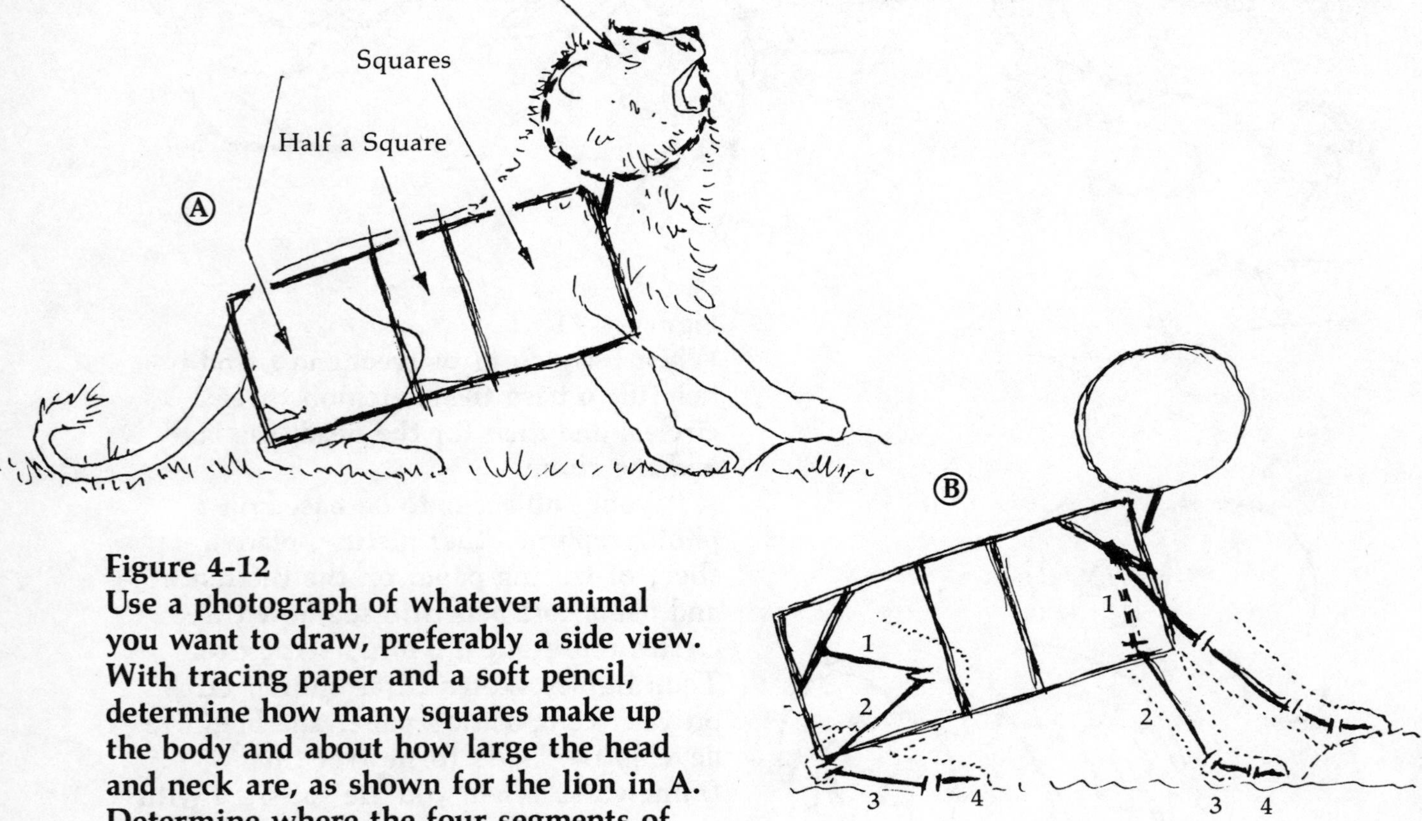
Circle
Squares
Half a Square
A
B
1
2
3
4
1
2
3
4

Figure 4-12
Use a photograph of whatever animal you want to draw, preferably a side view. With tracing paper and a soft pencil, determine how many squares make up the body and about how large the head and neck are, as shown for the lion in A. Determine where the four segments of each leg lie, as in B. This gives you the basic proportions you need to draw that animal.

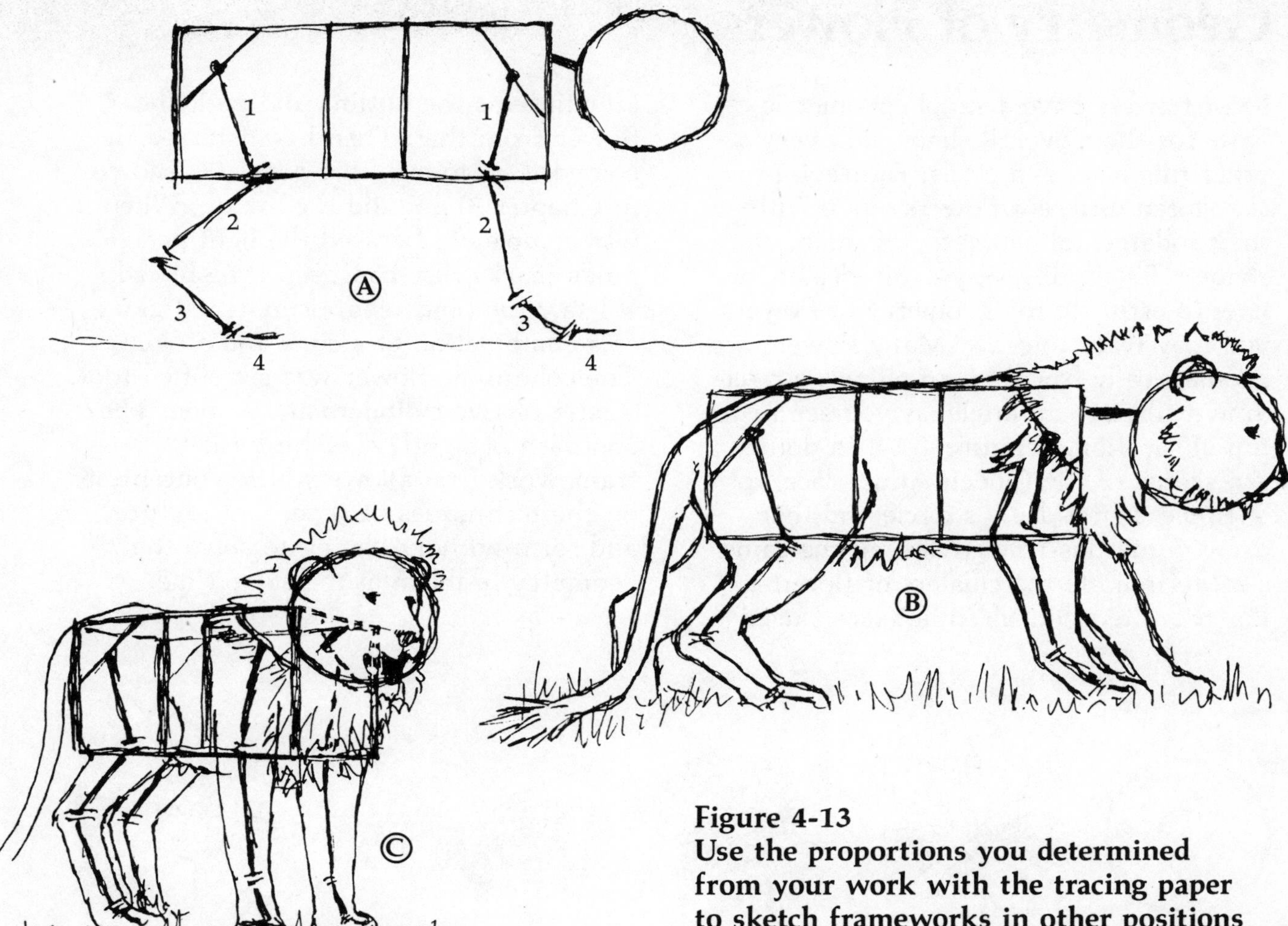
1
1
2
2
A
3
3
4
4
B
C

Figure 4-13
Use the proportions you determined from your work with the tracing paper to sketch frameworks in other positions (A), positions for which you do not have photographs. Then develop your animal on these frameworks, as in B and C.

This approach will greatly speed your freehand sketching of animals and will make your drawings more properly proportioned.

For whatever animal you want to draw freehand, get several good photographs, preferably side views, and play with some tracing paper and a soft pencil to determine a basic structure. Then, using the proportions you find, you can more easily draw the animal from the photo or you can change the pose and draw the animal in positions of which you do not have photographs. This scheme helps you more quickly make freehand sketches of animals that are more rewarding because they look right.

Geometry of Flowers

Most flowers have a simple geometric basis for their overall shape, and very often this basis is a circle. Figure 4-14 shows ten different flowers along with the fundamental geometry of their shapes. This will give you an idea about how to estimate the geometry of flowers you may want to draw. Many flowers are geometrically based on an ellipse, a circle drawn tilted at an angle, as you see in the top illustration of figure 4-14. In doing the sketch of the Queen Anne's lace, for example, I first drew a circle and then drew numerous tiny circles, all the same size, to indicate the clusters of florettes. For the tilted Queen Anne's lace I used an ellipse as the outline and built the flower from that. Then I transferred the composition to my final paper (as shown in Chapter 3) and did the inking. When it was completed, I erased the light pencil guide marks that had been transferred.

I saw the bindweed, or morning glory, as a combination of a cone and a circle. The columbine flower was simplified to a cluster of five cylinders and a cone. The approach of lightly sketching the framework first allows you to concentrate on the techniques of rendering texture and form without having to solve the geometry problem at the same time.

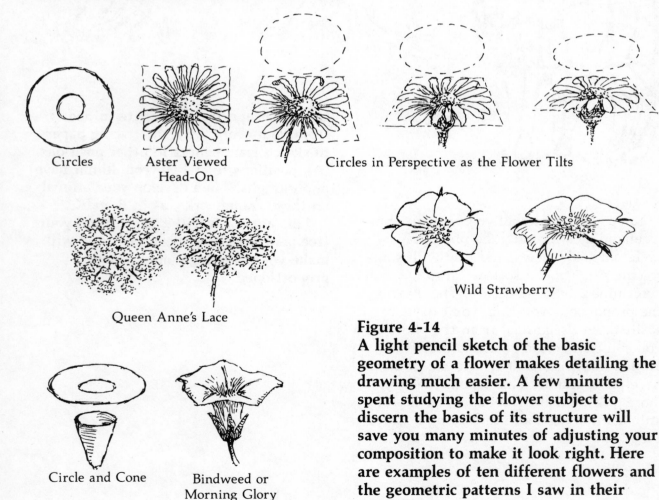

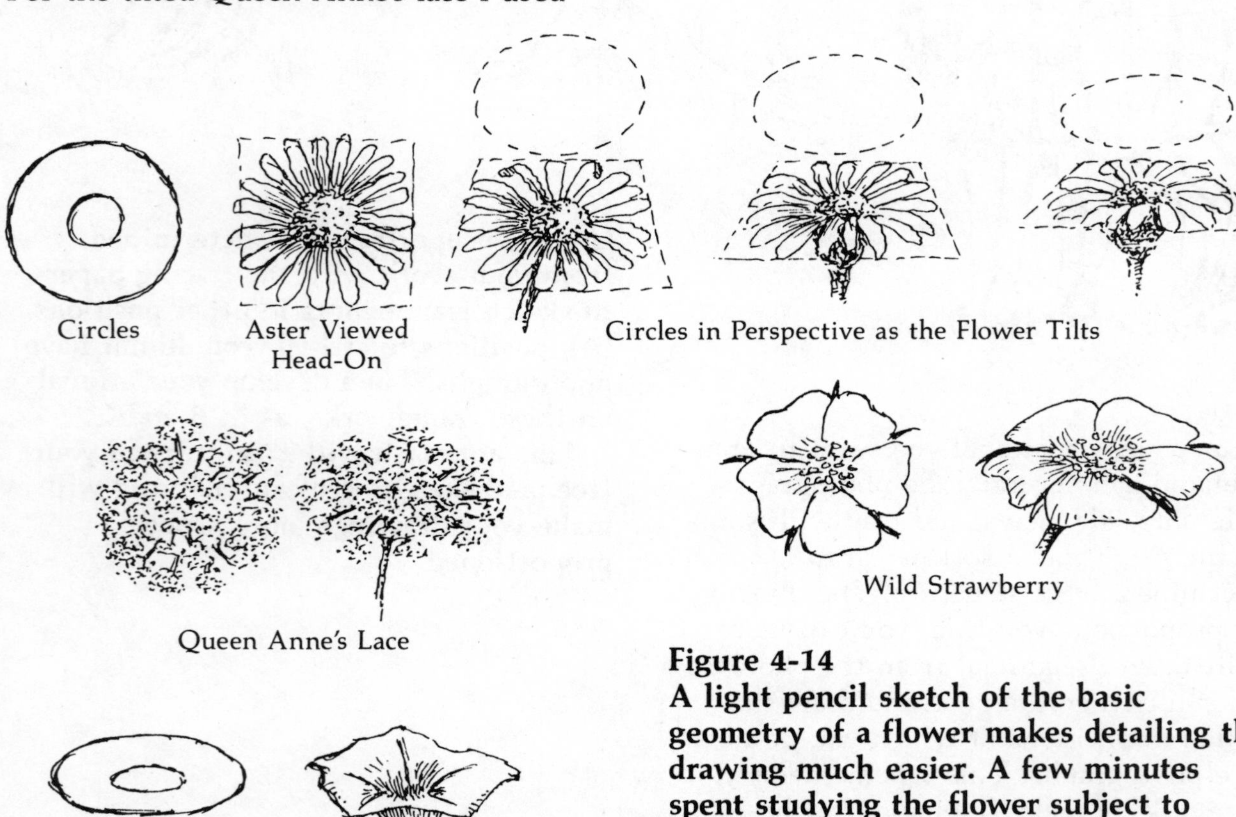
Circles
Aster Viewed Head-On
Circles in Perspective as the Flower Tilts
Wild Strawberry
Queen Anne's Lace
Circle and Cone
Bindweed or Morning Glory

Figure 4-14
A light pencil sketch of the basic geometry of a flower makes detailing the drawing much easier. A few minutes spent studying the flower subject to discern the basics of its structure will save you many minutes of adjusting your composition to make it look right. Here are examples of ten different flowers and the geometric patterns I saw in their structures.

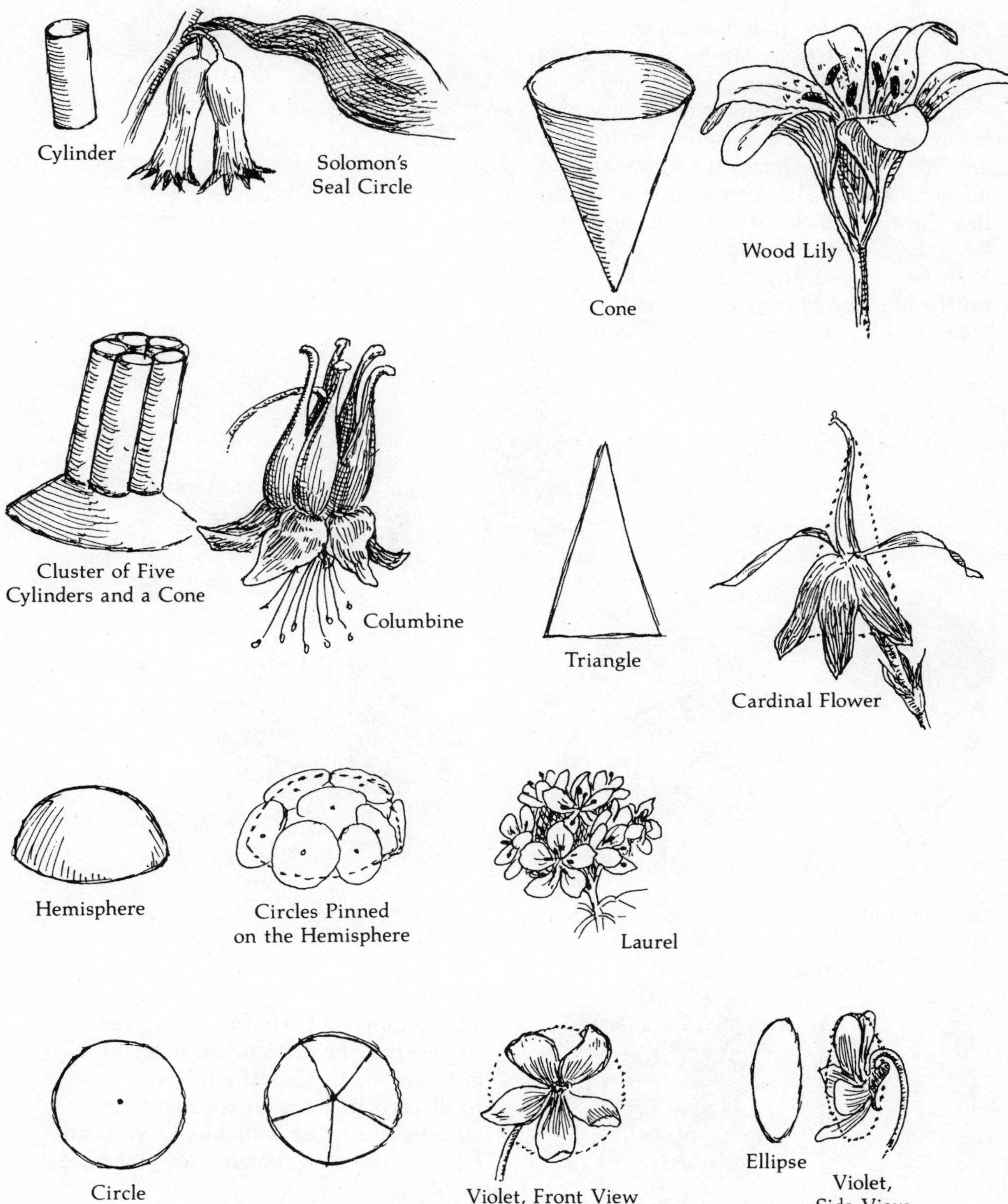
Cylinder
Solomon's Seal Circle
Cone
Wood Lily
Cluster of Five Cylinders and a Cone
Columbine
Triangle
Cardinal Flower
Hemisphere
Circles Pinned on the Hemisphere
Laurel
Circle
Violet, Front View
Ellipse
Violet, Side View

Geometry of Trees

Although usually quite irregular, the outline of most trees can be seen as being bounded roughly by regular geometric shapes. Figure 4-15 shows cases in which the cone, cone and hemisphere, cylinder, and sphere approximate the boundaries of different trees. The cottonwood is almost like the elm, but it carries branches much lower on the trunk, and its outer branches do not droop as much as those on the elm. I can still see an inverted cone as the basis for the tree, however.

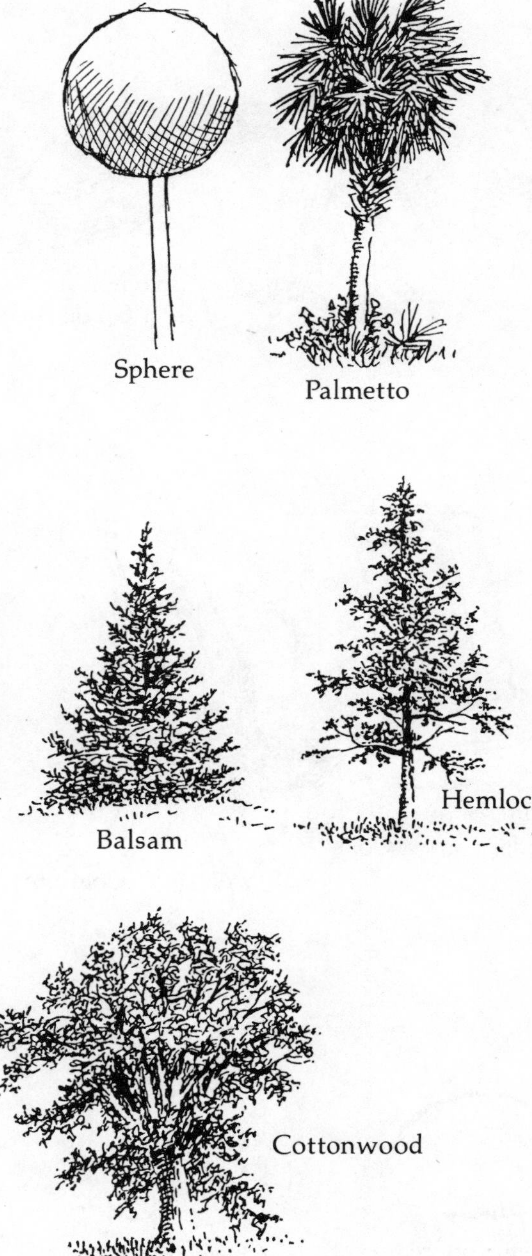
Sphere
Palmetto
Cone
White Spruce
Balsam
Hemlock

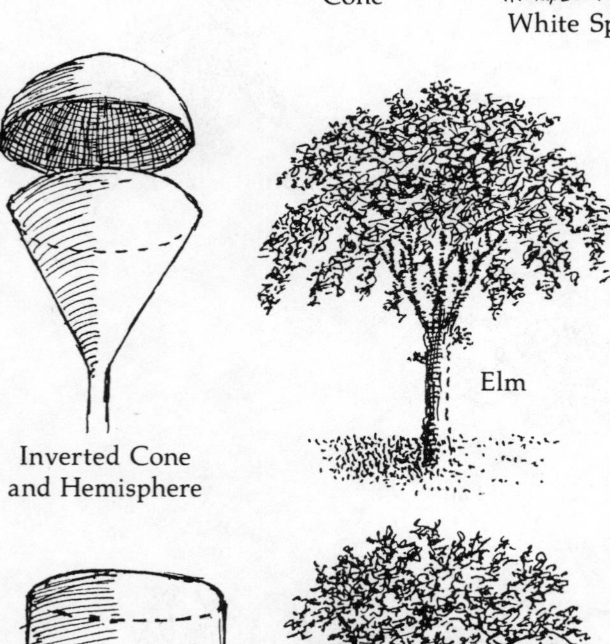
Inverted Cone
and Hemisphere
Elm
Cottonwood

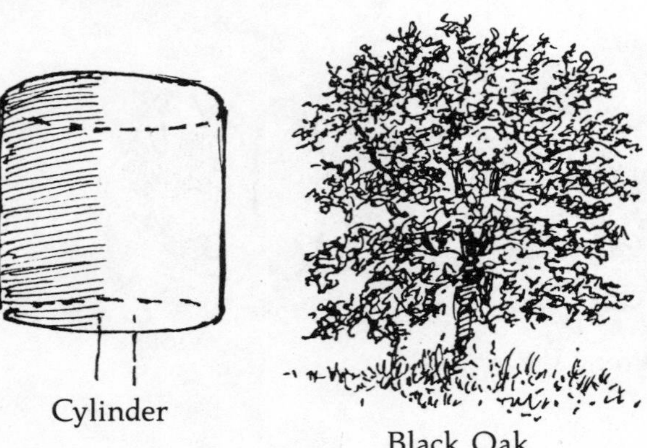
Cylinder
Black Oak

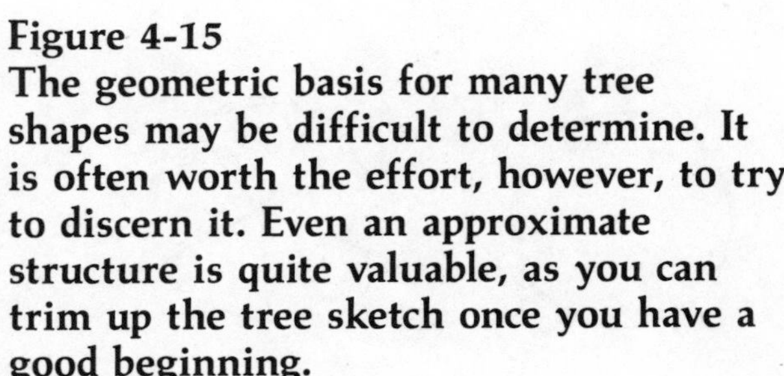

Figure 4-15
The geometric basis for many tree shapes may be difficult to determine. It is often worth the effort, however, to try to discern it. Even an approximate structure is quite valuable, as you can trim up the tree sketch once you have a good beginning.

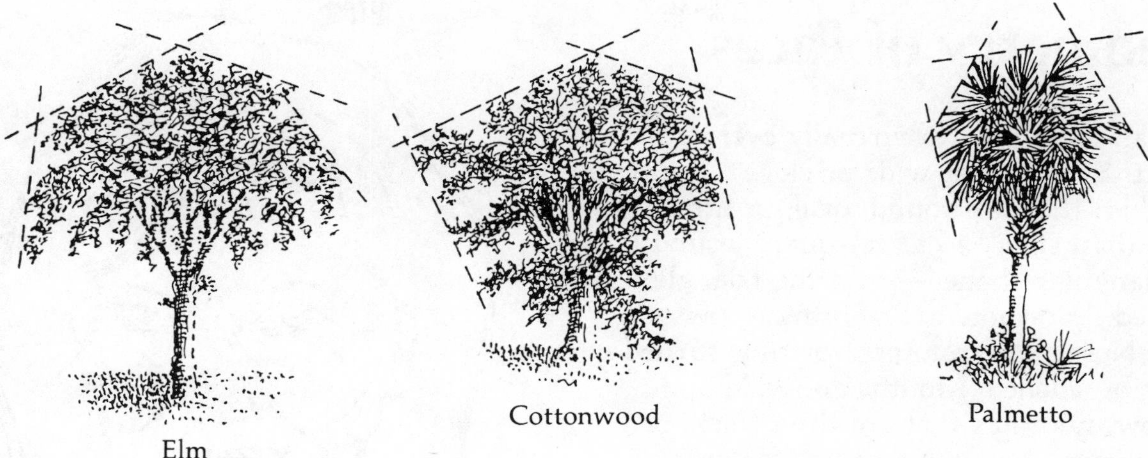
Elm
Cottonwood
Palmetto

Figure 4-16 shows you that the bounding lines of the foliage on trees most frequently are not curves, but rather a series of straight lines. Lollipop-shaped trees do not look realistic—trees do not grow that way (although they can be trimmed that way). Figure 4-17, based on Constable's *Hay Wain*, shows how the artist used straight lines to bound the middle-ground trees in this well-known landscape.

Figure 4-16
Trees seldom have a curved outline. This figure shows how some of the trees in figure 4-15 are bounded mostly by straight lines.

Figure 4-17
The outline of the middle-ground trees in John Constable's *Hay Wain* (National Gallery, London) consists of a series of straight lines.

Geometry of Faces

Human faces vary in virtually every aspect. Eyes are set wide or close together; they are round, oval, or little more than slits. Faces are square, round, or triangular-shaped—with the triangle pointed up or down. The brow is low or high. Noses are prominent or tiny, turned up or broadened. Mouths are wide or narrow, with lips that are thin, thick, or in-between. Any one face has features that are a combination of the variations listed, as suggested in figure 4-18. So how can you start to draw a face?

Oval or Elliptical

Figure 4-18
Faces are found with many different basic shapes.

Round

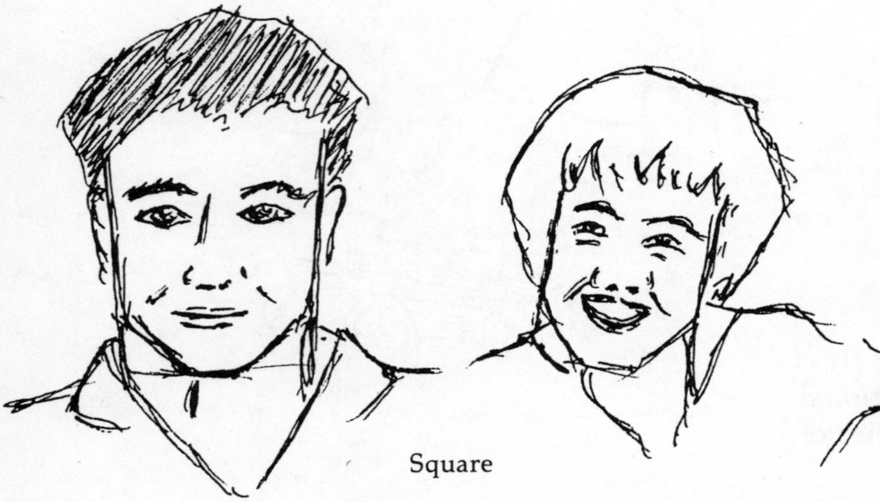

Square

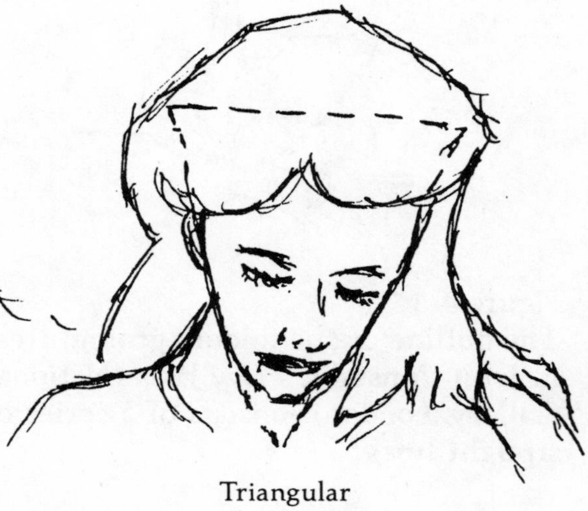

Triangular

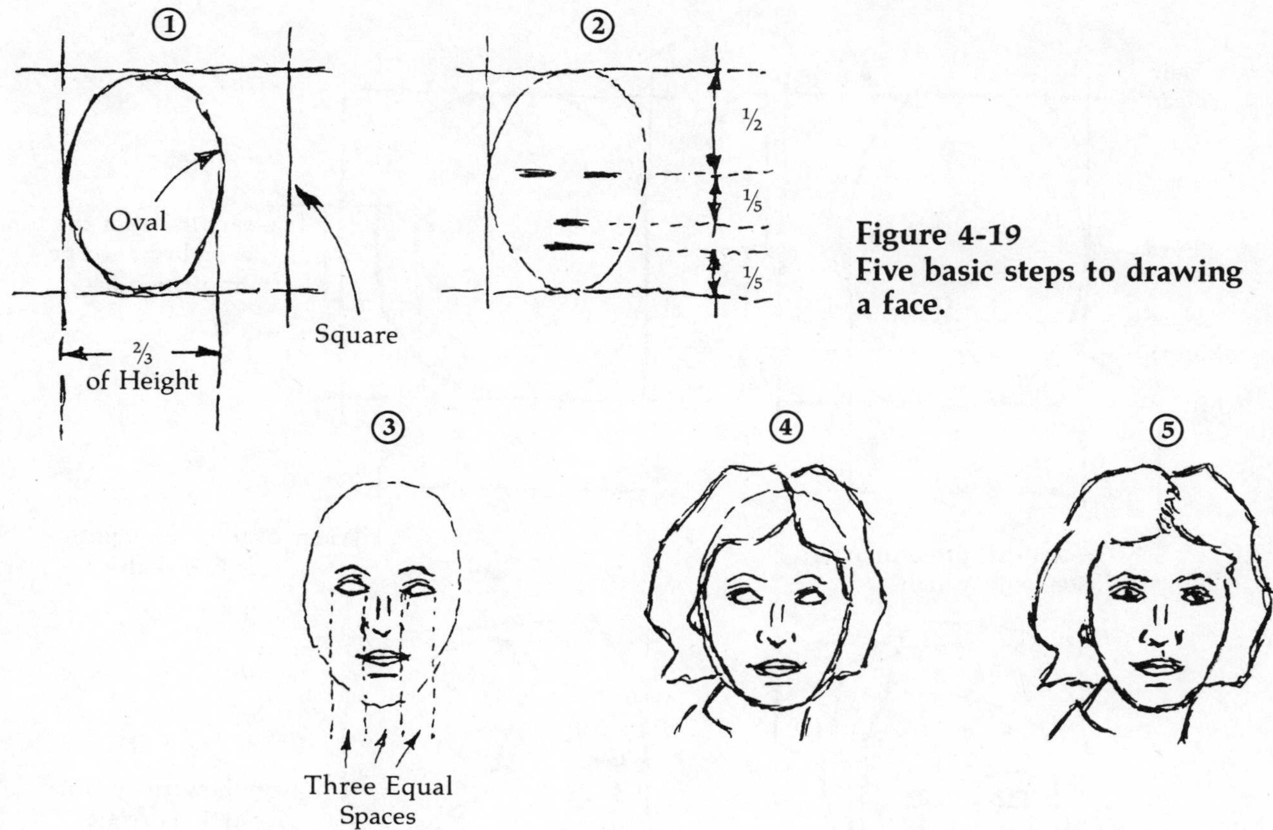
①
Oval
Square
⅔
of Height
②
½
⅕
⅕
③
Three Equal
Spaces
④
⑤

Figure 4-19
Five basic steps to drawing a face.

Faces can be thought of as variations on a basic set of proportions. If these proportions are roughed in, any particular face can be drawn by noting how it varies from this framework. Figure 4-19 suggests such a starting point. Sketch a square, and estimate two-thirds of it to contain the face, as in step 1. Place the eyes halfway between the top and the bottom of the square, place the bottom of the nose one-fifth of the height of the square down from the eyes, and place the mouth one-fifth up from the bottom (the chin), as in step 2. The eyes are spaced one eye-width apart, as in step 3. Rough in the hair, and you have a well-proportioned face, as in steps 4 and 5. Now you can start to make adjustments to create any particular face.

Basic Facial Proportions

Figure 4-20 shows a male face that takes three-quarters of the square's width and shows you how to estimate the location of the ears in full-face view as well as in profile and three-quarter view.
Remember that these proportions are not sacred! They are suggested only as a way to let you quickly rough in a well-proportioned face, which you can alter as necessary to produce the face that you want to draw. Some eyes are closer together; some are wider. Some faces have a greater distance between the bottom of the nose and the top of the lips. Some have a more prominent chin. Play with facial proportions on a piece of paper and see how small variations make great differences in the appearance of a face. Although they vary from individual to individual, facial features do not really wander all over the face. Only by playing with a pencil as I suggest will you appreciate this.

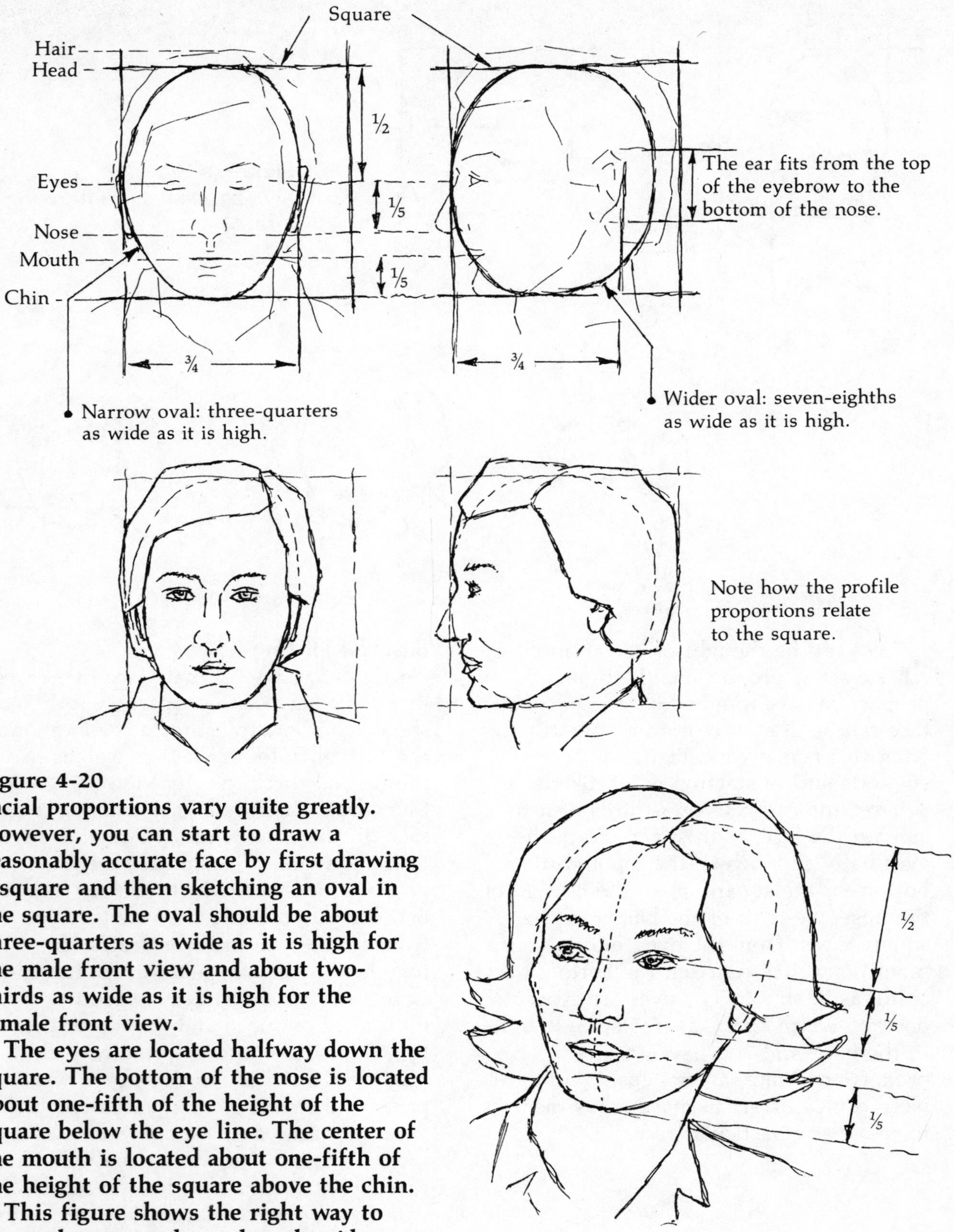

Square

Hair

Head

½

Eyes

⅕

Nose

Mouth

⅕

Chin

¾

¾

The ear fits from the top of the eyebrow to the bottom of the nose.

• Narrow oval: three-quarters as wide as it is high.

• Wider oval: seven-eighths as wide as it is high.

Note how the profile proportions relate to the square.

½
⅕
⅕

Figure 4-20
Facial proportions vary quite greatly. However, you can start to draw a reasonably accurate face by first drawing a square and then sketching an oval in the square. The oval should be about three-quarters as wide as it is high for the male front view and about two-thirds as wide as it is high for the female front view.

The eyes are located halfway down the square. The bottom of the nose is located about one-fifth of the height of the square below the eye line. The center of the mouth is located about one-fifth of the height of the square above the chin.

This figure shows the right way to locate the ears and to relate the side view, or *profile*, to the basic square.

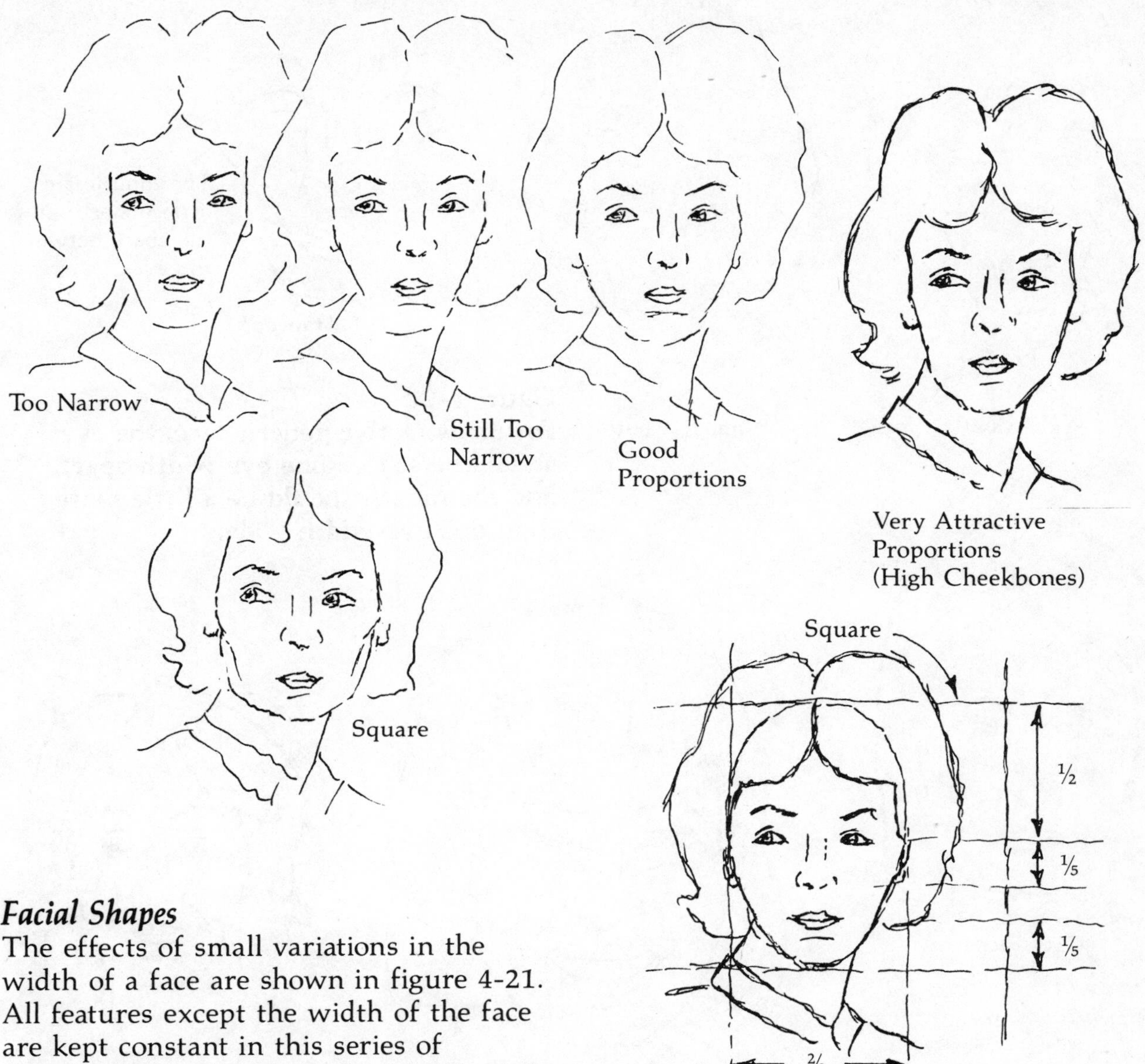
Too Narrow
Still Too Narrow
Good Proportions
Very Attractive Proportions (High Cheekbones)
Square
Square
½
⅕
⅕
⅔

Facial Shapes

The effects of small variations in the width of a face are shown in figure 4-21. All features except the width of the face are kept constant in this series of sketches. Figure 4-22 shows the effect of changing the width of the mouth, a bit smaller and a bit larger.

Facial Variations

Some additional variations of facial features are shown in figure 4-23. You should be wary of including too many lines in the pen drawing of a face. A few lines too many can turn a charming young face into that of a middle-aged woman, as you see in figure 4-24. This is the same face as that of the oval-faced girl drawn in figure 4-23, but with a few additional lines that suggest wrinkles.

Figure 4-21
Faces vary greatly in shape. Here you see proportions for an attractive female face that are narrowed and squared.

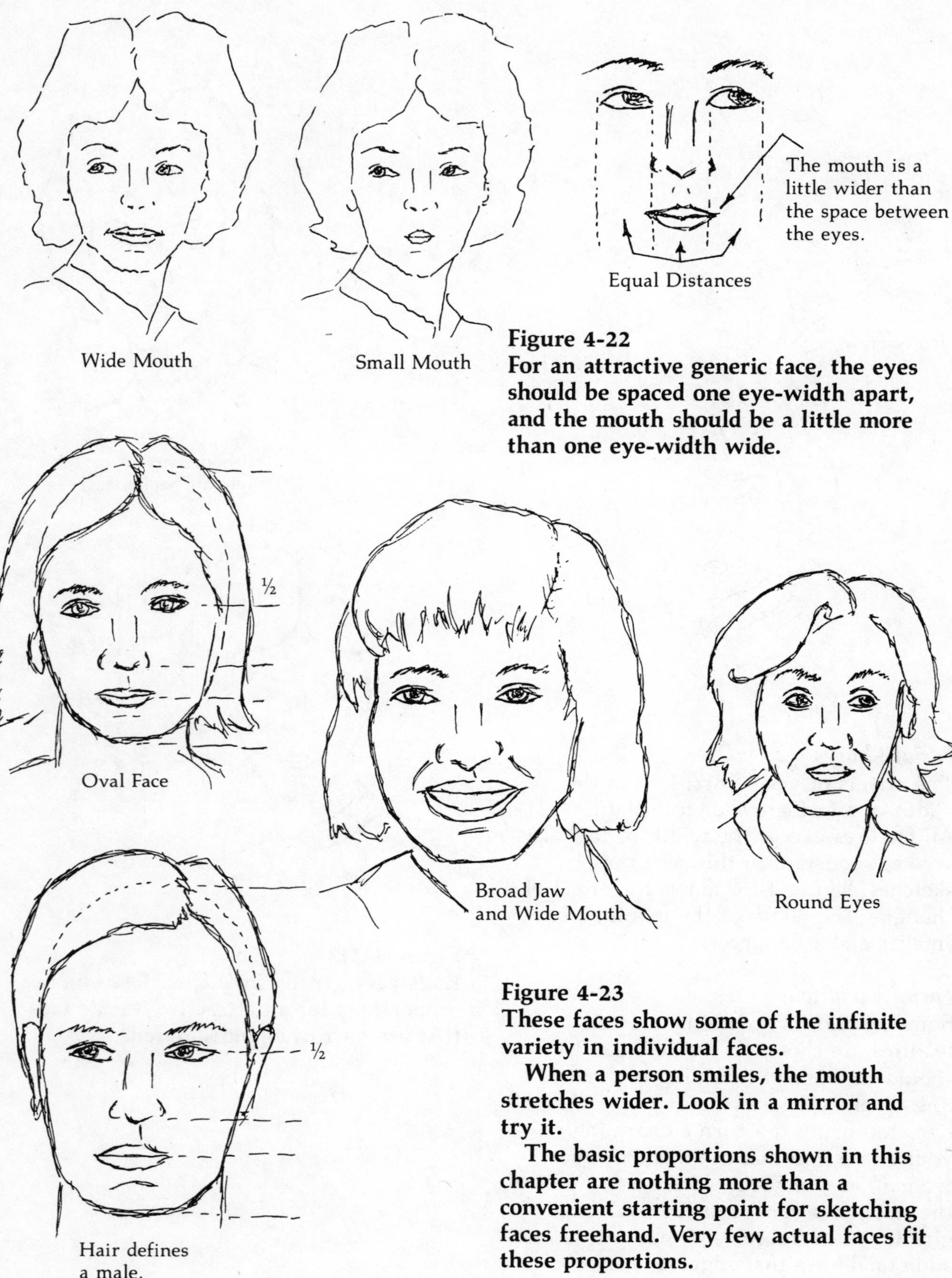
The mouth is a little wider than the space between the eyes.
Equal Distances
Wide Mouth
Small Mouth
½
Oval Face
Broad Jaw and Wide Mouth
Round Eyes
½
Hair defines a male.

Figure 4-22
For an attractive generic face, the eyes should be spaced one eye-width apart, and the mouth should be a little more than one eye-width wide.

Figure 4-23
These faces show some of the infinite variety in individual faces.

When a person smiles, the mouth stretches wider. Look in a mirror and try it.

The basic proportions shown in this chapter are nothing more than a convenient starting point for sketching faces freehand. Very few actual faces fit these proportions.

Figure 4-24
Be careful. . . . Adding just a few lines around the eyes, mouth, and forehead ages a youthful face. This is the same face as the "Oval Face" illustration in figure 4-23 with just a few lines added.

Human Figures

Human figures are three-dimensional. They represent *volume,* and so should your drawings of them. Even though your drawing of a person on a piece of paper is two-dimensional, it represents a solid volume. You should keep this roundness in mind as you draw human figures.

Figure 4-25 shows one way you can visualize the volume of your figure as a structure over which you stretch the smooth skin.

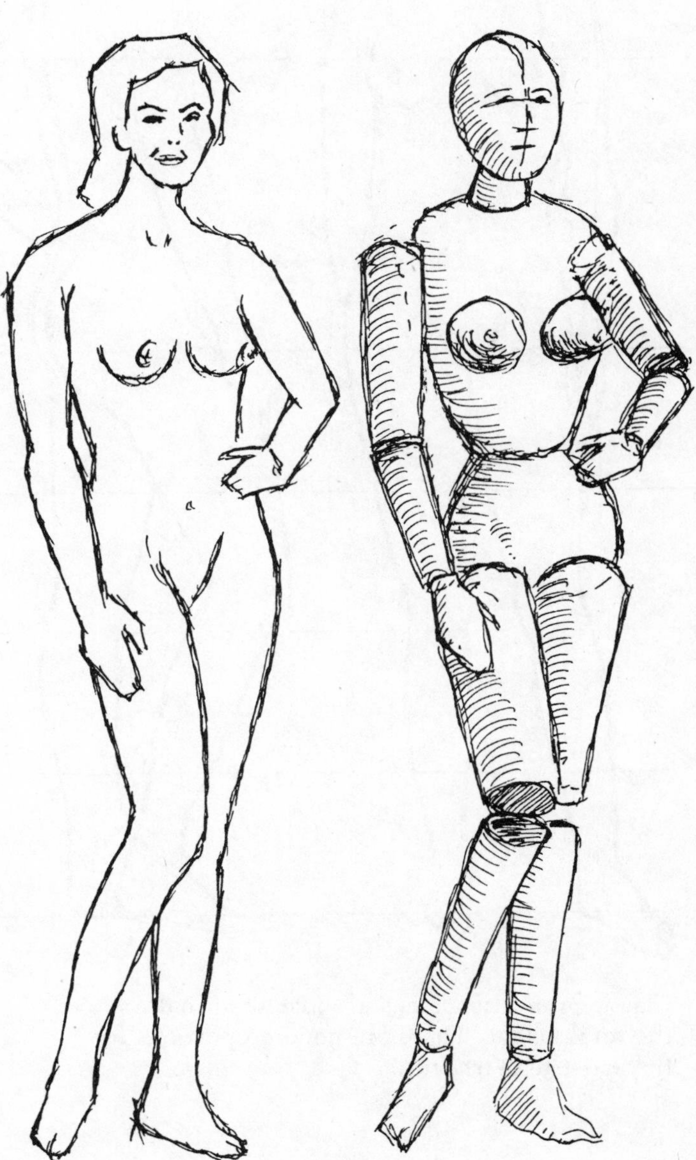

Figure 4-25
The *volume,* or three-dimensional properties, of the human figure should not be forgotten, even though some two-dimensional proportions are presented in this chapter.

Proportions, Female

People vary in body proportions just as they do in proportions of the face. Still, it is a good idea to rough in a well-proportioned, generic body as a start in your figure drawing and then alter it slightly to obtain the particular proportions of your subject. Figure 4-26 shows the proportions of a generic female. These are easy to remember, as the crotch divides the body in half, the breasts divide the upper half in half, and the knees divide the lower half in half. As shown to the right in this figure, most females are slightly longer in the trunk and shorter in the legs than the classic proportions.

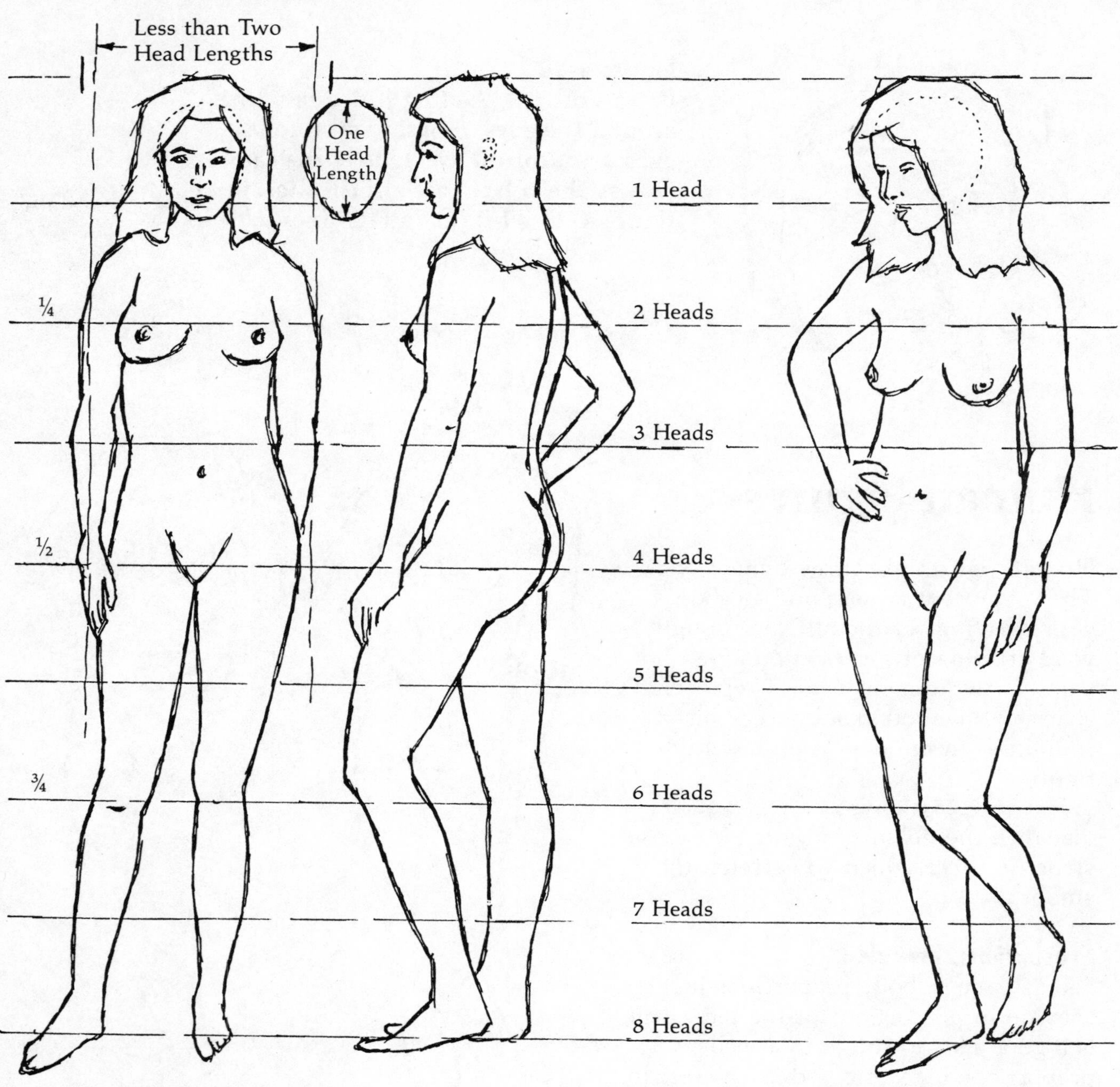
Less than Two Head Lengths
One Head Length
1 Head
2 Heads
3 Heads
4 Heads
5 Heads
6 Heads
7 Heads
8 Heads
¼
½
¾

Classic proportions: legs are just about half of the total height. These are good proportions for the artist to start with.

This figure has a slightly longer torso and slightly shorter legs, as most women do.

Figure 4-26
Women come in all proportions. A generic starting point, however, involves some easily remembered proportions. The knees, crotch, and breasts (almost) divide the figure in quarters. The head length, top to chin, is one-eighth of the total height. The width of the body is a little less than two head lengths.

Remember that most women have slightly longer torsos and slightly shorter legs than the classic proportions shown. Most women will be more like the figure on the right.

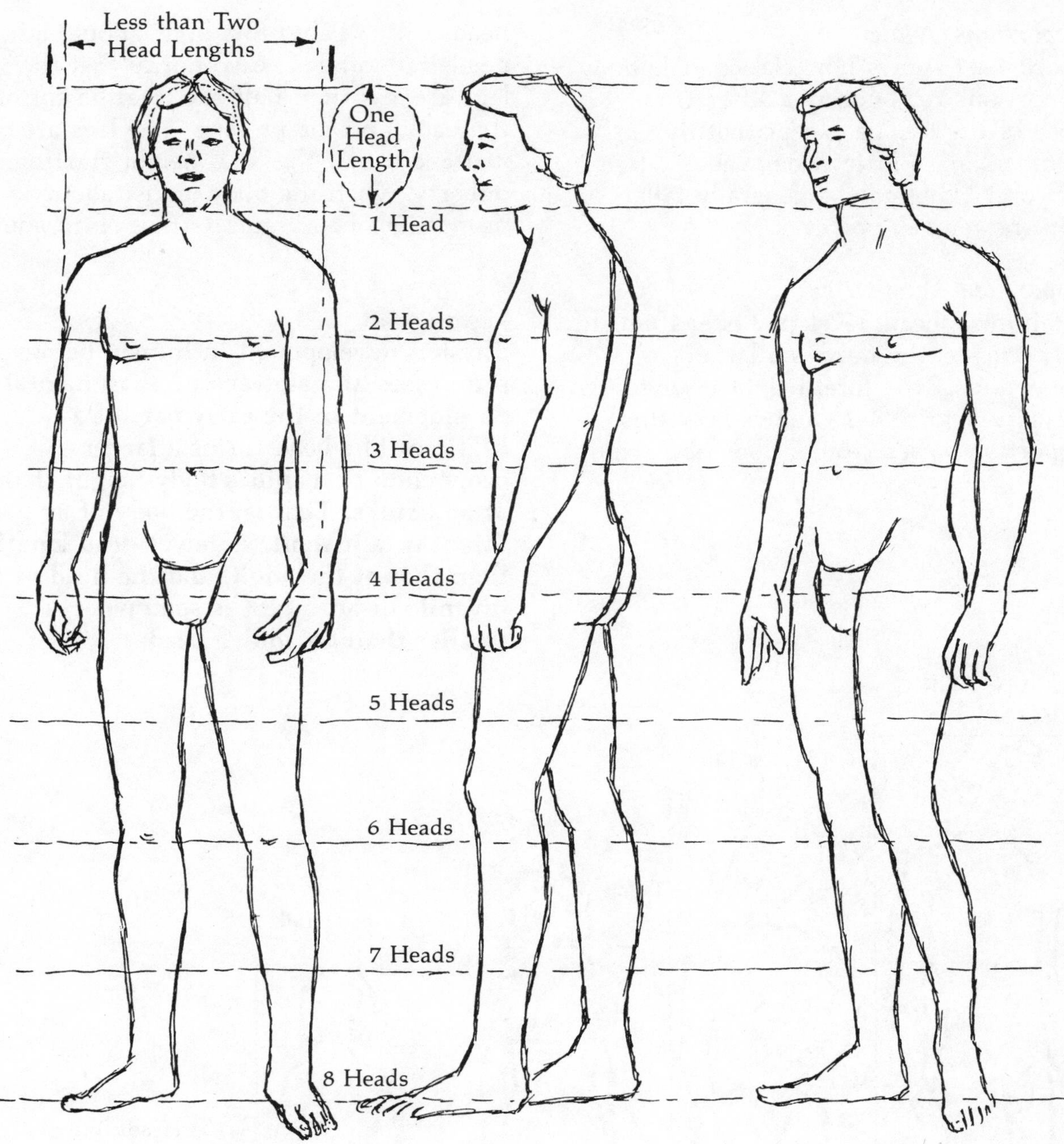
Less than Two
Head Lengths
One
Head
Length
1 Head
2 Heads
3 Heads
4 Heads
5 Heads
6 Heads
7 Heads
8 Heads

Figure 4-27
The classic proportions of the male body are about the same as those of the female figure. The knees, crotch, and breasts divide the total height in quarters. In both cases the body is eight heads high and a little less than two head lengths wide. The male shoulders are closer to being two head lengths wide, but the hips are narrower than those of the female.

As with the female proportions, those of the male vary widely among individuals. Those shown here should be used as a starting point and then modified for a particular individual.

Proportions, Male

Figure 4-27 shows how classic male body proportions really do not differ from those of the female except that the shoulders are a little wider and the hips narrower. The male is generally taller than the female, however.

Proportions Versus Age

The human head develops faster than the body. Hence, the head is a larger proportion of the total height prior to maturity. Figure 4-28 shows how this proportion varies from a body about four heads tall (a baby) to a body about eight heads tall (adults). Also notice that the legs are less than half the total height of the baby and the preteen. The legs are just about half the total height starting at puberty, when the body is just about proportioned the same as that of an adult.

Figure 4-28
Physical development in human beings progresses at a slower rate than mental development in the early part of a lifetime. The head forms a larger proportion of a child's body height than of an adult's. That is, the body of an infant or a juvenile is fewer head lengths than that of the adult, and the head of a juvenile or an infant is somewhat smaller than an adult's head.

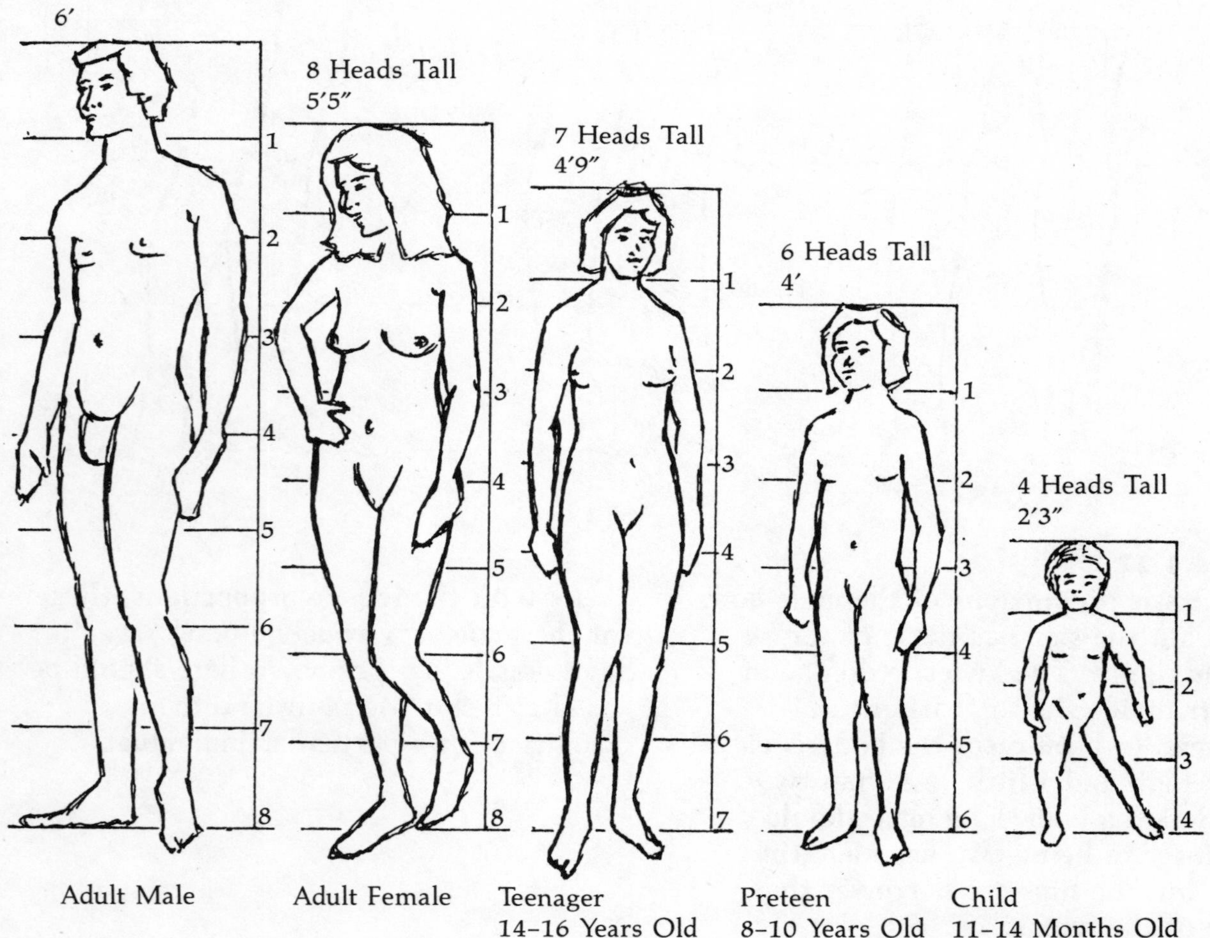
8 Heads Tall
6′
8 Heads Tall
5′5″
7 Heads Tall
4′9″
6 Heads Tall
4′
4 Heads Tall
2′3″
1
2
3
4
5
6
7
8
Adult Male
Adult Female
Teenager
14–16 Years Old
Preteen
8–10 Years Old
Child
11–14 Months Old

5
DRAWING TECHNIQUES

Pen Sketching Techniques

Pen Sketching Terms

Throughout this book I will be using terms such as *line, hatching, crosshatching,* and *stipple* or *stippling*. These are illustrated in figure 5-1. These terms refer to the ways that ink is applied to the paper in order to suggest shapes, various tones, textures, and visual effects such as volume and distance.

Line defines contour and is an important design element in itself. A few short lines can be used to suggest texture, as you see in A.

Tone is important in rendering the solidity of form. Tone is simply shading that creates a contrast with the white of the paper. Tone involves a gray scale from almost white to black. Hatching (B), crosshatching (C), and stippling (D) are used to cover more or less of the white paper with tone in order to produce darker passages. In pen-and-black-ink drawing and in black-pencil drawing, we do not have the added dimension of color, so colors must be suggested by the careful use of tone.

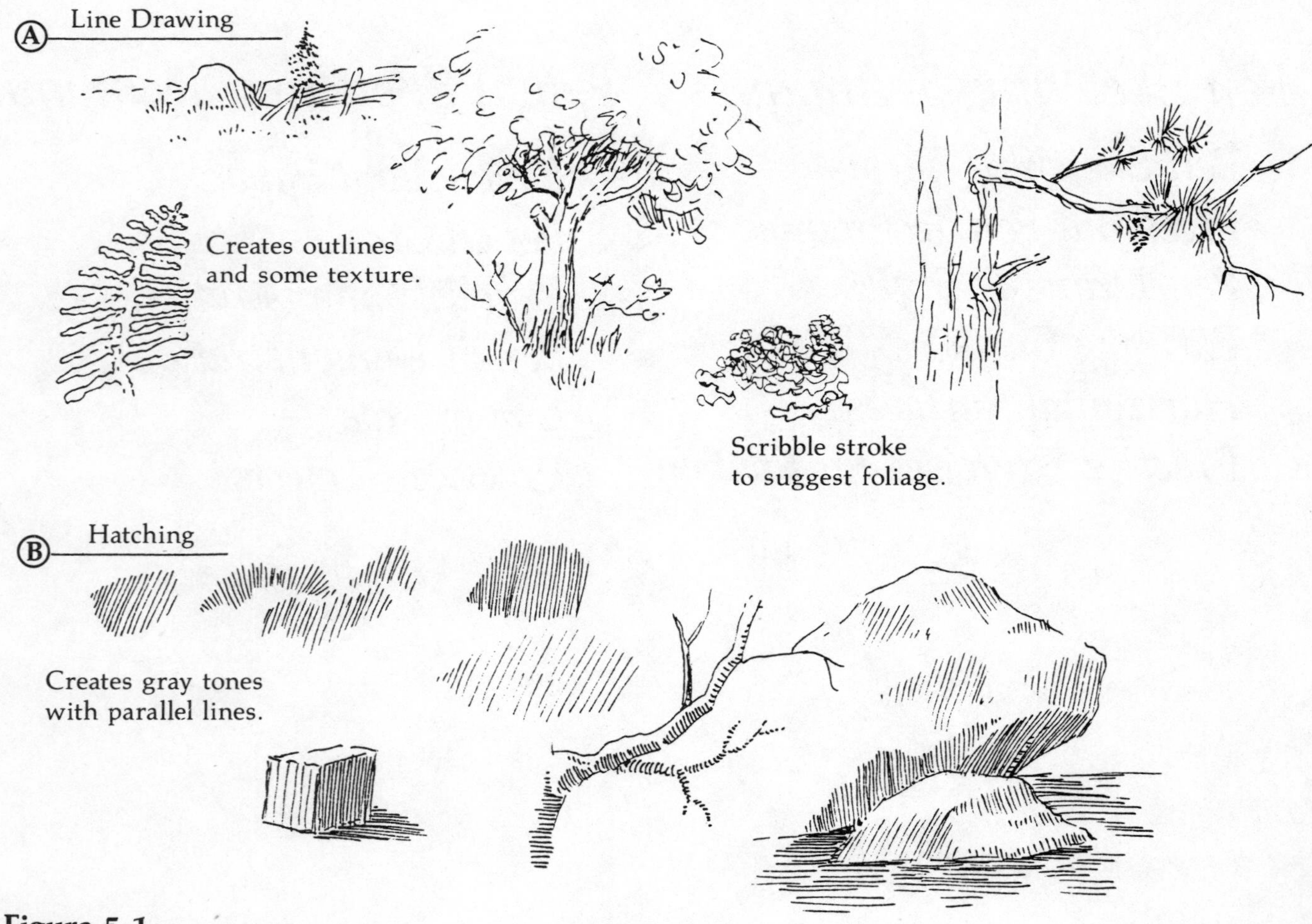
A
Line Drawing
Creates outlines
and some texture.
Scribble stroke
to suggest foliage.
B
Hatching
Creates gray tones
with parallel lines.

Figure 5-1
These are several of the ways to use ink linework to render subject matter.

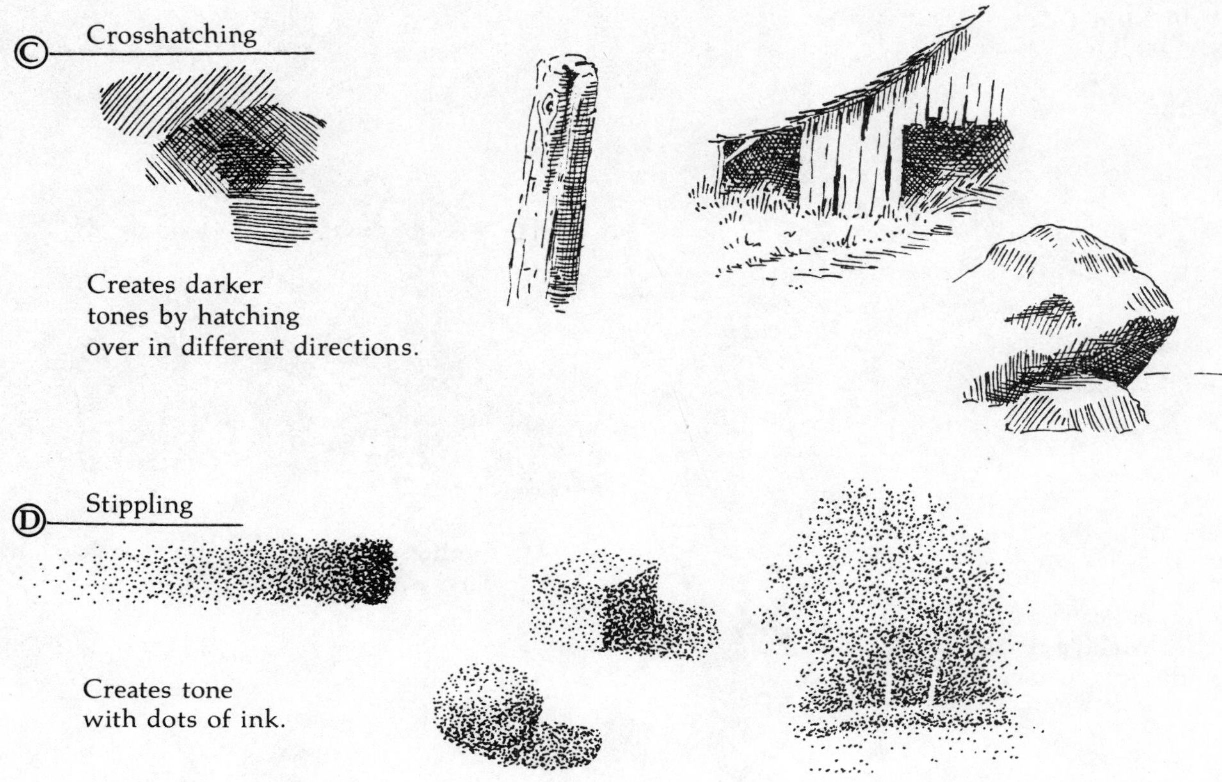
C Crosshatching
Creates darker
tones by hatching
over in different directions.
D Stippling
Creates tone
with dots of ink.

Freehand Pen Techniques

For our purposes here, technique and style refer to the particular ways that you use the pen to produce your drawing. In executing any particular composition, there are many techniques to choose from. Figure 5-2 shows the same subject, a portion of a country church in Sandringham, England, drawn using five different techniques. Although line is a very important drawing element, it is not always necessary to use line in a drawing if the edges and form of the subject can be expressed with tone alone. A and E show sketches completed with no use of line whatever to assist in indicating the edges of the subject. D shows a minimal use of line; B, a maximum use of line. Note the softness of the subject in A and E, where there are no lines as such. The use of a finer pen allows development of finer details. The coarse pen used in C presents a bolder impression, but with this pen the drawing is accomplished more quickly, since a greater volume of ink is applied with each stroke. It takes much more time to complete a stipple drawing (E), since each motion of the pen applies only a minute amount of ink. None of these techniques is any "righter" than any other; they are simply different. If you draw often you will soon develop a style of your own based on these techniques.

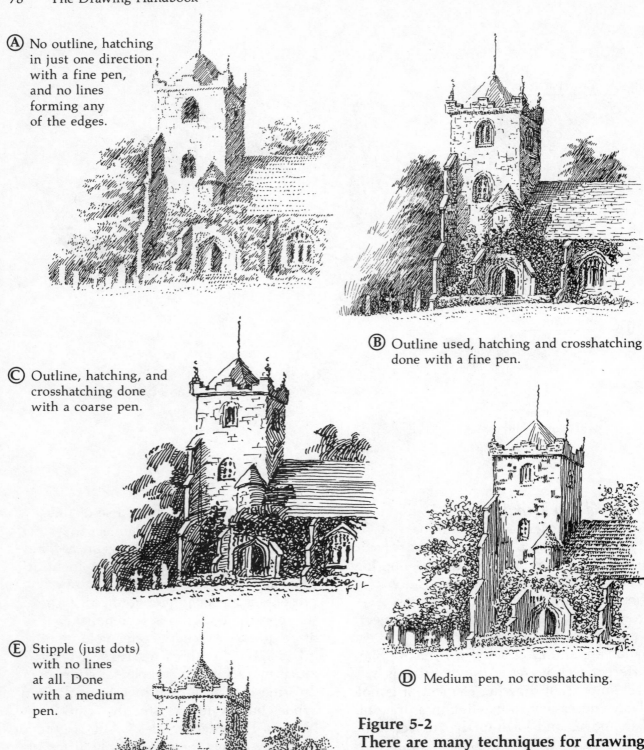

(A) No outline, hatching in just one direction with a fine pen, and no lines forming any of the edges.

(B) Outline used, hatching and crosshatching done with a fine pen.

(C) Outline, hatching, and crosshatching done with a coarse pen.

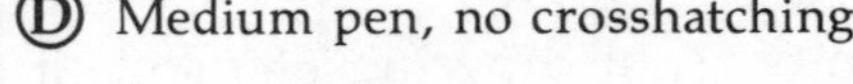

(D) Medium pen, no crosshatching.

(E) Stipple (just dots) with no lines at all. Done with a medium pen.

Figure 5-2
There are many techniques for drawing with the pen. Over time you will develop your own. It is not that one single technique is correct and the others are wrong—they are simply different. You should experiment to find what is most pleasing to *you*. Study the differences among these pen techniques.

Pen Drawing Styles

Two styles of pen drawing are illustrated in figure 5-3: *realistic* and *stylistic.* Realistic drawings make an attempt to show or suggest the actual texture, form, and detail of the subject (A). Stylistic drawing abstracts the subject's essence and by great simplification and distortion creates a more decorative effect. The mangrove tree drawn stylistically in B (next page) shows the leaves in a pleasing but unnatural manner. The leaves are shown considerably larger in proportion to the trunk and roots than they are in life.

This approach is good for a poster or an interpretive sign in a nature preserve, since it does get the idea of the mangrove tree across simply and attractively. It shows the characteristic root system and the shape of the leaves. It makes recognition of that tree easy, even though no mangrove tree really looks just like that.

Ⓐ

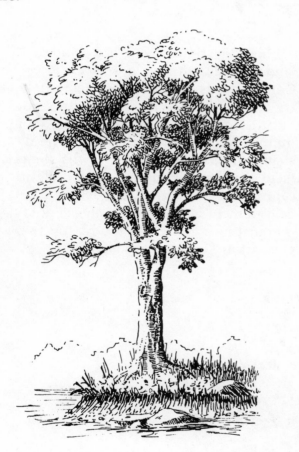

Figure 5-3
The two trees shown in A are drawn in a *realistic* manner while the subjects in B (next page) are drawn in a *stylistic* manner. The scene in C (next page) is drawn *loosely* although realistically. Compare this with the *tight* drawing of the tree on the left in A and the very tight drawing of the tree on the right in B.

Ⓑ

Shown in figure 5-3C is a winter landscape drawn in a loose style. Compare this with the very tight style of the mangrove tree in B. *Loose* does not mean sloppy or careless; in a loose style, minute detail is ignored for the overall shape and tone impression of the subject. Field sketches are often done loosely to capture a composition for further development at home. The choice of style is sometimes guided by the reason the piece of art is being produced.

Ⓒ

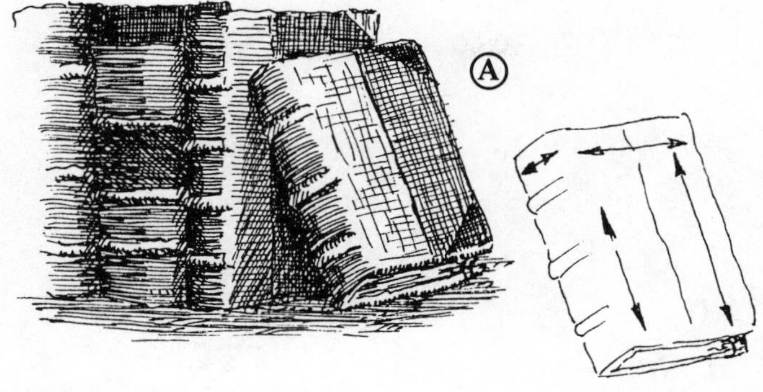
A
B
C
D
E

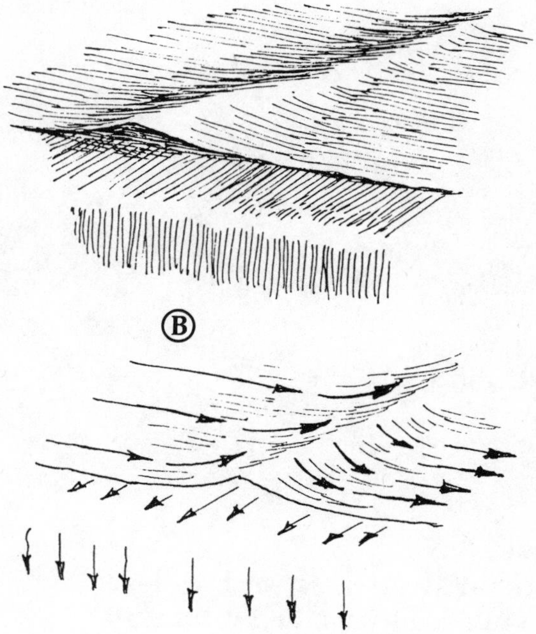

Figure 5-4
Line direction helps the eye see how surfaces lie. It is generally a good idea to have your toning lines parallel to the edges of subjects that have edges, such as the books in A, the tablecloth in B, and the roof in C. Lines also indicate by their slope the direction of the surface that they texture, as with the wrinkle in the tablecloth in B and the changing slope of the ground in D. The different surfaces of the rock in E are suggested by the direction of the lines on each surface.

Forming Surfaces

Outline, hatching, and crosshatching each use line to produce the effect. Line has direction and therefore tends to assist the viewer in interpreting the drawing by suggesting direction. When you draw square or rectangular things, such as the books in figure 5-4A, let your lines run parallel to the edges of the item you are texturing. Most but not all the linework on the old books follows this suggestion. There are enough lines parallel to the edges of the books, however, to establish at a glance how these surfaces lie. In figure 5-4B the linework parallels the edges of the tablecloth. Note that here the lines curve to follow the curvature of the surface. This and the inclusion of a highlight and shadow help to tell viewers that they are looking at a wrinkle in the tablecloth. The shingles in figure 5-4C are indicated by lines that run parallel to the edges of the roof. It would be more

A

Figure 5-5
Horizontal surfaces, such as level ground, roadways, and calm water, should be toned with horizontal strokes. This will tend to make them appear flat, as in A and B. Note the vertical waterfall lines in B.

Shadows on smooth horizontal surfaces like the roadway in A should be shown with horizontal strokes, as shown along the right side of the roadway.

Shadow on grass is best shown by packing vertical grass marks together tightly as under the big tree in B.

B

difficult to interpret this as a roof if the lines that I used for texturing ran in other directions.

By their direction the *grass marks,* rows of very short lines or dots, in figure 5-4D serve the purpose of indicating whether the ground is level, rising, or falling. In figure 5-4E the planes of the rocks are obvious because of the direction of the lines that texture them.

It is important to remember that surfaces are formed and are more readily perceived by the viewer when the texturing and shading line directions assist that perception.

Horizontal Surfaces

One of the most important times to be sure your line direction is proper is when you are indicating horizontal surfaces, such as roadways, level ground, and water. Each of these can be difficult for the viewer to interpret if the major linework is not horizontal, as shown in figure 5-5A and B. Also, shadows on smooth, horizontal surfaces should be drawn with horizontal strokes, as in the road shown in A. When you show shadows on grass, however, the shadow is best rendered by the same strokes as the grass itself: short vertical lines packed

Hatching (parallel lines) to show tone.

Crosshatching to show darker tone.

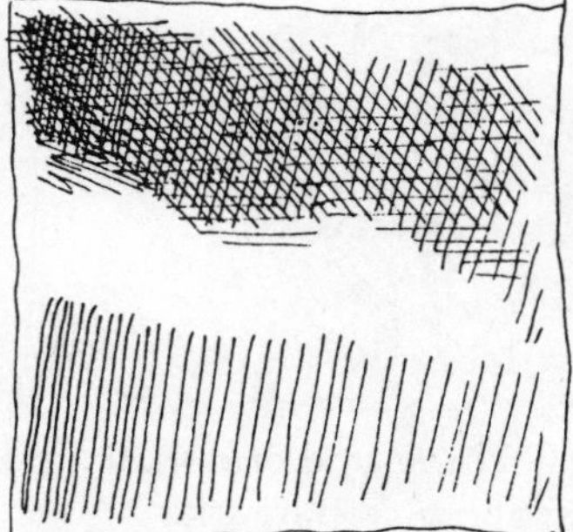

Graded tone (dark to light).

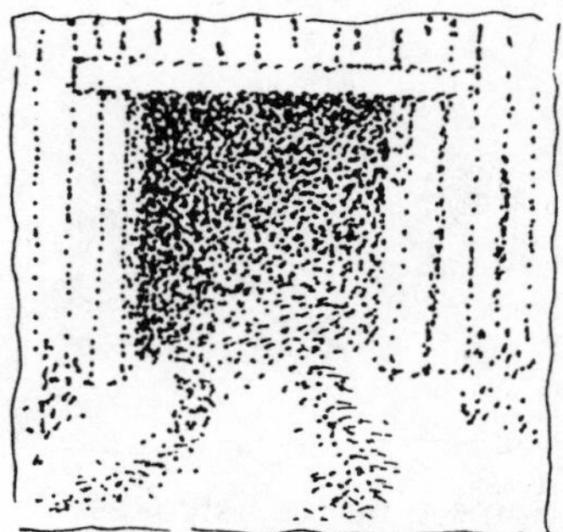

Stipple (just dots).

Scribble lines to show foliage.

Hatching to show distant foliage.

together closely. This technique maintains the texture of the grass. You can see this in B.

Practice Exercises for the Pen

It will benefit you to do a few practice exercises. This way you can try some of the things discussed in this chapter so far and get used to using the pen if it is new to you as a drawing instrument. Draw twelve squares of about an inch and one-half on a side on some paper, and try to copy the exercises in figure 5-6. You may want to do this several times if you are new to the pen. If you do, you will be surprised at how easy it is to create effects with the pen once you become a little familiar with using it.

Figure 5-6
Practice is the basis for success in learning any skill. The practice exercises shown here feature techniques that are used in many of the subjects in the rest of this book. Draw some squares about an inch and one-half on a side on a sheet of paper, and try to duplicate the studies shown in this figure.

Hatching and crosshatching to show stonework.

Never draw every brick or stone you see; use hatching to break the monotony in some areas.

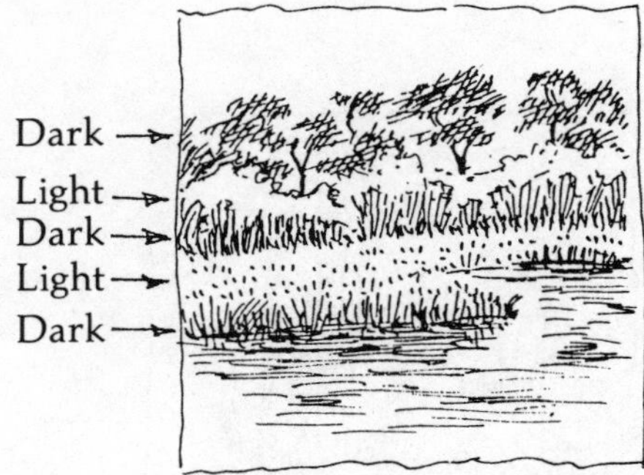
Dark
Light
Dark
Light
Dark
Alternate light and dark to show successive layers of foliage.

Grass marks show how the ground rises, falls, or lies flat.

Show the surface of level water with horizontal lines.

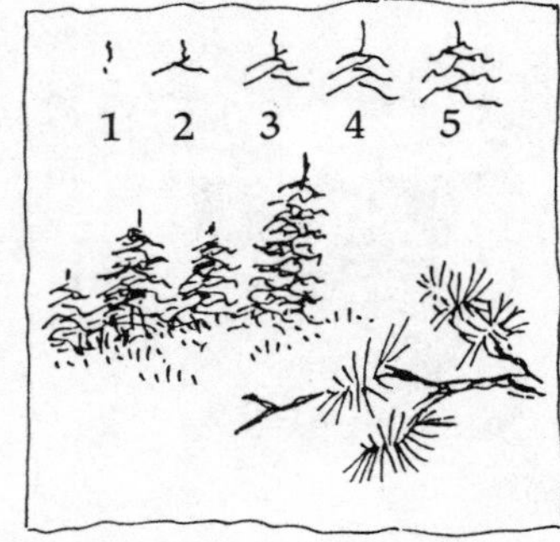
1 2 3 4 5
Some pine tree strokes. After step 5, darken each tree with additional strokes.

Pencil Sketching Techniques

Pencils and Paper

The way that graphite takes to paper is determined by the roughness of the paper surface. A very smooth surface does not hold the graphite well, so softer pencils are needed to make darker marks on paper with a very smooth surface. Paper with a rough surface holds a good deal of graphite, so the softer pencils produce marks that are all about the same. To get lighter tones on paper with a rough surface, you must either press a kneaded eraser on the graphite from a soft pencil or use some of the harder pencils. Figure 5-7 shows how a range of pencils from 2H to 6B marked different kinds of paper. Note that the roughest papers, the 140 pound watercolor paper and the tracing vellum, show no perceptible difference between the HB, B, 3B, and 6B pencils. A range from 6H (very hard) to HB would be appropriate for these papers.

You will find it quite helpful to make charts like this on all the different kinds of paper you will use so you can determine which pencils you will need before you start a drawing.

You *can* draw with just one pencil, producing a range of tones by lightly touching the paper with the pencil to produce light tones and pressing heavily

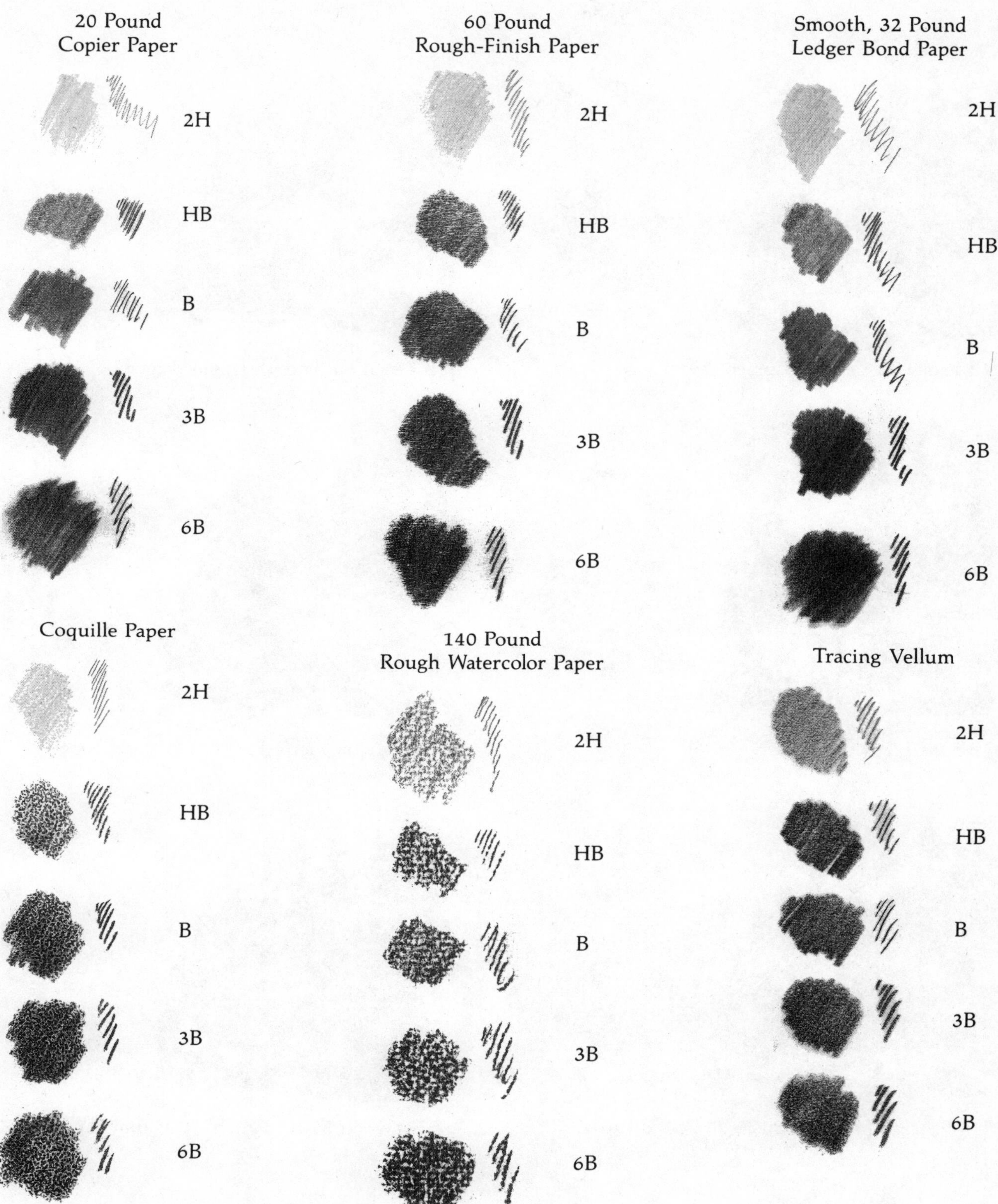
20 Pound
Copier Paper
2H
HB
B
3B
6B
60 Pound
Rough-Finish Paper
2H
HB
B
3B
6B
Smooth, 32 Pound
Ledger Bond Paper
2H
HB
B
3B
6B
Coquille Paper
2H
HB
B
3B
6B
140 Pound
Rough Watercolor Paper
2H
HB
B
3B
6B
Tracing Vellum
2H
HB
B
3B
6B

Figure 5-7
Pencil strokes take differently on different paper, depending on the roughness of the finish. You should make yourself a test chart like this one, with all of your drawing pencils on the types of paper you intend to use.

Ⓐ

4B Pencil on Smooth Copier Paper.

Ⓑ

HB Pencil on Smooth Copier Paper.

Ⓒ

4B Pencil on Linen Paper.

Ⓓ

2H Pencil on Matte-Finish, 70 Pound Paper.

Ⓔ

HB Pencil on Matte-Finish, 70 Pound Paper.

Ⓕ

4B Pencil on Matte-Finish, 70 Pound Paper.

Figure 5-8
These illustrations demonstrate how different paper surfaces take pencil. For instance, you can see how the harder pencil, 2H, made a darker impression on a rougher paper surface (D) than the softer HB pencil did on a smoother surface (B). Smooth paper picks up less graphite.

to produce dark ones, and by using the kneaded eraser. This is illustrated in figure 5-8, where the same subject is shown drawn using six different paper and pencil combinations.

Pencil Strokes

The most important thing to do when learning to draw with the pencil is to start drawing. You will learn so much in a short time. Figure 5-9 shows the same subject drawn with three different combinations of pencils. In each case the end result is about the same. This is to

Figure 5-9
The pencils you use are not as important as your getting started on some experimenting to see for yourself what happens. This figure shows some different combinations used to accomplish just about the same result.

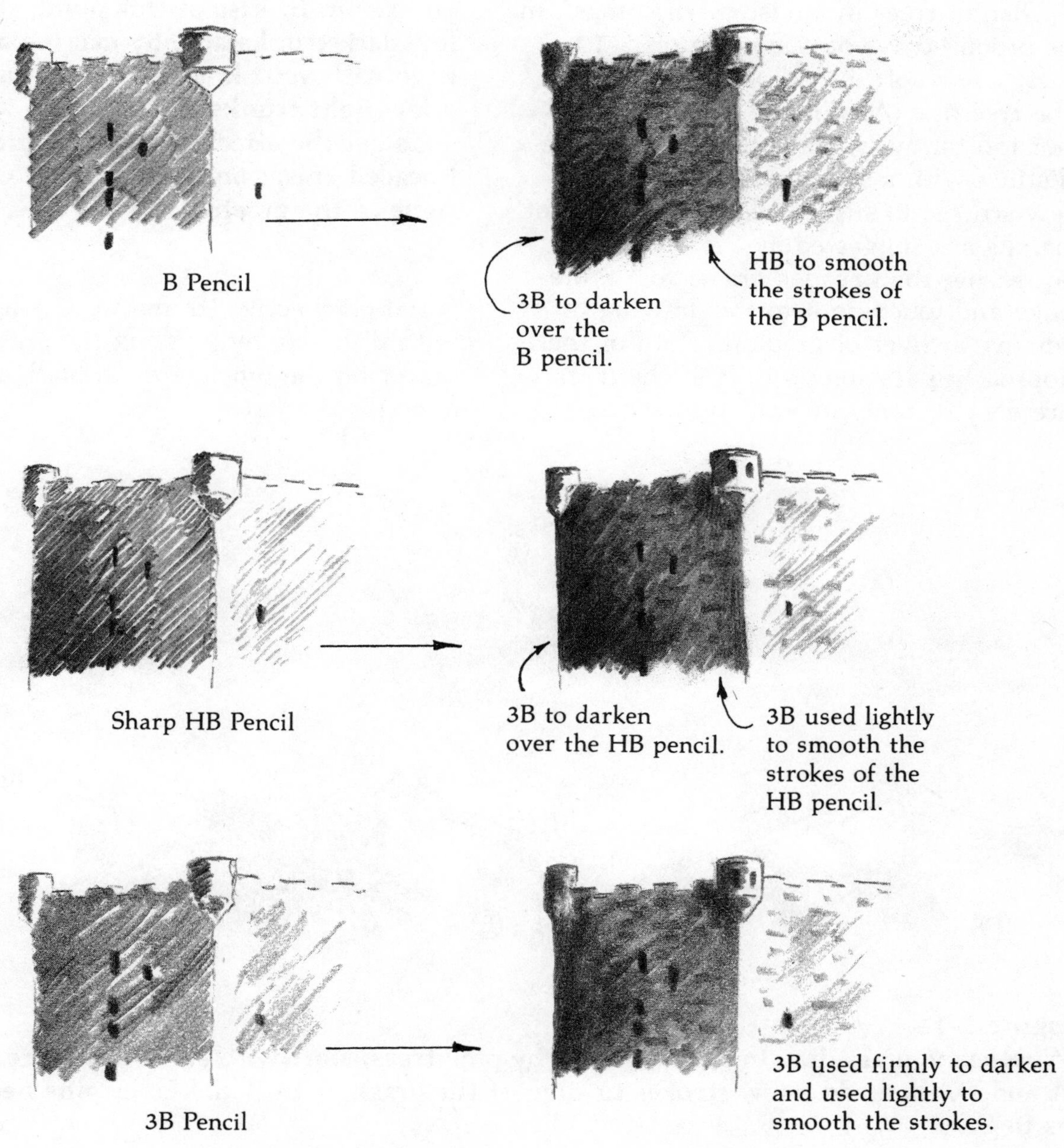
B Pencil
3B to darken over the B pencil.
HB to smooth the strokes of the B pencil.
Sharp HB Pencil
3B to darken over the HB pencil.
3B used lightly to smooth the strokes of the HB pencil.
3B Pencil
3B used firmly to darken and used lightly to smooth the strokes.

A
B
C

show you that the particular set of pencils you use is not critical to the result you will get, so it is best to get on with the drawing and see for yourself what happens. You will quickly learn what combination works best for you.

Distant trees in landscape drawings can be produced as you see in figure 5-10. First use a soft, broad pencil to block in the tree line (A). Then, if the trees are not too far away, make the outline more distinct with a sharp point and put in a few strokes to suggest dark trunks. Light trunks are suggested by the result of squeezing the kneaded eraser to a knife-edge and touching it to the drawing to remove a sliver of graphite. Both of these approaches are shown in B. If the trees are very distant you can suggest the aerial perspective (things appear lighter with distance) by pressing the kneaded eraser on the whole area to be lightened, as in C.

Figure 5-10
To suggest distant trees, first block them in with a broad, soft pencil, such as a 3B, as shown in A.

Next, sharpen the edges of the foliage with a sharp pencil, such as an HB, as you see in B. Also at this point, show a few dark trunks and, by making a knife-edge with your kneaded eraser, touch in a few light trunks.

To get the effect of distance, press the kneaded eraser on the drawing to remove some of the graphite, as in C.

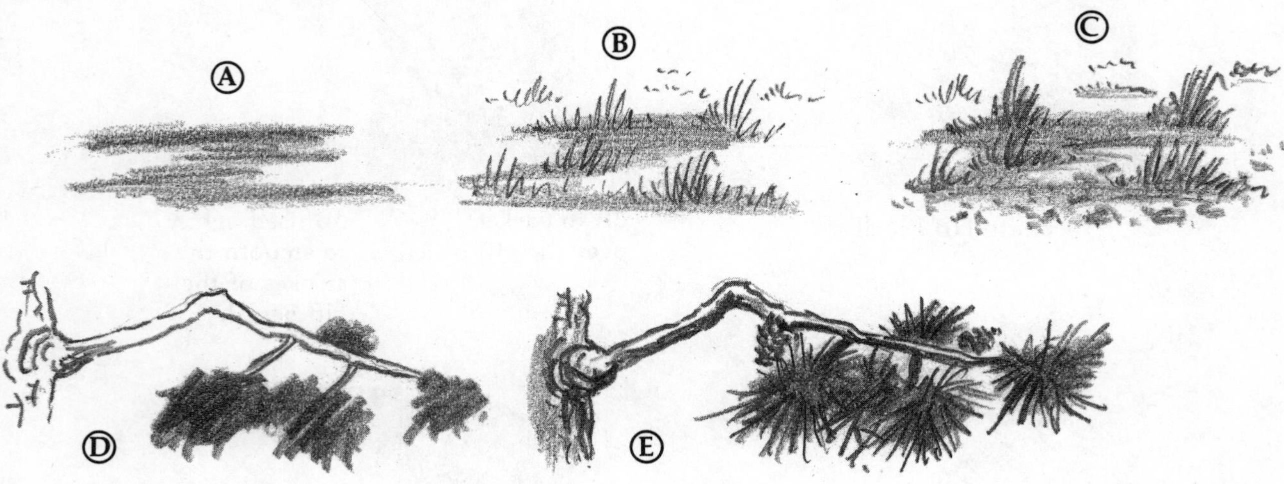
A
B
C
D
E

Figure 5-11
Whether you are drawing grass or nearby pine trees, start with some toned areas, as in A and D, then add a few strokes to suggest the grass, as in B and C, or pine needles, as in E.

A
B

Figure 5-12
Lines suggest how surfaces lie. Anything that is horizontal, like roads and the surface of smooth water, should be textured with horizontal lines, as shown at A. Grass marks indicate the slope of the stream banks, at B.

Grass and some foliage is usually rendered by first indicating mass with a soft pencil and then suggesting detail with a sharp pencil. This is illustrated in figure 5-11, where grass is shown in A, B, and C, and pine tree foliage is shown in D and E.

As in pen drawing, the direction of strokes in pencil drawings suggests the nature of the surface being drawn. Horizontal surfaces should be suggested by horizontal strokes; surfaces running upward or downward, by slanted strokes (figure 5-12).

Pencil Demonstration 1

Some uses of different pencils, the kneaded eraser, and the erasing shield are demonstrated in figure 5-13. The letters pointing out parts of the finished drawing (top) correspond with the letters of the partially completed drawings in the lower half of the figure so you can see the sequence I followed in completing each part of the drawing.

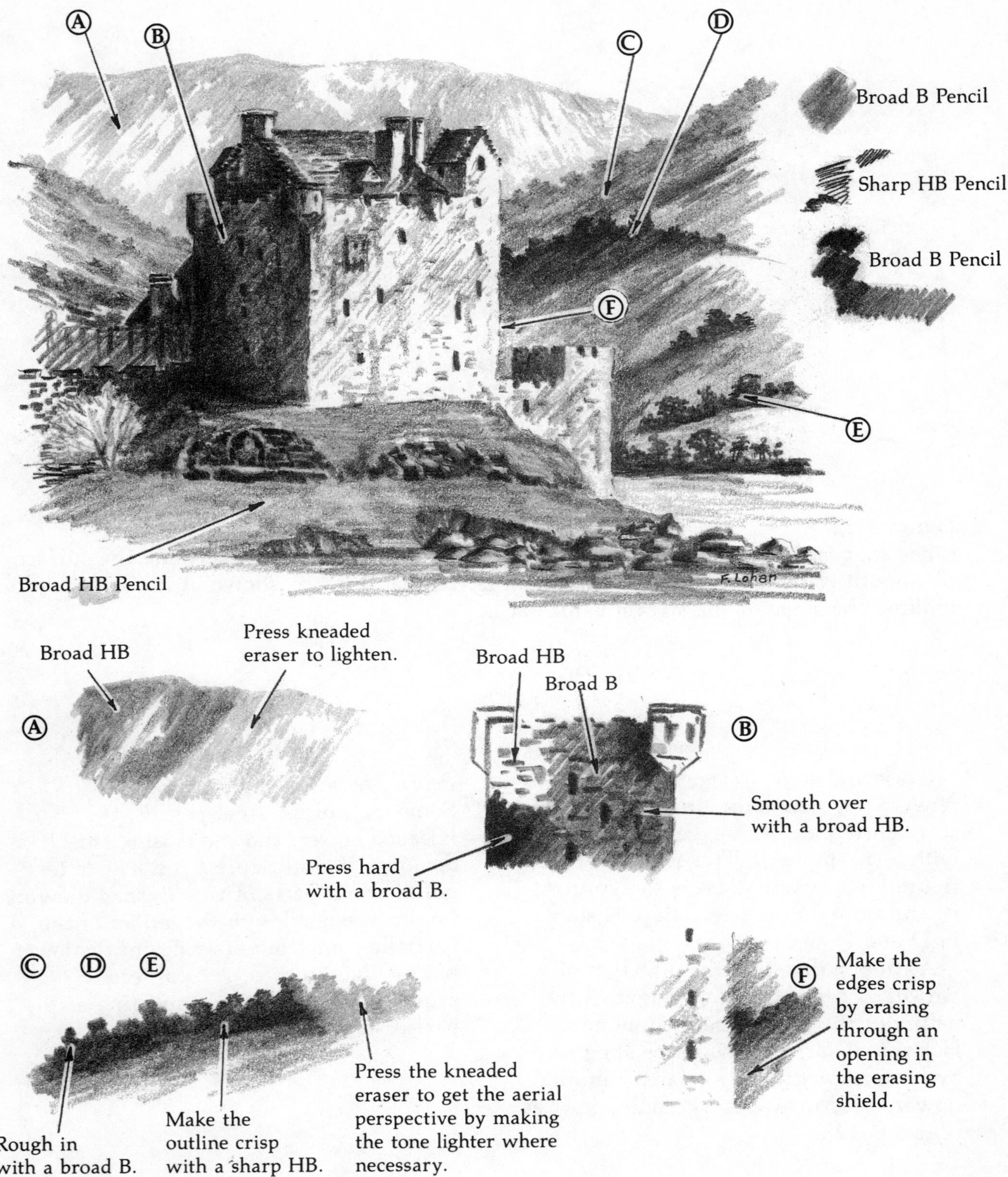
Ⓐ
Ⓑ
Ⓒ
Ⓓ
Broad B Pencil
Sharp HB Pencil
Broad B Pencil
Ⓕ
Ⓔ
Broad HB Pencil
F. Lohan
Broad HB
Press kneaded eraser to lighten.
Ⓐ
Broad HB
Broad B
Ⓑ
Smooth over with a broad HB.
Press hard with a broad B.
Ⓒ Ⓓ Ⓔ
Ⓕ
Make the edges crisp by erasing through an opening in the erasing shield.
Rough in with a broad B.
Make the outline crisp with a sharp HB.
Press the kneaded eraser to get the aerial perspective by making the tone lighter where necessary.

Figure 5-13
This is a demonstration of how the different pencils, kneaded eraser, and erasing shield are used in a sketch.

F. Lohan

Figure 5-14
Demonstration 1 was done using three different pencils. This demonstration shows the results obtained with just one pencil. A kneaded eraser was used to lighten the more distant trees.

Pencil Demonstration 2

The demonstration landscape in figure 5-14 was done with just one pencil, a broad-point 4B on a matte-finish paper. The distant trees were lightened with the kneaded eraser (remember to just press it rather than rub with it). The light areas on the foreground rocks were created by using the broad-point pencil very lightly on the paper.

Linen Paper

Figure 5-15 shows the effect produced by drawing on linen paper with a soft, broad-point pencil. This pattern can be quite attractive when there are some dark areas in a study. You will have a chance to try this pencil drawing later, in Part 2, where it is the subject of a step-by-step exercise.

FJL

Figure 5-15
This is a 3B pencil drawing on linen paper. The pattern in the paper shows when soft, broad-point pencils are used.
This study, a bust of Thalia, the Greek Muse of comedy, is the subject of a pencil exercise in Part 2 of this book, where step-by-step suggestions for its completion are provided.

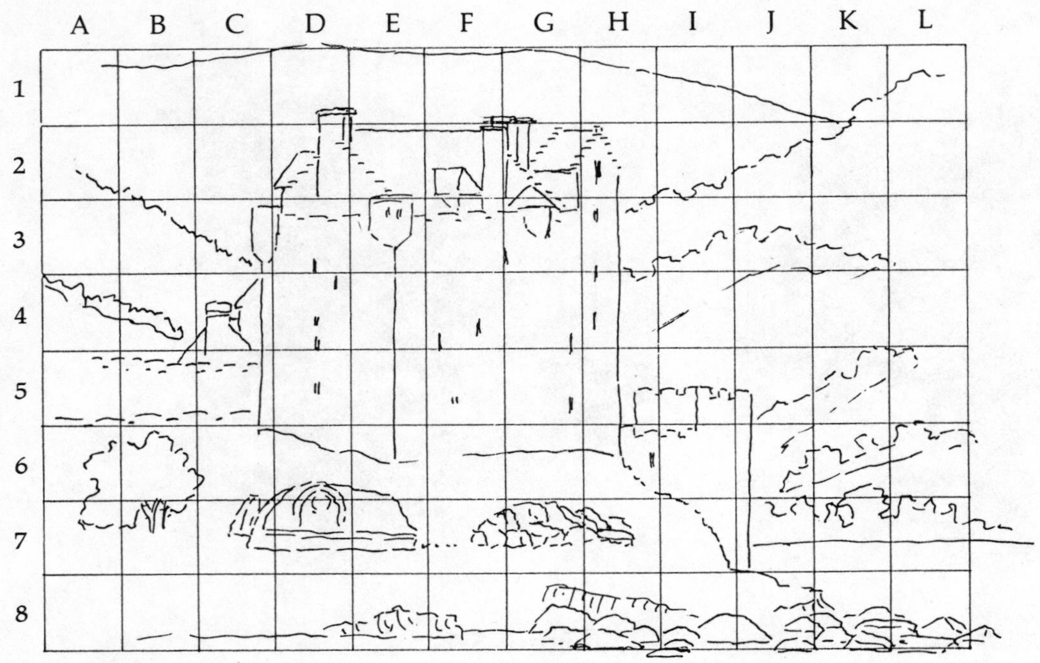
A B C D E F G H I J K L
1
2
3
4
5
6
7
8

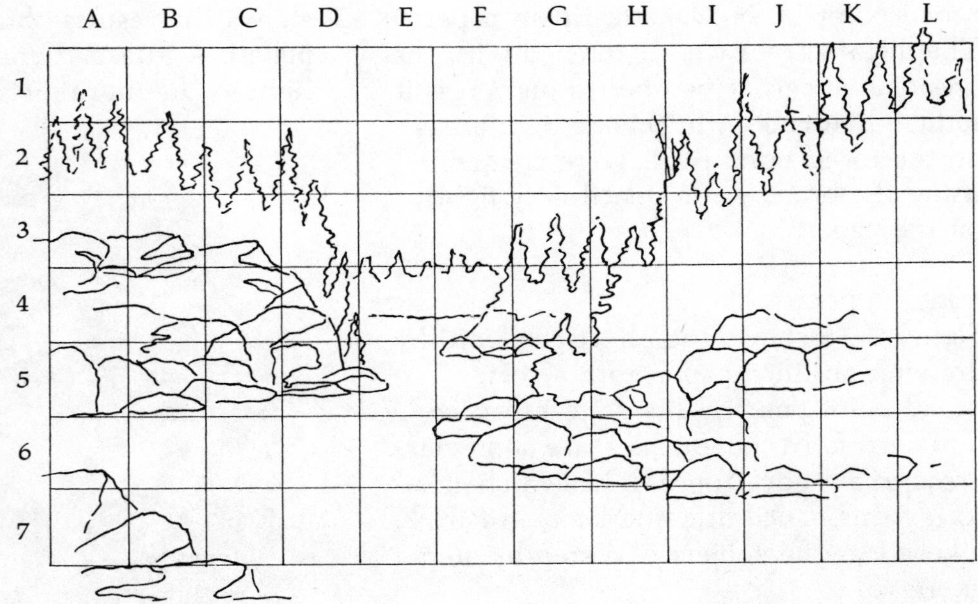
A B C D E F G H I J K L
1
2
3
4
5
6
7

Practice Subjects

You should try drawing the two demonstration subjects in figure 5-16 for practice with the pencil. Use the gridded compositions (as discussed in Chapter 3) to assist you in getting your composition outlined and transferred to your final paper quickly.

Figure 5-16
These are the gridded composition drawings for the two pencil demonstration figures. It will be good practice for you to draw these subjects yourself. Use these gridded outlines to make your own composition outlines to transfer to your final paper (as discussed in Chapter 3).

PART 2
DRAWING EXERCISES

Landscapes

Architecture

Artifacts

Birds

Animals

Flowers

Faces and Clothing

On Your Own

Part 2 concentrates on drawing techniques for the pen and the pencil. It contains various drawing exercises, some in pen and ink and some in pencil, organized in chapters under the titles listed above. Each exercise includes the completed study, a gridded outline composition of the subject, and a partially completed study offering some suggestions as to how you might best proceed to draw that subject.

You should use a gridded outline, as discussed in Chapter 3, to quickly and easily reproduce the composition at the exact size you want your final drawing to be. Then you can transfer the outline to your final paper and get to work on it.

I have indicated the pens or pencils I used for each exercise in the caption for the completed drawing. Where paper is not mentioned, I used 70 pound, vellum-finish drawing paper.

6
Landscapes

A Forest Brook

Misty Vermont Morn

The Cliffs, Hunstanton

The Itchen River Near Winchester

Bell Rock, Sedona, Arizona

Plane Tree

Shark Valley Slough, Florida

Stream, Great Smoky Mountains

Georgian Bay, Canada

Carter County, Kentucky

Florida Everglades

For Sale

Several of the exercises in this chapter were done with a very fine 5×0 technical pen. You can use the finest crowquill pen you have or try these exercises with the finest pen you own. Although the appearance of your drawing may differ from that of mine if you use a coarser pen, your drawing will be just as valid. You cannot create very fine detail with a coarse pen at the size of the drawings in these exercises, so do the best you can if you do not have a fine-point pen to work with.

The next chapter illustrates more fully the difference between finished products created with coarse pens and those created with fine pens.

A Forest Brook

F. Lohan

Figure 6-1
A 5×0 (a very fine point) technical pen drawing of a small waterfall on a shady forest brook.

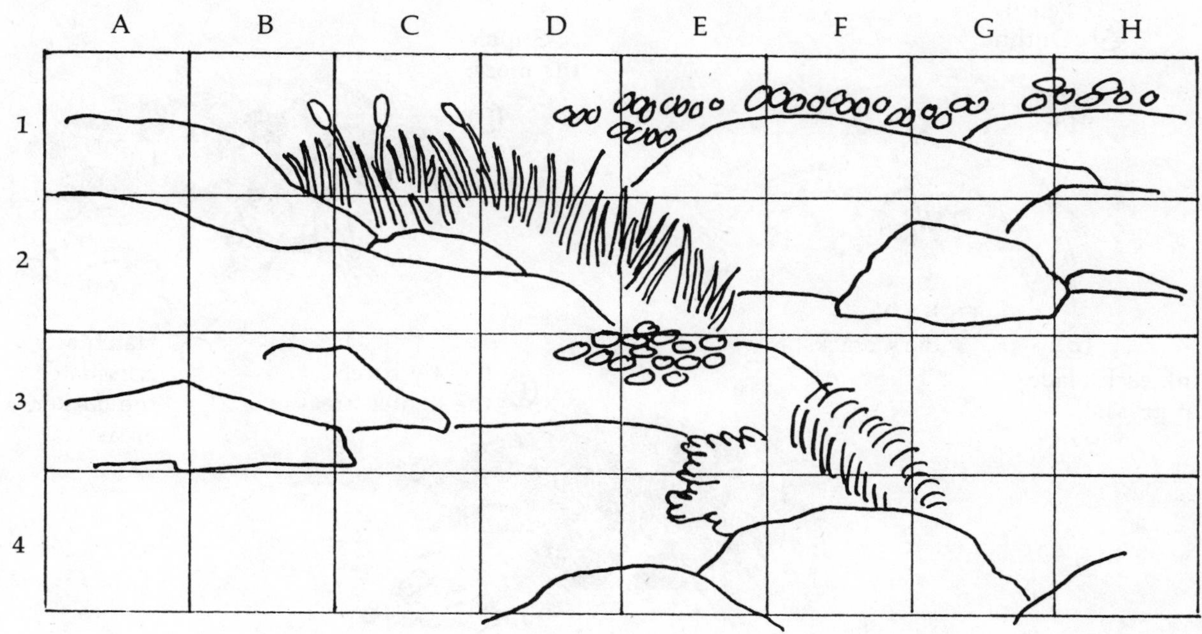
A
B
C
D
E
F
G
H
1
2
3
4

Figure 6-2
Use this gridded figure to assist your preparation of your own outline drawing of this study.

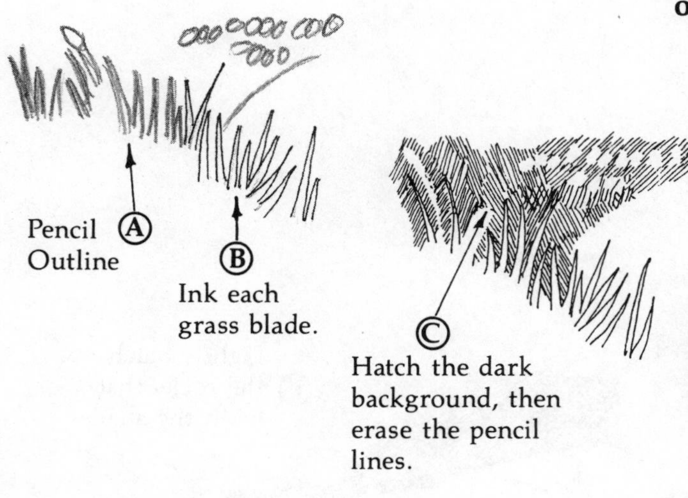
Pencil Outline Ⓐ
Ⓑ Ink each grass blade.
Ⓒ Hatch the dark background, then erase the pencil lines.

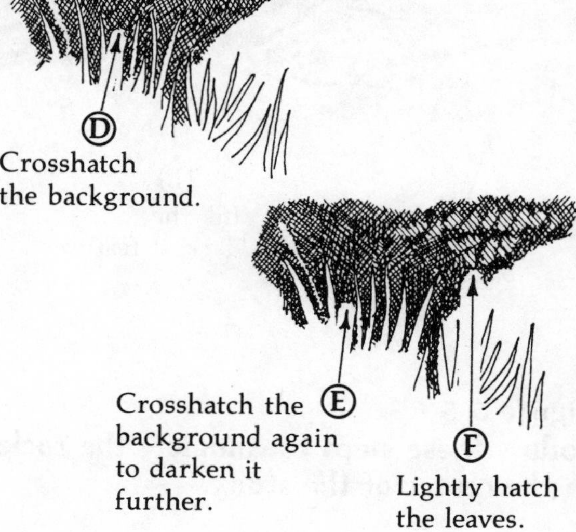
Ⓓ Crosshatch the background.
Crosshatch the background again to darken it further. Ⓔ
Ⓕ Lightly hatch the leaves.

Figure 6-3
Follow these steps to complete the dark background behind the rocks.

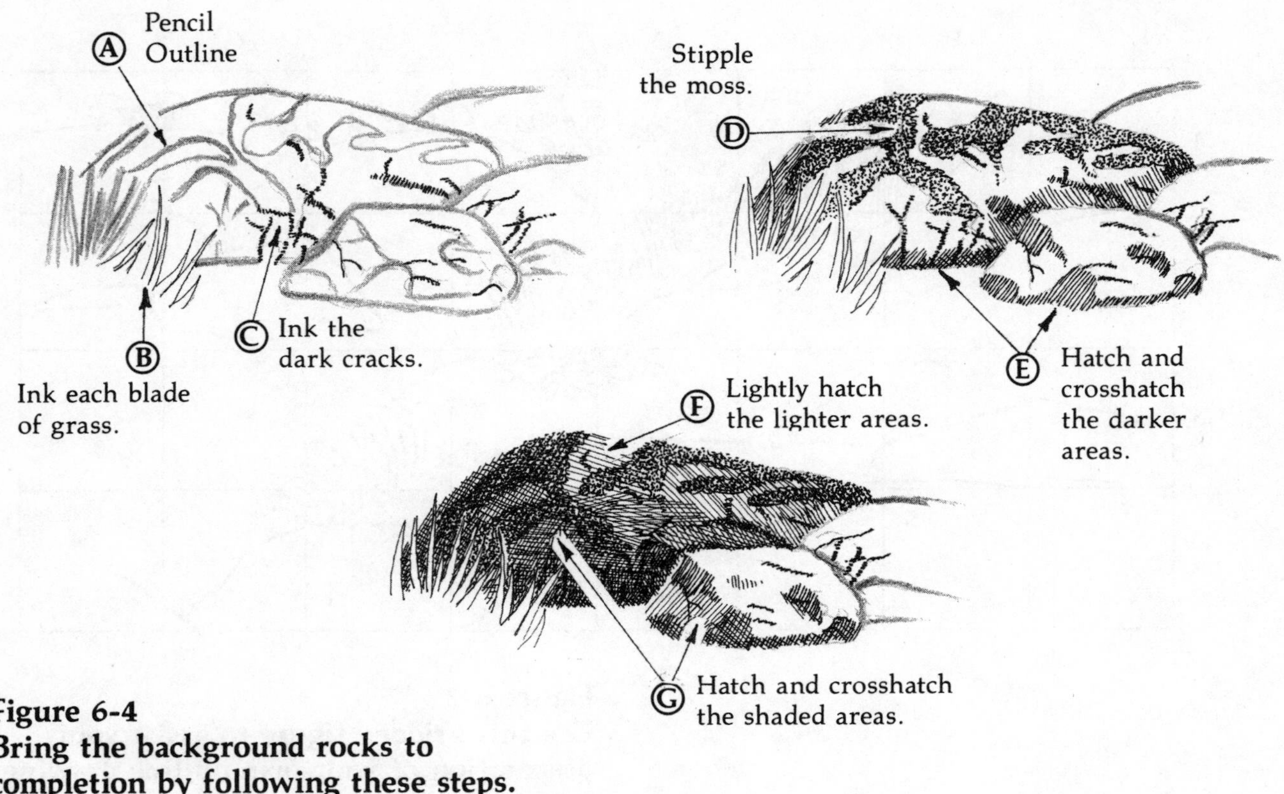
Pencil
Ⓐ Outline
Stipple
the moss.
Ⓓ
Ⓑ
Ink each blade
of grass.
Ⓒ Ink the
dark cracks.
Ⓔ Hatch and
crosshatch
the darker
areas.
Ⓕ Lightly hatch
the lighter areas.
Ⓖ Hatch and crosshatch
the shaded areas.

Figure 6-4
Bring the background rocks to completion by following these steps.

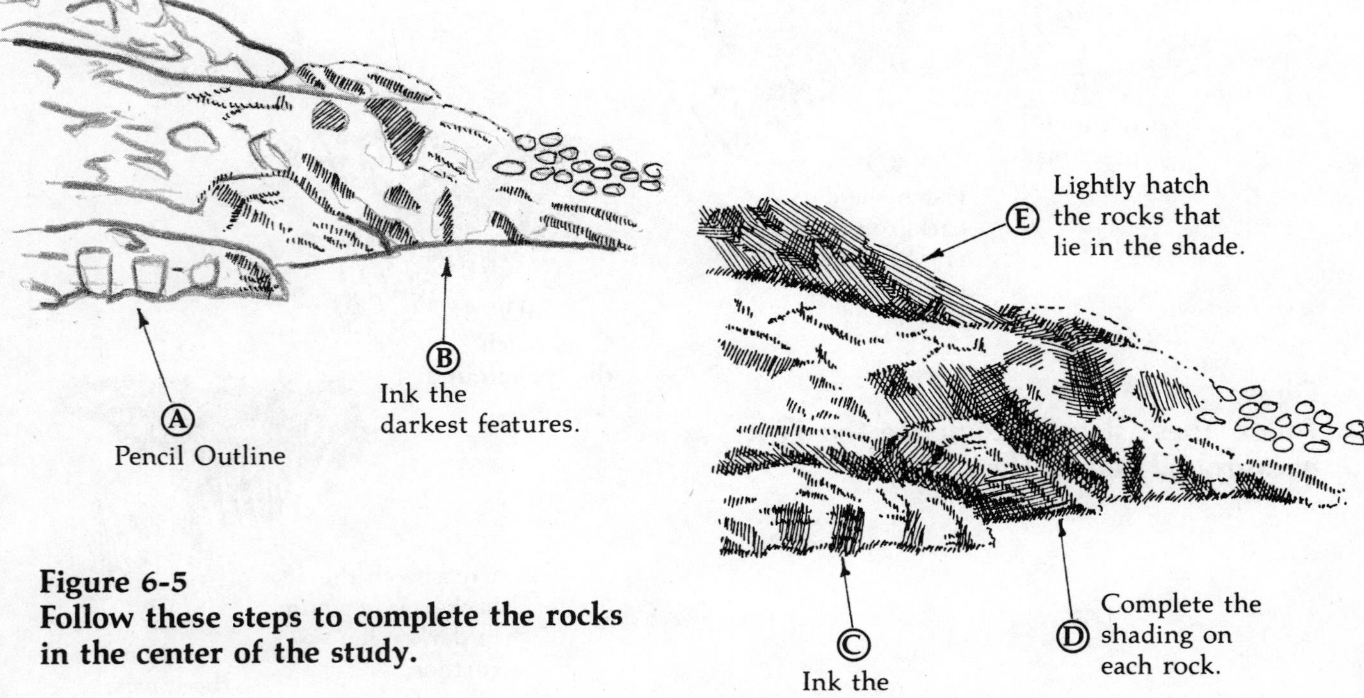
Ⓐ
Pencil Outline
Ⓑ
Ink the
darkest features.
Lightly hatch
Ⓔ the rocks that
lie in the shade.
Ⓒ
Ink the
dark features.
Complete the
Ⓓ shading on
each rock.

Figure 6-5
Follow these steps to complete the rocks in the center of the study.

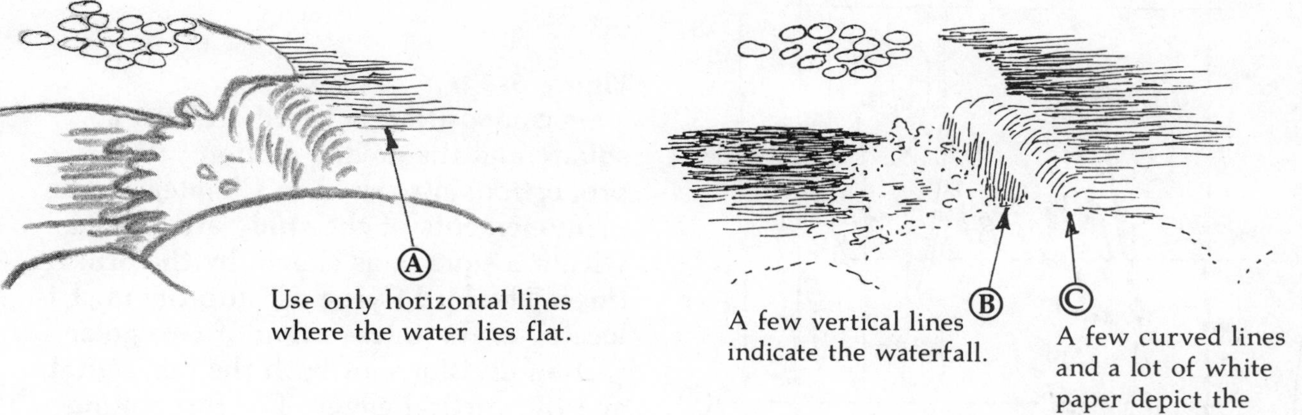
Ⓐ
Use only horizontal lines where the water lies flat.
Ⓑ
A few vertical lines indicate the waterfall.
Ⓒ
A few curved lines and a lot of white paper depict the edge of the waterfall.

Figure 6-6
Follow these steps to complete the water. Be sure to leave plenty of white paper showing at the edge of the waterfall and in the foamy splash area.

Misty Vermont Morn

F. Lohan

Figure 6-7
This misty woodland scene is the result of the use of three pencils: sharp- and broad-point B pencils and a broad-point 3B pencil. A kneaded eraser was also used on this study on vellum-finish paper. The original measures three by five inches.

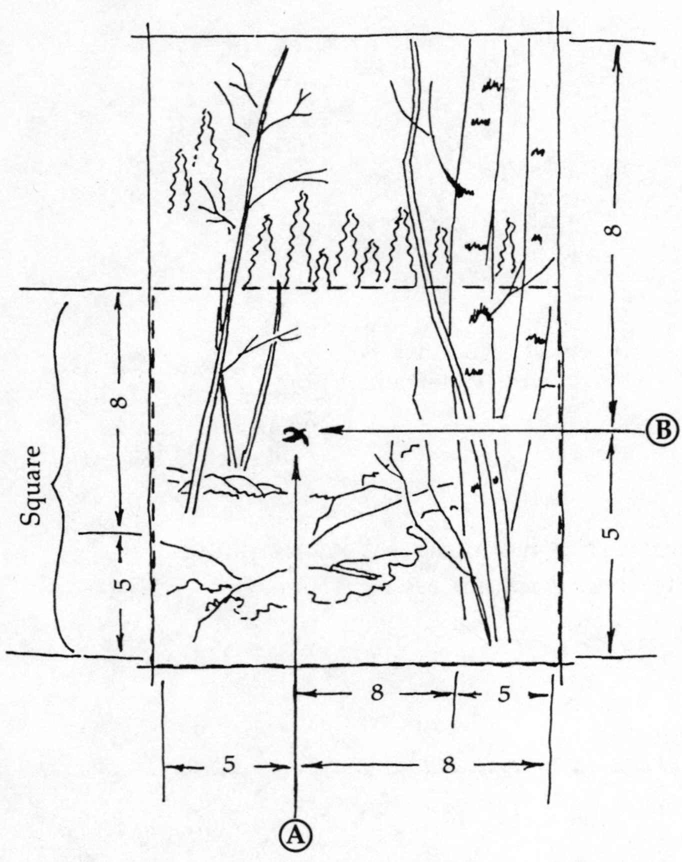
Square
8
5
8
5
B
8
5
5
8
A

Figure 6-8
This composition is based on both a square and the golden section proportions discussed in Chapter 1. The main elements of the study are located within a square, as shown by the broken lines. The bird flying off into the mist is located at the intersection of two golden section divisions, of both the horizontal and the vertical edges. The foreground birch trees are within a golden section subdivision of the bottom edge from the bird to the right side.

Figure 6-9
Use the gridded outline in this figure to assist you as you make your own composition outline (according to the instructions in Chapter 3).

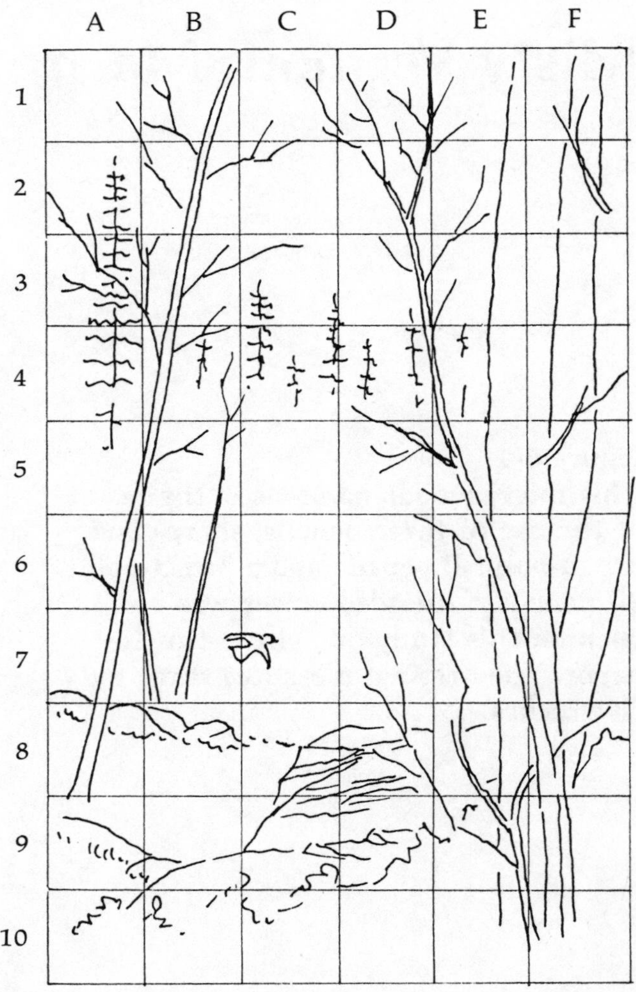
A
B
C
D
E
F
1
2
3
4
5
6
7
8
9
10

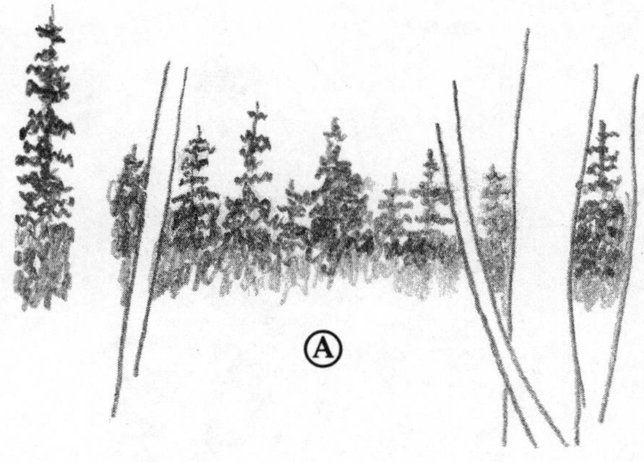
A

B

C
D

Figure 6-10
A Put the background trees in place with your broad-point B pencil.
B Press the kneaded eraser on the drawing a few times to get the light, misty effect.
C Use your sharp B pencil to put the nearest pine tree in place.
D Continue the pine tree right down into the mist. Use your kneaded eraser to blend the lower part of the tree into the mist.

A
B
C
D

Figure 6-11
A Use your broad-point and sharp B pencils to start the forest and rocks in the middle ground at the edge of the mist.
B Press your kneaded eraser on the area.
C Reemphasize the shaded part of the rocks.
D Use the kneaded eraser gingerly until the rocks have distinction but are not overly prominent. Getting this right is a back-and-forth process in which you use the pencil, touch the kneaded eraser to the drawing, and use more pencil if necessary, repeating until you are satisfied.

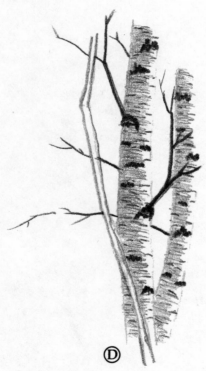

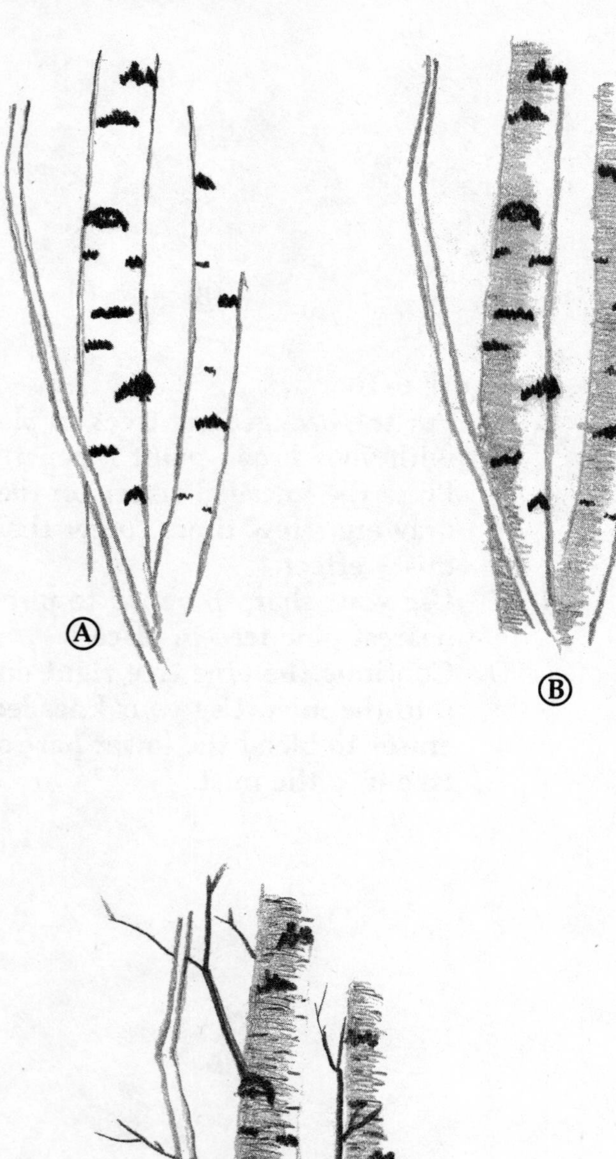
A
B

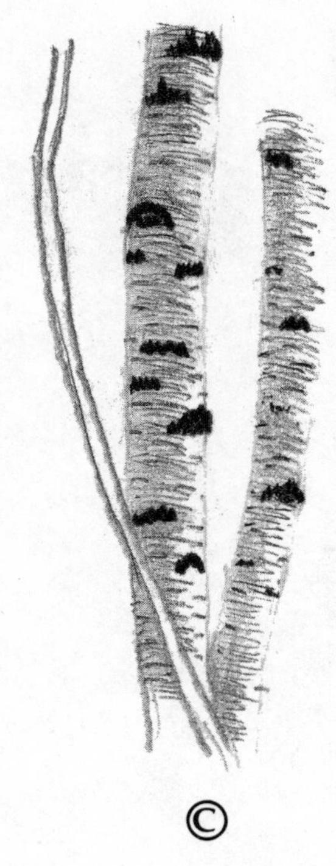
C

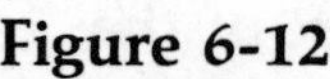
C1
C2

Figure 6-12

A Use your 3B pencil for the darkest markings.

B Use your broad-point B pencil to shade the left side of each tree.

C Use your sharp B pencil, as at C1, then add dark dashes, as at C2.

D Finally, add a few branches . . . but not too many.

F. Lohan

Figure 6-13
This is a fine-point pen rendition of the misty woodland scene. Note the use of stipple (dots) for the misty effect. Lines of ink cannot produce the same range of delicate tones that the pencil can. I used a 5×0 (five-zero) technical pen for this exercise.

Use the outline you prepared for the pencil exercise to prepare another final sheet and try this pen approach.

The Cliffs, Hunstanton

F. Lohan

Figure 6-14
These massive cliffs in Norfolk are composed of a relatively hard, white layer of stone over a softer, red-colored stratum. The sea erodes the red layer and the harder, light-colored layer falls to the beach, sometimes in giant slabs. I used a 3×0 technical pen here.

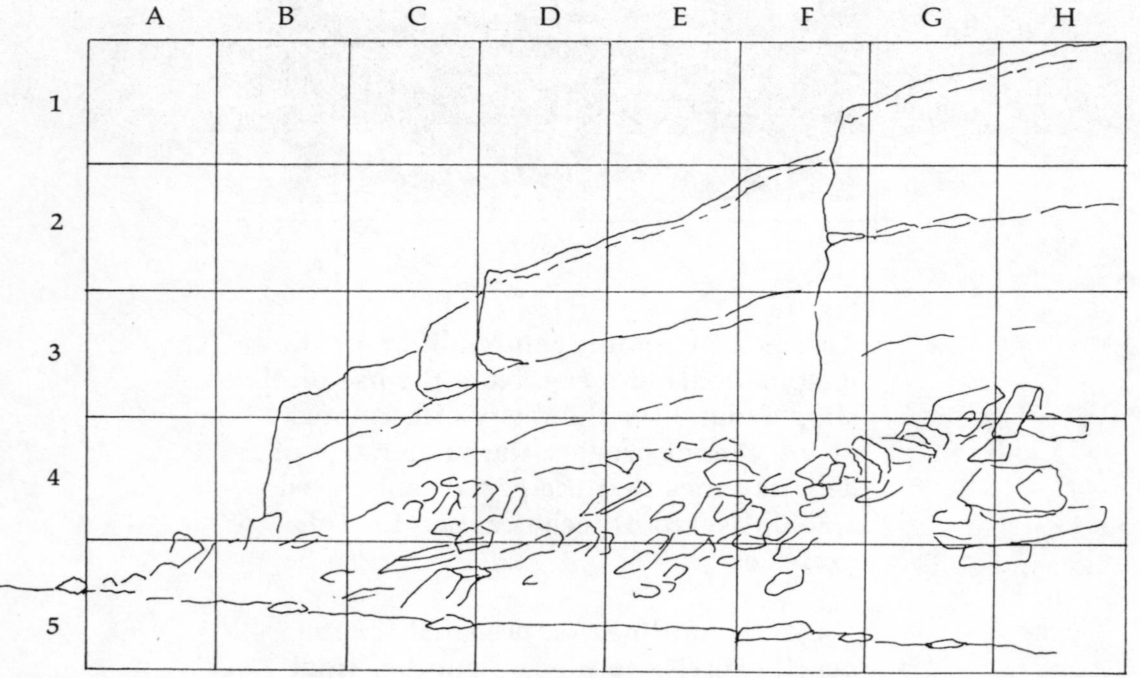
A
B
C
D
E
F
G
H
1
2
3
4
5

Figure 6-15
Use this gridded composition to make your faintly drawn pencil outline over which you will do your pen work.

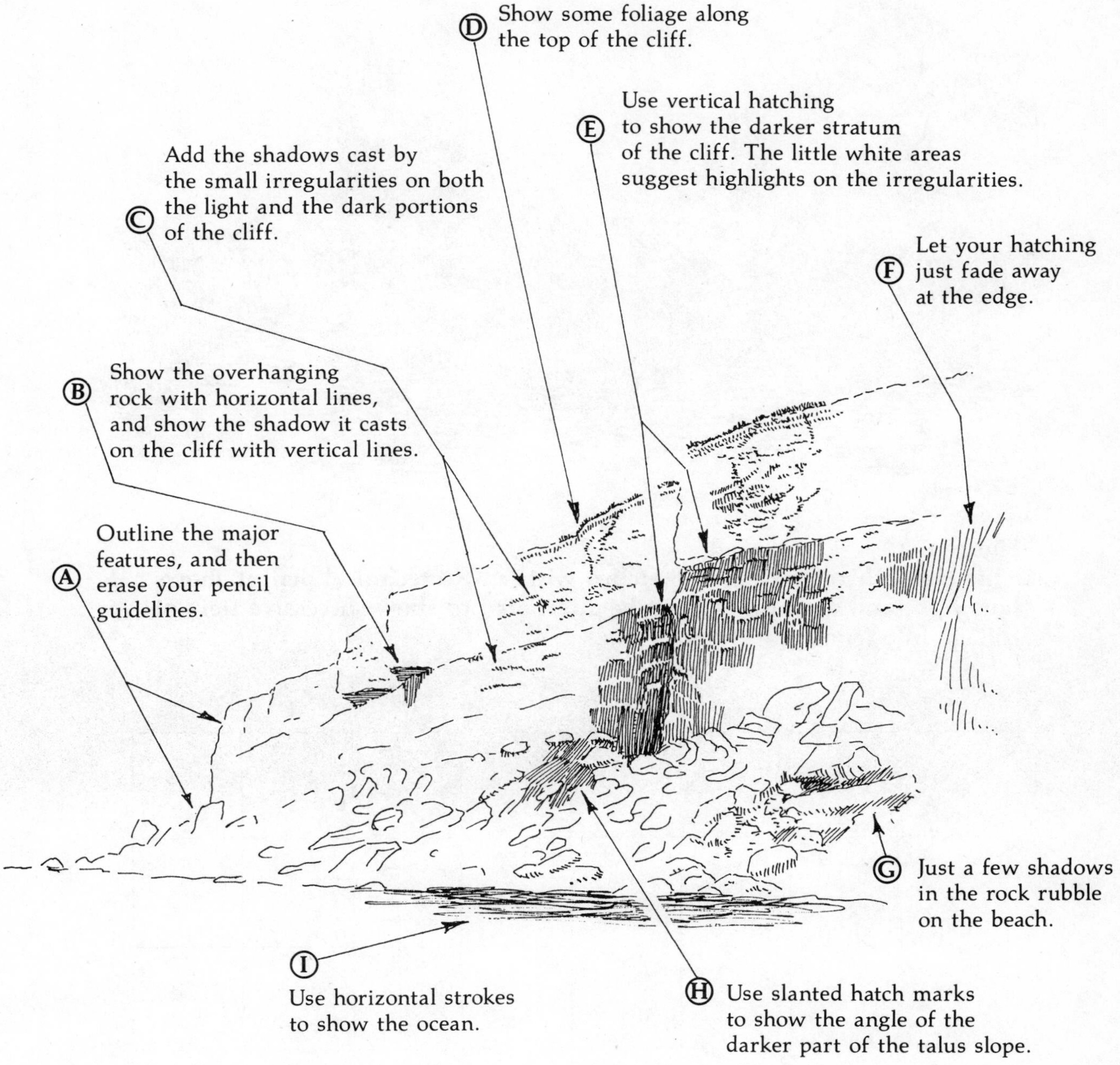
Ⓓ Show some foliage along the top of the cliff.
Ⓔ Use vertical hatching to show the darker stratum of the cliff. The little white areas suggest highlights on the irregularities.
Ⓒ Add the shadows cast by the small irregularities on both the light and the dark portions of the cliff.
Ⓕ Let your hatching just fade away at the edge.
Ⓑ Show the overhanging rock with horizontal lines, and show the shadow it casts on the cliff with vertical lines.
Ⓐ Outline the major features, and then erase your pencil guidelines.
Ⓖ Just a few shadows in the rock rubble on the beach.
Ⓘ Use horizontal strokes to show the ocean.
Ⓗ Use slanted hatch marks to show the angle of the darker part of the talus slope.

Figure 6-16
Use these suggestions and refer to the completed ink study in figure 6-14 to complete your own ink sketch.

The Itchen River Near Winchester

F. Lohan

Figure 6-17
This Hampshire scene was sketched with a 3×0 technical pen. It shows how light and dark tones must be alternated to show successive tiers of foliage in a landscape study.

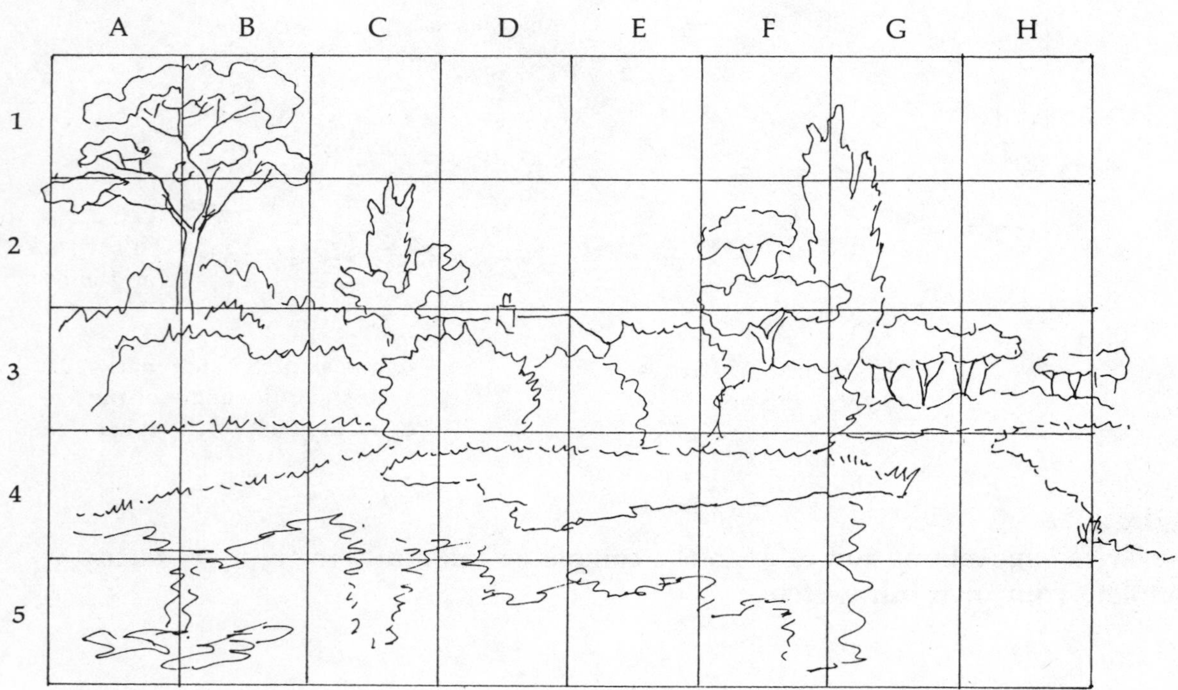
A
B
C
D
E
F
G
H
1
2
3
4
5

Figure 6-18
Use this gridded composition to prepare your light pencil drawing over which you will do your inking.

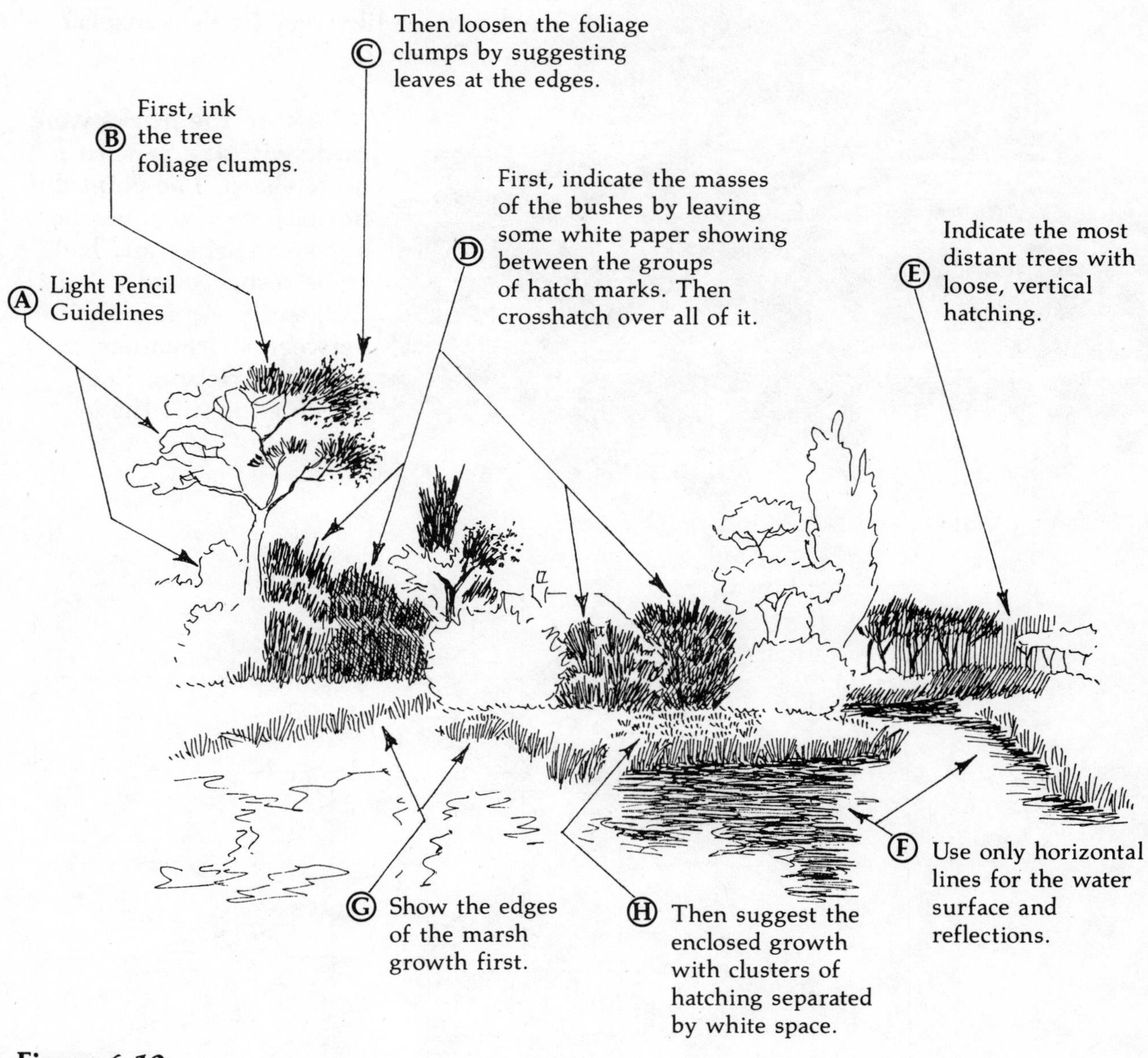
Then loosen the foliage
Ⓒ clumps by suggesting
leaves at the edges.
First, ink
Ⓑ the tree
foliage clumps.
First, indicate the masses
of the bushes by leaving
some white paper showing
Ⓓ between the groups
of hatch marks. Then
crosshatch over all of it.
Indicate the most
distant trees with
Ⓔ loose, vertical
hatching.
Ⓐ Light Pencil
Guidelines
Ⓕ Use only horizontal
lines for the water
surface and
reflections.
Ⓖ Show the edges
of the marsh
growth first.
Ⓗ Then suggest the
enclosed growth
with clusters of
hatching separated
by white space.

Figure 6-19
Use these suggestions and the completed study (figure 6-17) to guide the completion of your drawing.

Bell Rock, Sedona, Arizona

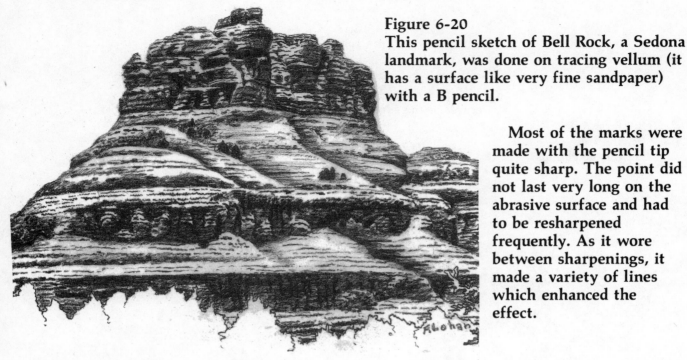

Figure 6-20
This pencil sketch of Bell Rock, a Sedona landmark, was done on tracing vellum (it has a surface like very fine sandpaper) with a B pencil.

Most of the marks were made with the pencil tip quite sharp. The point did not last very long on the abrasive surface and had to be resharpened frequently. As it wore between sharpenings, it made a variety of lines which enhanced the effect.

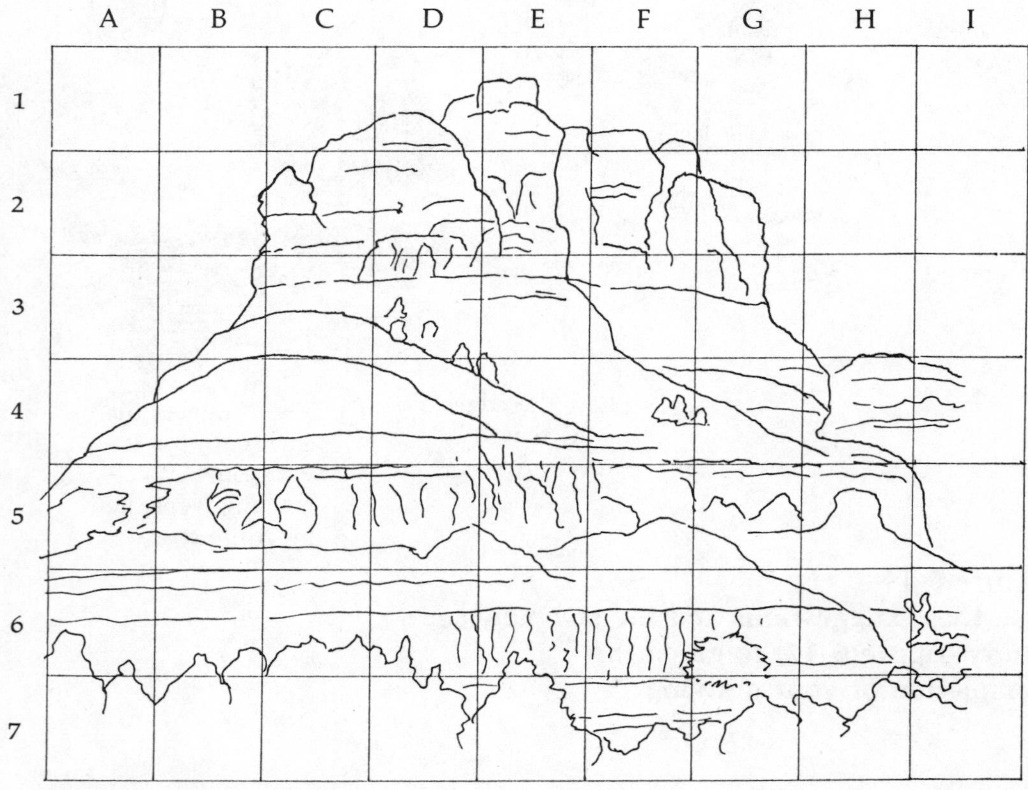
A B C D E F G H I
1
2
3
4
5
6
7

Figure 6-21
Use this gridded outline and the instructions in Chapter 3 to prepare your own composition drawing for this study.

B
C
A
B
C

Figure 6-22

A Make your outline very light, as it cannot be erased the way it can with an ink drawing.

B Make the dark cracks and strata marks first, working one section at a time. I worked with Plexiglas under my paper when I did this drawing. A softer underlying surface will give you a somewhat different final appearance.

C Shade over your detail work to create the forms on the rock face.

Figure 6-23
This drawing was done on regular 70 pound, vellum-finish paper. Note the difference in the final result as compared with figure 6-20.

Plane Tree

F. Lohan

Figure 6-24
I used a 3×0 technical pen for this study of a plane tree, or sycamore, in late autumn. Hyde Park and Kensington Gardens in London have some magnificent examples of trees of different species.

Note the lack of outlines in this drawing. The tone itself defines most of the edges.

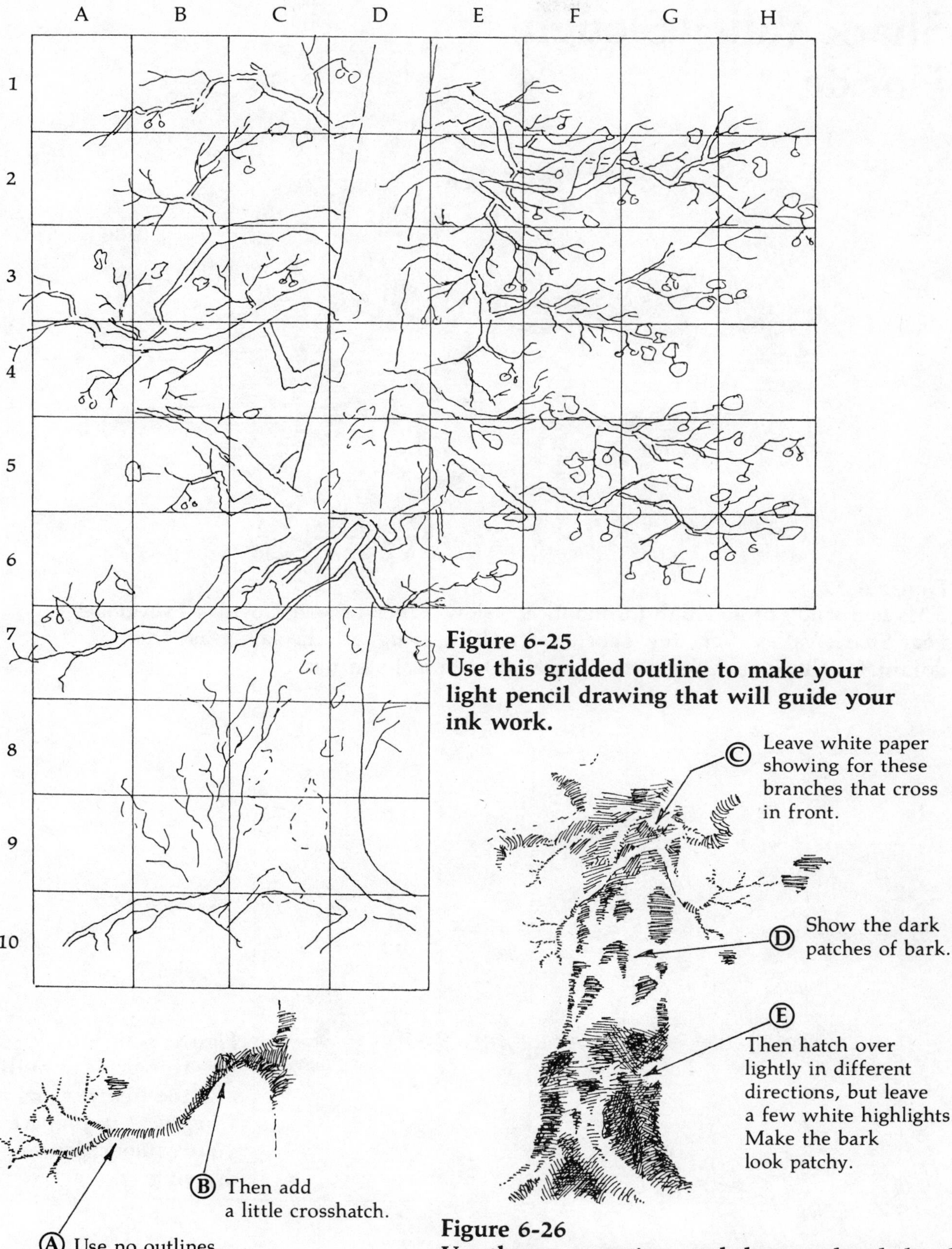
A B C D E F G H
1
2
3
4
5
6
7
8
9
10
Ⓒ Leave white paper showing for these branches that cross in front.
Ⓓ Show the dark patches of bark.
Ⓔ Then hatch over lightly in different directions, but leave a few white highlights. Make the bark look patchy.
Ⓑ Then add a little crosshatch.
Ⓐ Use no outlines, just hatch marks.

Figure 6-25
Use this gridded outline to make your light pencil drawing that will guide your ink work.

Figure 6-26
Use these suggestions and the completed sketch (figure 6-24) to guide you in completing your ink drawing of this subject.

Shark Valley Slough, Florida

F. Lohan

Figure 6-27
This is a study of a slough (pronounced "slew") in southern Florida's Everglades near Shark Valley. Very few short, vertical lines suggest the saw grass that dominates the Everglades. I used a size 0 technical pen here.

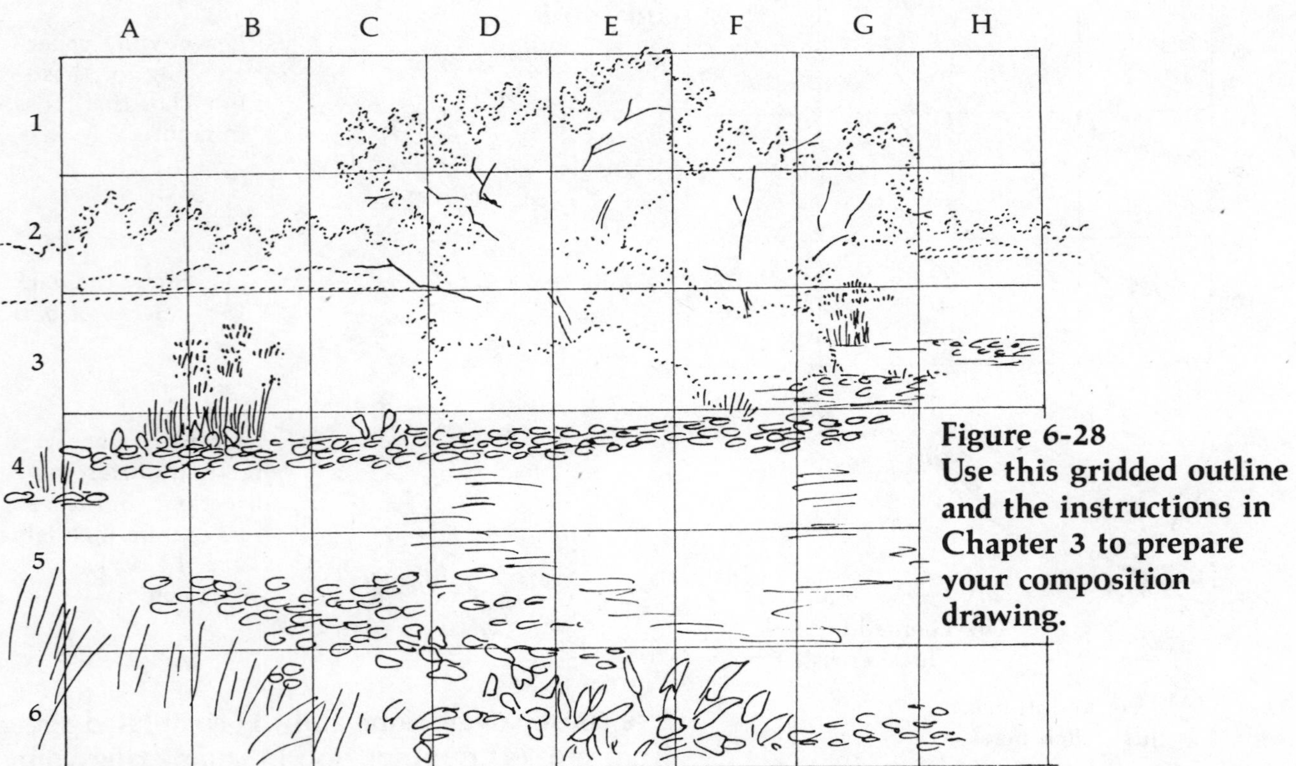
A
B
C
D
E
F
G
H
1
2
3
4
5
6

Figure 6-28
Use this gridded outline and the instructions in Chapter 3 to prepare your composition drawing.

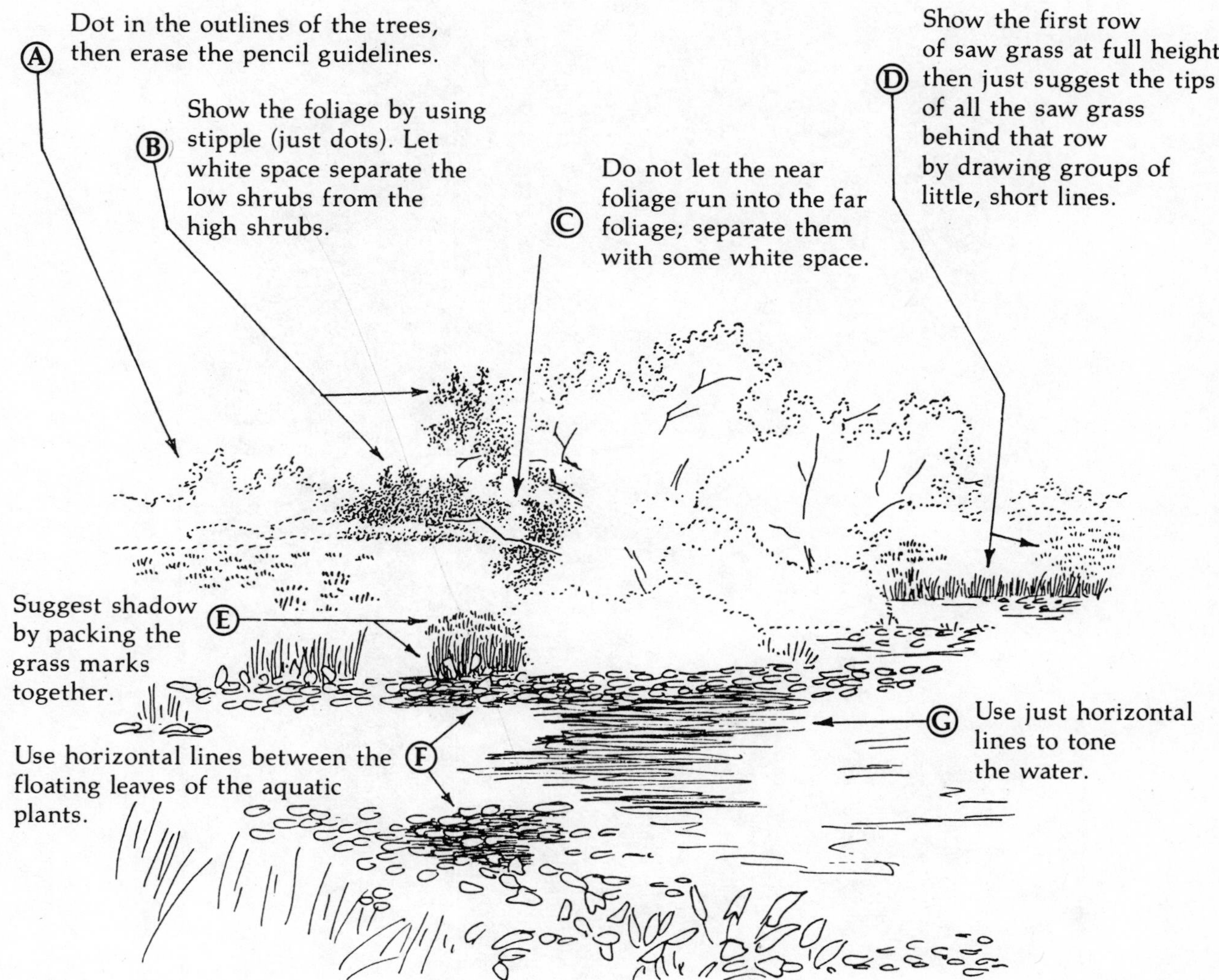
Ⓐ Dot in the outlines of the trees, then erase the pencil guidelines.
Ⓑ Show the foliage by using stipple (just dots). Let white space separate the low shrubs from the high shrubs.
Ⓒ Do not let the near foliage run into the far foliage; separate them with some white space.
Ⓓ Show the first row of saw grass at full height, then just suggest the tips of all the saw grass behind that row by drawing groups of little, short lines.
Ⓔ Suggest shadow by packing the grass marks together.
Ⓕ Use horizontal lines between the floating leaves of the aquatic plants.
Ⓖ Use just horizontal lines to tone the water.

Figure 6-29
Use these suggestions to complete the ink work on your study of the slough.

Stream, Great Smoky Mountains

F.Lohan

Figure 6-30
This is a 3×0 technical pen study of a stream in the Great Smoky Mountains near Gatlinburg, Tennessee. The area offers thousands of such vistas, each one different from all the others.

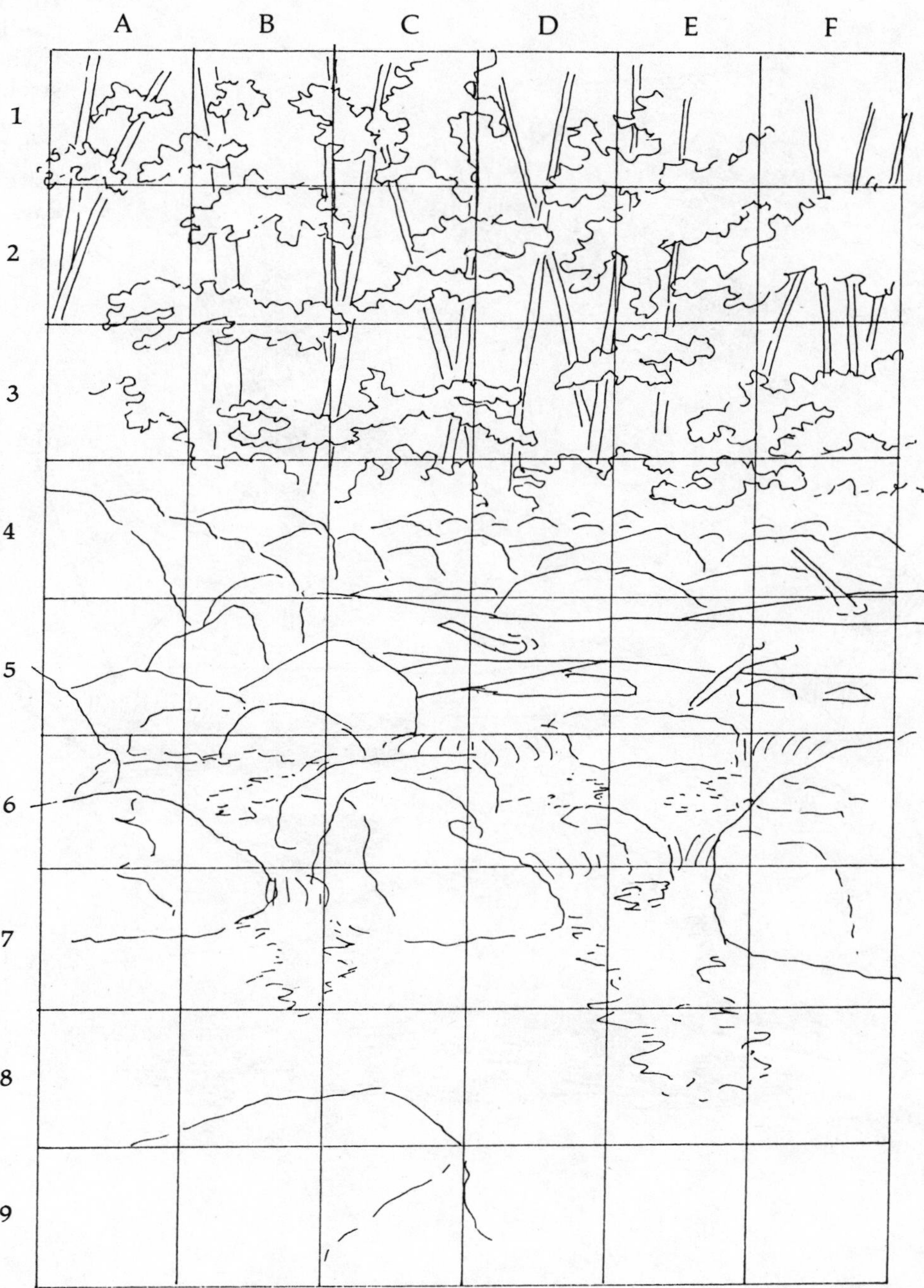
A
B
C
D
E
F
1
2
3
4
5
6
7
8
9

Figure 6-31
Use this gridded figure to help prepare your own composition drawing of this subject.

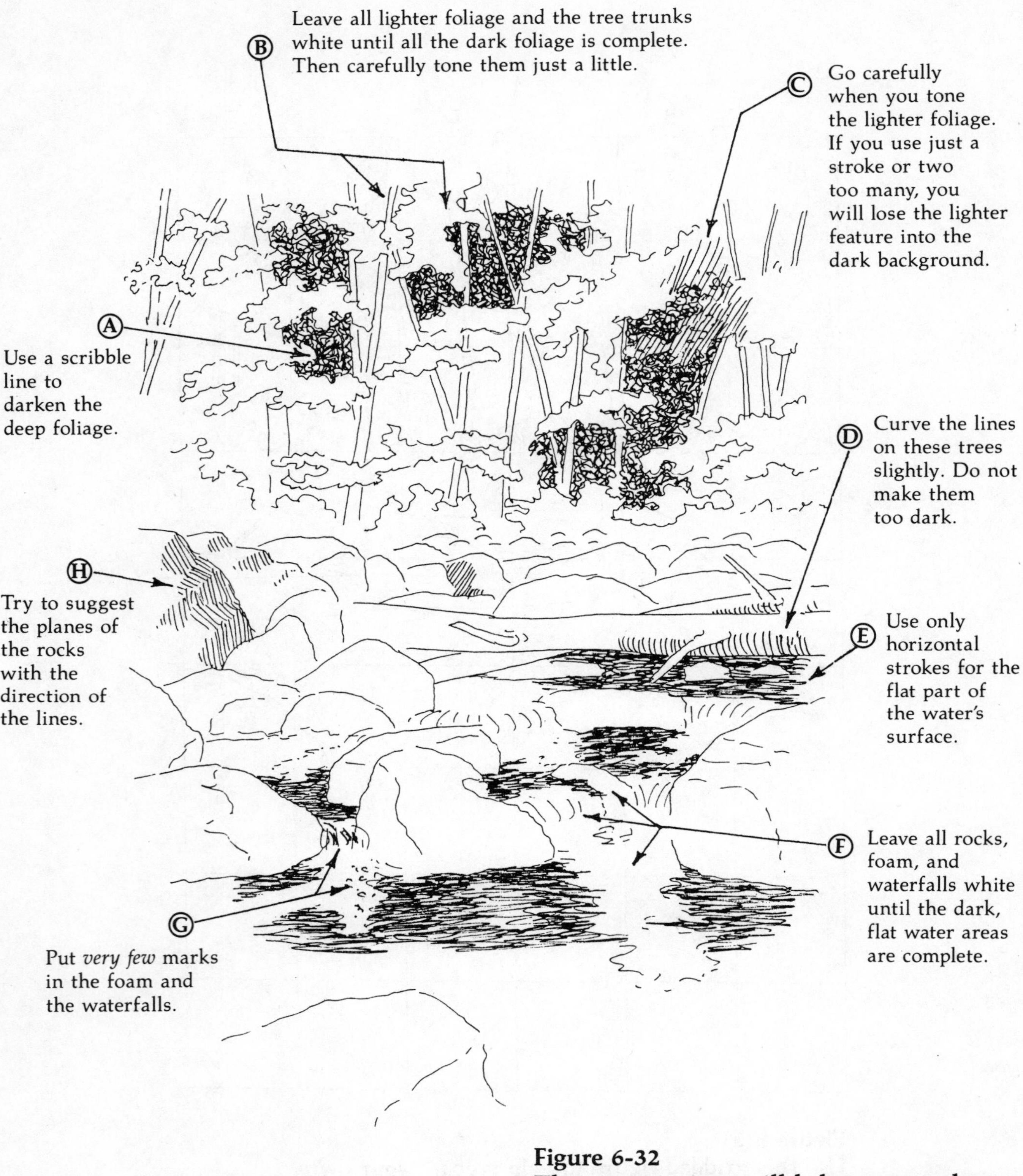
B
Leave all lighter foliage and the tree trunks white until all the dark foliage is complete. Then carefully tone them just a little.
C
Go carefully when you tone the lighter foliage. If you use just a stroke or two too many, you will lose the lighter feature into the dark background.
A
Use a scribble line to darken the deep foliage.
D
Curve the lines on these trees slightly. Do not make them too dark.
H
Try to suggest the planes of the rocks with the direction of the lines.
E
Use only horizontal strokes for the flat part of the water's surface.
F
Leave all rocks, foam, and waterfalls white until the dark, flat water areas are complete.
G
Put *very few* marks in the foam and the waterfalls.

Figure 6-32
These suggestions will help you complete your drawing of the mountain stream.

Georgian Bay, Canada

F.Lohan

Figure 6-33
This is a headland in Cyprus Lake Provincial Park on Georgian Bay in Ontario. I used a 3×0 technical pen for this study of the rugged Niagara escarpment on the Bruce peninsula near Tobermory.

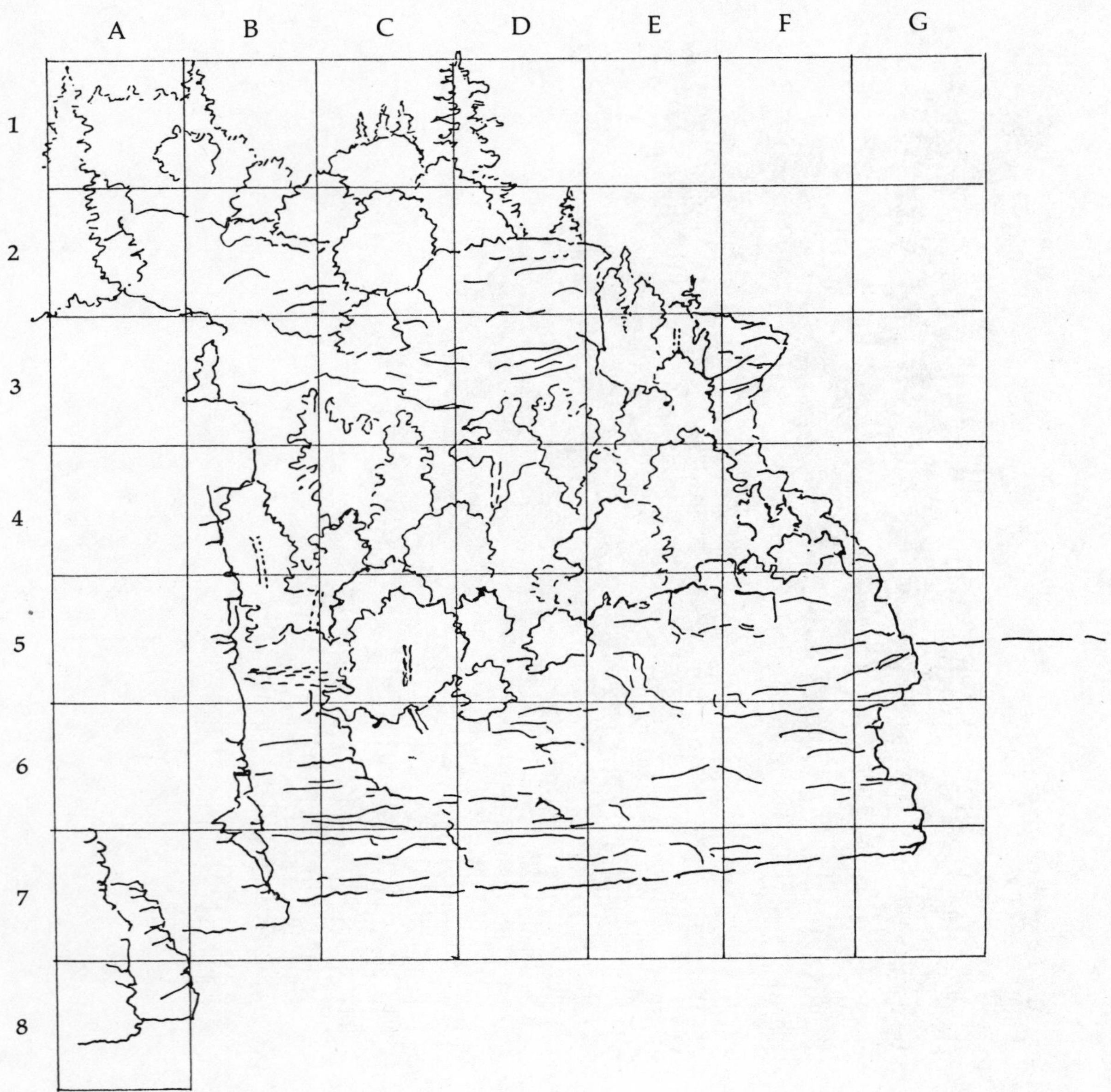
A
B
C
D
E
F
G
1
2
3
4
5
6
7
8

Figure 6-34
Use this figure to help establish your composition drawing.

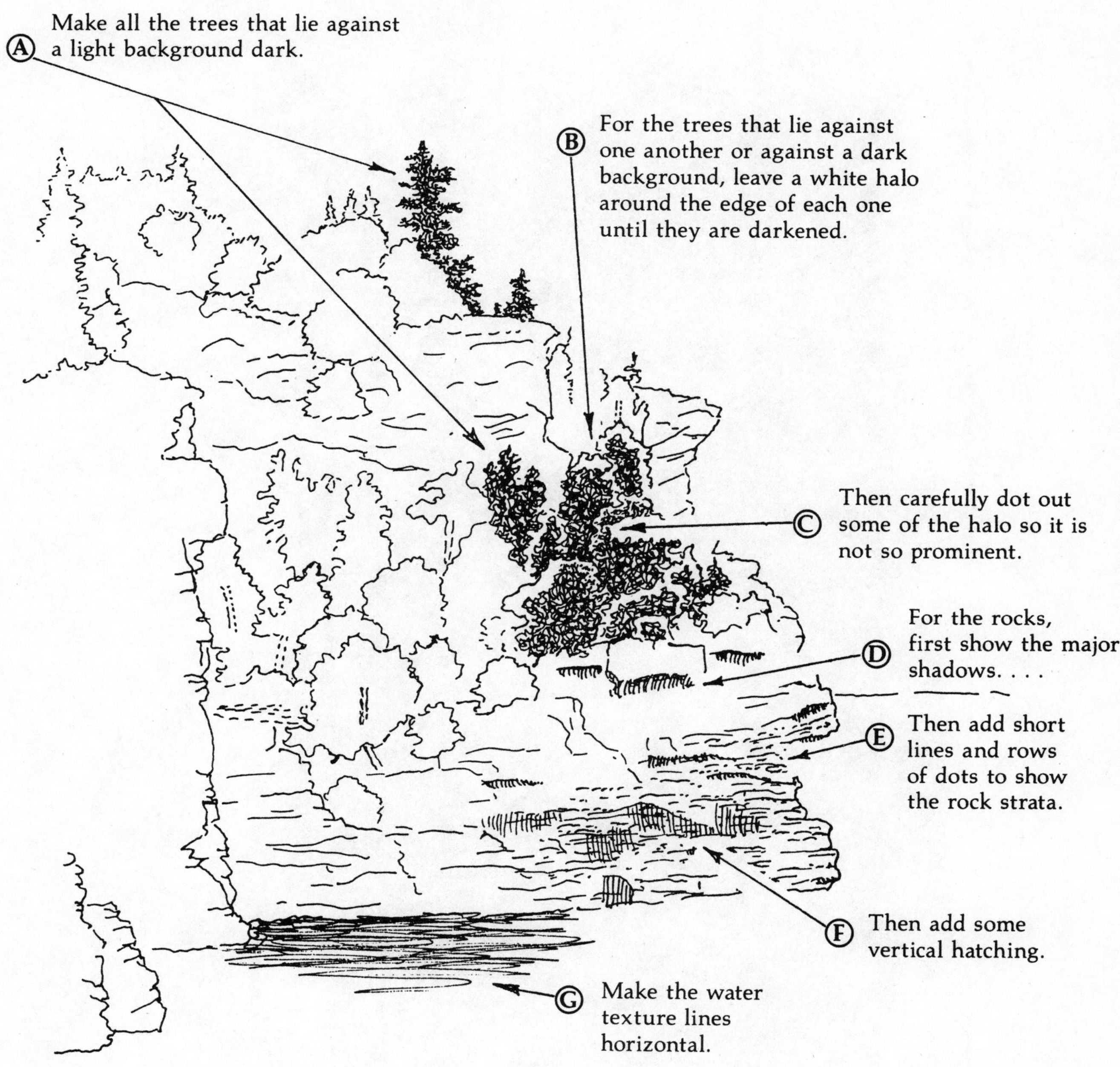
A Make all the trees that lie against a light background dark.
B For the trees that lie against one another or against a dark background, leave a white halo around the edge of each one until they are darkened.
C Then carefully dot out some of the halo so it is not so prominent.
D For the rocks, first show the major shadows. . . .
E Then add short lines and rows of dots to show the rock strata.
F Then add some vertical hatching.
G Make the water texture lines horizontal.

Figure 6-35
These suggestions will help you complete your ink drawing of this scene.

Carter County, Kentucky

F. Lohan
CARTER CAVES, KY.

Figure 6-36
This pencil sketch of a scene in Carter Caves State Park, Kentucky, shows one of the many magnificent limestone bluffs you encounter in the forest. This drawing was done on tracing vellum (an abrasive surface) with sharp and broad-point HB and B pencils.

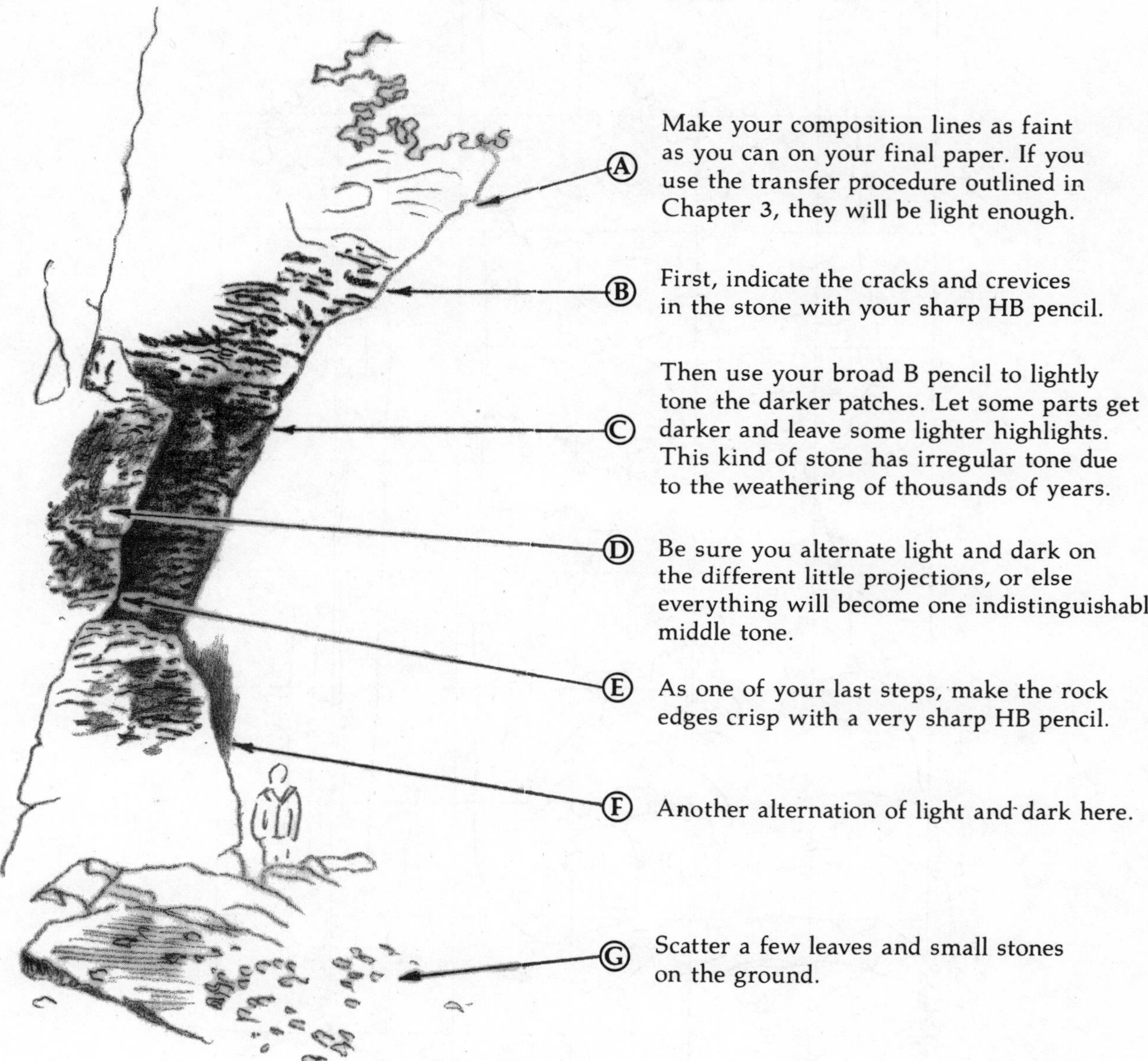

A
Make your composition lines as faint as you can on your final paper. If you use the transfer procedure outlined in Chapter 3, they will be light enough.
B
First, indicate the cracks and crevices in the stone with your sharp HB pencil.
C
Then use your broad B pencil to lightly tone the darker patches. Let some parts get darker and leave some lighter highlights. This kind of stone has irregular tone due to the weathering of thousands of years.
D
Be sure you alternate light and dark on the different little projections, or else everything will become one indistinguishable middle tone.
E
As one of your last steps, make the rock edges crisp with a very sharp HB pencil.
F
Another alternation of light and dark here.
G
Scatter a few leaves and small stones on the ground.

Figure 6-37
Use these suggestions as you work on your drawing of the limestone bluff and old beech tree. I put the person in to give a feeling for scale.

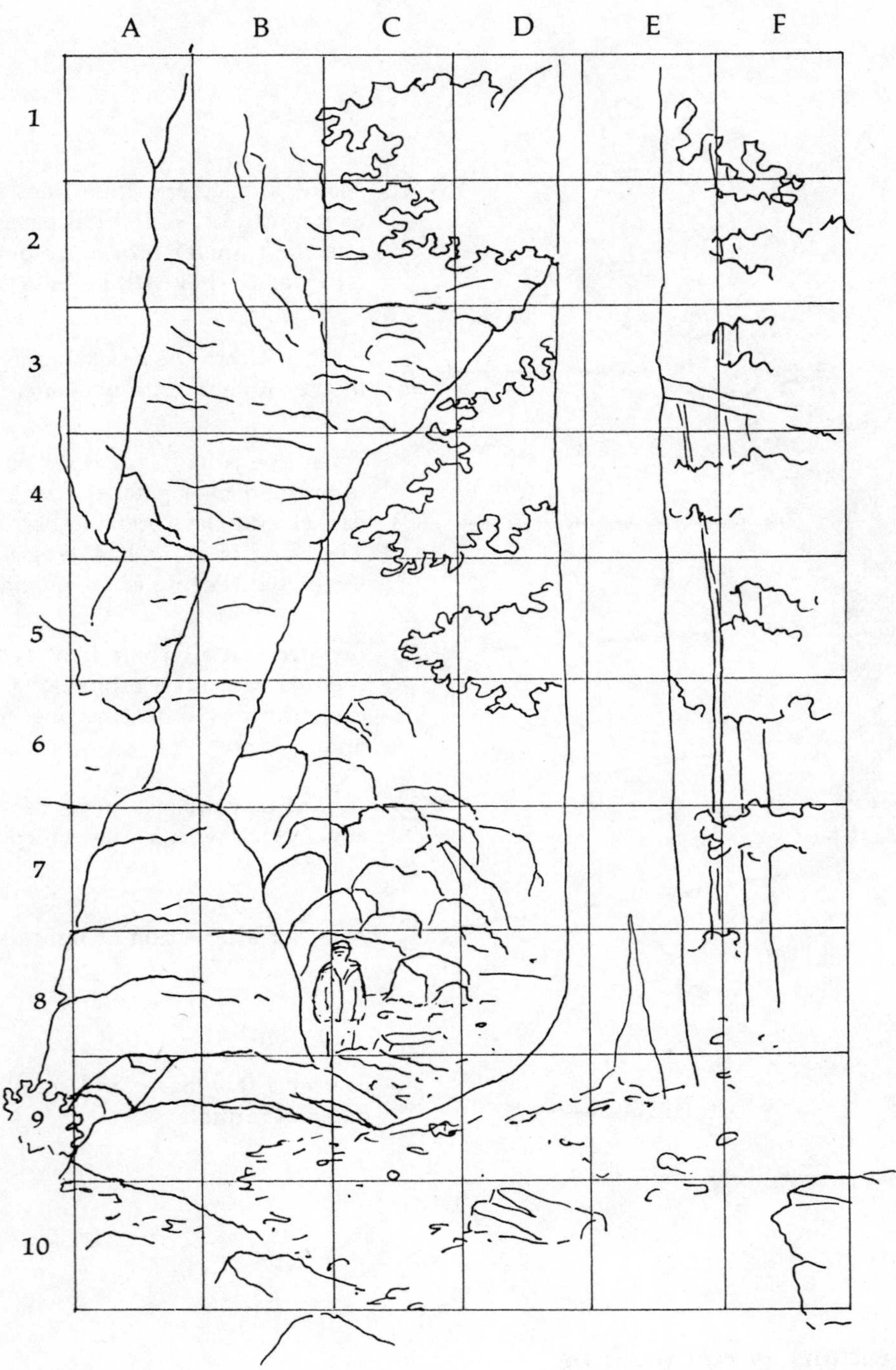
A
B
C
D
E
F
1
2
3
4
5
6
7
8
9
10

Figure 6-38
Use this gridded outline and the instructions in Chapter 3 to make your composition drawing for this subject.

Florida Everglades

Figure 6-39
This is a 3×0 technical pen sketch of a stand of Melaleuca trees. The Melaleuca tree is native to Australia and is now an exotic in the Everglades that displaces native vegetation.

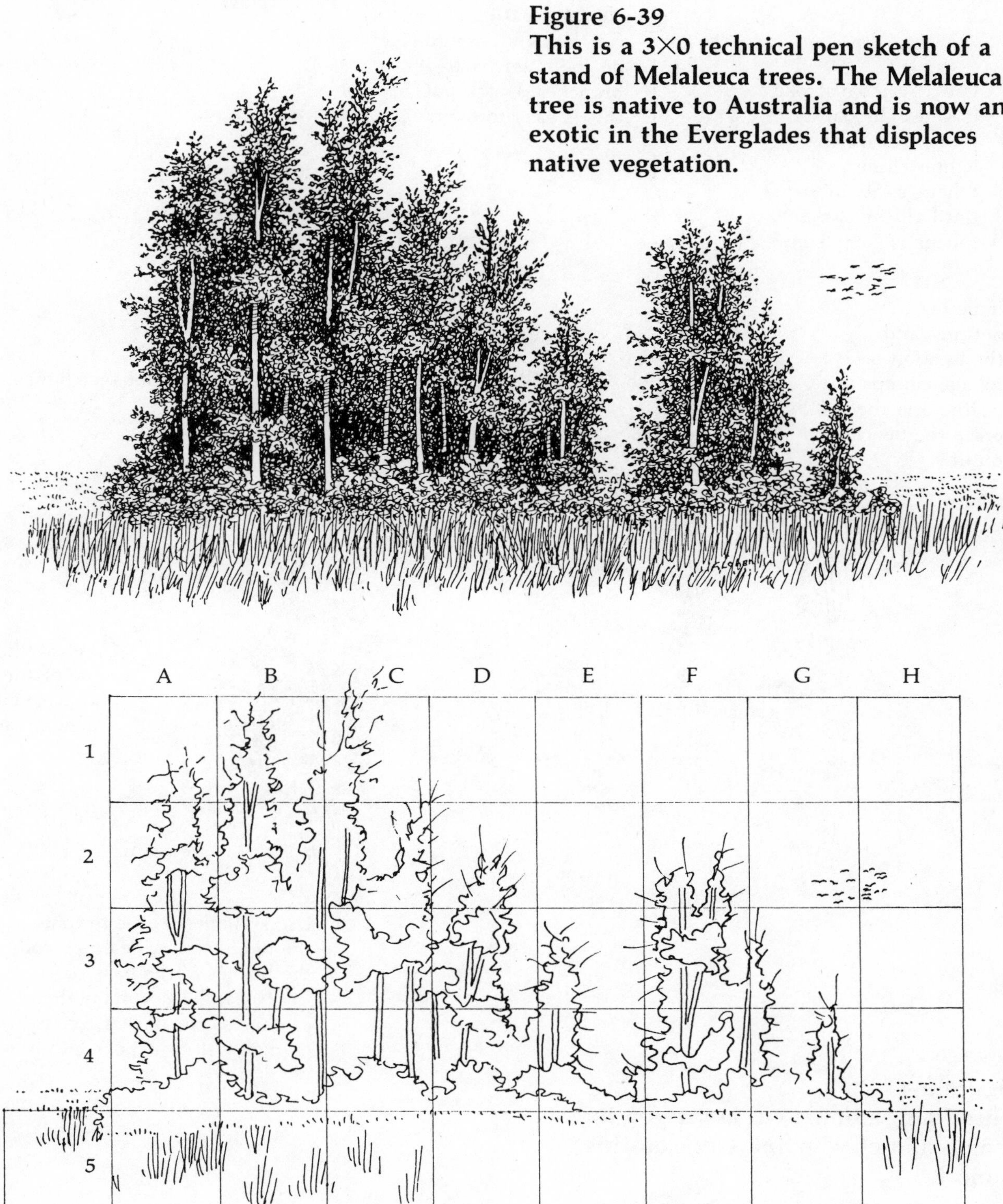
A
B
C
D
E
F
G
H
1
2
3
4
5

Figure 6-40
Use this gridded outline to assist you in making your composition drawing for this study. See Chapter 3 for instructions on copying and transferring a drawing.

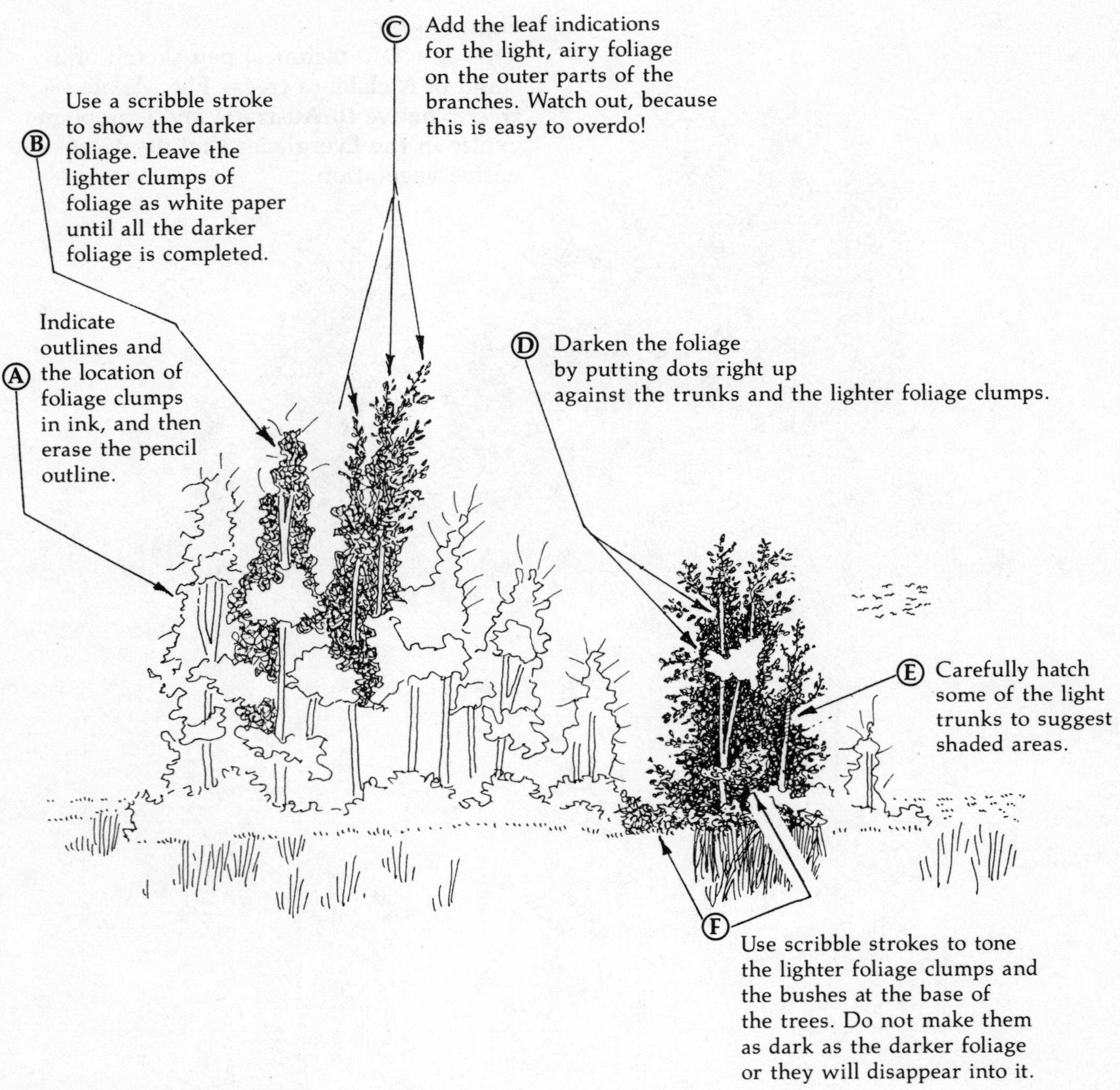
Ⓒ Add the leaf indications for the light, airy foliage on the outer parts of the branches. Watch out, because this is easy to overdo!
Ⓑ Use a scribble stroke to show the darker foliage. Leave the lighter clumps of foliage as white paper until all the darker foliage is completed.
Ⓐ Indicate outlines and the location of foliage clumps in ink, and then erase the pencil outline.
Ⓓ Darken the foliage by putting dots right up against the trunks and the lighter foliage clumps.
Ⓔ Carefully hatch some of the light trunks to suggest shaded areas.
Ⓕ Use scribble strokes to tone the lighter foliage clumps and the bushes at the base of the trees. Do not make them as dark as the darker foliage or they will disappear into it.

Figure 6-41
These suggestions will assist you in completion of your ink work on this subject.

For Sale

F. Lohan

Figure 6-42
I used a 3×0 technical pen for this sketch of an abandoned farmhouse along Route 12 in southern Michigan. Note the use of different textures as well as different tones to distinguish one tree from another.

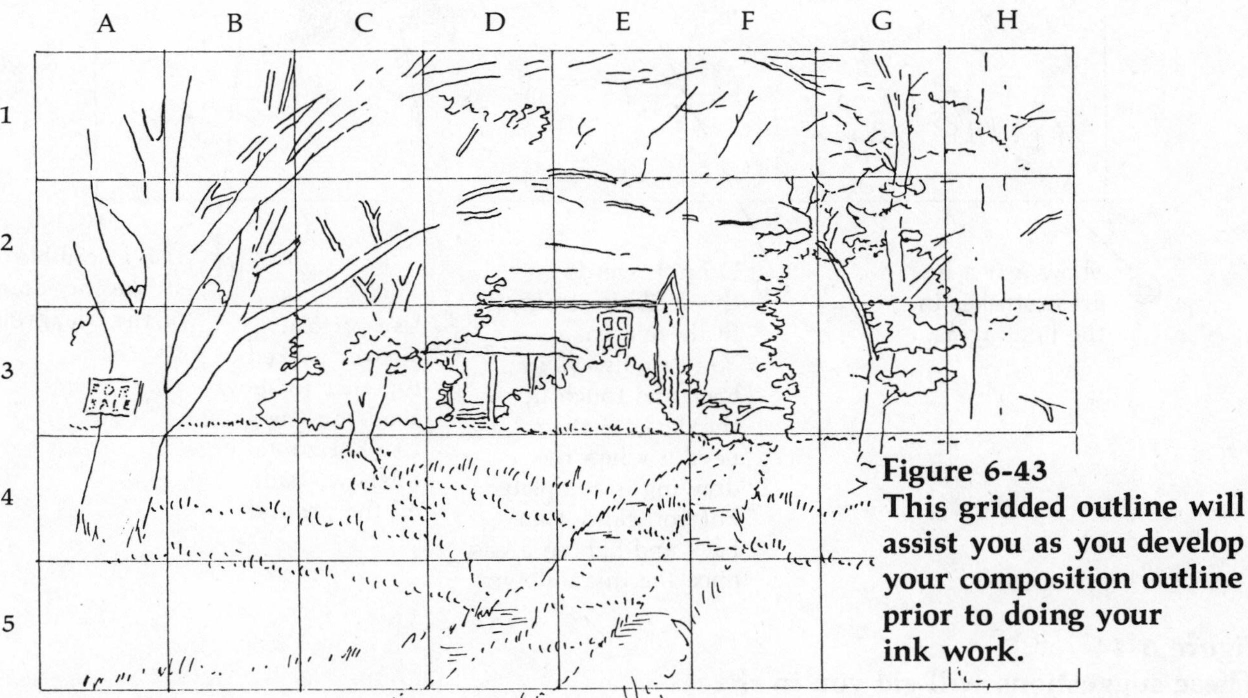
A B C D E F G H
1
2
3
4
5
FOR SALE

Figure 6-43
This gridded outline will assist you as you develop your composition outline prior to doing your ink work.

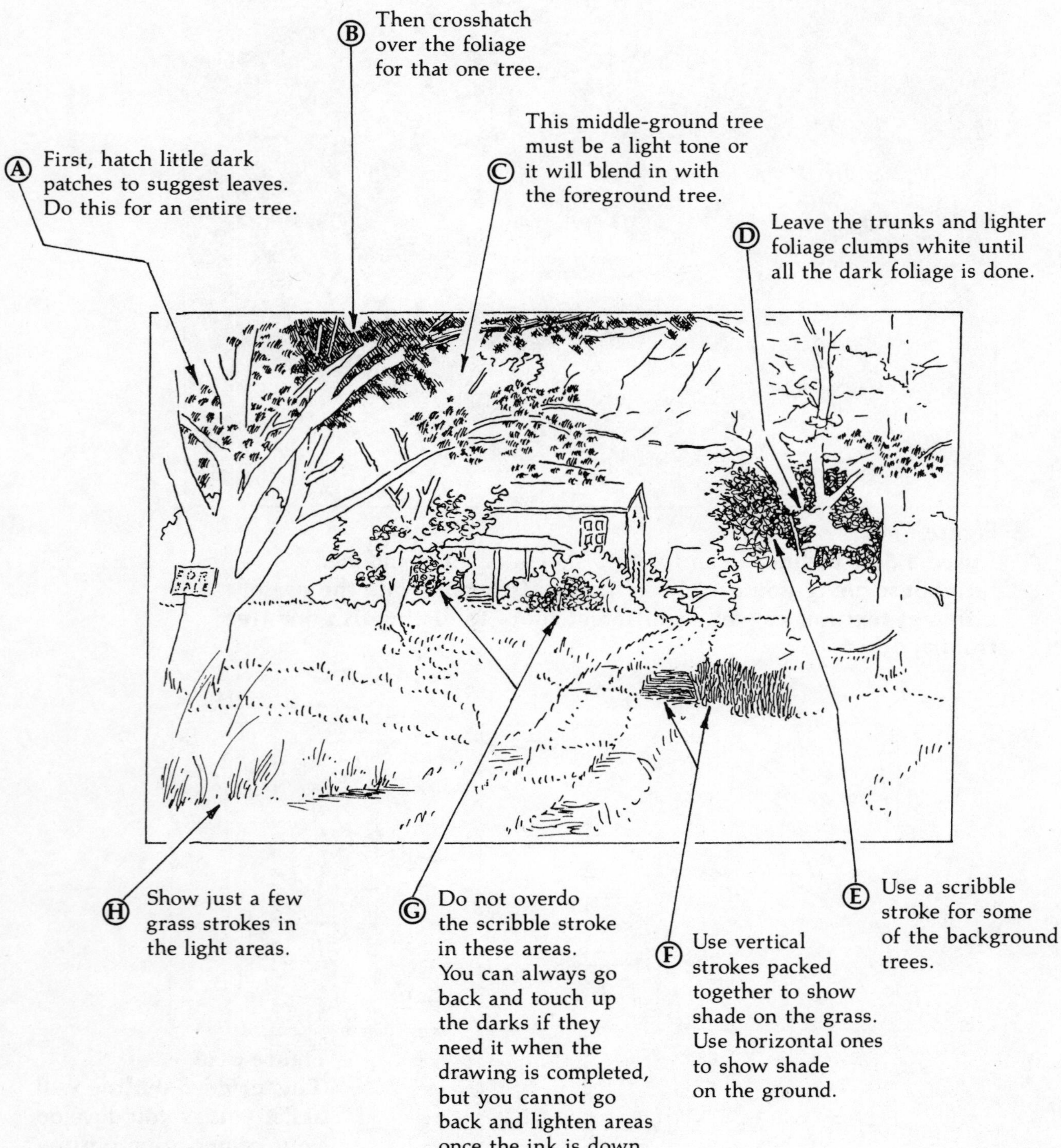
Ⓑ Then crosshatch over the foliage for that one tree.
Ⓐ First, hatch little dark patches to suggest leaves. Do this for an entire tree.
Ⓒ This middle-ground tree must be a light tone or it will blend in with the foreground tree.
Ⓓ Leave the trunks and lighter foliage clumps white until all the dark foliage is done.
FOR SALE
Ⓗ Show just a few grass strokes in the light areas.
Ⓖ Do not overdo the scribble stroke in these areas. You can always go back and touch up the darks if they need it when the drawing is completed, but you cannot go back and lighten areas once the ink is down.
Ⓕ Use vertical strokes packed together to show shade on the grass. Use horizontal ones to show shade on the ground.
Ⓔ Use a scribble stroke for some of the background trees.

Figure 6-44
These suggestions will aid you in the completion of your sketch of this scene.

7
Architecture

St. Giles	*Clovelly*
Tintagel, Cornwall	*Bridge over River Derwent*
The Cotswolds	*Lord Leycester's Hospital*
Sandringham	*Spicer House*
St. John the Baptist	*Illinois Barn*
Salisbury Cathedral	*Ightham Mote, Kent*
Masada	*Windsor Castle*

I did the first six subjects in this chapter as part of a study of different towers and steeples on British churches. The first subject has neither tower nor steeple . . . just a quaint bell cote. The second has a tower with a flat roof; the third, a small peaked roof; and so on, to the sixth study, that of the spectacular tower and spire of Salisbury Cathedral.

The first five exercises were drawn with coarse pens: a size 0 technical pen for the first, an even heavier artist's fountain pen for the next three, and a 3×0 technical pen for Salisbury Cathedral.

Two pencil exercises are included: a tight study at Masada and a loose study of the Spicer House in Michigan. These give you a chance to try both ways of drawing with the pencil.

St. Giles

Figure 7-1
I used a size 0 technical pen for this study of an early English, gothic-style church. Note that the church has a pretty bell cote instead of a tower and steeple.

A B C D E F G H I
1
2
3
4
5
6

Figure 7-2
Use this gridded outline to prepare your light pencil outline, and then follow the suggestions in figure 7-3 to complete your ink drawing of this subject.

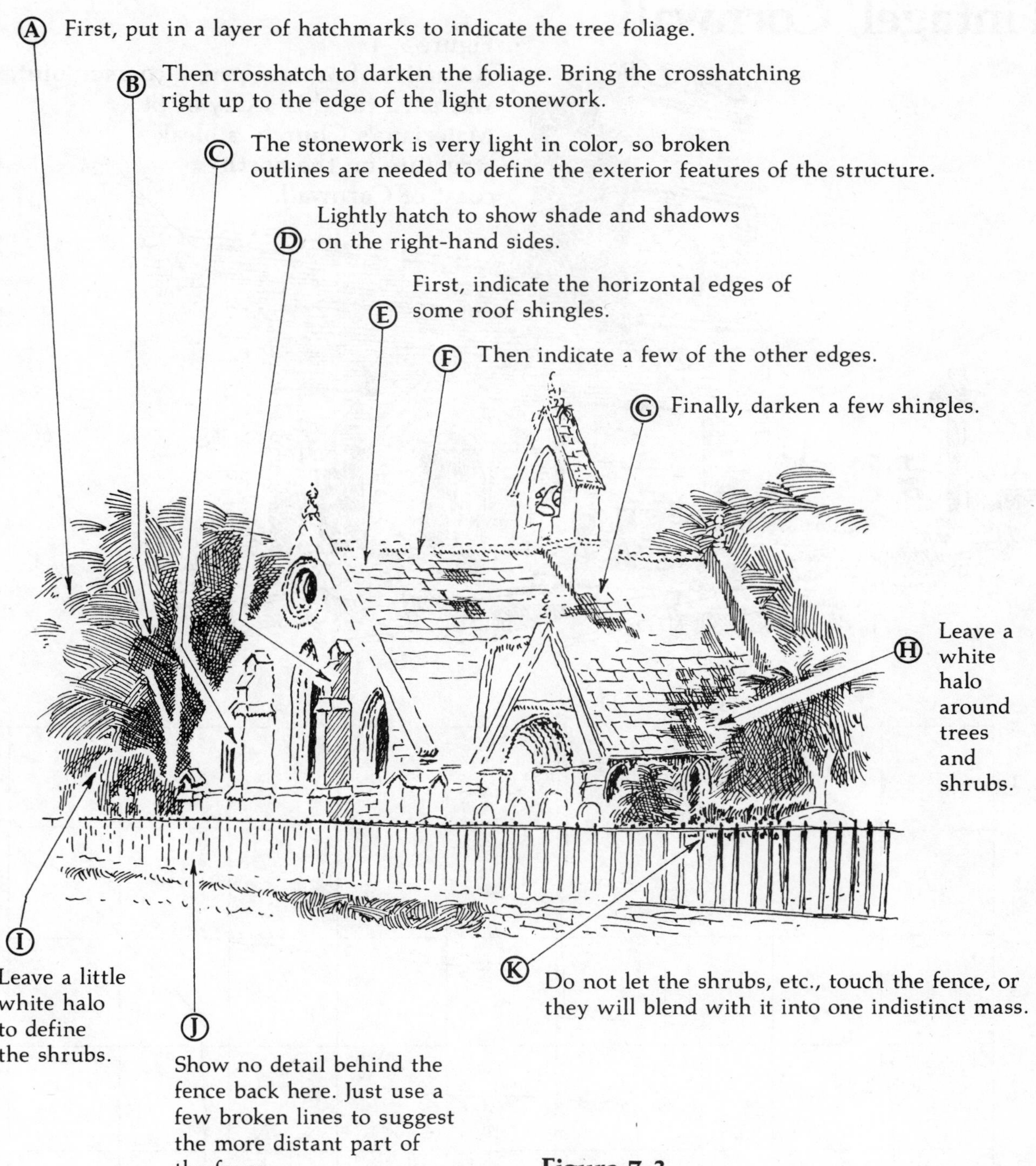
A First, put in a layer of hatchmarks to indicate the tree foliage.
B Then crosshatch to darken the foliage. Bring the crosshatching right up to the edge of the light stonework.
C The stonework is very light in color, so broken outlines are needed to define the exterior features of the structure.
D Lightly hatch to show shade and shadows on the right-hand sides.
E First, indicate the horizontal edges of some roof shingles.
F Then indicate a few of the other edges.
G Finally, darken a few shingles.
H Leave a white halo around trees and shrubs.
I Leave a little white halo to define the shrubs.
J Show no detail behind the fence back here. Just use a few broken lines to suggest the more distant part of the fence.
K Do not let the shrubs, etc., touch the fence, or they will blend with it into one indistinct mass.

Figure 7-3
Follow these suggestions as you use the gridded outline in figure 7-1 to guide your completion of the ink study. As your last step, put a few indications of the stonework in both the sunny parts and the shaded parts of the building. Do not overdo this or you will make these areas too dark and the stone won't look light.

Tintagel, Cornwall

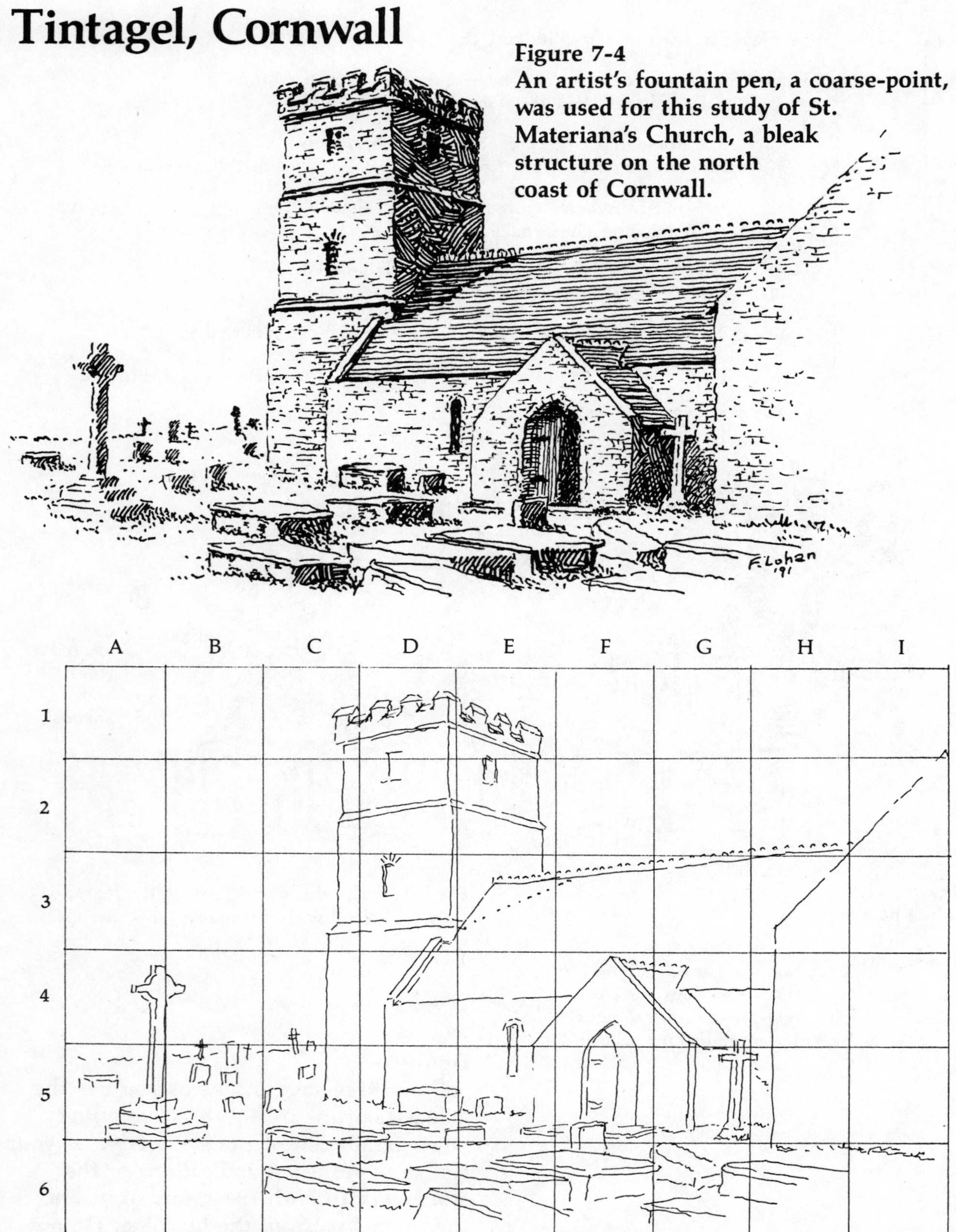
F. Lohan '91
A B C D E F G H I
1
2
3
4
5
6

Figure 7-4
An artist's fountain pen, a coarse-point, was used for this study of St. Materiana's Church, a bleak structure on the north coast of Cornwall.

Figure 7-5
Use this gridded outline to guide the development of your composition drawing.

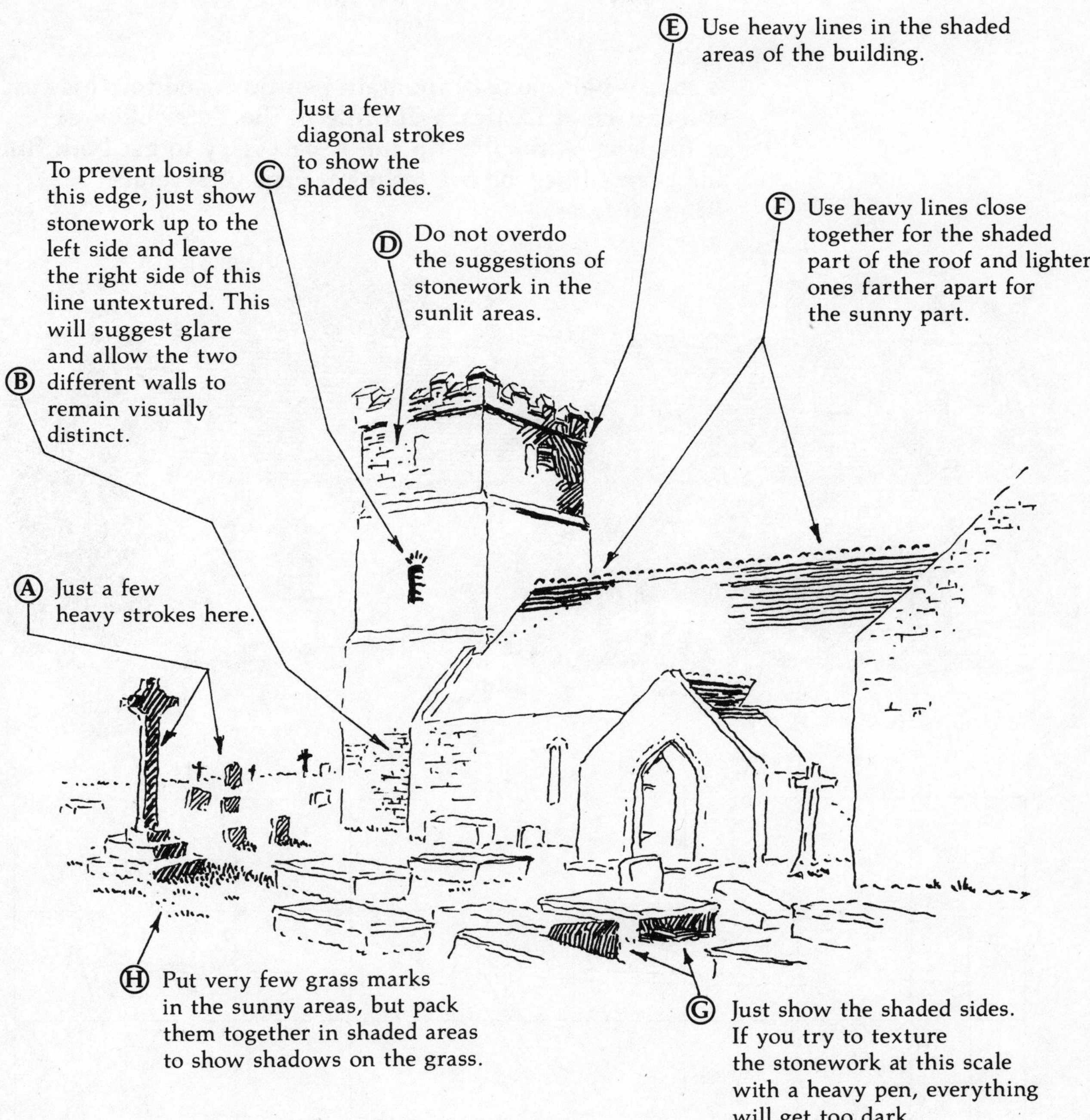
Ⓔ Use heavy lines in the shaded areas of the building.
Just a few diagonal strokes to show the shaded sides.
To prevent losing this edge, just show stonework up to the left side and leave the right side of this line untextured. This will suggest glare and allow the two different walls to remain visually distinct.
Ⓒ
Ⓓ Do not overdo the suggestions of stonework in the sunlit areas.
Ⓕ Use heavy lines close together for the shaded part of the roof and lighter ones farther apart for the sunny part.
Ⓑ
Ⓐ Just a few heavy strokes here.
Ⓗ Put very few grass marks in the sunny areas, but pack them together in shaded areas to show shadows on the grass.
Ⓖ Just show the shaded sides. If you try to texture the stonework at this scale with a heavy pen, everything will get too dark.

Figure 7-6
A flexible-point pen, like a crowquill, a replaceable-nib pen, or an artist's fountain pen, is necessary for this study, since both thick and thin lines are needed. With the flexible-tip pens, you simply press a little harder to get a wider line. If you do this with a technical pen you will break it.

The Cotswolds

Figure 7-7
A coarse-point artist's fountain pen was used for this study of a church at Eastleach-Turville in the Cotswold area of England. A flexible-tip pen is necessary to get both fine and coarse lines, or use technical pens of several different sizes.

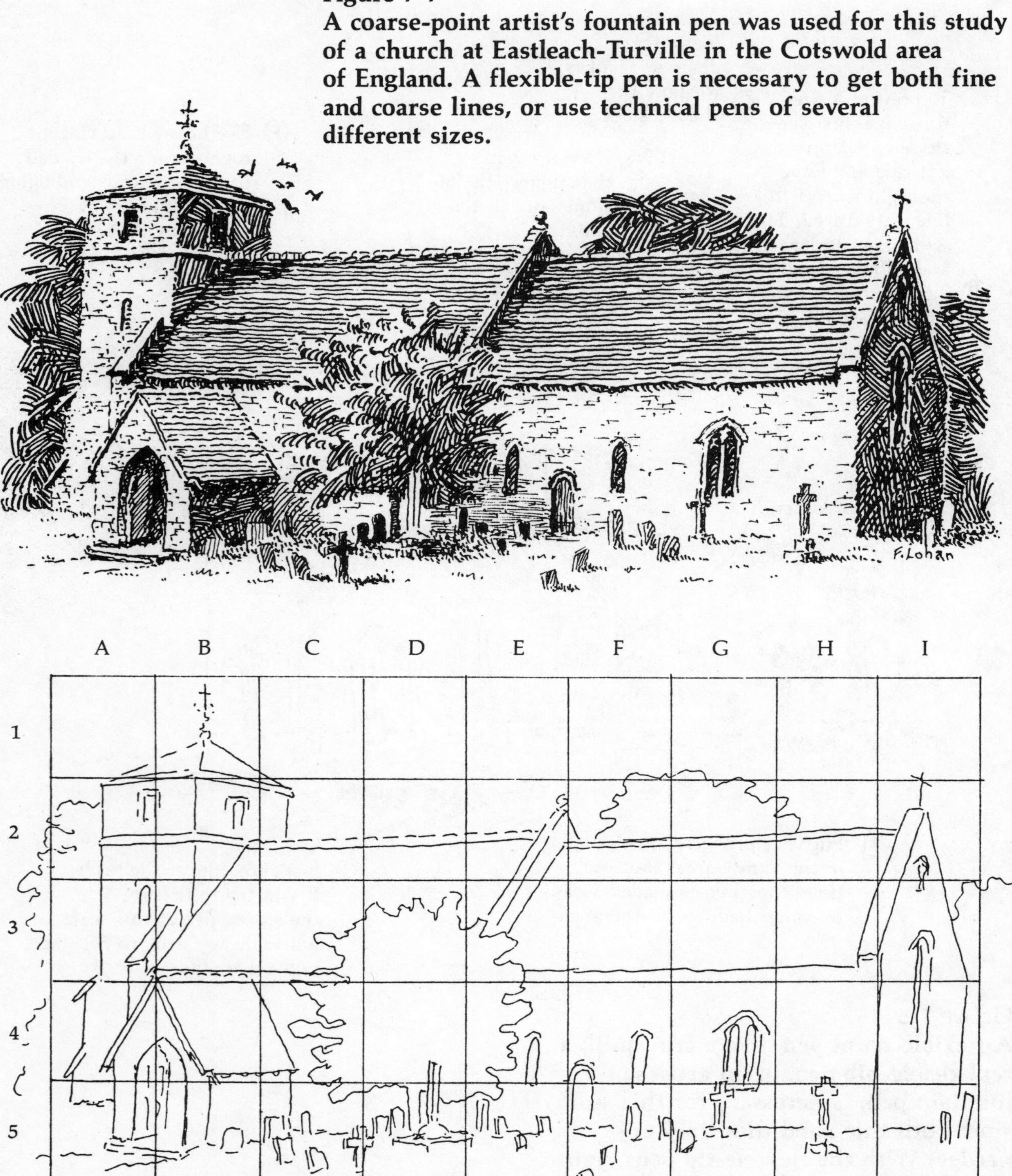
F. Lohan
A B C D E F G H I
1
2
3
4
5

Figure 7-8
This gridded outline will assist you in the preparation of your composition drawing.

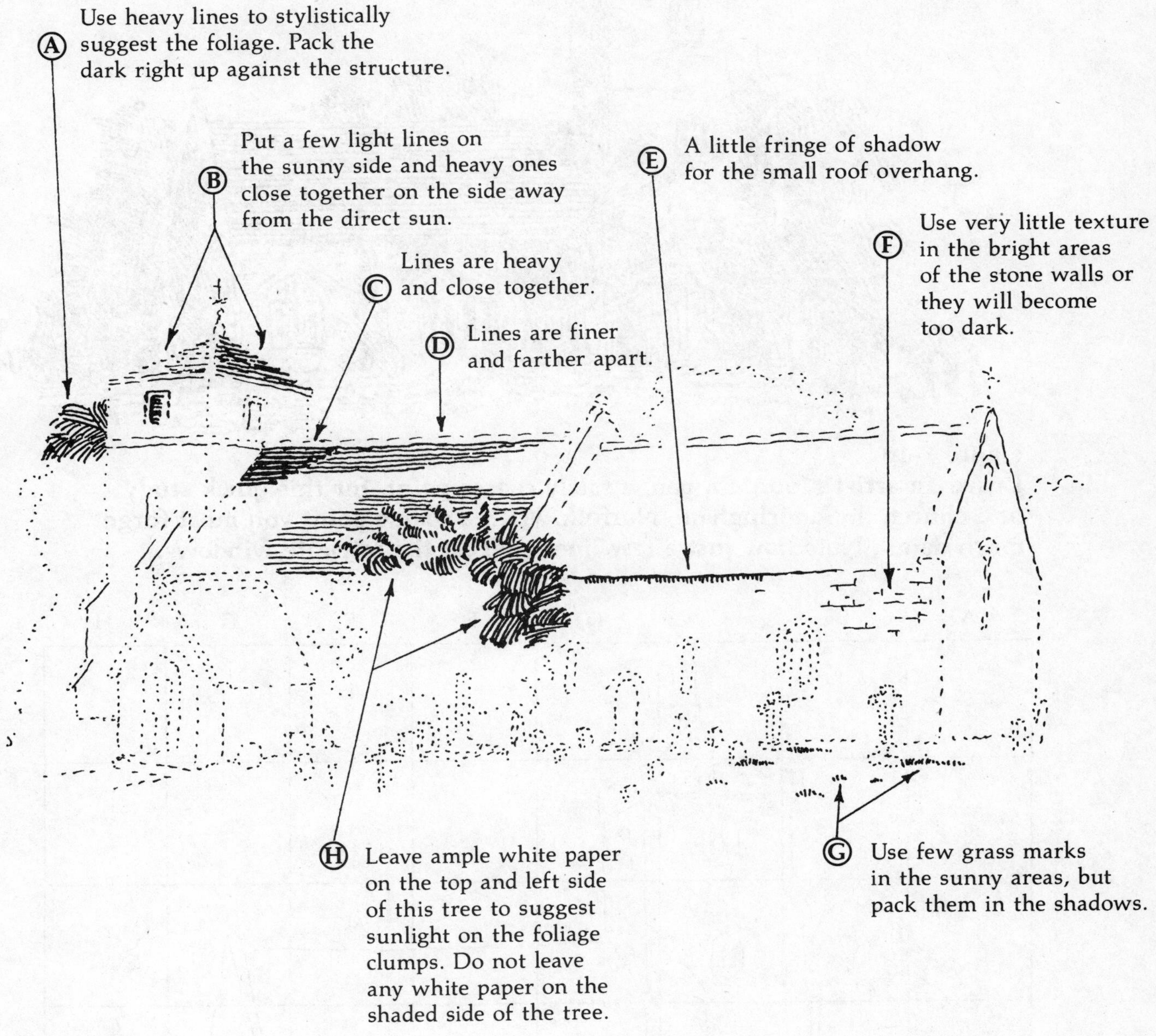

A Use heavy lines to stylistically suggest the foliage. Pack the dark right up against the structure.
B Put a few light lines on the sunny side and heavy ones close together on the side away from the direct sun.
C Lines are heavy and close together.
D Lines are finer and farther apart.
E A little fringe of shadow for the small roof overhang.
F Use very little texture in the bright areas of the stone walls or they will become too dark.
H Leave ample white paper on the top and left side of this tree to suggest sunlight on the foliage clumps. Do not leave any white paper on the shaded side of the tree.
G Use few grass marks in the sunny areas, but pack them in the shadows.

Figure 7-9
These suggestions will help you complete your drawing. Use a flexible-point pen, such as a crowquill or any other nib pen or an artist's fountain pen.

Sandringham

Figure 7-10
I used an artist's fountain pen, a fairly coarse point, for this quick study of a church in Sandringham, Norfolk. With a coarse point you must forgo much detail. Note how just a few lines suggest the intricate windows.

A B C D E F G H
1
2
3
4
5

Figure 7-11
Use this gridded outline and the instructions in Chapter 3 to complete your composition drawing of this subject.

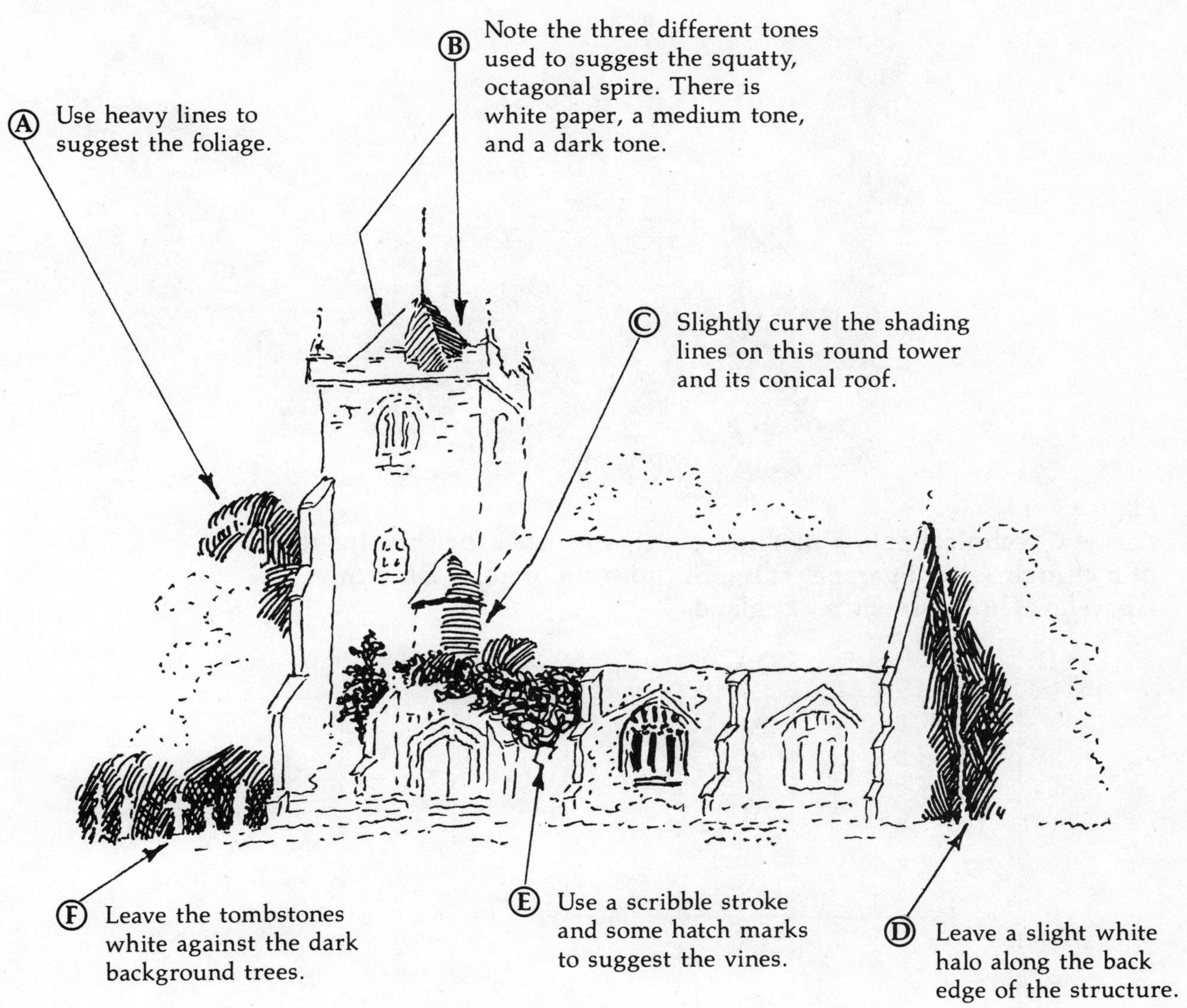
(A) Use heavy lines to suggest the foliage.
(B) Note the three different tones used to suggest the squatty, octagonal spire. There is white paper, a medium tone, and a dark tone.
(C) Slightly curve the shading lines on this round tower and its conical roof.
(D) Leave a slight white halo along the back edge of the structure.
(E) Use a scribble stroke and some hatch marks to suggest the vines.
(F) Leave the tombstones white against the dark background trees.

Figure 7-12
Use a flexible-nib pen, not a technical pen, and these suggestions to work on your drawing of this subject. Use a coarse- rather than a fine-point pen.

St. John the Baptist

Fichan

Figure 7-13
A size 0 technical pen, a medium-point, was used for this drawing of a church with a parapet spire, St. John the Baptist Church at Chaceley, Gloucestershire, England.

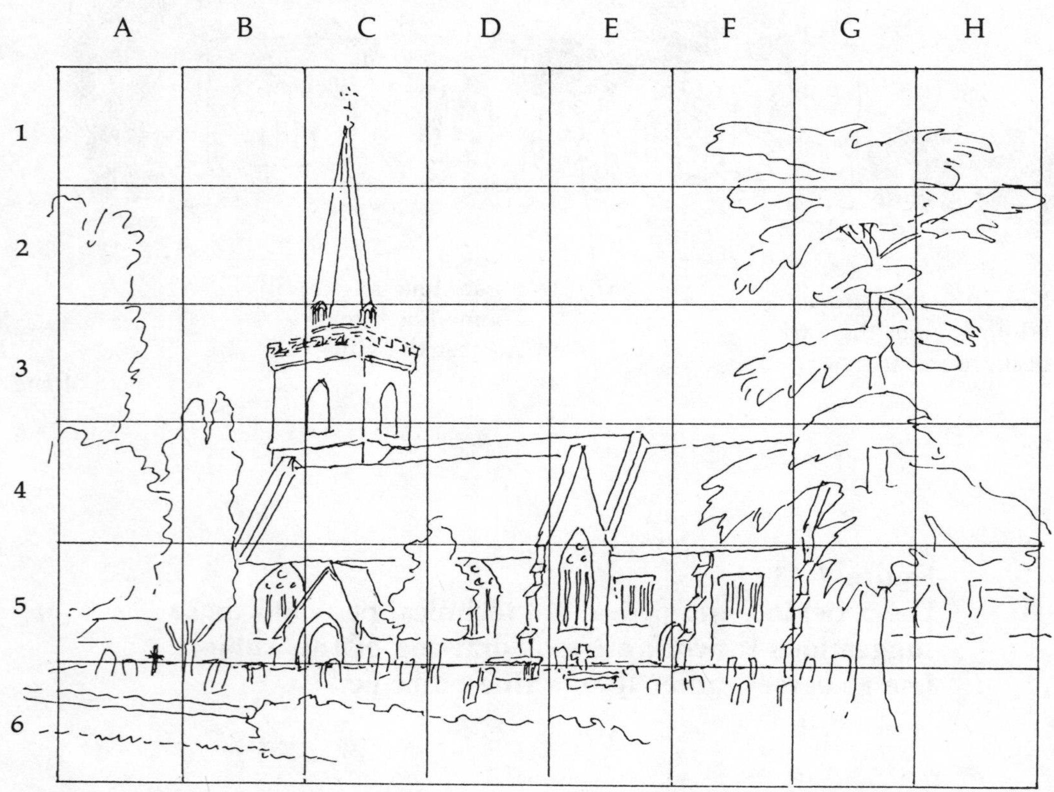

A B C D E F G H
1
2
3
4
5
6

Figure 7-14
Use this gridded composition to lay out a light pencil sketch over which you can do your ink work.

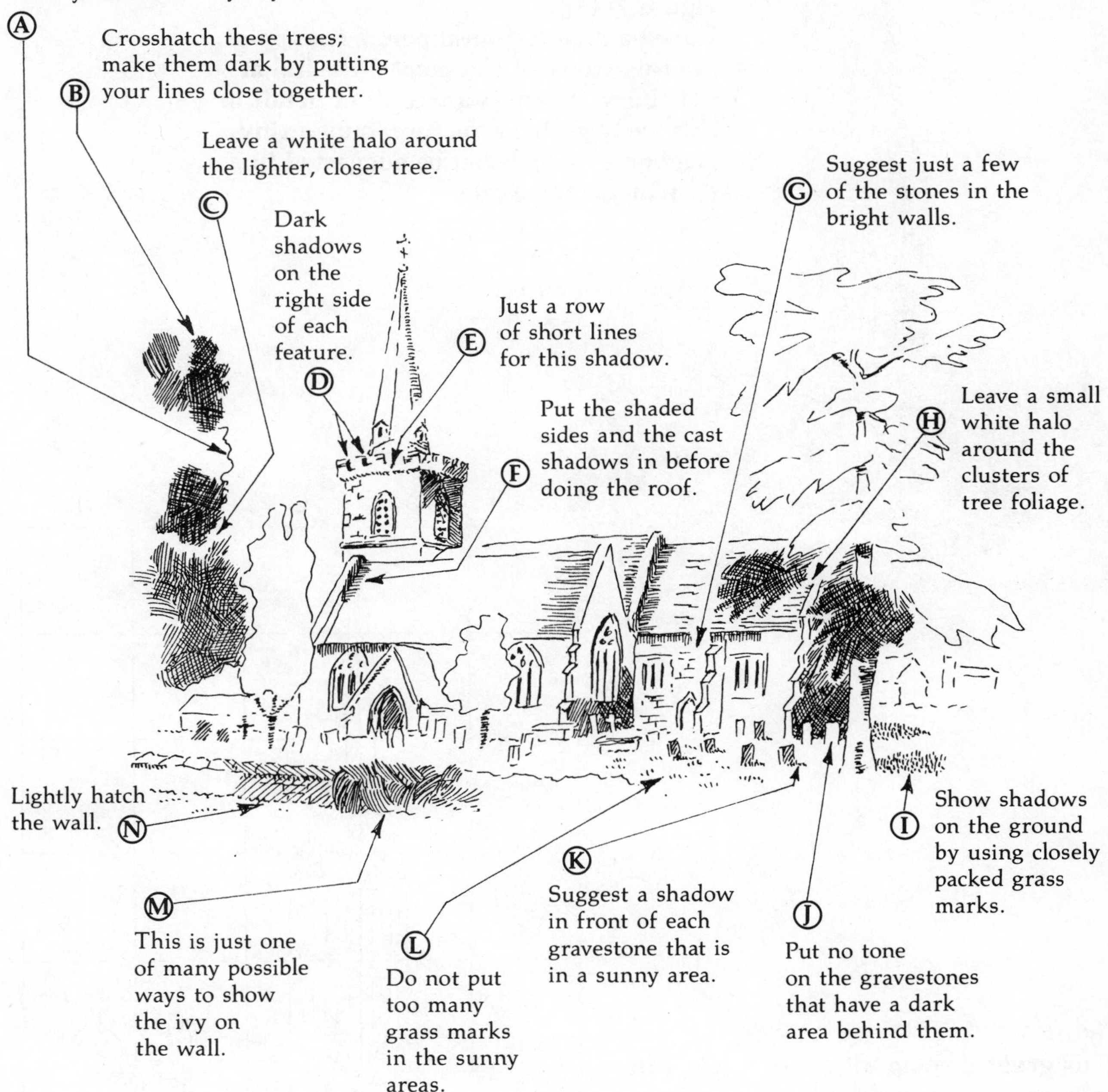
This is the light
pencil outline.
Lightly erase this
after your ink is very dry.
A
Crosshatch these trees;
make them dark by putting
B your lines close together.
Leave a white halo around
the lighter, closer tree.
C
Dark
shadows
on the
right side
of each
feature.
D
Just a row
of short lines
for this shadow.
E
Put the shaded
sides and the cast
shadows in before
doing the roof.
F
G
Suggest just a few
of the stones in the
bright walls.
H
Leave a small
white halo
around the
clusters of
tree foliage.
Lightly hatch
the wall.
N
Show shadows
I on the ground
by using closely
packed grass
marks.
K
Suggest a shadow
in front of each
gravestone that is
in a sunny area.
M
This is just one
of many possible
ways to show
the ivy on
the wall.
L
Do not put
too many
grass marks
in the sunny
areas.
J
Put no tone
on the gravestones
that have a dark
area behind them.

Figure 7-15
Use these suggestions and the completed study (figure 7-13) to guide you as you complete your work on this subject.

Salisbury Cathedral

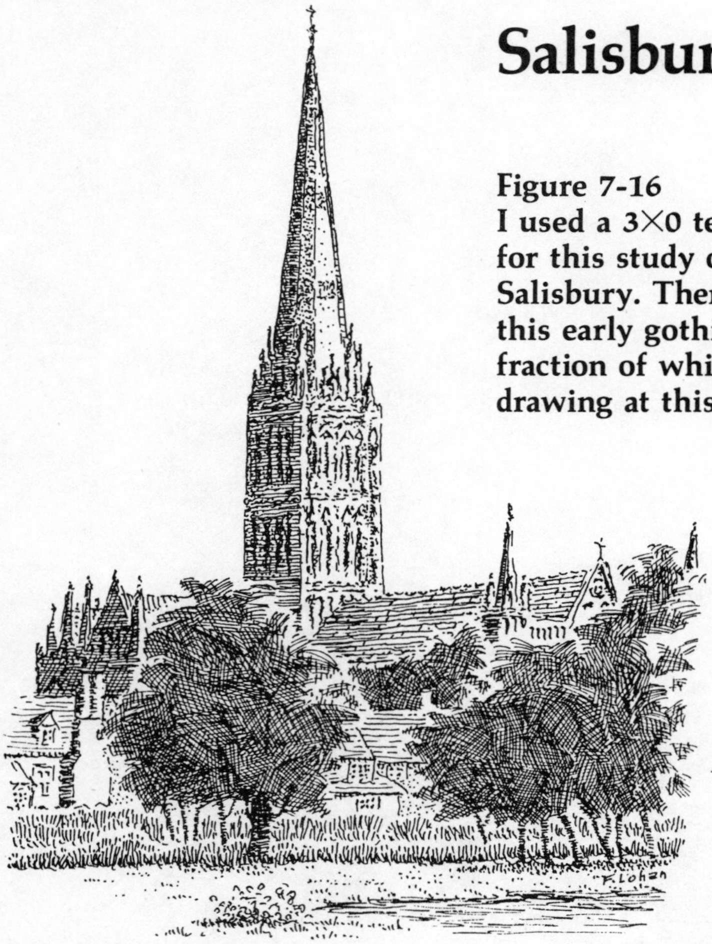

Figure 7-16
I used a 3×0 technical pen, a fine-point, for this study of the great cathedral at Salisbury. There is a wealth of detail in this early gothic structure, only a tiny fraction of which can be suggested in a drawing at this scale.

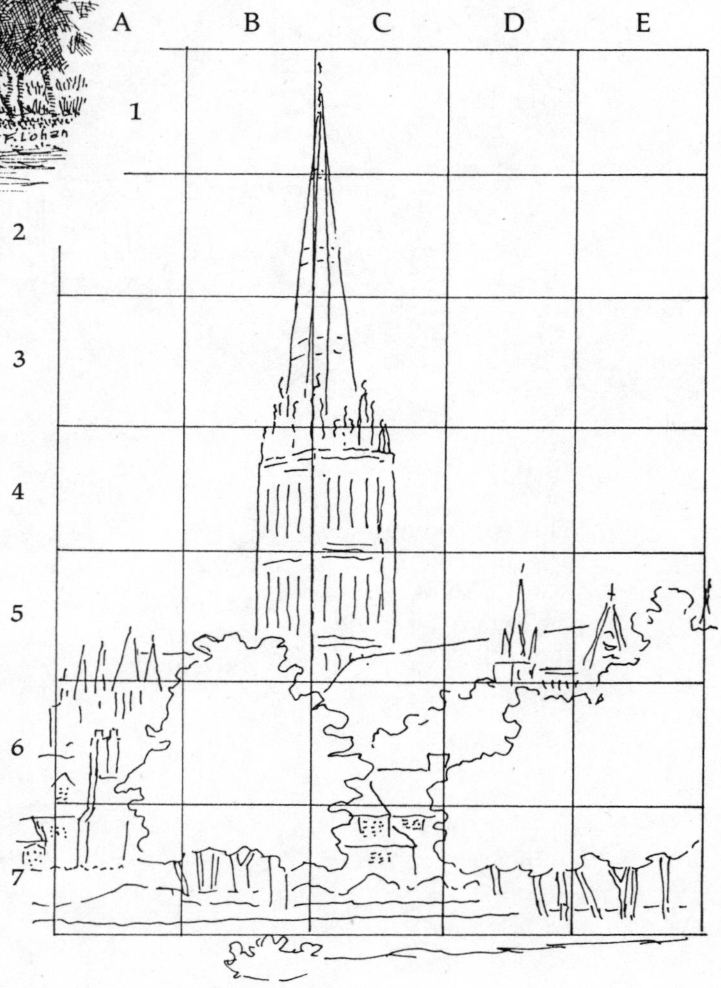

Figure 7-17
This gridded composition will help you prepare your faint pencil outline, over which you will do your ink work.

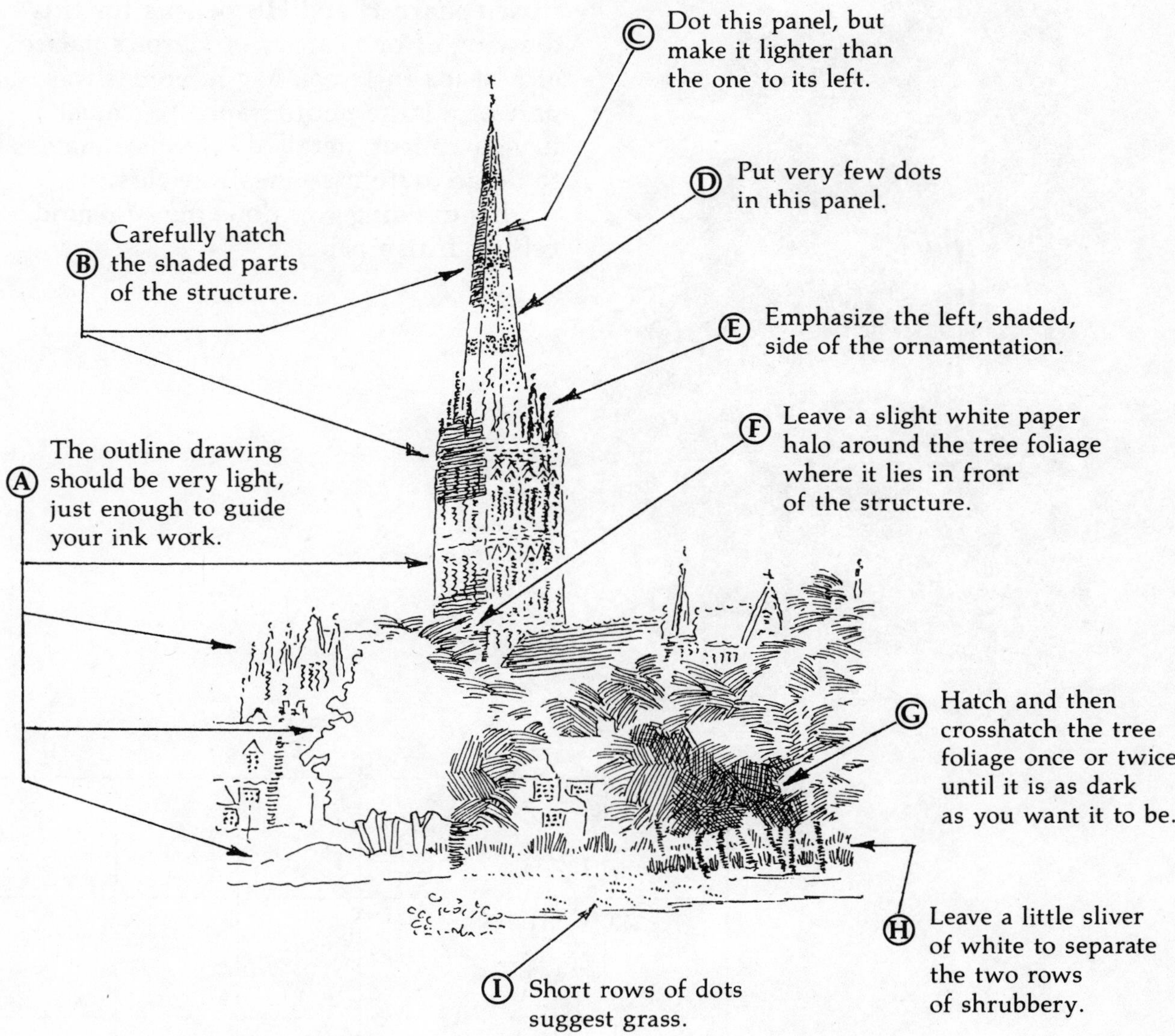
Ⓒ Dot this panel, but make it lighter than the one to its left.
Ⓓ Put very few dots in this panel.
Ⓑ Carefully hatch the shaded parts of the structure.
Ⓔ Emphasize the left, shaded, side of the ornamentation.
Ⓕ Leave a slight white paper halo around the tree foliage where it lies in front of the structure.
Ⓐ The outline drawing should be very light, just enough to guide your ink work.
Ⓖ Hatch and then crosshatch the tree foliage once or twice until it is as dark as you want it to be.
Ⓗ Leave a little sliver of white to separate the two rows of shrubbery.
Ⓘ Short rows of dots suggest grass.

Figure 7-18
Follow these suggestions and refer to the completed sketch (figure 7-16) to complete your ink study of Salisbury Cathedral. This is a tiny study of a highly intricate subject. All you can do is establish an accurately proportioned figure of the well-known tower and spire and suggest some of the ornamentation with a few dots and short dashes.

Masada

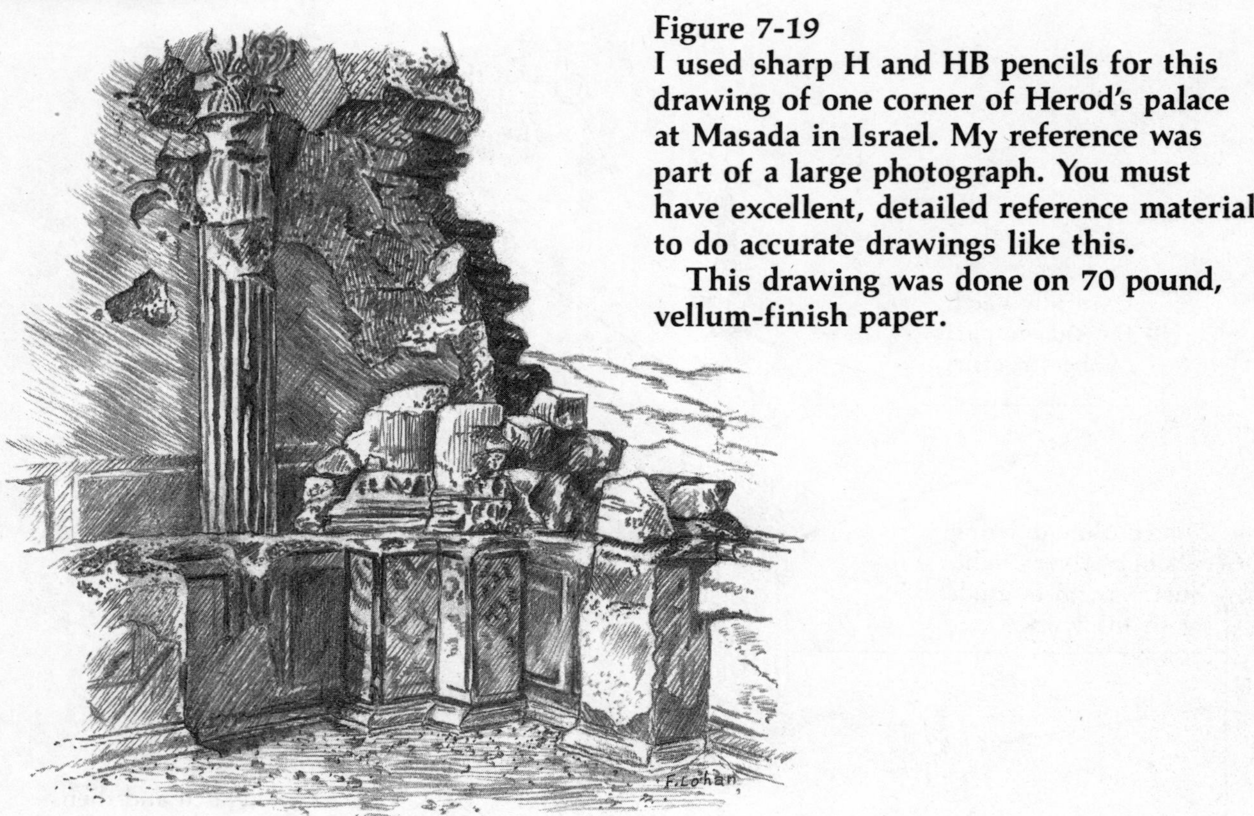
F. Lohan

Figure 7-19
I used sharp H and HB pencils for this drawing of one corner of Herod's palace at Masada in Israel. My reference was part of a large photograph. You must have excellent, detailed reference material to do accurate drawings like this.

This drawing was done on 70 pound, vellum-finish paper.

A B C D E F

1 2 3 4 5 6

Figure 7-20
Use this gridded composition to establish your light pencil outline on which you will do your final work.

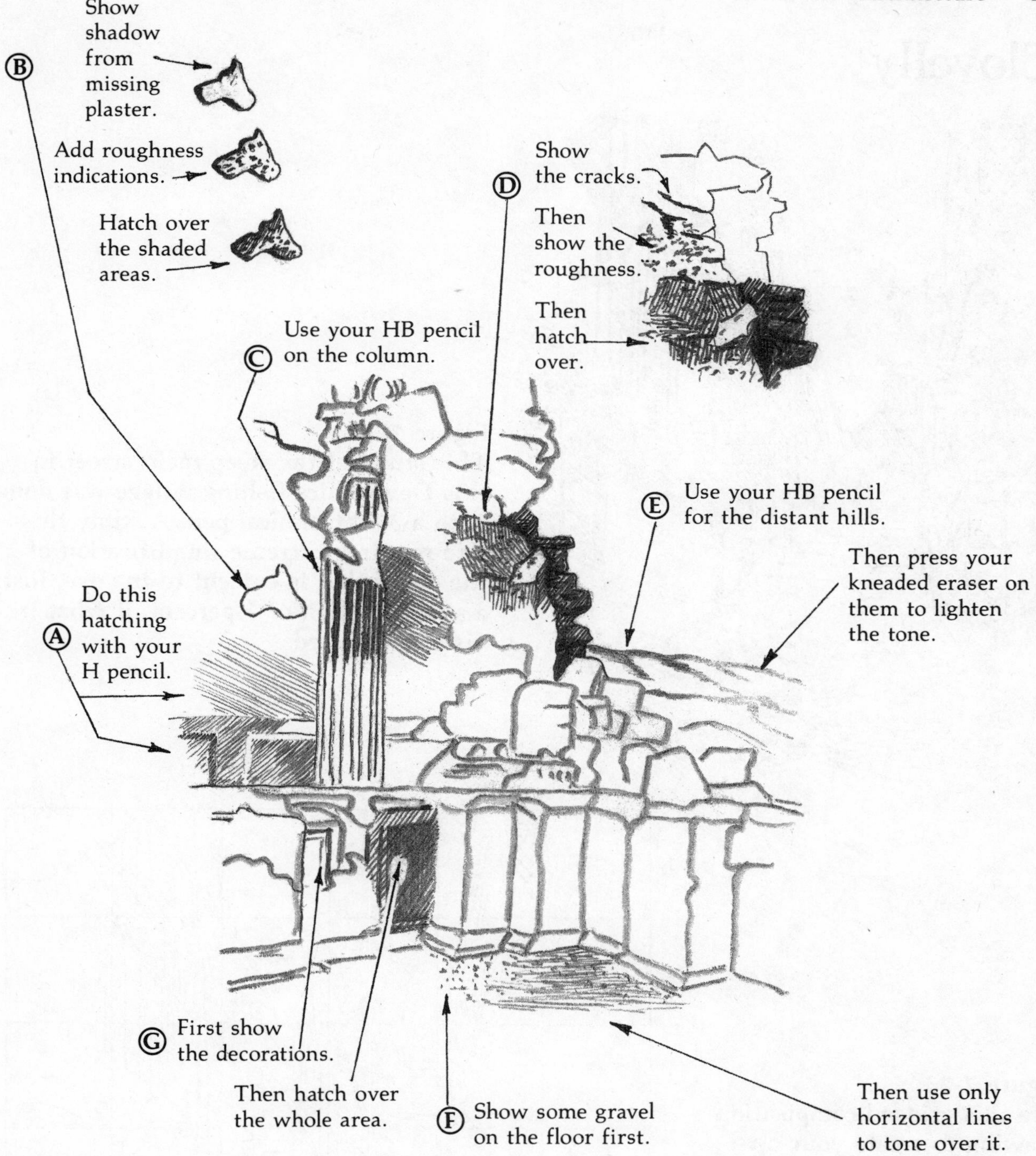
B
Show
shadow
from
missing
plaster.
Add roughness
indications.
Hatch over
the shaded
areas.
D
Show
the cracks.
Then
show the
roughness.
Then
hatch
over.
C
Use your HB pencil
on the column.
E
Use your HB pencil
for the distant hills.
Then press your
kneaded eraser on
them to lighten
the tone.
A
Do this
hatching
with your
H pencil.
G
First show
the decorations.
Then hatch over
the whole area.
F
Show some gravel
on the floor first.
Then use only
horizontal lines
to tone over it.

Figure 7-21
These suggestions will help you complete your version of this study. Use your kneaded eraser wherever you think a pencil area is too dark. Note: Your pencil outline should be very light. My outline in this figure is shown dark where the drawing is unfinished only to ensure its visibility when printed.

Clovelly

Lohan

Figure 7-22
This study of the steep main street in this Devonshire fishing village was done with a 3×0 technical pen. A study this size requires extreme simplification of the detail that is evident to the eye. Just a small fraction of 1 percent of what is visible was used.

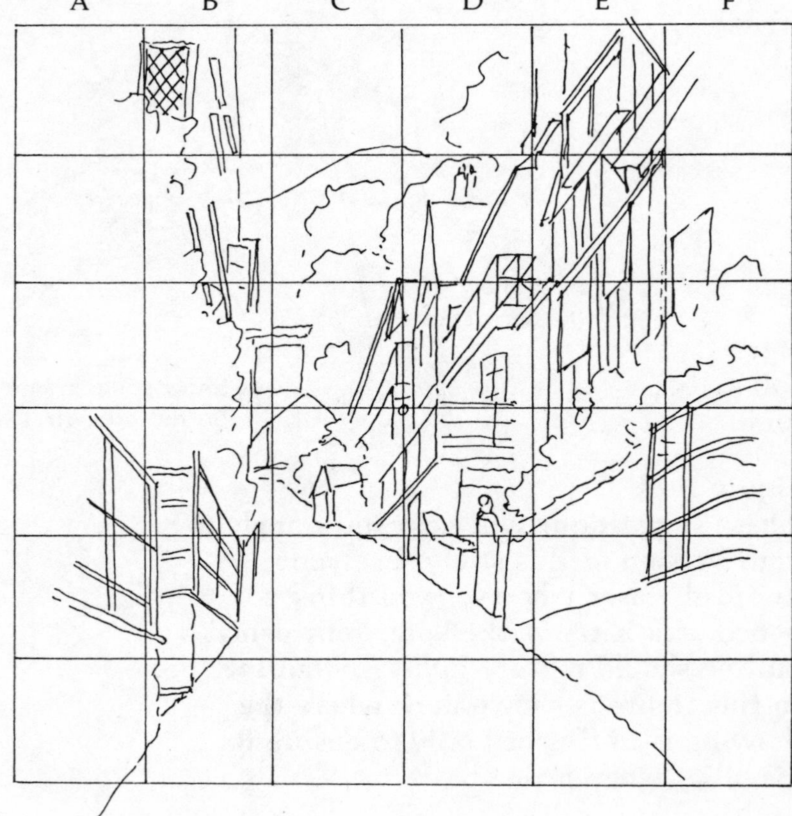
A
B
C
D
E
F
1
2
3
4
5
6

Figure 7-23
Use this gridded composition drawing to create your own faint pencil sketch, which will guide your ink work.

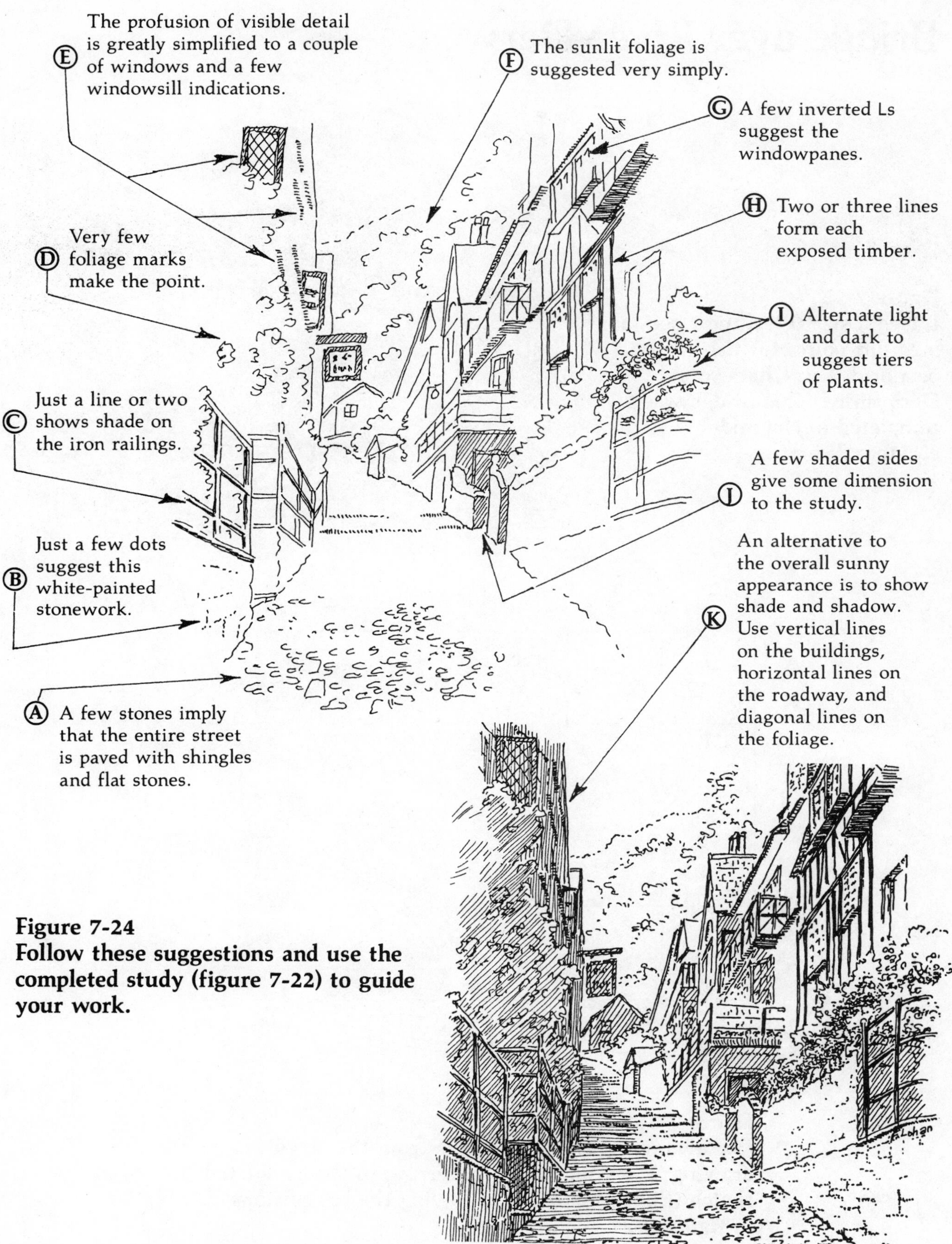
Ⓔ The profusion of visible detail is greatly simplified to a couple of windows and a few windowsill indications.
Ⓕ The sunlit foliage is suggested very simply.
Ⓖ A few inverted Ls suggest the windowpanes.
Ⓗ Two or three lines form each exposed timber.
Ⓓ Very few foliage marks make the point.
Ⓘ Alternate light and dark to suggest tiers of plants.
Ⓒ Just a line or two shows shade on the iron railings.
Ⓙ A few shaded sides give some dimension to the study.
Ⓑ Just a few dots suggest this white-painted stonework.
Ⓚ An alternative to the overall sunny appearance is to show shade and shadow. Use vertical lines on the buildings, horizontal lines on the roadway, and diagonal lines on the foliage.
Ⓐ A few stones imply that the entire street is paved with shingles and flat stones.

Figure 7-24
Follow these suggestions and use the completed study (figure 7-22) to guide your work.

Bridge over River Derwent

F. Lohan

Figure 7-25
I used a size 0 technical pen, a medium-point, for this study of a bridge in Chatsworth, Derbyshire. This bridge was completed in the mid-eighteenth century.

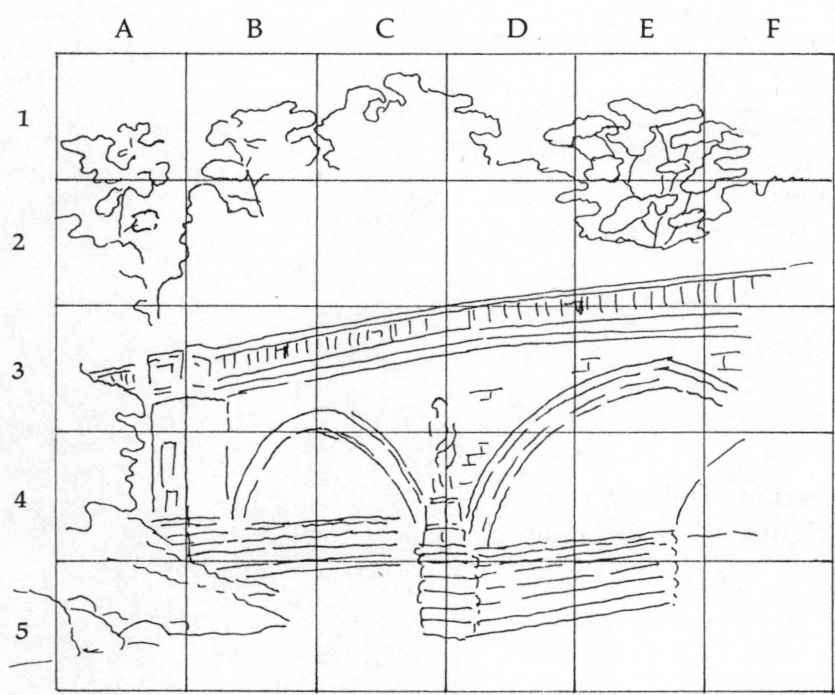
A
B
C
D
E
F
1
2
3
4
5

Figure 7-26
Make your light pencil outline from this gridded drawing, then ink over it, referring to the completed sketch (figure 7-25) and following the suggestions in figure 7-27.

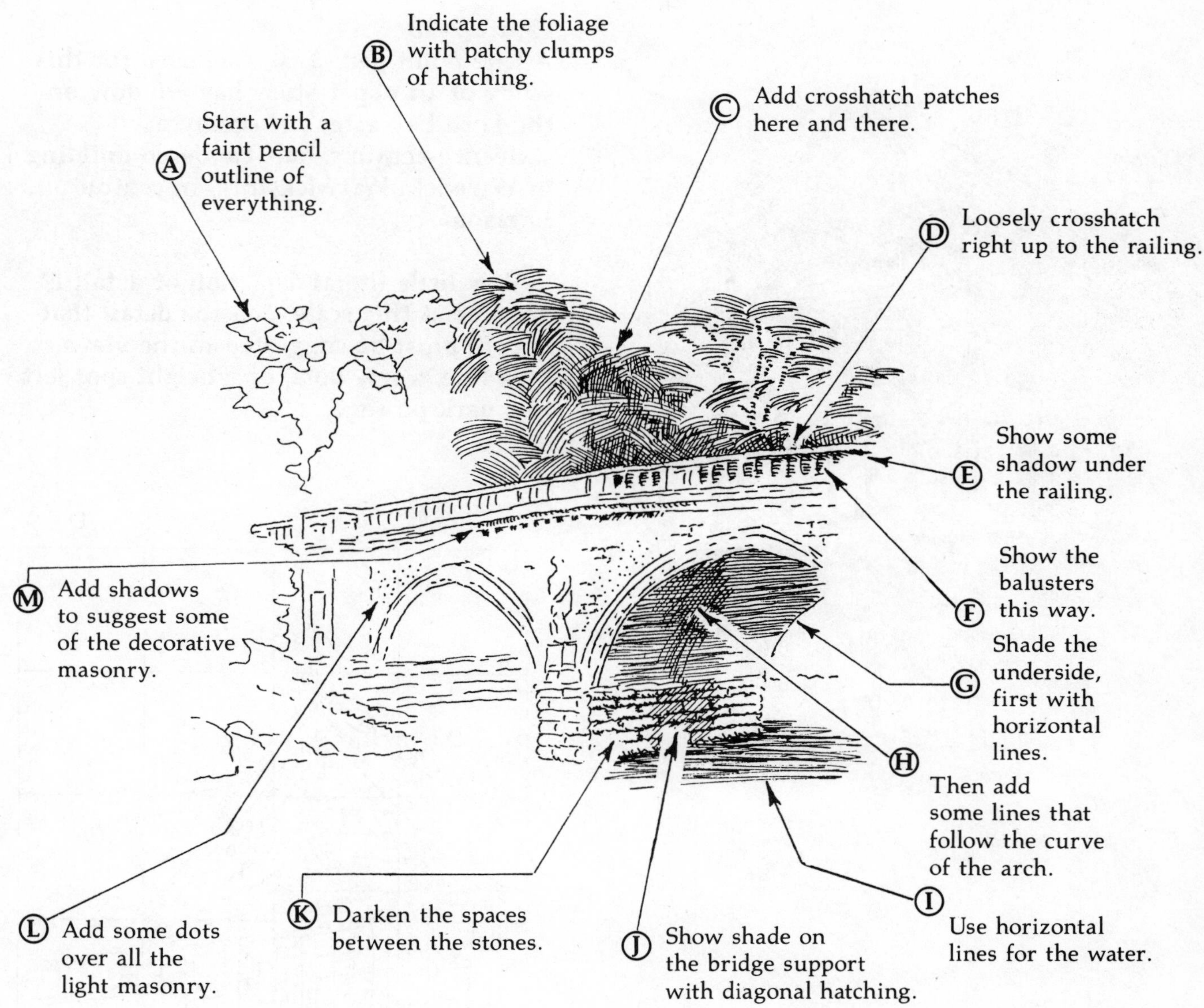
Ⓑ Indicate the foliage with patchy clumps of hatching.
Ⓒ Add crosshatch patches here and there.
Ⓐ Start with a faint pencil outline of everything.
Ⓓ Loosely crosshatch right up to the railing.
Ⓔ Show some shadow under the railing.
Ⓕ Show the balusters this way.
Ⓜ Add shadows to suggest some of the decorative masonry.
Ⓖ Shade the underside, first with horizontal lines.
Ⓗ Then add some lines that follow the curve of the arch.
Ⓘ Use horizontal lines for the water.
Ⓛ Add some dots over all the light masonry.
Ⓚ Darken the spaces between the stones.
Ⓙ Show shade on the bridge support with diagonal hatching.

Figure 7-27
Follow these suggestions and refer to the completed sketch (figure 7-25) to do your version.

Lord Leycester's Hospital

Figure 7-28
A fine-point pen, 3×0, was used for this study of an upper-story bay window on the Lord Leycester's Hospital, a sixteenth-century, half-timbered building in Warwick, Warwickshire, in central England.

Very little literal depiction of detail is possible at this scale, and the detail that is here must be suggested to the viewer by a line, a few dots, or a bright spot left in a dark passage.

A B C D

1
2
3
4
5
6
7

Figure 7-29
Use this gridded composition drawing to prepare your pencil outline. Then follow the suggestions in figure 7-30 and refer to the completed drawing (figure 7-28) to finish your drawing.

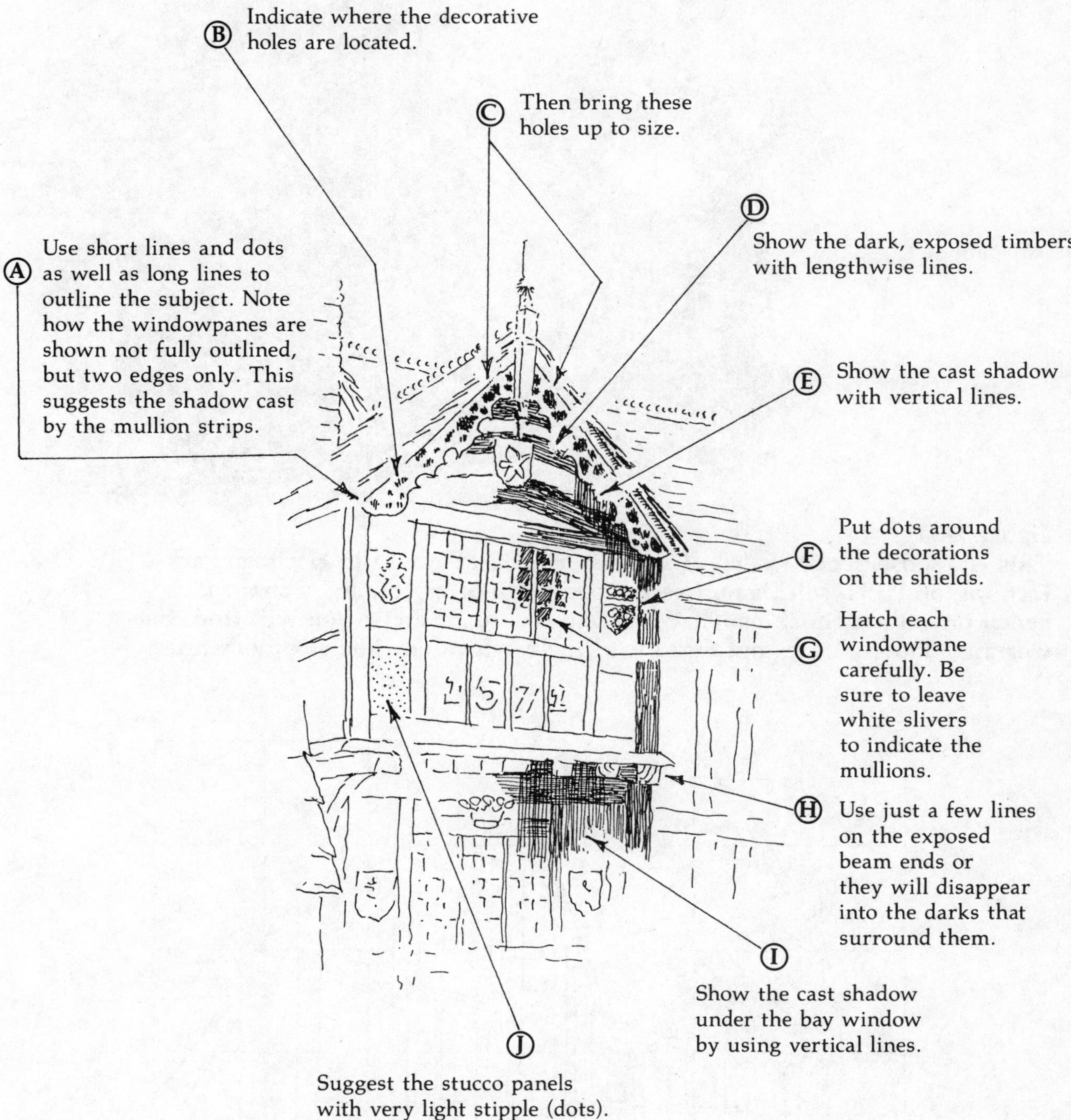
B Indicate where the decorative holes are located.
C Then bring these holes up to size.
D Show the dark, exposed timbers with lengthwise lines.
A Use short lines and dots as well as long lines to outline the subject. Note how the windowpanes are shown not fully outlined, but two edges only. This suggests the shadow cast by the mullion strips.
E Show the cast shadow with vertical lines.
F Put dots around the decorations on the shields.
G Hatch each windowpane carefully. Be sure to leave white slivers to indicate the mullions.
H Use just a few lines on the exposed beam ends or they will disappear into the darks that surround them.
I Show the cast shadow under the bay window by using vertical lines.
J Suggest the stucco panels with very light stipple (dots).

Figure 7-30
Follow these suggestions and refer to the completed drawing (figure 7-28) to complete your ink drawing. Do not complete the drawing right out to the edges of the composition outline. Rather, let the drawing sort of fade away as you approach the edges. This focuses the viewer's attention on the center of interest: the beautiful, timbered bay window.

Spicer House

F. Lohan

Figure 7-31
This is a loose pencil sketch of the historic Spicer House in Heritage Park, Farmington Hills, Michigan. Use a broad-point 3B pencil and a sharp B pencil on vellum-finish paper. When you try this exercise you will find that working "loosely" does not mean working carelessly or in a sloppy manner.

A
B
C
D
E
F
G
1
2
3
4
5

Figure 7-32
Use this gridded outline to prepare your final outline. Remember to keep your outline as faint as possible.

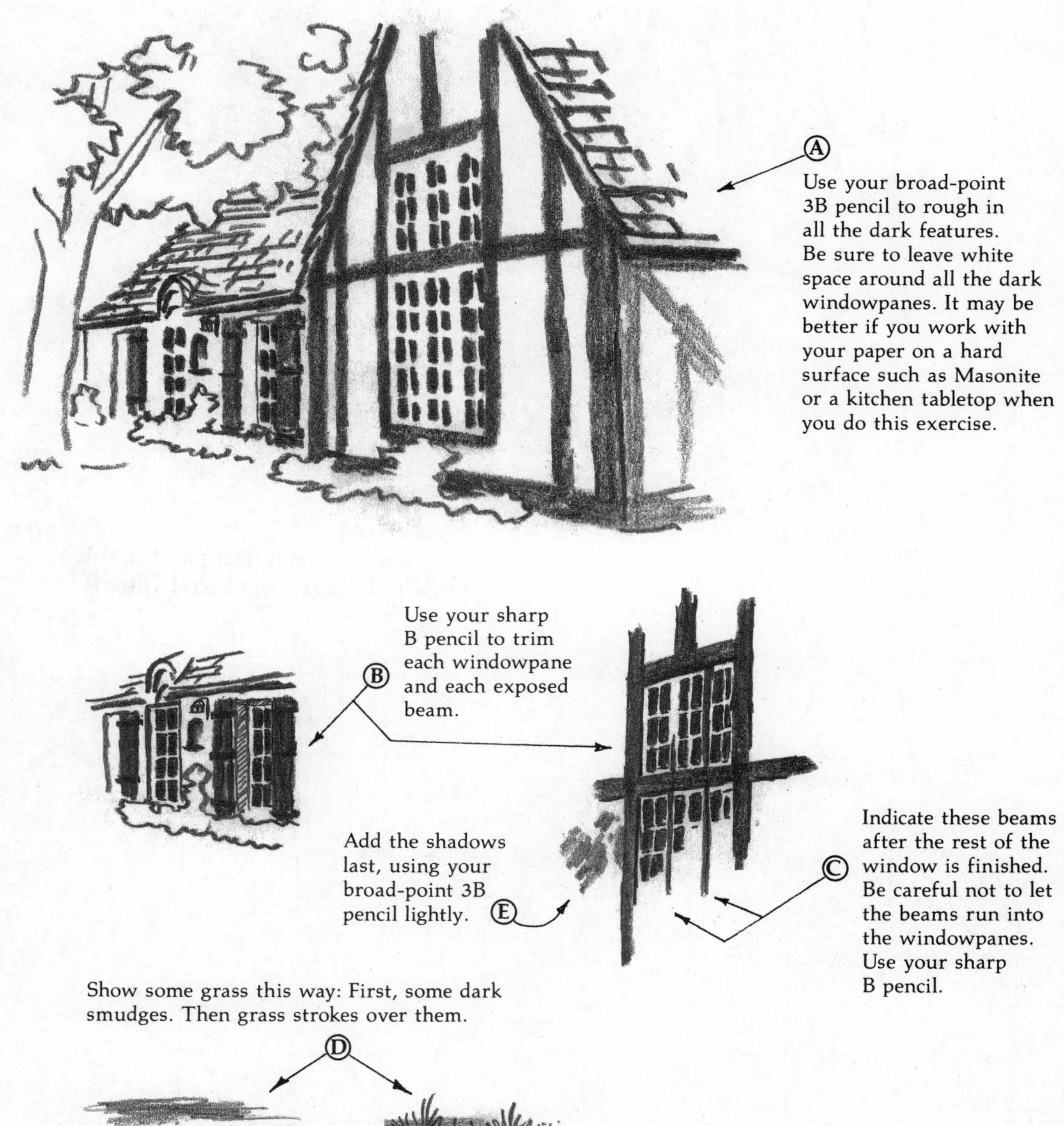
A
Use your broad-point 3B pencil to rough in all the dark features. Be sure to leave white space around all the dark windowpanes. It may be better if you work with your paper on a hard surface such as Masonite or a kitchen tabletop when you do this exercise.
B
Use your sharp B pencil to trim each windowpane and each exposed beam.
C
Indicate these beams after the rest of the window is finished. Be careful not to let the beams run into the windowpanes. Use your sharp B pencil.
E
Add the shadows last, using your broad-point 3B pencil lightly.
D
Show some grass this way: First, some dark smudges. Then grass strokes over them.

Figure 7-33
These suggestions may help you to complete your version of this pencil exercise.

Illinois Barn

Figure 7-34
I used a 3×0 technical pen for this sketch of a barn in central Illinois.

A
B
C
D
E
F
G
H
1
2
3
4
5

Figure 7-35
Use this gridded figure and the instructions in Chapter 3 to prepare your own composition drawing.

Note: Complete the trees first, then do the barns so they do not interfere with the trees.

Light

Ⓑ Then add hatching to tone the shaded side of the tree. Make each group of hatching go in slightly different directions.

If your bark marks start to disappear, just darken them as you go along. Be sure to leave some white paper as highlights on the two nearer trees.

Ⓐ First put the bark marks all over the tree trunk. Complete one tree at a time.

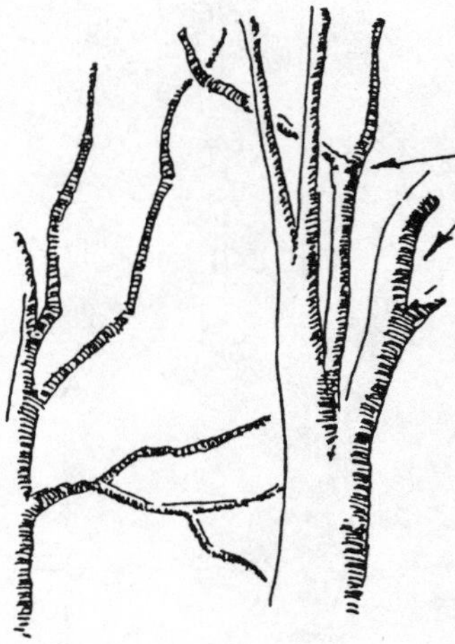

Ⓒ Start the two far trees this way.

Then add the bark texture.

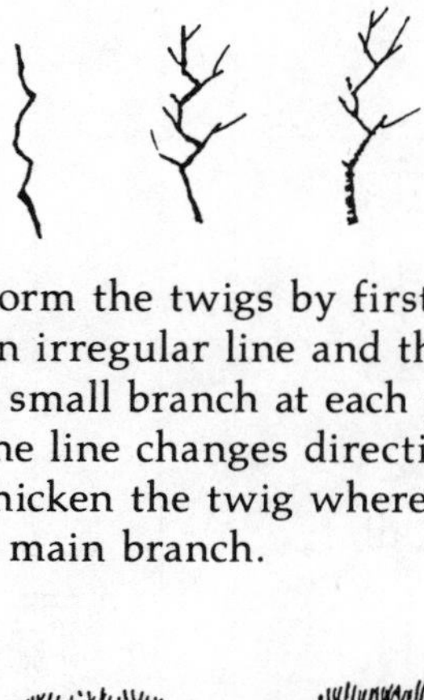

Ⓔ Leave a few blades of grass showing at the base.

Ⓕ Form the twigs by first drawing an irregular line and then putting a small branch at each place where the line changes direction. Finally, thicken the twig where it joins a main branch.

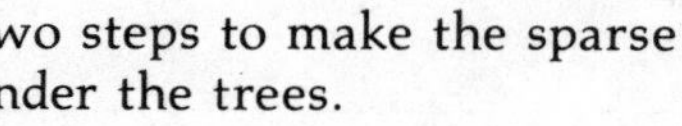

Ⓖ Two steps to make the tree shadows.

Ⓓ Leave a thin white strip where the dark tree crosses the dark part of the barn.

Ⓗ Two steps to make the sparse grass under the trees.

Figure 7-36
These suggestions will assist you in finishing your version of this sketch.

Ightham Mote, Kent

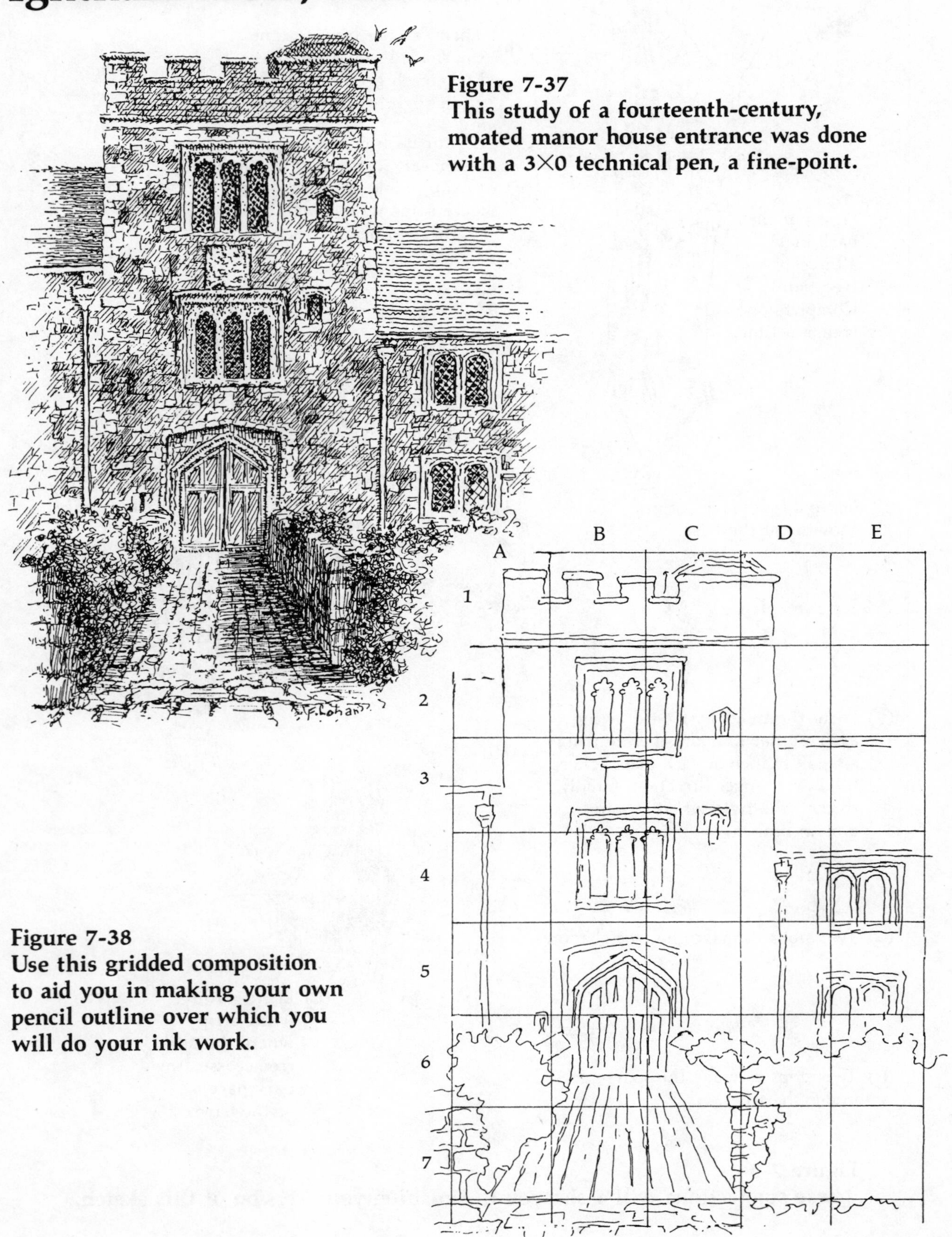
A
B
C
D
E
1
2
3
4
5
6
7

Figure 7-37
This study of a fourteenth-century, moated manor house entrance was done with a 3×0 technical pen, a fine-point.

Figure 7-38
Use this gridded composition to aid you in making your own pencil outline over which you will do your ink work.

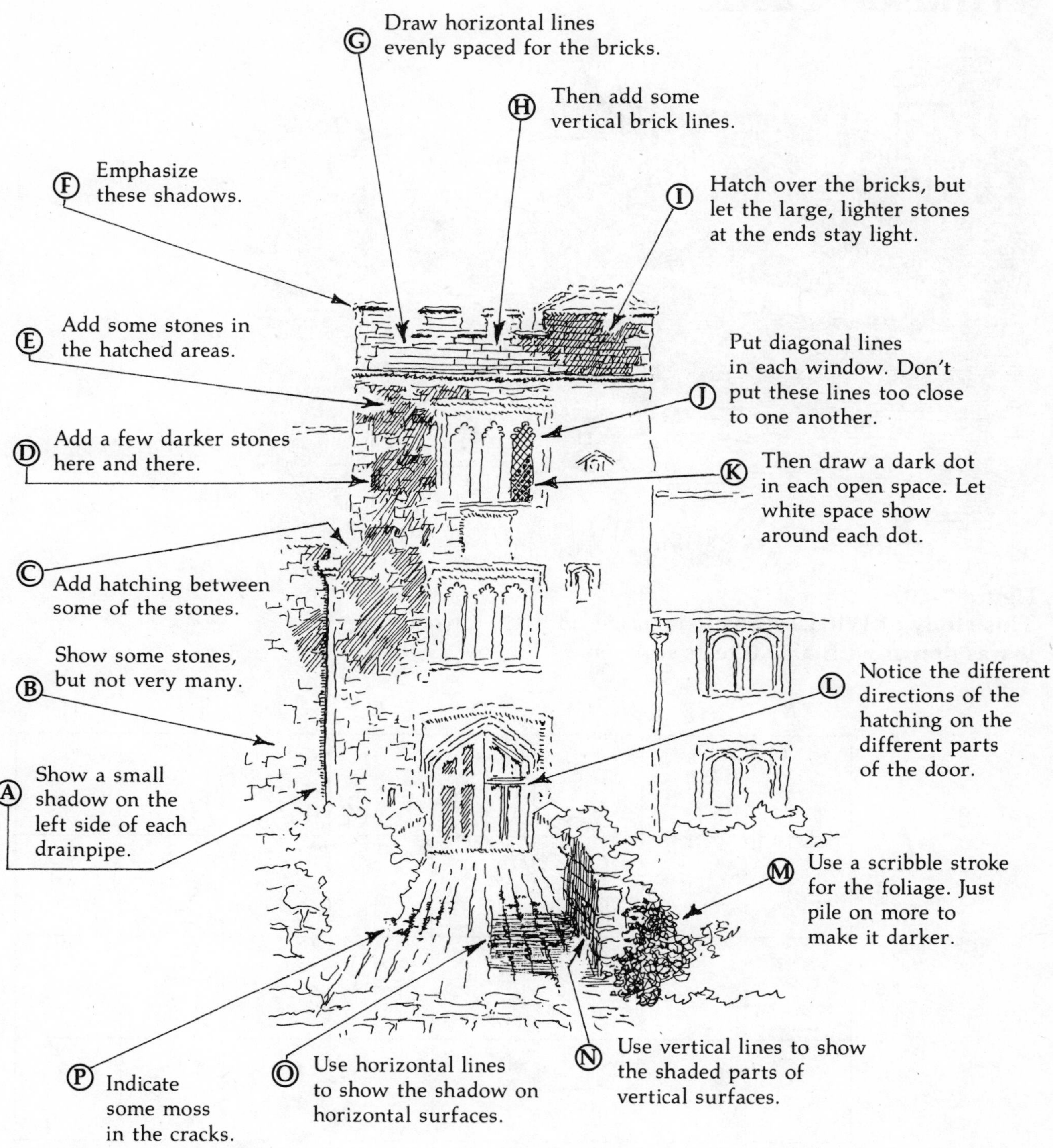
G Draw horizontal lines evenly spaced for the bricks.
H Then add some vertical brick lines.
F Emphasize these shadows.
I Hatch over the bricks, but let the large, lighter stones at the ends stay light.
E Add some stones in the hatched areas.
J Put diagonal lines in each window. Don't put these lines too close to one another.
D Add a few darker stones here and there.
K Then draw a dark dot in each open space. Let white space show around each dot.
C Add hatching between some of the stones.
B Show some stones, but not very many.
L Notice the different directions of the hatching on the different parts of the door.
A Show a small shadow on the left side of each drainpipe.
M Use a scribble stroke for the foliage. Just pile on more to make it darker.
P Indicate some moss in the cracks.
O Use horizontal lines to show the shadow on horizontal surfaces.
N Use vertical lines to show the shaded parts of vertical surfaces.

Figure 7-39
Follow these steps and refer to the completed pen drawing (figure 7-37) to guide your work on this exercise.

Windsor Castle

Figure 7-40
This study of Windsor Castle is based on a 1915 woodcut. It was drawn with a 3×0 technical pen.

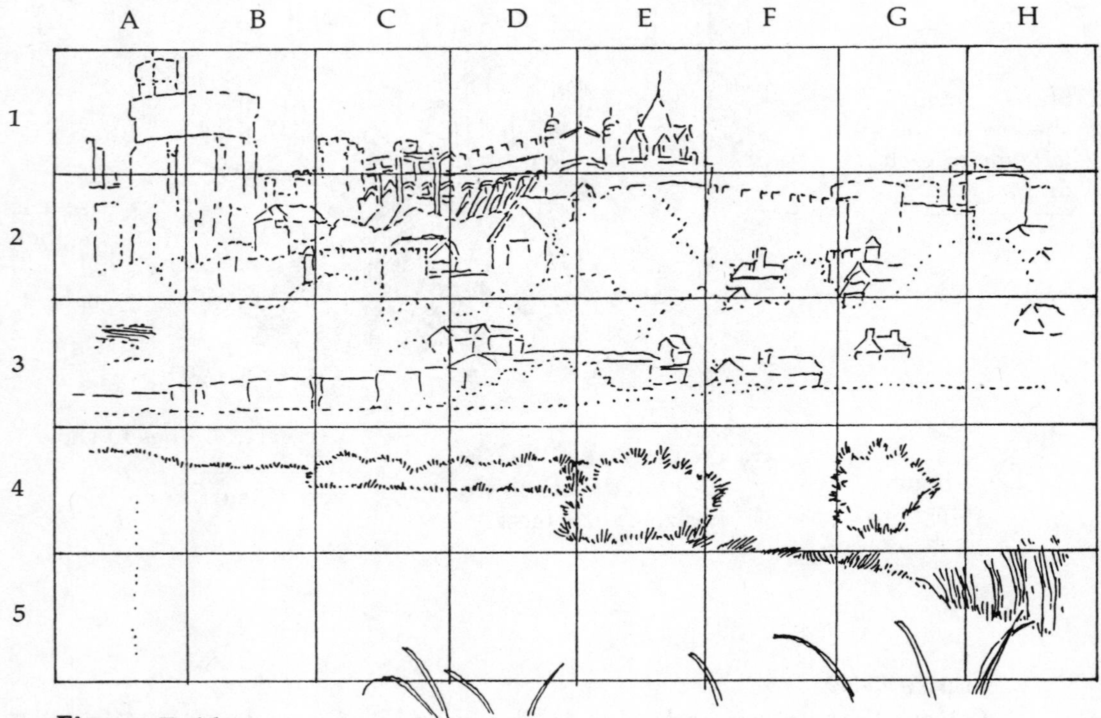
A
B
C
D
E
F
G
H
1
2
3
4
5

Figure 7-41
Use this gridded composition to assist the preparation of your composition.

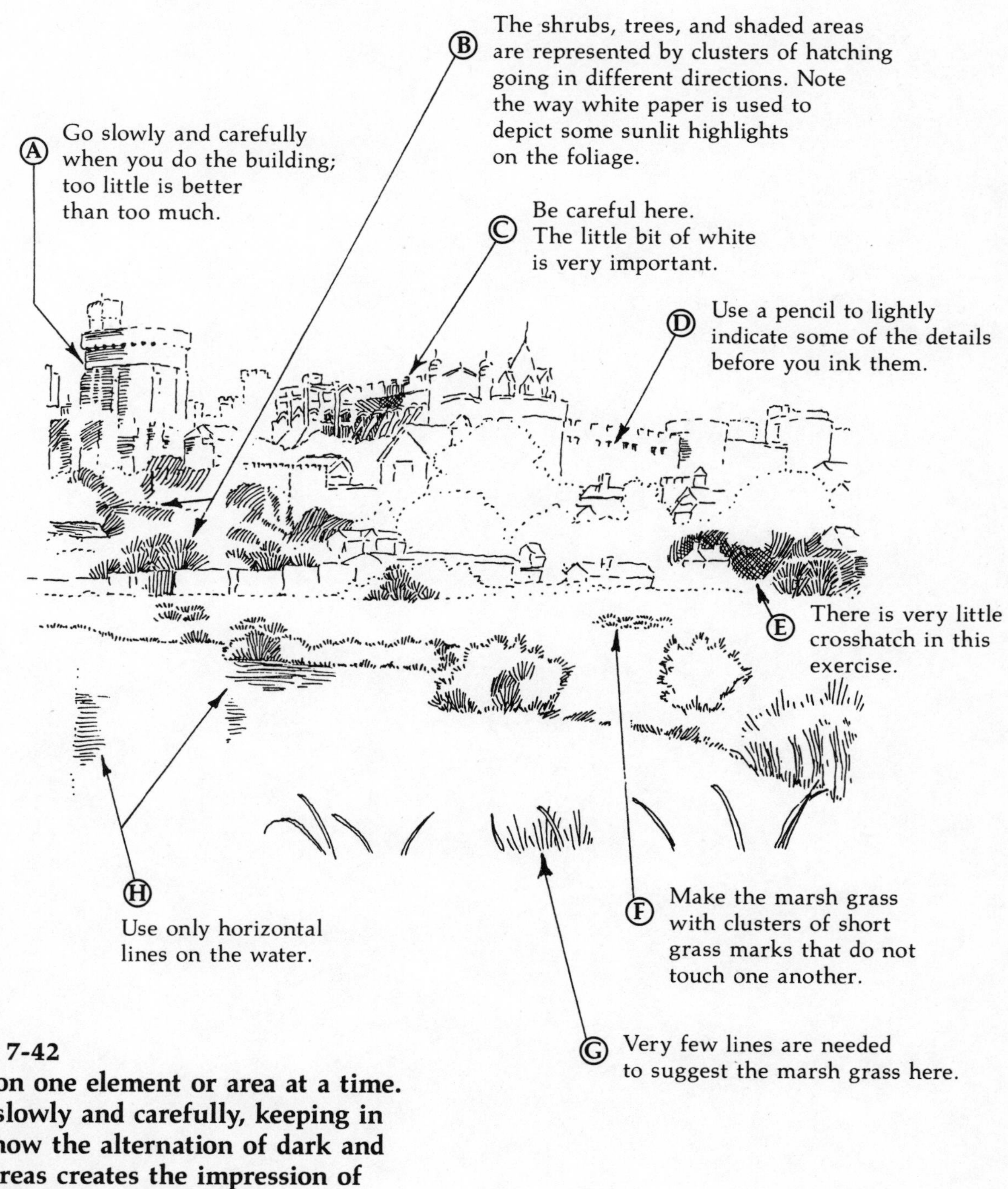
A
Go slowly and carefully when you do the building; too little is better than too much.
B
The shrubs, trees, and shaded areas are represented by clusters of hatching going in different directions. Note the way white paper is used to depict some sunlit highlights on the foliage.
C
Be careful here. The little bit of white is very important.
D
Use a pencil to lightly indicate some of the details before you ink them.
E
There is very little crosshatch in this exercise.
F
Make the marsh grass with clusters of short grass marks that do not touch one another.
G
Very few lines are needed to suggest the marsh grass here.
H
Use only horizontal lines on the water.

Figure 7-42
Work on one element or area at a time. Work slowly and carefully, keeping in mind how the alternation of dark and light areas creates the impression of form, texture, and distance.

8 Artifacts

The first exercise in this section on artifacts (products of human workmanship) is an imaginary scene involving old books. There is so much ink on the paper in this sketch that it might be difficult for a beginning artist to decide just how to proceed. As figure 8-3 shows, just take one book at a time, do them all individually, and then add the shelves and dark tones under them.

Seven of the exercises in this chapter involve drawings of stone circles in Great Britain. These sketches are a part of a series I did on several of these ancient monuments. The stone circles at Avebury, for instance, are said to date back to about 3000 B.C. The first two stone circle studies involve the same scene at Avebury; one uses the ink stipple technique and the other a pencil. You can try both the pencil and the pen version and see the difference in the final products and in the relative ease of producing them. The other stone monolith studies involve the conventional use of ink line, hatching, and crosshatching.

Old Books

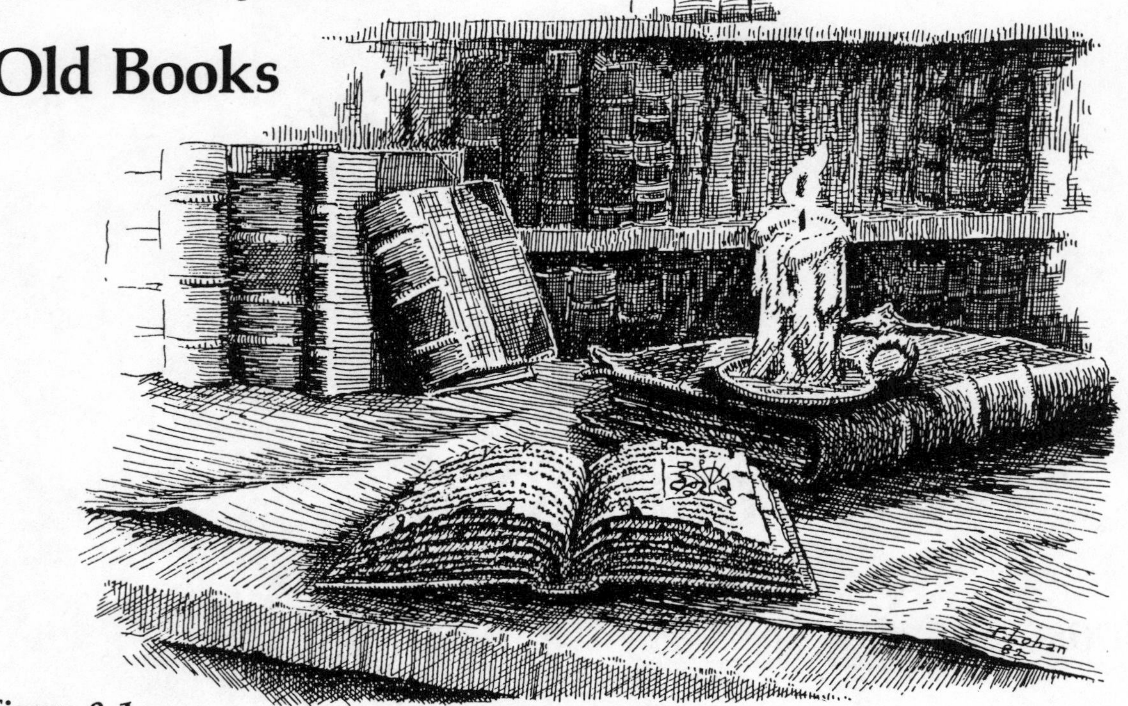

Figure 8-1
I used my 3×0 technical pen here. The hatching line directions help form the surfaces of the books, table, and tablecloth. Most of the lines on the books run parallel to one of the edges of the books, and diagonal lines are used for some deeper toning and shading only.

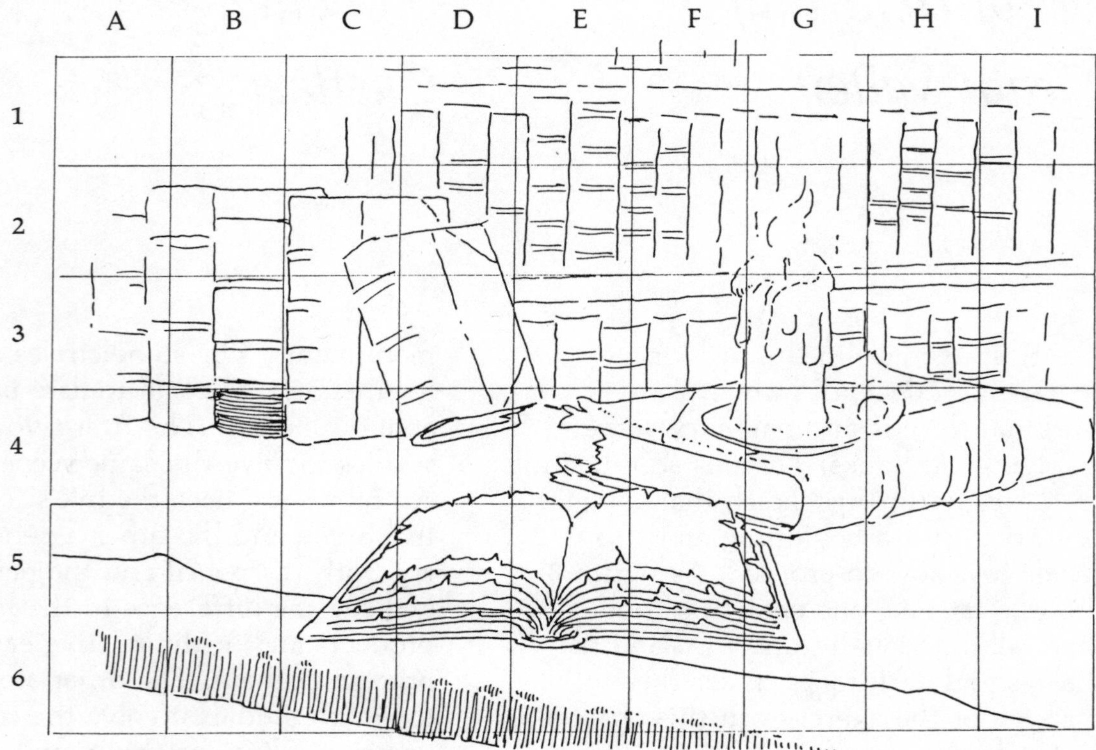
A B C D E F G H I
1
2
3
4
5
6

Figure 8-2
This gridded composition will assist you in creating your own light pencil outline, which will guide your pen work.

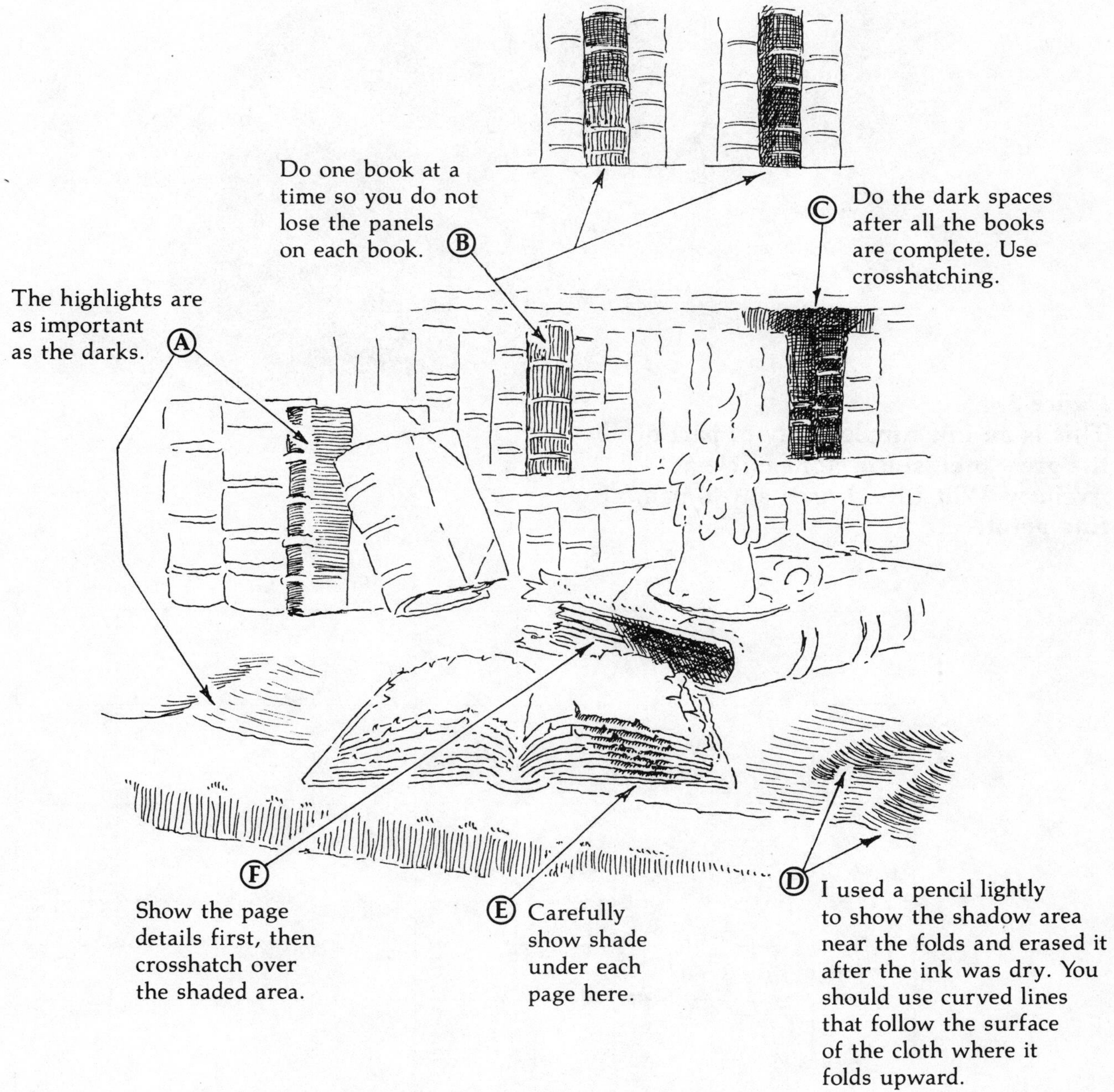
Do one book at a time so you do not lose the panels on each book. Ⓑ
Ⓒ Do the dark spaces after all the books are complete. Use crosshatching.
The highlights are as important as the darks. Ⓐ
Ⓕ Show the page details first, then crosshatch over the shaded area.
Ⓔ Carefully show shade under each page here.
Ⓓ I used a pencil lightly to show the shadow area near the folds and erased it after the ink was dry. You should use curved lines that follow the surface of the cloth where it folds upward.

Figure 8-3
These suggestions will make your work on this exercise easier.

Avebury, Study 1

Figure 8-4
This is an ink stipple study of part of the great prehistoric stone circle at Avebury, Wiltshire. I used a 3×0 pen, a fine-point.

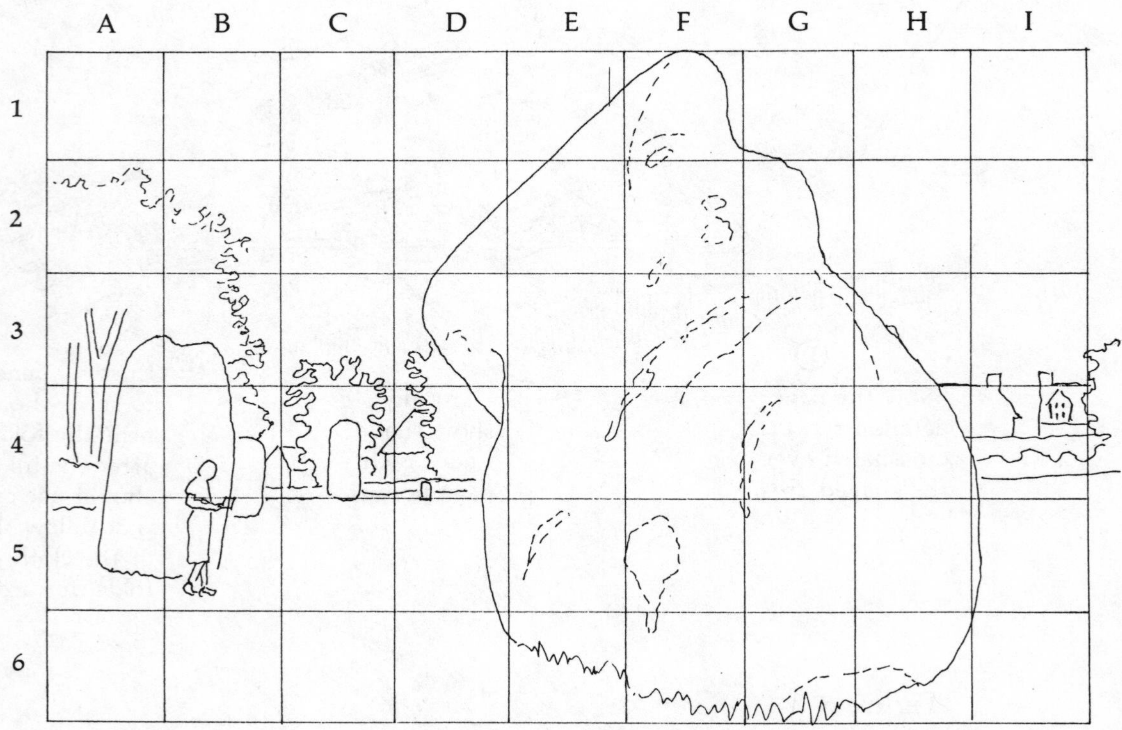
A
B
C
D
E
F
G
H
I
1
2
3
4
5
6

Figure 8-5
This gridded composition will assist you in establishing your pencil outline, which will guide your pen work.

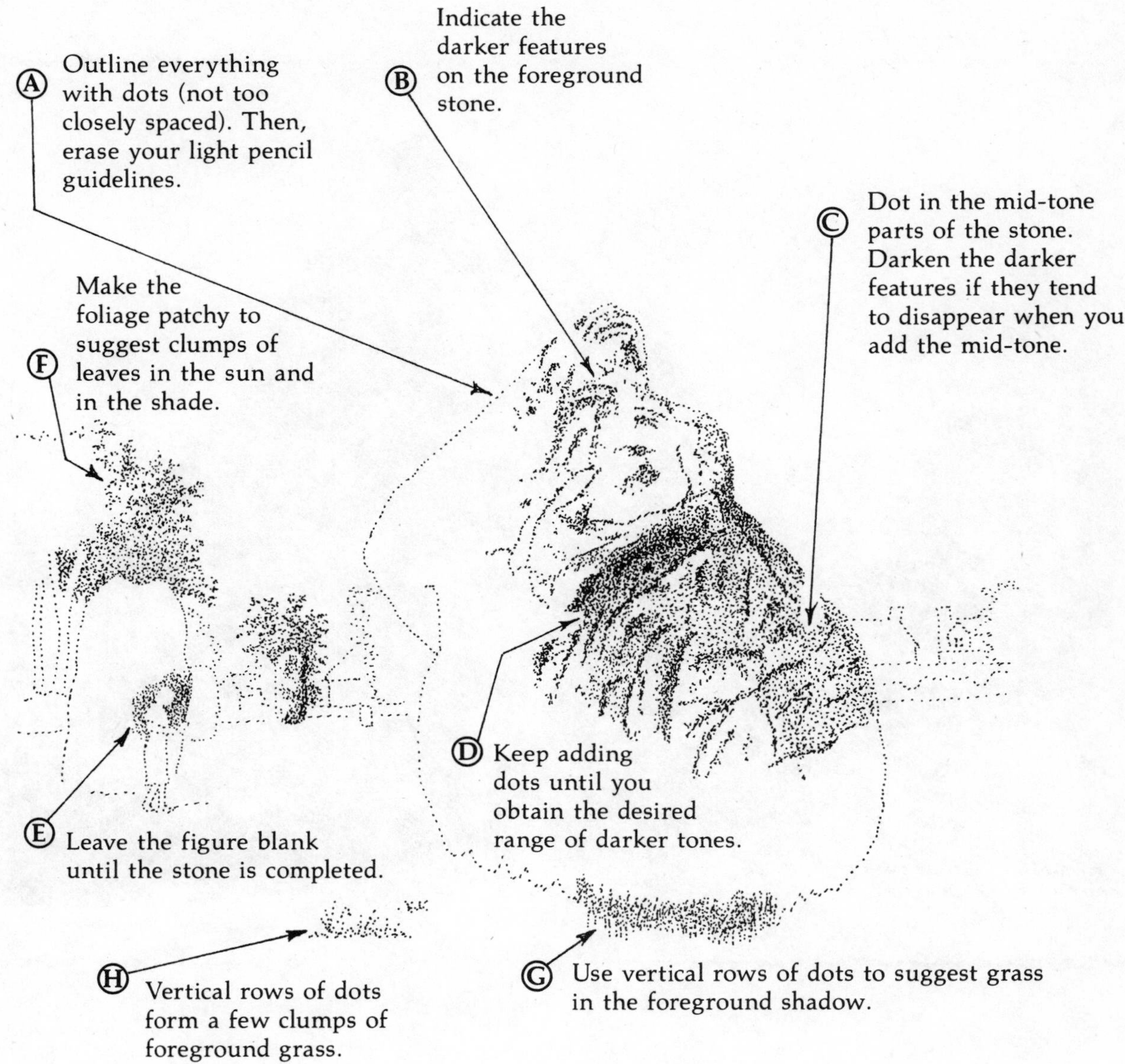
Indicate the
darker features
on the foreground
stone.
Outline everything
with dots (not too
closely spaced). Then,
erase your light pencil
guidelines.
Dot in the mid-tone
parts of the stone.
Darken the darker
features if they tend
to disappear when you
add the mid-tone.
Make the
foliage patchy to
suggest clumps of
leaves in the sun and
in the shade.
Keep adding
dots until you
obtain the desired
range of darker tones.
Leave the figure blank
until the stone is completed.
Vertical rows of dots
form a few clumps of
foreground grass.
Use vertical rows of dots to suggest grass
in the foreground shadow.

Figure 8-6
These suggestions will help you complete your drawing of the Avebury stones.

Complete all stones first, and then do the trees. Work carefully where the trees touch the stones; do not let them touch where they are the same tone or they will blend together visually and lose their distinction. Make sure that one item is either darker or lighter than the other where they touch.

Avebury, Study 2

AVEBURY, WILTSHIRE
SOUTH CIRCLE
F.Lohan

Figure 8-7
Smooth, 70 pound paper and broad-point B and 6B pencils as well as sharp B and HB pencils and a kneaded eraser were used for this closeup study of one of the great stones at the Avebury site. Compare this study with Study 1 in which ink stipple was used to draw the same subject.

Use figure 8-5 for your composition drawing on this study.

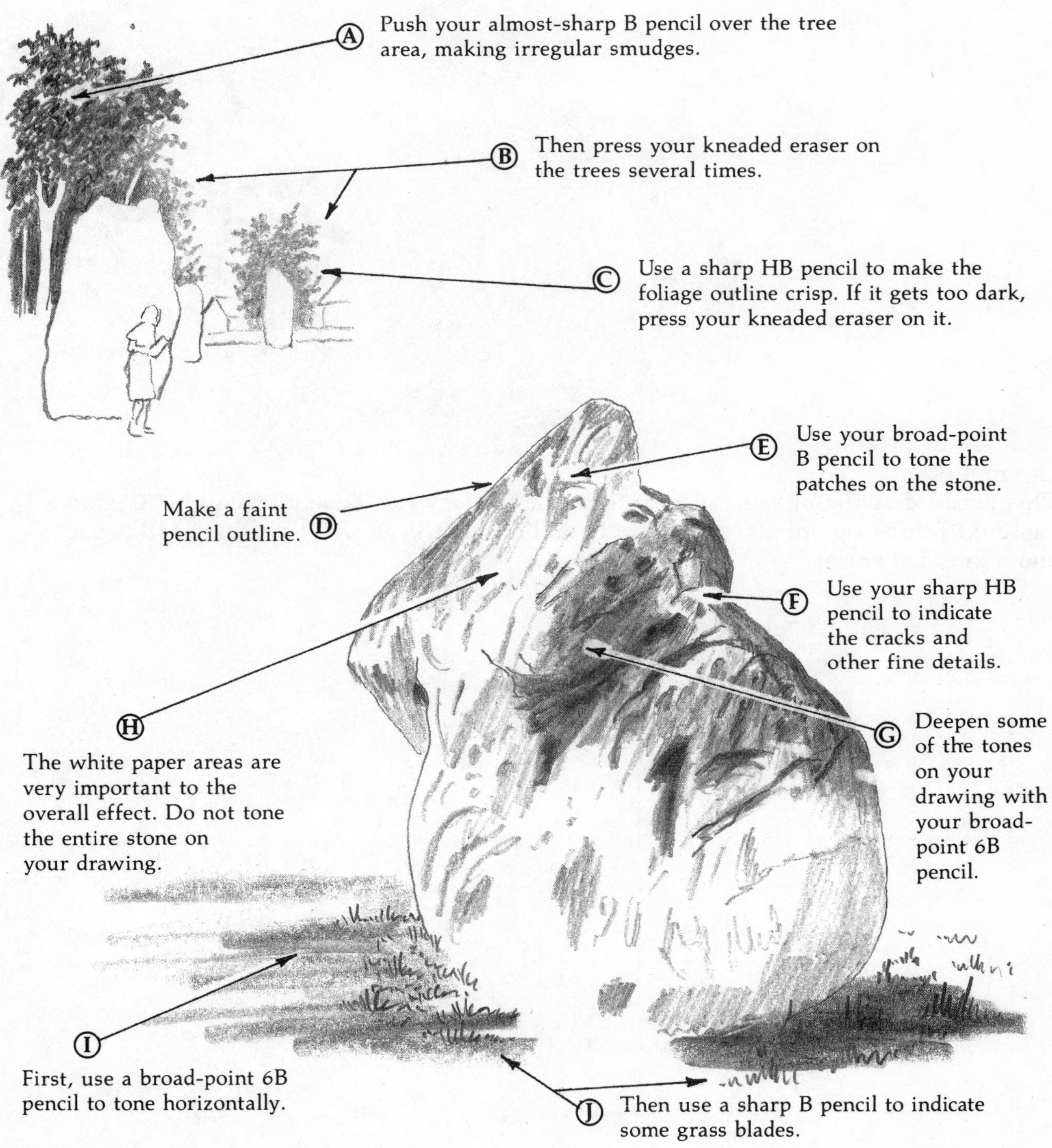
A
Push your almost-sharp B pencil over the tree area, making irregular smudges.
B
Then press your kneaded eraser on the trees several times.
C
Use a sharp HB pencil to make the foliage outline crisp. If it gets too dark, press your kneaded eraser on it.
E
Use your broad-point B pencil to tone the patches on the stone.
D
Make a faint pencil outline.
F
Use your sharp HB pencil to indicate the cracks and other fine details.
H
The white paper areas are very important to the overall effect. Do not tone the entire stone on your drawing.
G
Deepen some of the tones on your drawing with your broad-point 6B pencil.
I
First, use a broad-point 6B pencil to tone horizontally.
J
Then use a sharp B pencil to indicate some grass blades.

Figure 8-8
These suggestions will help you complete your drawing.

Avebury, Study 3

Figure 8-9
This pencil drawing of some of the stones at Avebury was done on smooth, 70 pound paper with broad-point and sharp B, 3B, and 6B pencils as well as a sharp HB pencil and a kneaded eraser.

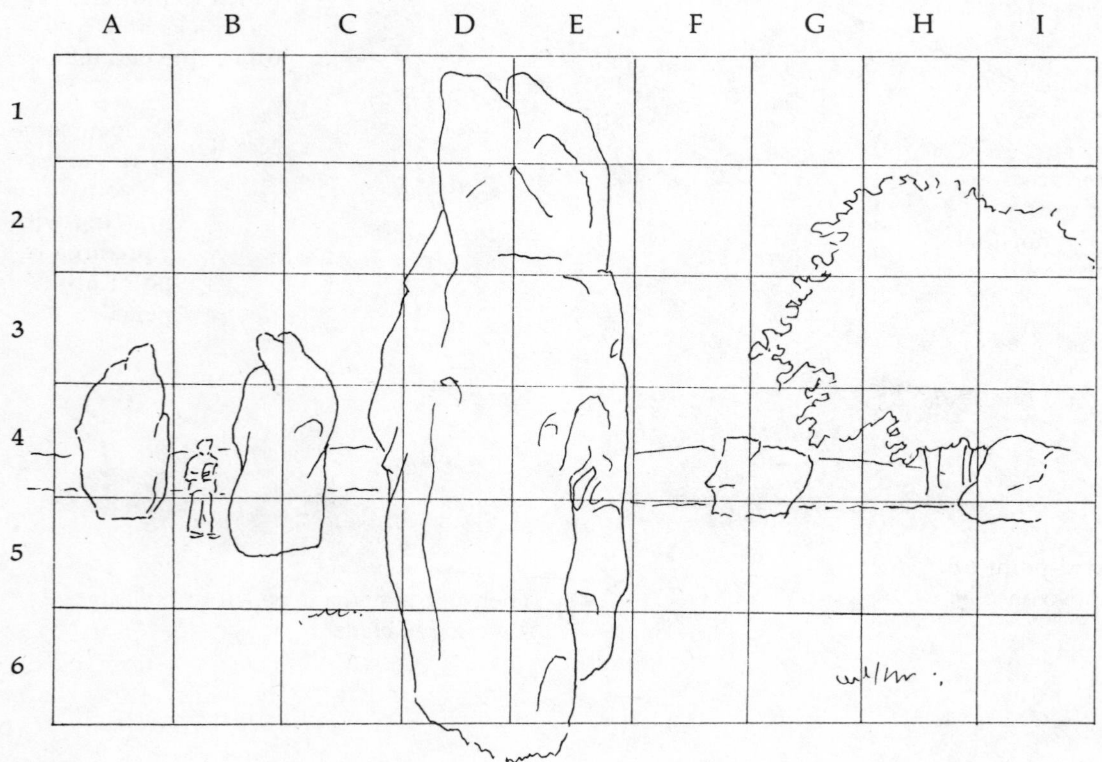
A B C D E F G H I
1
2
3
4
5
6

Figure 8-10
Use this gridded outline to prepare your composition drawing for this exercise.

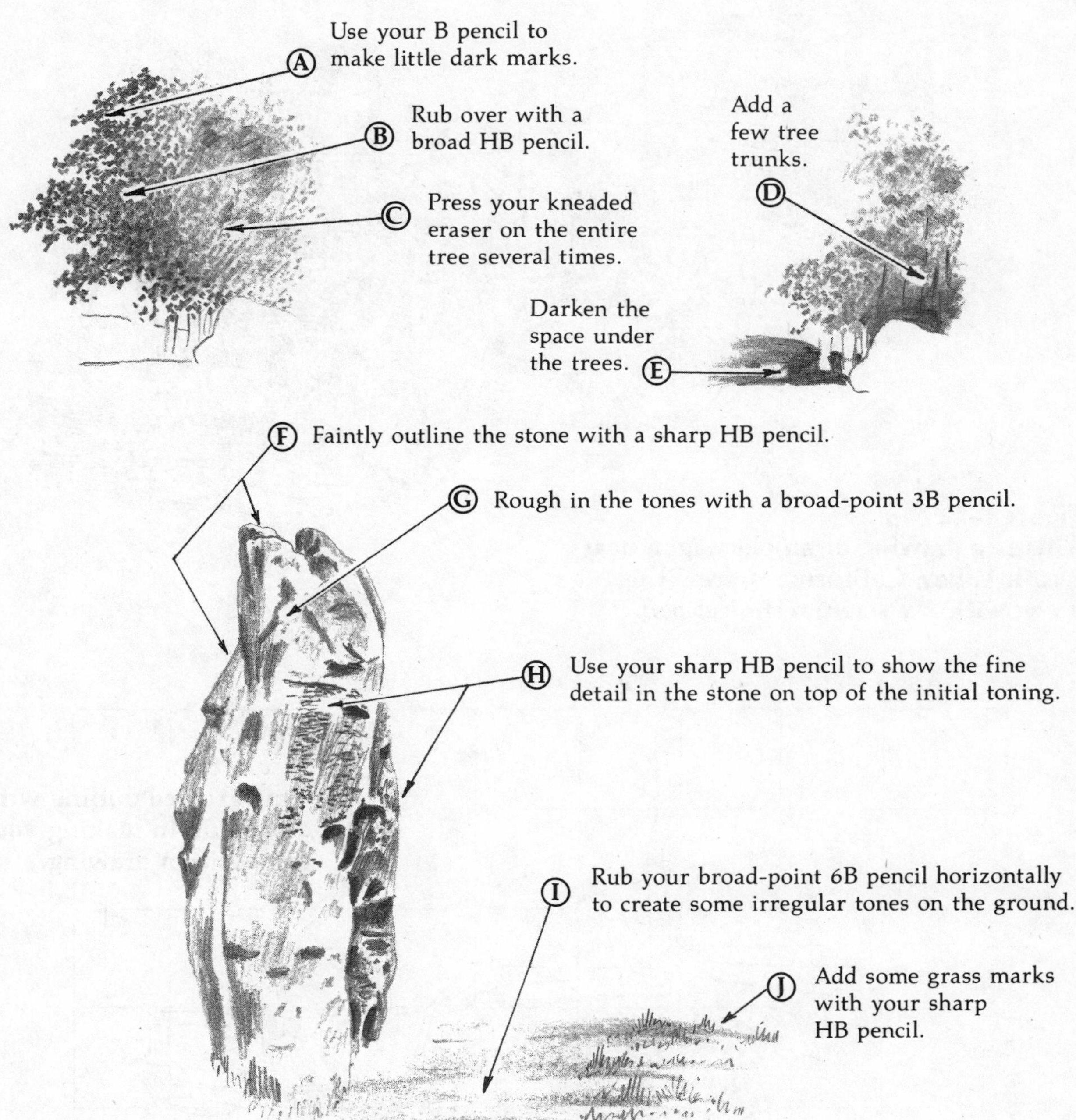
Ⓐ Use your B pencil to make little dark marks.
Ⓑ Rub over with a broad HB pencil.
Ⓒ Press your kneaded eraser on the entire tree several times.
Add a few tree trunks. Ⓓ
Darken the space under the trees. Ⓔ
Ⓕ Faintly outline the stone with a sharp HB pencil.
Ⓖ Rough in the tones with a broad-point 3B pencil.
Ⓗ Use your sharp HB pencil to show the fine detail in the stone on top of the initial toning.
Ⓘ Rub your broad-point 6B pencil horizontally to create some irregular tones on the ground.
Ⓙ Add some grass marks with your sharp HB pencil.

Figure 8-11
These suggestions and the careful use of your kneaded eraser when necessary will help you complete your drawing of this subject.

Death Valley

Figure 8-12
This is a drawing of an old wagon near Death Valley, California. I drew this scene with my size 0 technical pen.

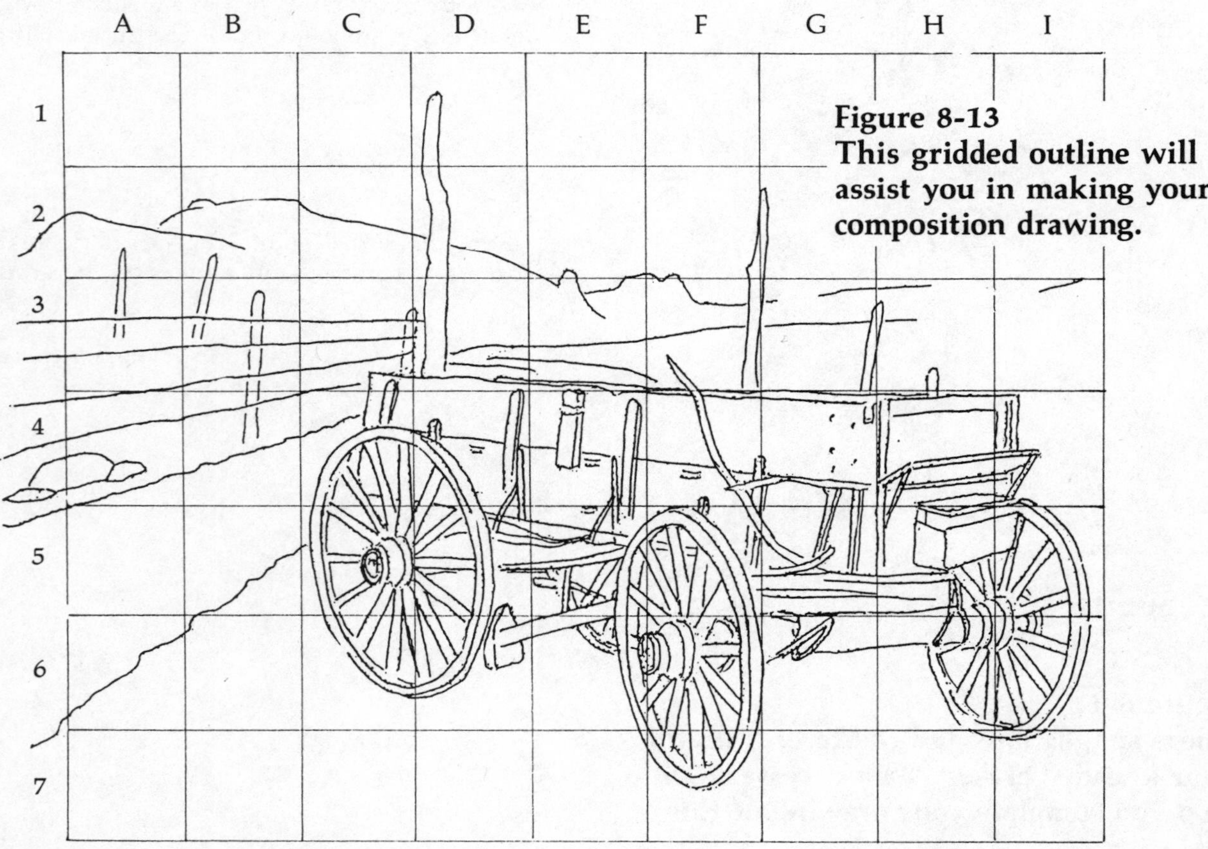
A
B
C
D
E
F
G
H
I
1
2
3
4
5
6
7

Figure 8-13
This gridded outline will assist you in making your composition drawing.

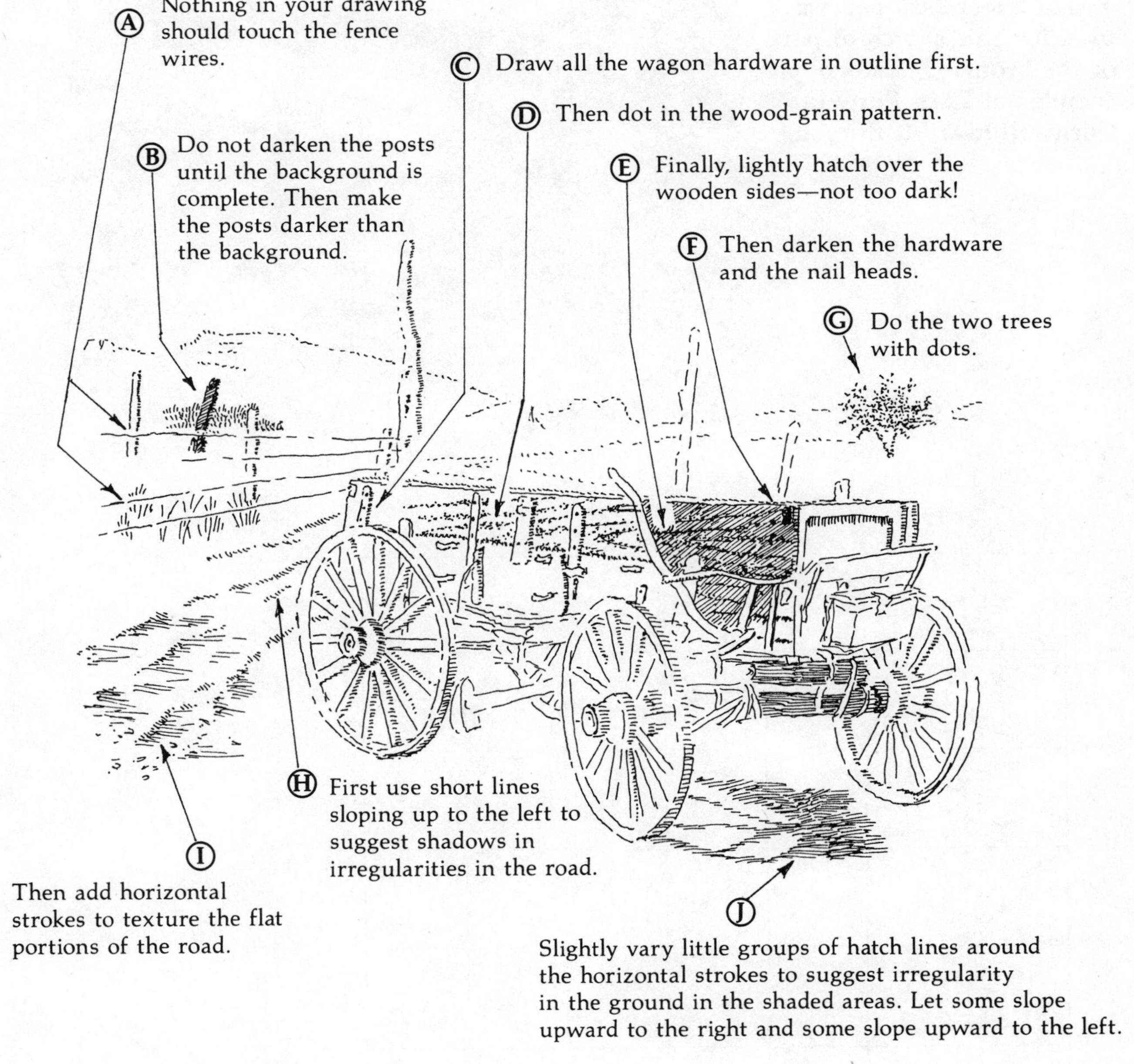
(A) Nothing in your drawing should touch the fence wires.
(B) Do not darken the posts until the background is complete. Then make the posts darker than the background.
(C) Draw all the wagon hardware in outline first.
(D) Then dot in the wood-grain pattern.
(E) Finally, lightly hatch over the wooden sides—not too dark!
(F) Then darken the hardware and the nail heads.
(G) Do the two trees with dots.
(H) First use short lines sloping up to the left to suggest shadows in irregularities in the road.
(I) Then add horizontal strokes to texture the flat portions of the road.
(J) Slightly vary little groups of hatch lines around the horizontal strokes to suggest irregularity in the ground in the shaded areas. Let some slope upward to the right and some slope upward to the left.

Figure 8-14
Follow these suggestions as you complete your drawing of the wagon.

Carn Euny

F. Lohan

Figure 8-15
A size 0 technical pen was used for this sketch of part of the bronze-age stone complex at Carn Euny in Cornwall near St. Buryan.

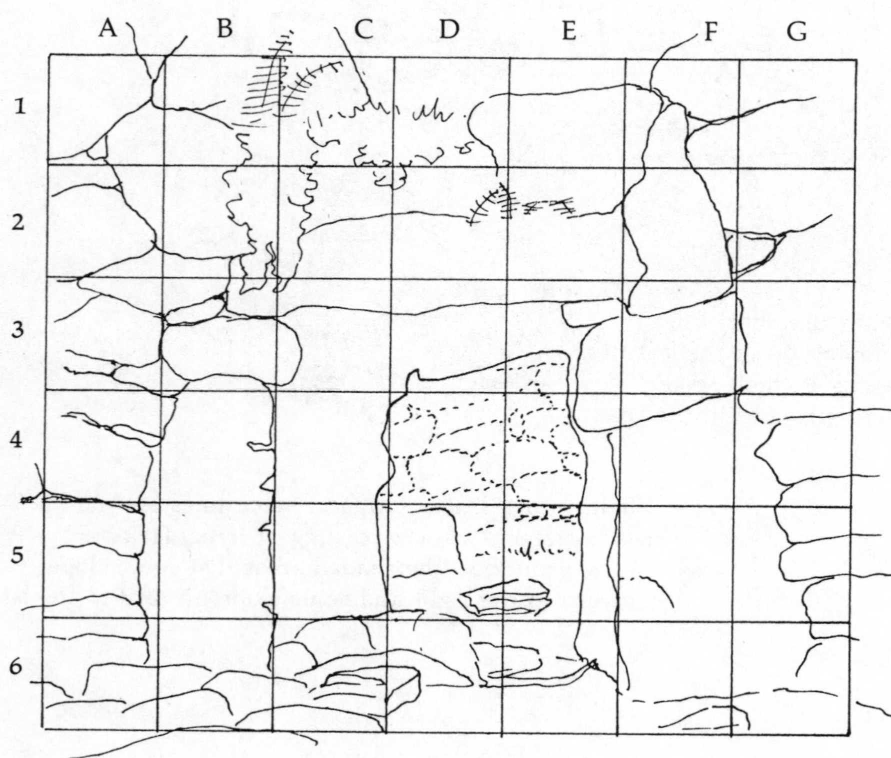
A
B
C
D
E
F
G
1
2
3
4
5
6

Figure 8-16
Use this gridded outline to prepare your working drawing for this subject.

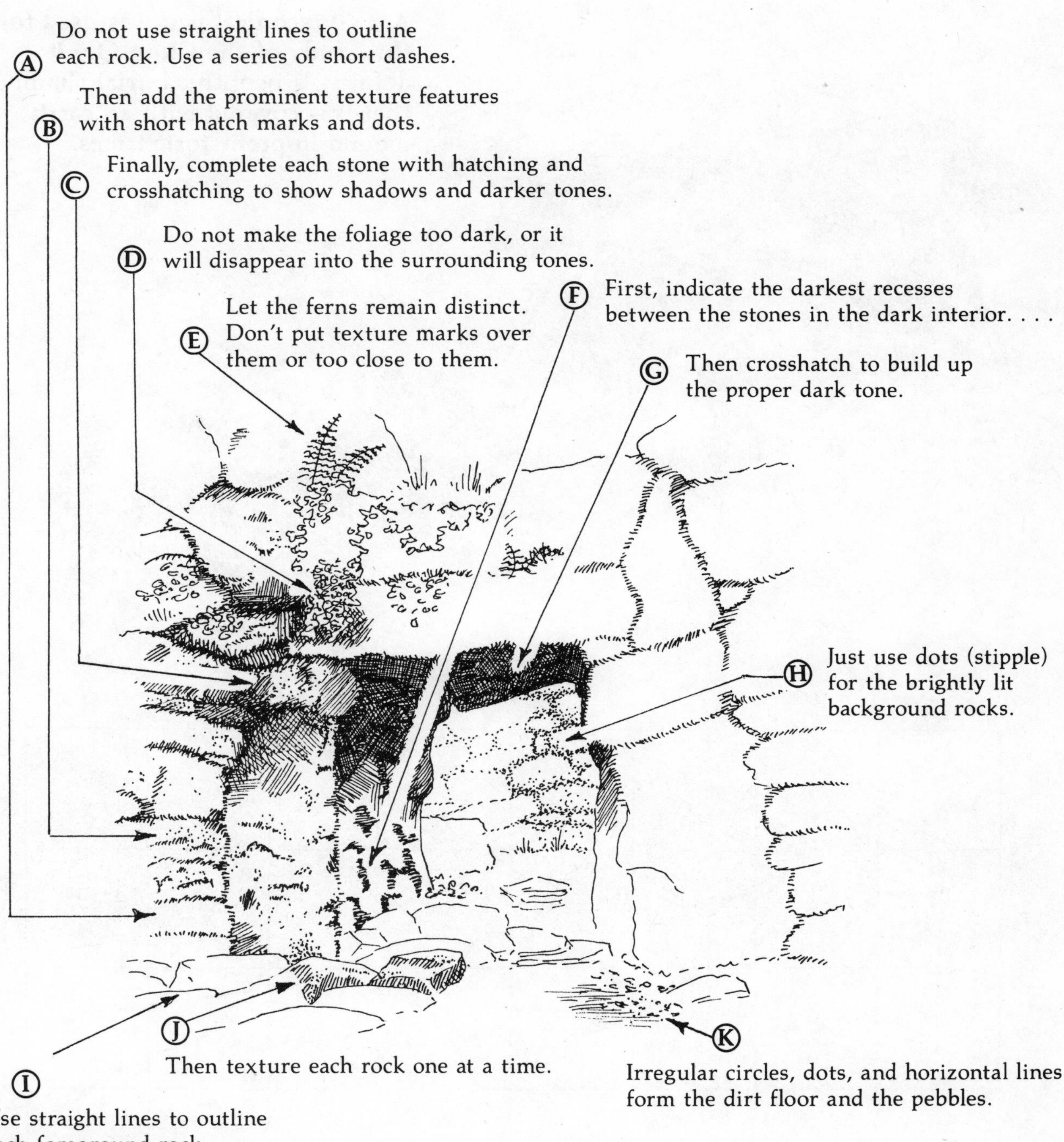
Do not use straight lines to outline each rock. Use a series of short dashes.
Then add the prominent texture features with short hatch marks and dots.
Finally, complete each stone with hatching and crosshatching to show shadows and darker tones.
Do not make the foliage too dark, or it will disappear into the surrounding tones.
Let the ferns remain distinct. Don't put texture marks over them or too close to them.
First, indicate the darkest recesses between the stones in the dark interior. . . .
Then crosshatch to build up the proper dark tone.
Just use dots (stipple) for the brightly lit background rocks.
Then texture each rock one at a time.
Irregular circles, dots, and horizontal lines form the dirt floor and the pebbles.
Use straight lines to outline each foreground rock. . . .

Figure 8-17
Use these suggestions as you complete your ink drawing of Carn Euny.

Chun Quoit

F. Lohan

Figure 8-18
A 3×0 technical pen was used for this study of the Chun Quoit dolmen, a neolithic burial chamber that was covered with an earth mound in prehistoric times.

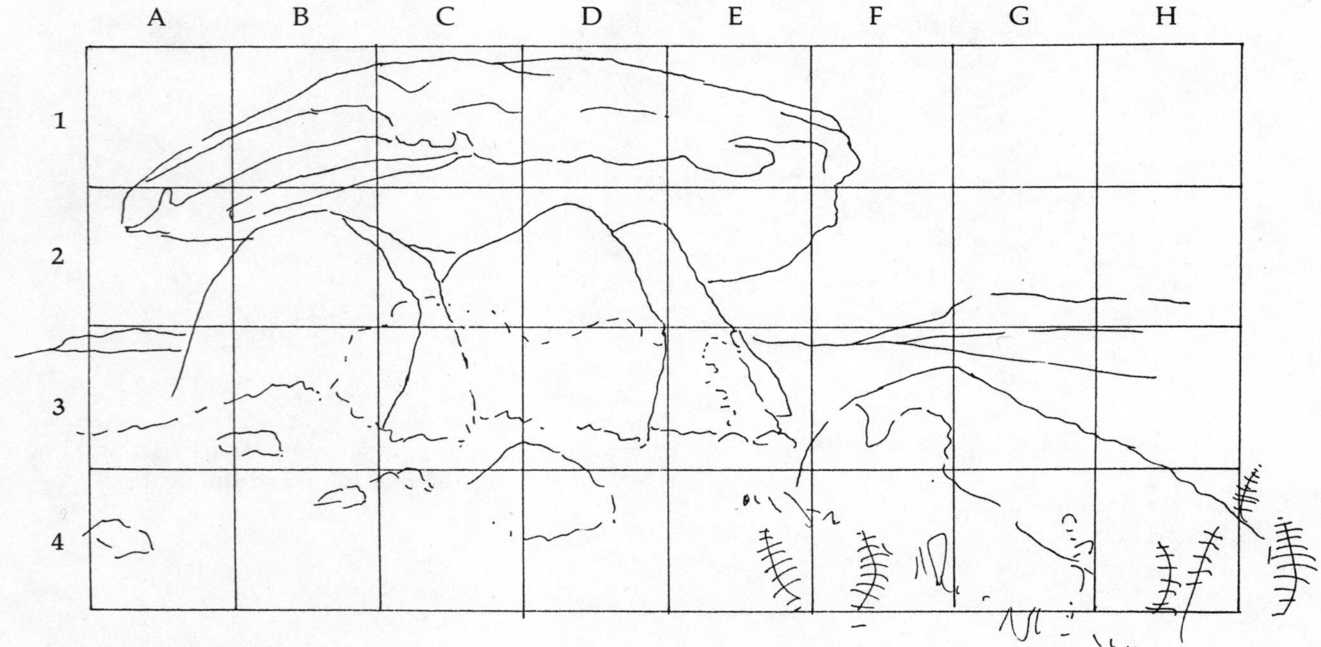
A
B
C
D
E
F
G
H
1
2
3
4

Figure 8-19
Use this gridded composition to prepare your pencil outline of Chun Quoit for your ink work.

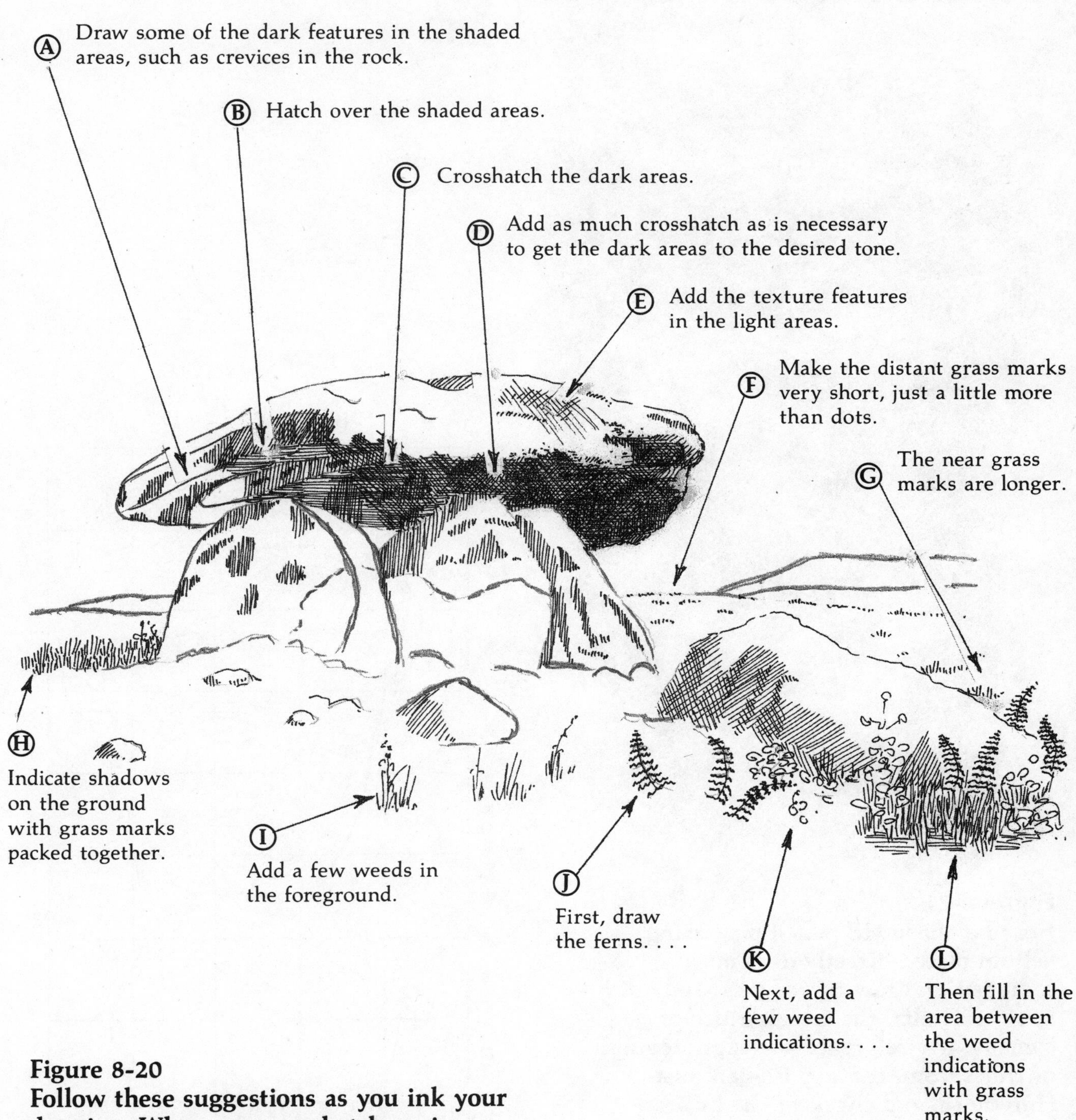
Ⓐ Draw some of the dark features in the shaded areas, such as crevices in the rock.
Ⓑ Hatch over the shaded areas.
Ⓒ Crosshatch the dark areas.
Ⓓ Add as much crosshatch as is necessary to get the dark areas to the desired tone.
Ⓔ Add the texture features in the light areas.
Ⓕ Make the distant grass marks very short, just a little more than dots.
Ⓖ The near grass marks are longer.
Ⓗ Indicate shadows on the ground with grass marks packed together.
Ⓘ Add a few weeds in the foreground.
Ⓙ First, draw the ferns. . . .
Ⓚ Next, add a few weed indications. . . .
Ⓛ Then fill in the area between the weed indications with grass marks.

Figure 8-20
Follow these suggestions as you ink your drawing. When you crosshatch, as in steps C and D, remember to keep your lines close together. If you do your hatching with widely spaced lines, you have a hard time making an area dark. The darkest areas in my sketch have just four layers of lines.

Thalia, Muse of Comedy

Thalia

Figure 8-21
I used a sharp HB pencil on tracing vellum placed directly over my composition drawing for this study of a bust of Thalia, the Greek Muse of comedy. My reference was a photograph of this second-century Roman bust. The chin, nose, and cheek of the bust are damaged.

A
B
C
D
E
1
2
3
4
5
6
7
8
9

Figure 8-22
Use this gridded outline to prepare your outline drawing.

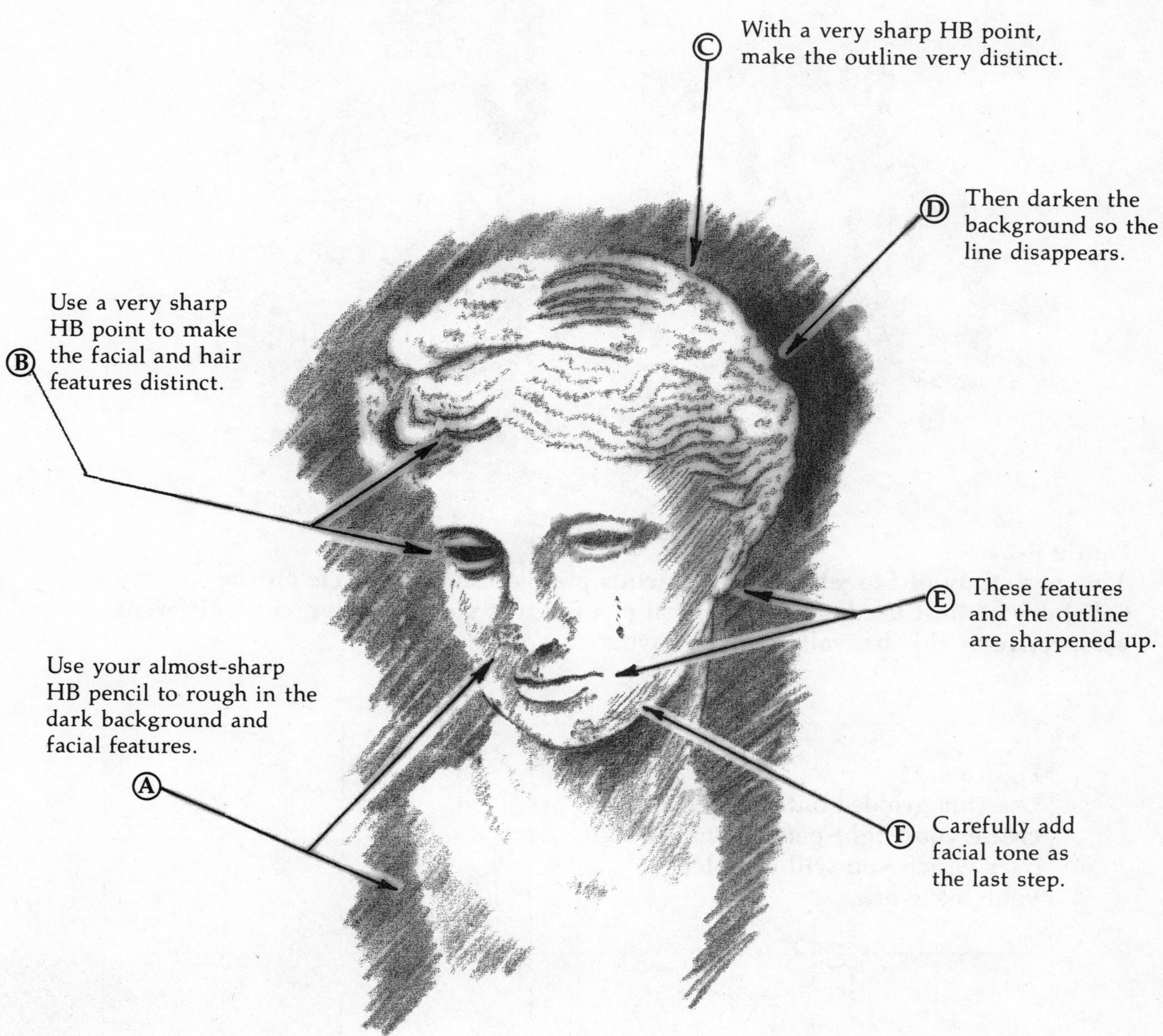
With a very sharp HB point, make the outline very distinct.
Then darken the background so the line disappears.
Use a very sharp HB point to make the facial and hair features distinct.
These features and the outline are sharpened up.
Use your almost-sharp HB pencil to rough in the dark background and facial features.
Carefully add facial tone as the last step.

Figure 8-23
Use these suggestions to guide your rendition of this subject. Your kneaded eraser, squeezed to a point and pressed on small areas of your drawing, will be helpful as you work, as it is easy to get marks too dark at first.

Stonehenge

Figure 8-24
This is a study of Stonehenge, the famous prehistoric stone circle on the Salisbury plain. I used a 3×0 technical pen for this view, which gives a different perspective of this basically circular layout.

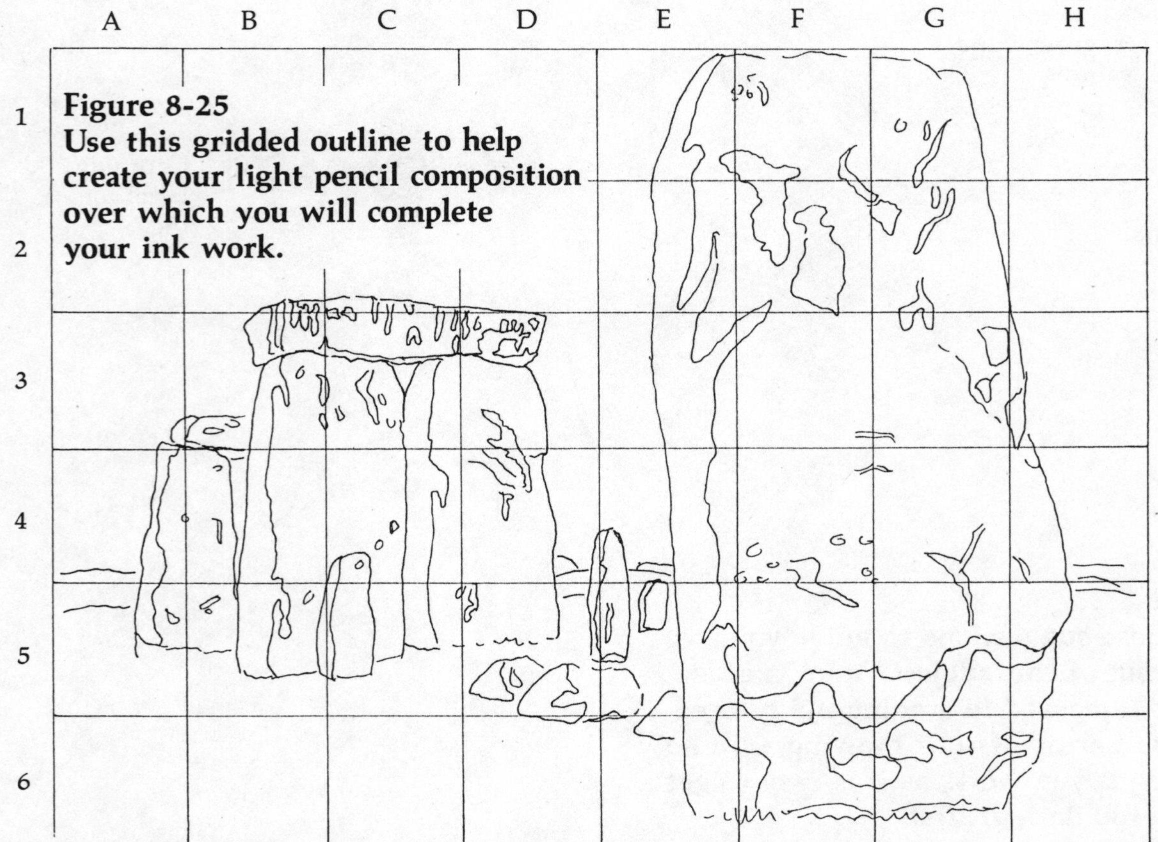
A B C D E F G H
1
2
3
4
5
6

Figure 8-25
Use this gridded outline to help create your light pencil composition over which you will complete your ink work.

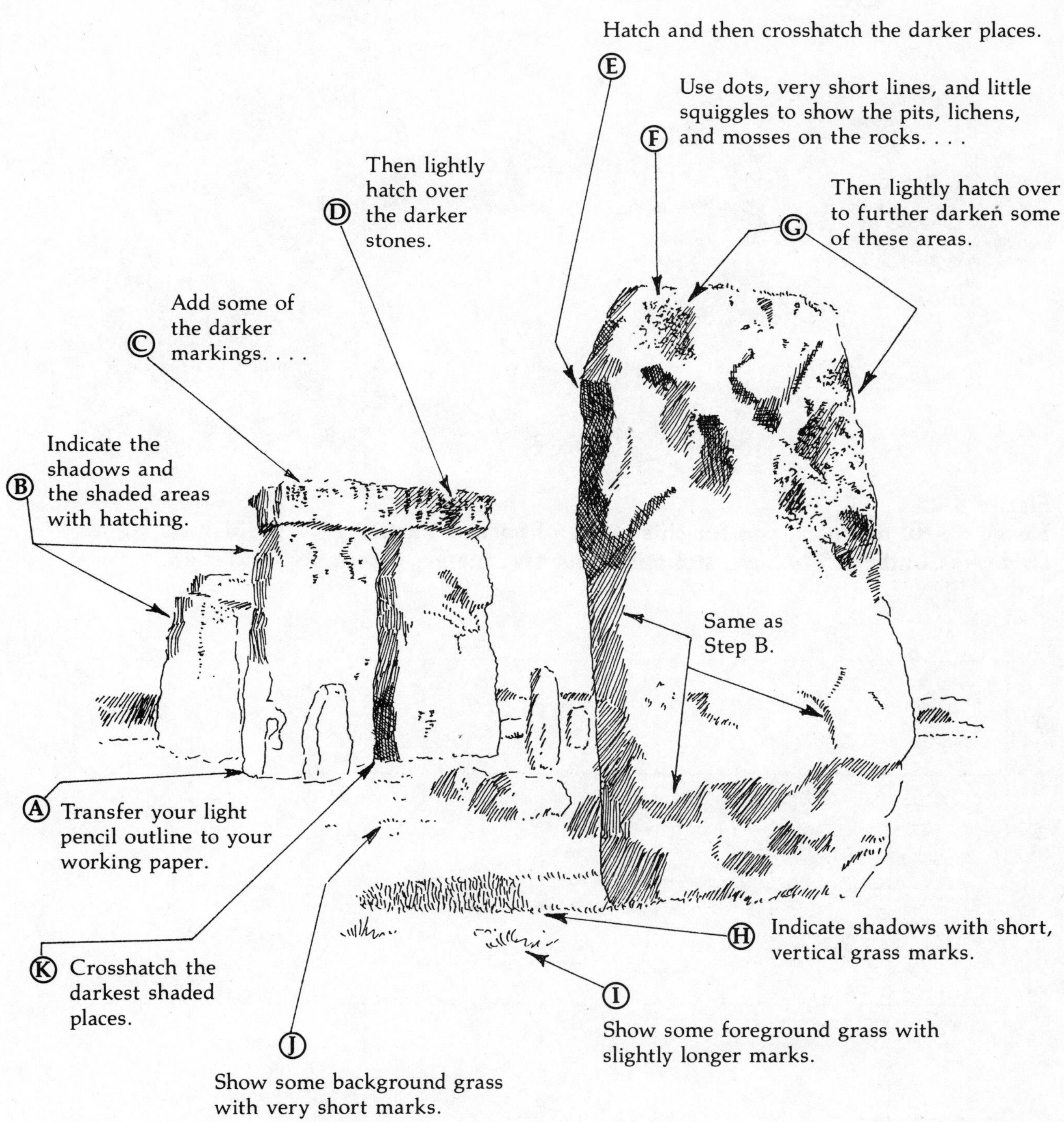
Hatch and then crosshatch the darker places.
E
Use dots, very short lines, and little squiggles to show the pits, lichens, and mosses on the rocks. . . .
F
Then lightly hatch over to further darken some of these areas.
G
Then lightly hatch over the darker stones.
D
Add some of the darker markings. . . .
C
Indicate the shadows and the shaded areas with hatching.
B
Same as Step B.
A
Transfer your light pencil outline to your working paper.
H
Indicate shadows with short, vertical grass marks.
K
Crosshatch the darkest shaded places.
I
Show some foreground grass with slightly longer marks.
J
Show some background grass with very short marks.

Figure 8-26
These are some suggestions for completing your version of this ink study.

Castlerigg

F. Lohan

Figure 8-27
I used a 3×0 technical pen for this study of part of Castlerigg, a prehistoric stone circle in Cumbria. The near stone is about two meters (about six feet) high.

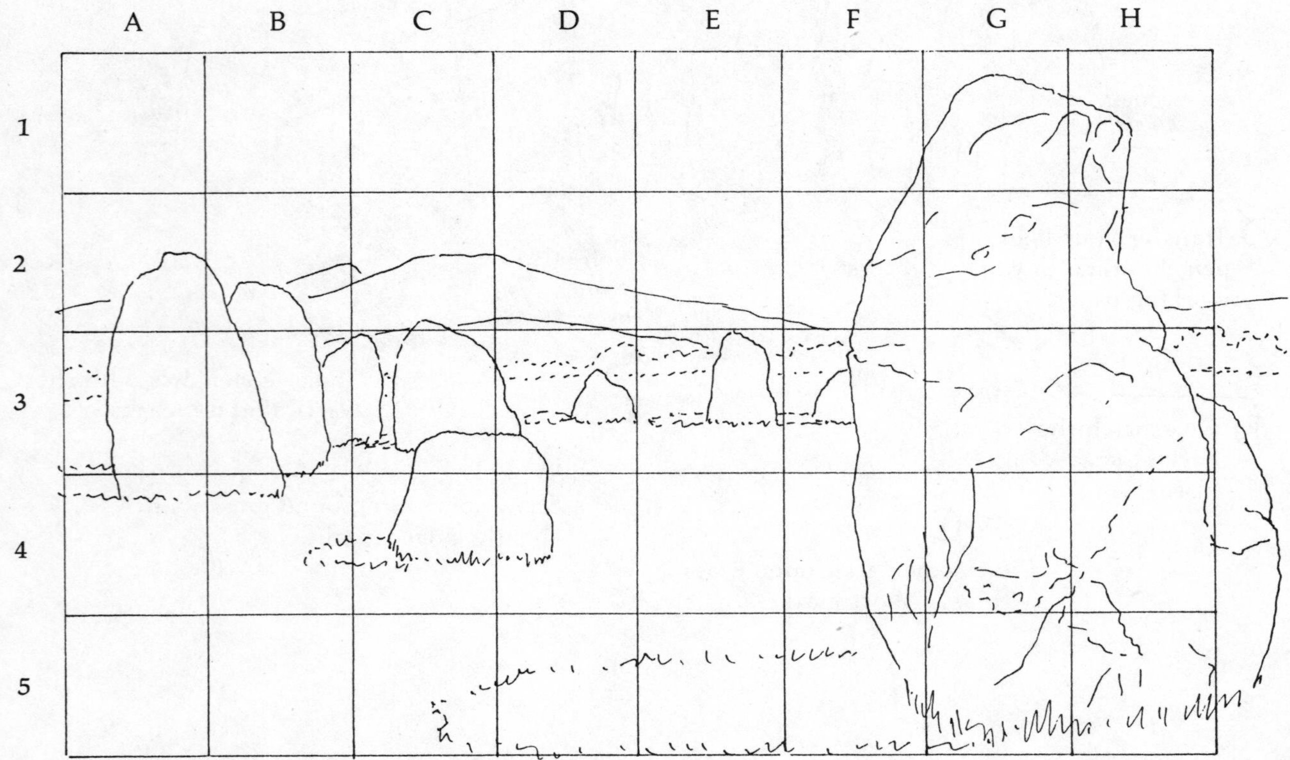
A
B
C
D
E
F
G
H
1
2
3
4
5

Figure 8-28
Use this gridded composition of the Castlerigg stones to help create your light pencil outline.

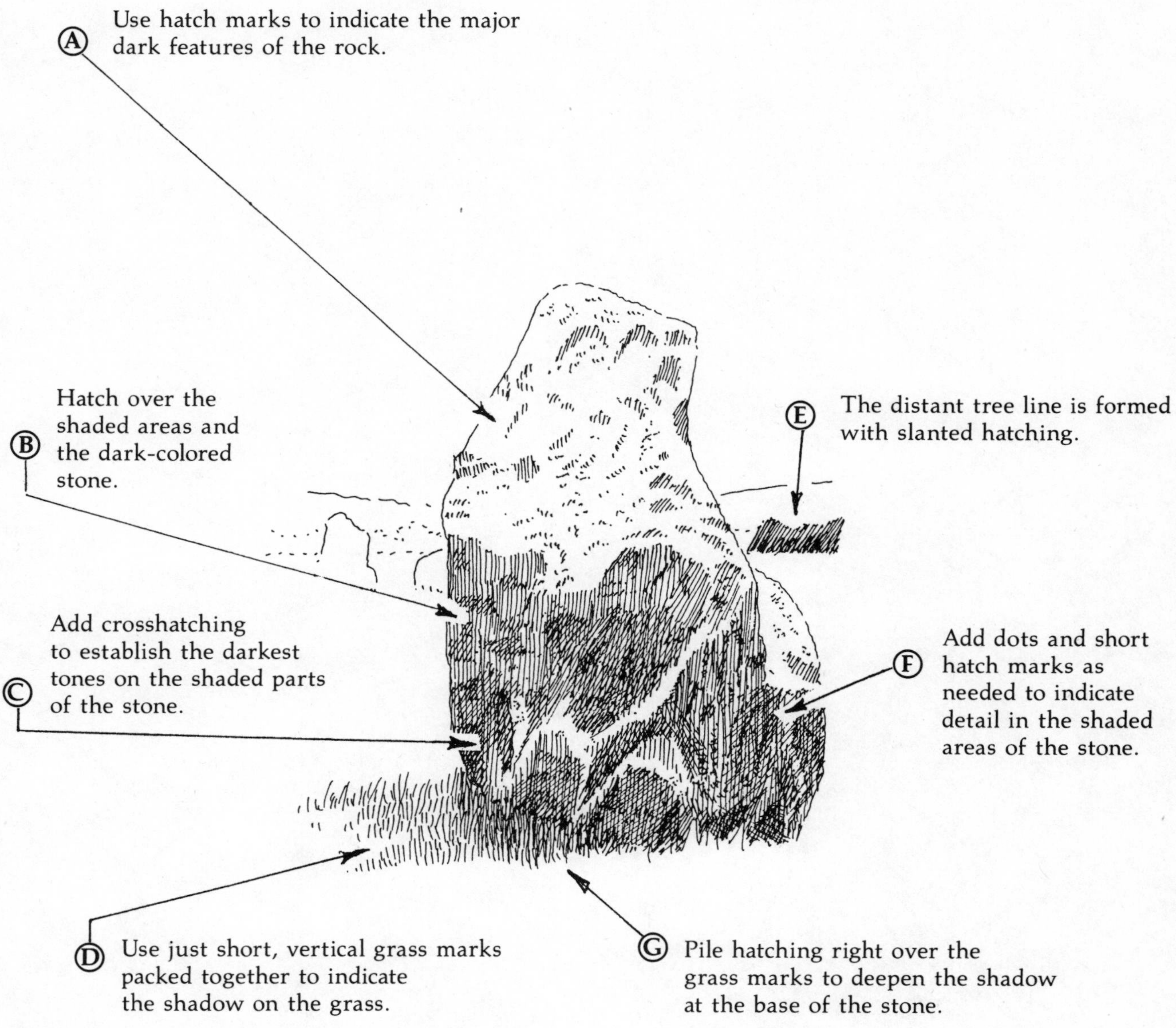

Ⓐ Use hatch marks to indicate the major dark features of the rock.
Ⓑ Hatch over the shaded areas and the dark-colored stone.
Ⓒ Add crosshatching to establish the darkest tones on the shaded parts of the stone.
Ⓓ Use just short, vertical grass marks packed together to indicate the shadow on the grass.
Ⓔ The distant tree line is formed with slanted hatching.
Ⓕ Add dots and short hatch marks as needed to indicate detail in the shaded areas of the stone.
Ⓖ Pile hatching right over the grass marks to deepen the shadow at the base of the stone.

Figure 8-29
Follow steps A, B, and C to complete each of the stones. The more distant stones require less detailed treatment and are established primarily with outline and shade indications.

9
Birds

Osprey
Mockingbird
Chickadee
Canada Goose
Mallard

One of the main things to keep in mind about drawing birds is that the drawing should suggest the bird's feathers to the viewer properly. Most often this means that each feather must be carefully darkened, and a white sliver must be left around each one. You will see this in both the ink and the pencil exercises that follow except the last one, mallard. In that exercise, the dark tone itself gives enough indication of the individual feathers in the wings. Notice, though, that in the mallard drawing no attempt was made to show each feather on the body, as there was in the Canada goose drawing in the next-to-last exercise. It is all a matter of the scale of the drawing. Once, I did a sketch of a flying black duck for an interpretive sign at a national wildlife refuge. The drawing was large; the bird measured about twenty inches from beak to tip of tail. I drew perhaps five or six dozen individual feathers on the duck's body (see figure 3-23 for a reproduction of this drawing).

When you want to draw detailed studies of birds, you need excellent photographic references in order to see the detail you want to include. Remember, you cannot draw what you cannot see or do not know *very* thoroughly.

Osprey

F.Lohan
Ⓐ Start with the eye.
Ⓑ Complete the beak and dark head feathers.
Ⓒ Then gently tone the light areas on the head. Leave the little highlight on the eye white—do not tone it. Don't lose the highlight on the beak either.
Ⓓ Make each dark feather black, but leave a sliver of white paper around each one. Keep your pencil sharp for this step.
Ⓔ Then lightly tone over the dark feathers with a broad-point B pencil.
A B C D E F G
1
2
3
4
5
6
7
8
9

Figure 9-1
Use a sharp-point B pencil for most of this sketch and vellum-finish paper or some paper with a little tooth. Use the pencil gently to indicate the lighter areas. Step D, in which you make the dark feathers black using a sharp point, will work better if your sheet of paper is on a hard surface such as a smooth Formica tabletop.

Mockingbird

P. Lohan
Ⓓ Be sure to leave white between the dark feather indications.
Ⓔ Go over those feather marks that must be darker.

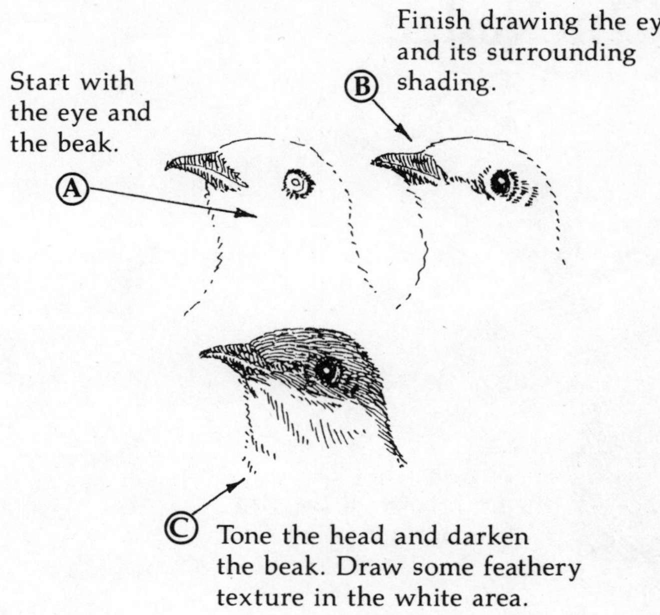
Start with the eye and the beak.
Ⓐ
Ⓑ Finish drawing the eye and its surrounding shading.
Ⓒ Tone the head and darken the beak. Draw some feathery texture in the white area.

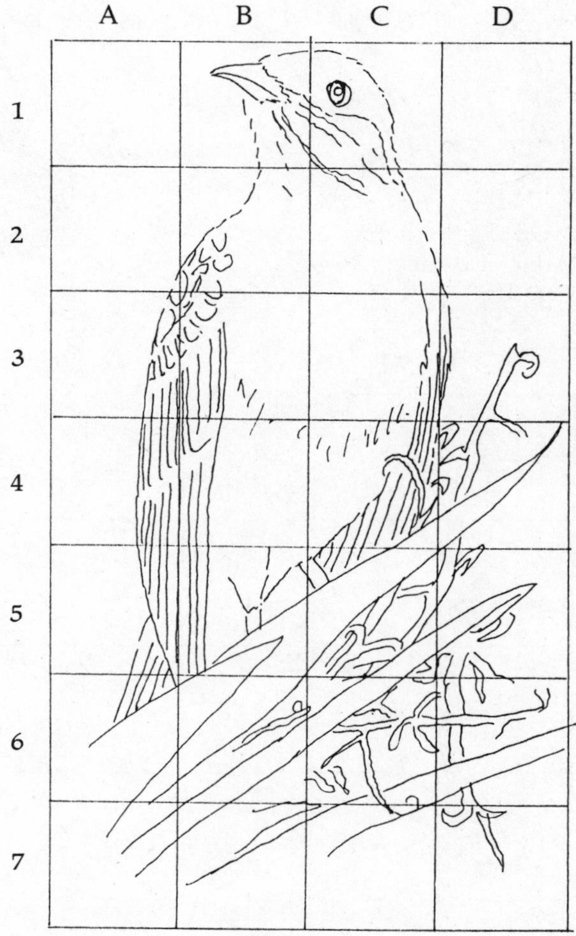
A
B
C
D
1
2
3
4
5
6
7

Figure 9-2
This exercise was done with a 3×0 technical pen on vellum-finish paper.

Chickadee

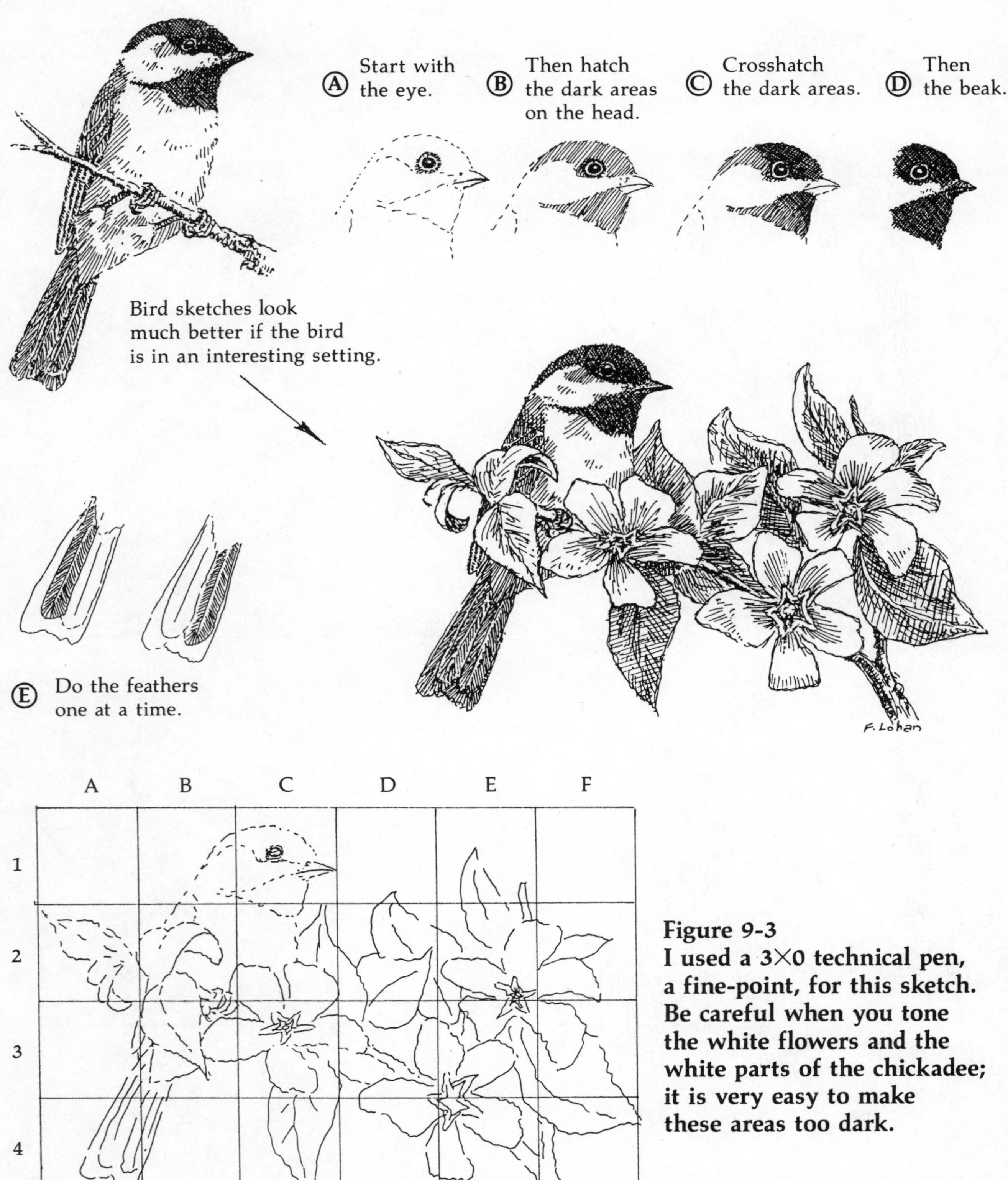

Ⓐ Start with the eye.
Ⓑ Then hatch the dark areas on the head.
Ⓒ Crosshatch the dark areas.
Ⓓ Then the beak.
Bird sketches look much better if the bird is in an interesting setting.
Ⓔ Do the feathers one at a time.
F. Lohan
A
B
C
D
E
F
1
2
3
4

Figure 9-3
I used a 3×0 technical pen, a fine-point, for this sketch. Be careful when you tone the white flowers and the white parts of the chickadee; it is very easy to make these areas too dark.

Canada Goose

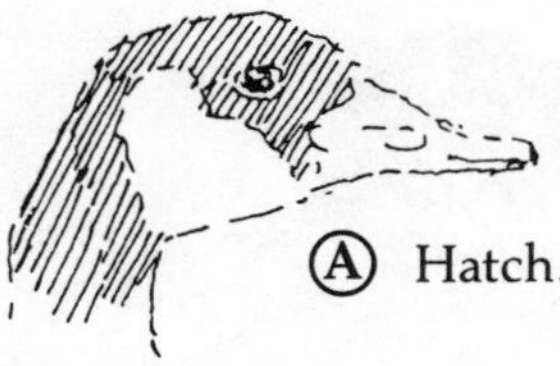

Ⓐ Hatch.

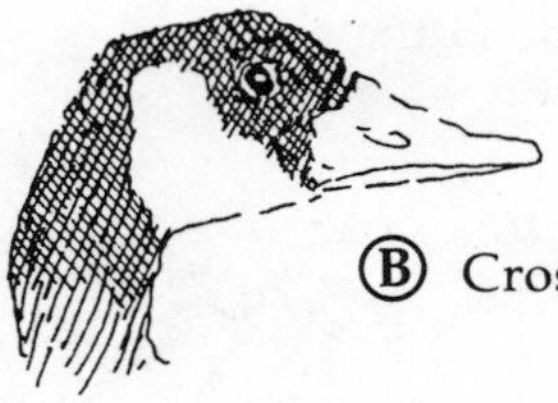

Ⓑ Crosshatch.

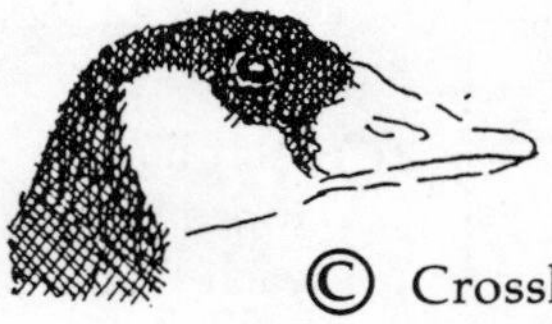

Ⓒ Crosshatch again.

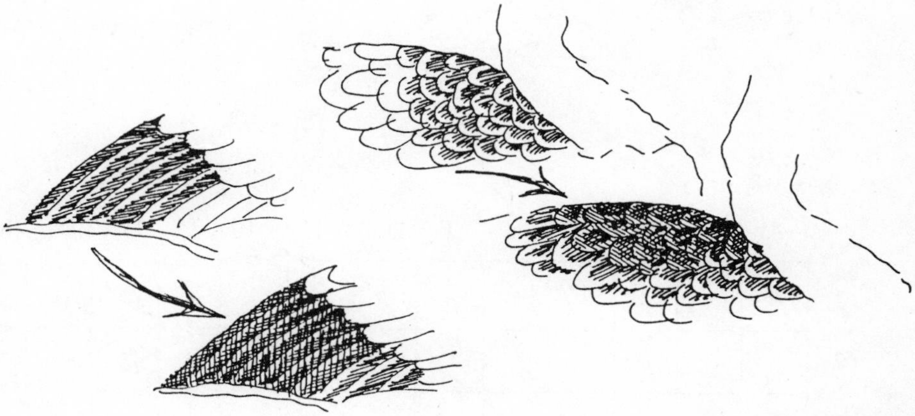

Ⓓ Hatch and then crosshatch each individual feather.

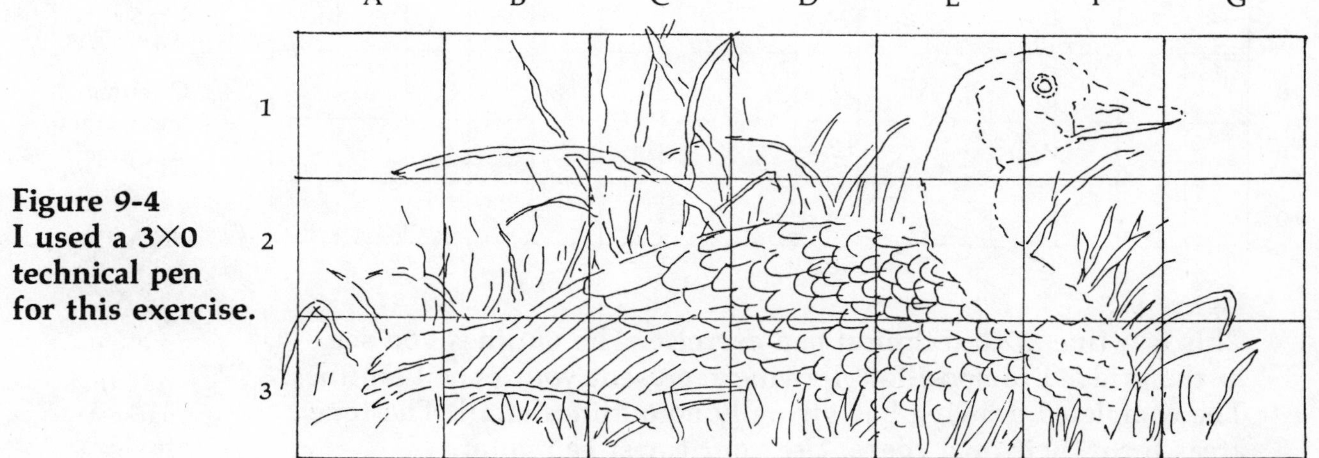
A
B
C
D
E
F
G
1
2
3

Figure 9-4
I used a 3×0 technical pen for this exercise.

Mallard

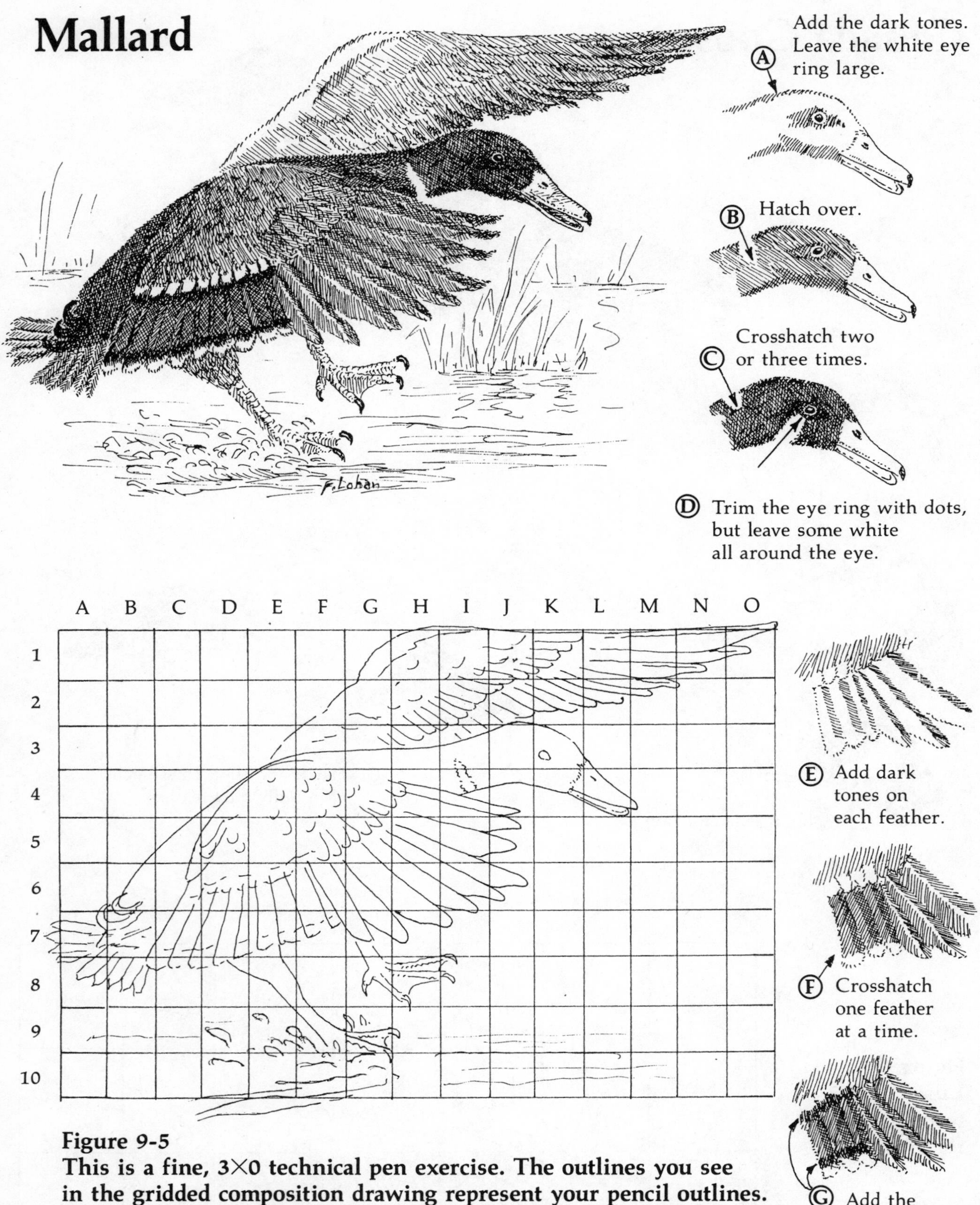
Add the dark tones. Leave the white eye ring large.
A
B
Hatch over.
Crosshatch two or three times.
C
D
Trim the eye ring with dots, but leave some white all around the eye.
F. Lohan
A B C D E F G H I J K L M N O
1
2
3
4
5
6
7
8
9
10
E
Add dark tones on each feather.
F
Crosshatch one feather at a time.
G
Add the darkest feathers.

Figure 9-5
This is a fine, 3×0 technical pen exercise. The outlines you see in the gridded composition drawing represent your pencil outlines. The completed drawing has virtually no outlines at all. The toned areas form their own edges. Use your finest pen point.

10
Animals

Gray Fox
Chipmunk
Indian Tiger
Hippopotamus
African Elephant

When drawing furred animals, you can count on getting a furry appearance by using short pen or pencil strokes in the direction that the fur lies on the animal. This technique is used in the first two exercises (one is for the pen, and the other is for the pencil).

Attention to the geometry of the subject makes establishing the composition for the tiger portrait in the third exercise easier. The animal's face is based on a circle, gridded with the horizontal and vertical diameters broken into four parts each. The facial features are then aligned on this grid, in figure 10-3. Always look for relationships like this when you are drawing animals. It makes the establishment of your composition drawing, the starting point for your detail work, much easier.

Gray Fox

Ⓐ
Ⓑ
Ⓒ
F. Lohan

Darken the eyeball slightly.

Figure 10-1
Use short strokes to indicate fur on the face and legs. Use slightly longer ones on the rest of the fox. The strokes follow the direction of the fur.

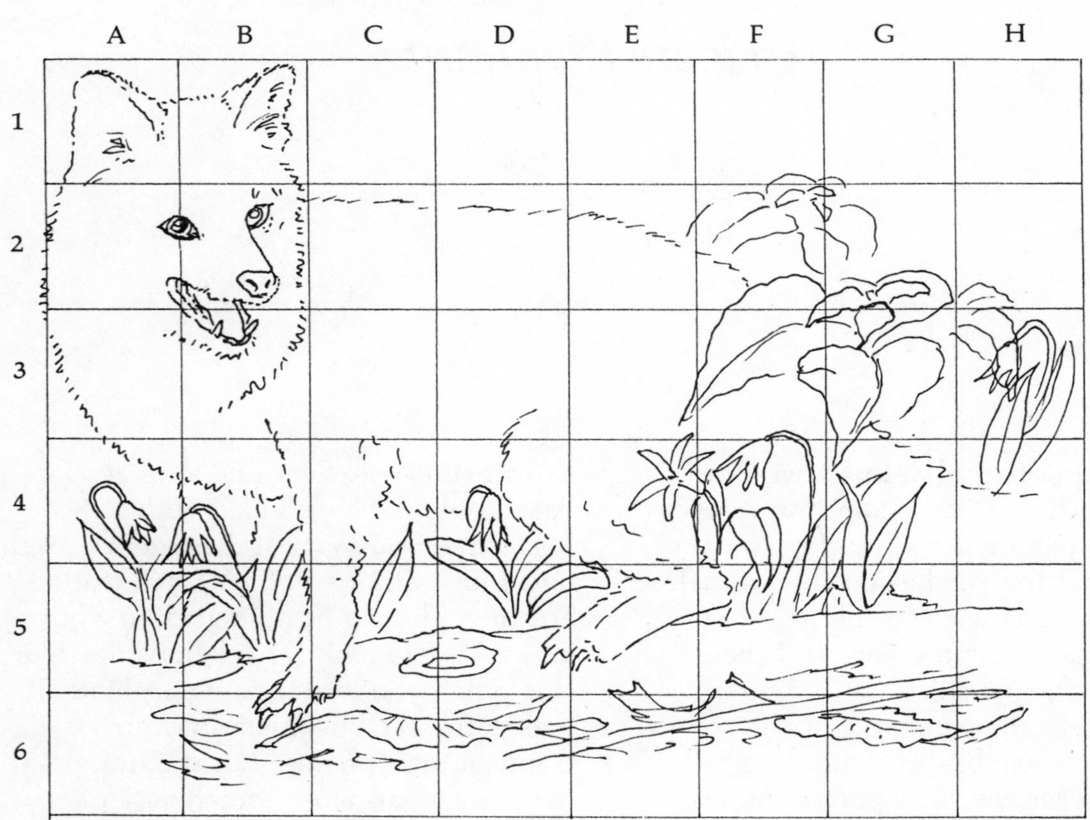
A B C D E F G H
1
2
3
4
5
6

Chipmunk

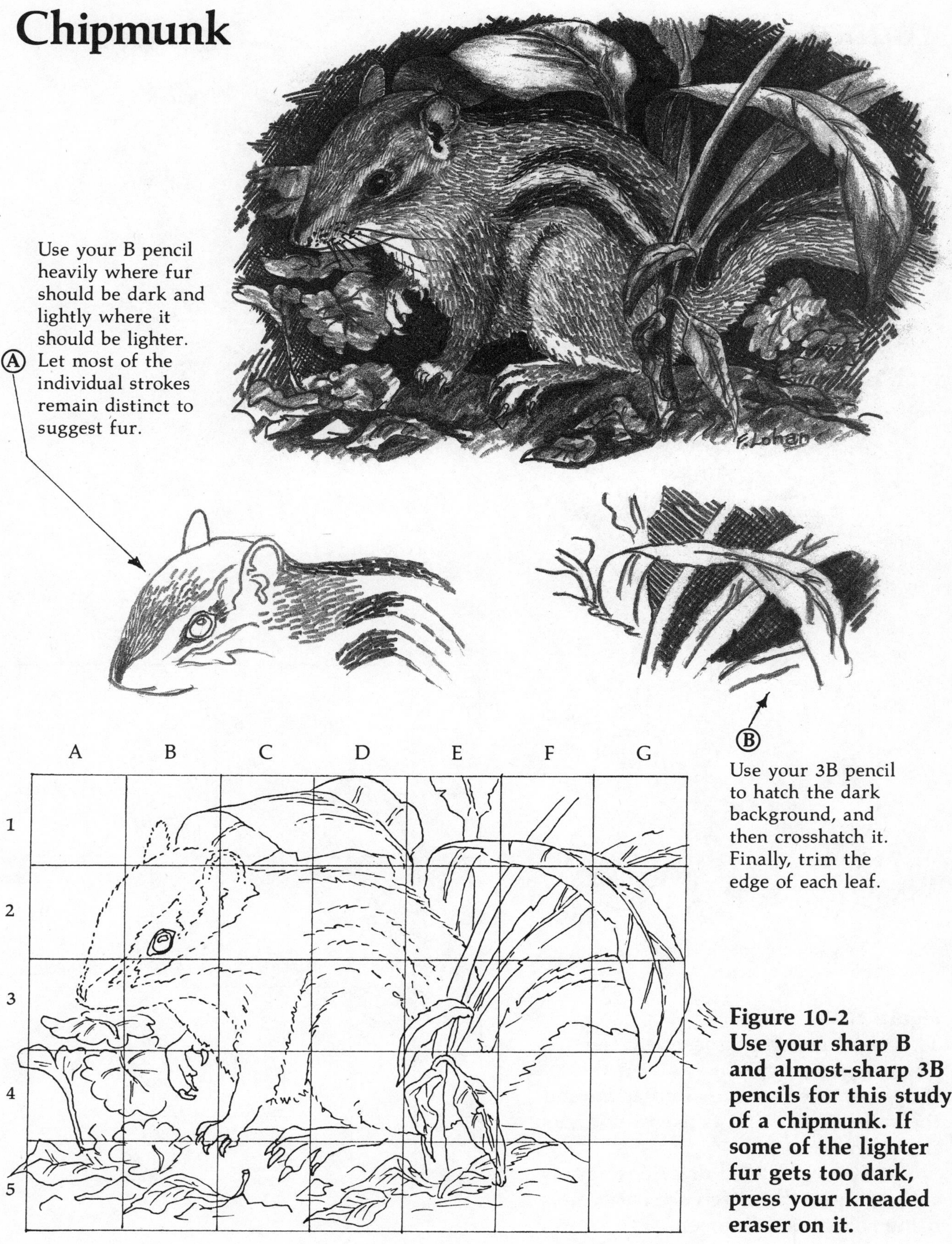
A
B
C
D
E
F
G
1
2
3
4
5

Ⓐ Use your B pencil heavily where fur should be dark and lightly where it should be lighter. Let most of the individual strokes remain distinct to suggest fur.

Ⓑ Use your 3B pencil to hatch the dark background, and then crosshatch it. Finally, trim the edge of each leaf.

Figure 10-2
Use your sharp B and almost-sharp 3B pencils for this study of a chipmunk. If some of the lighter fur gets too dark, press your kneaded eraser on it.

Indian Tiger

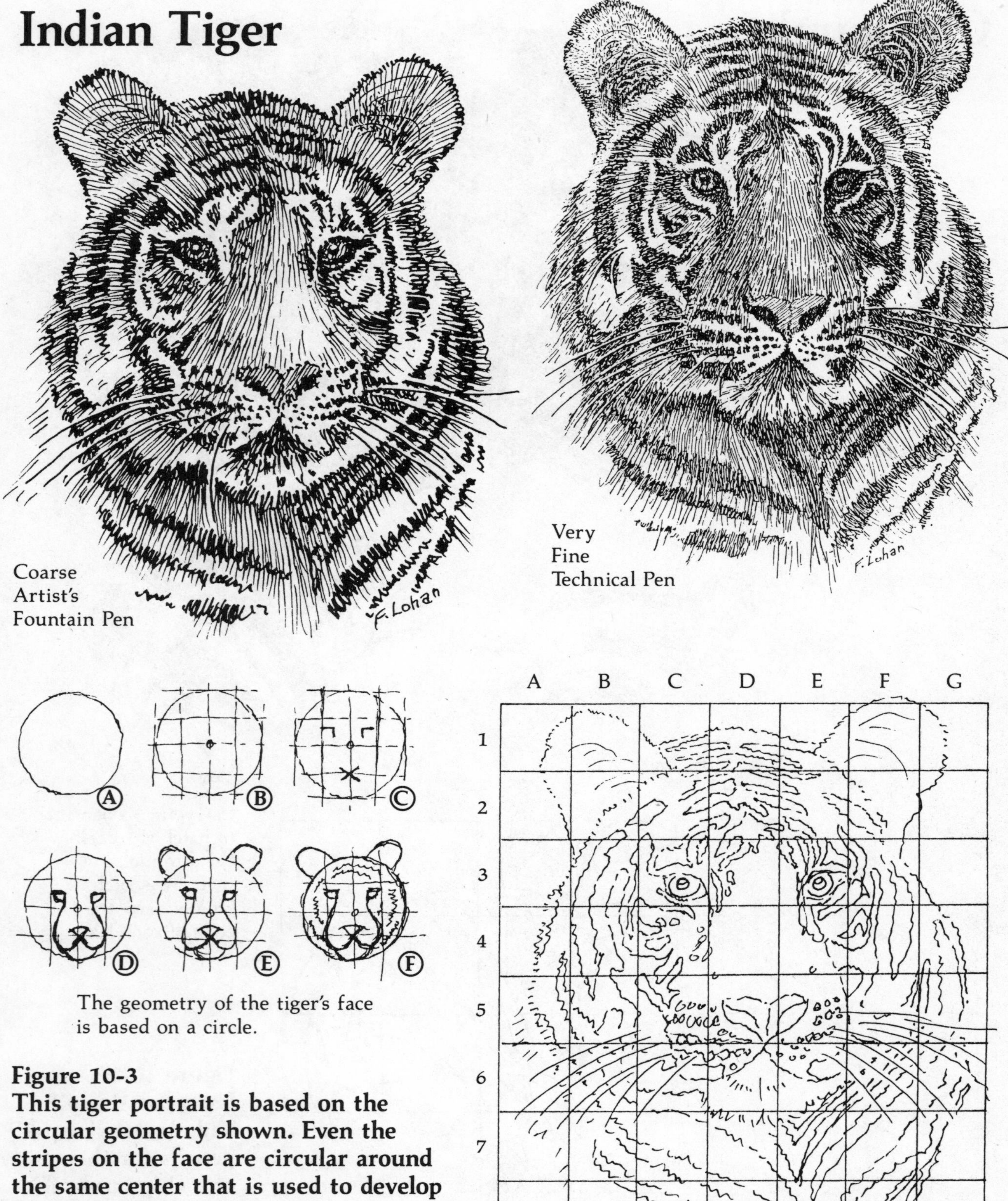
Coarse
Artist's
Fountain Pen
F. Lohan
Very
Fine
Technical Pen
F. Lohan
A B C D E F G
1
2
3
4
5
6
7
8
A
B
C
D
E
F

The geometry of the tiger's face is based on a circle.

Figure 10-3
This tiger portrait is based on the circular geometry shown. Even the stripes on the face are circular around the same center that is used to develop the other features.

The two completed drawings of this subject show the difference between using coarse and fine pens.

Hippopotamus

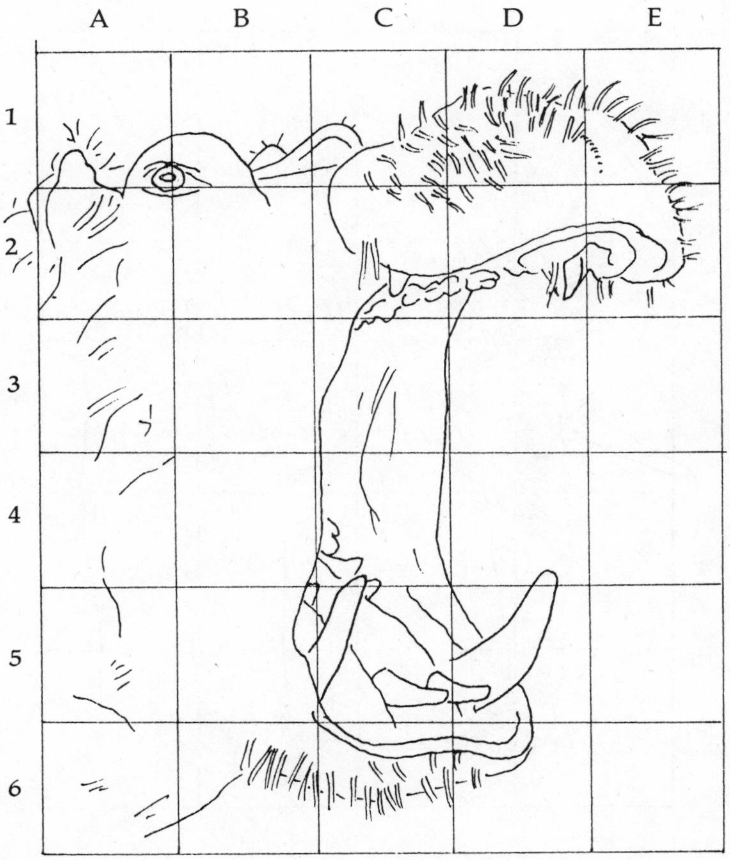

F. Lohan
Use double lines for the whiskers. Draw them first.
A
Add the spots and dots all over the nose. 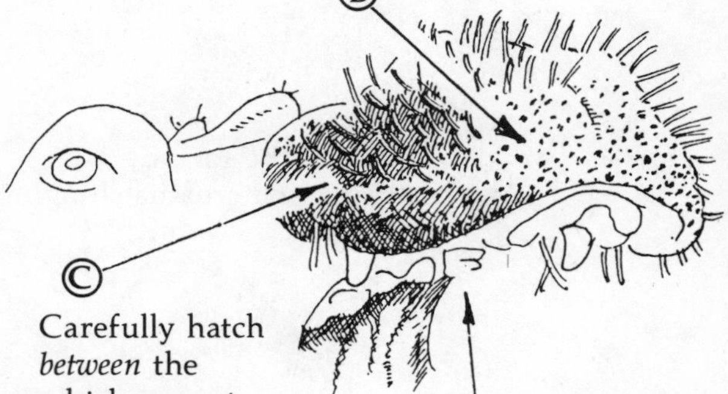
B
C
Carefully hatch *between* the whiskers, not over them.
D
Leave all the teeth white until the inside of the mouth is done. 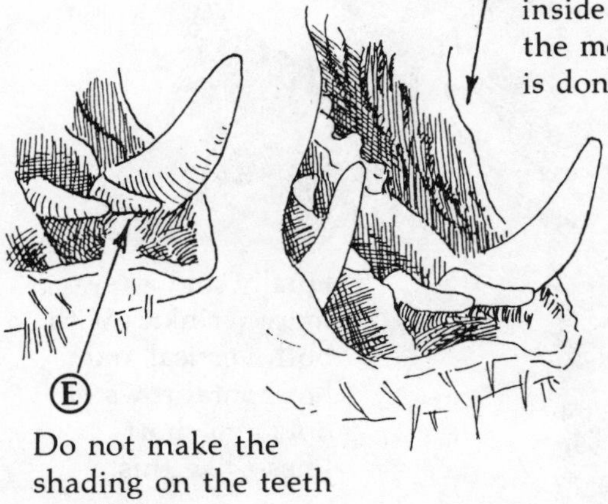
E
Do not make the shading on the teeth too dark.
A
B
C
D
E
1
2
3
4
5
6

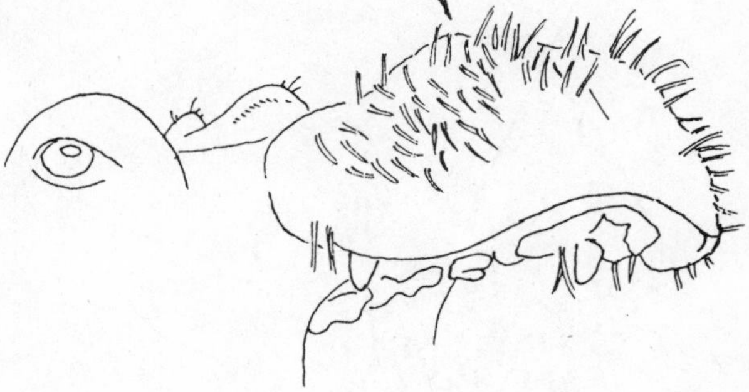

Figure 10-4
A 3×0 technical pen was used for this exercise.

African Elephant

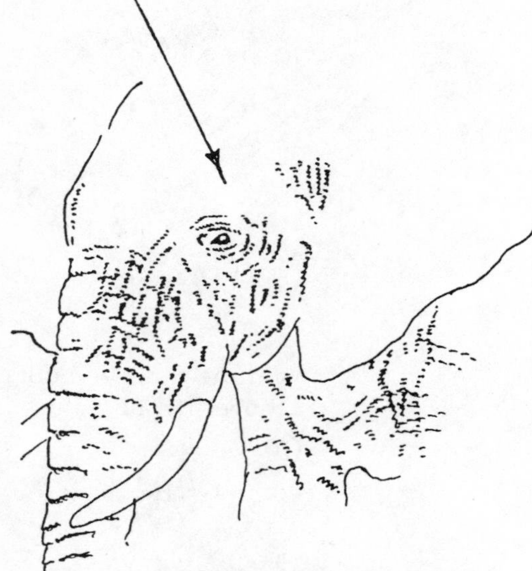
Ⓐ
First, show most of the creases
with rows of short lines.

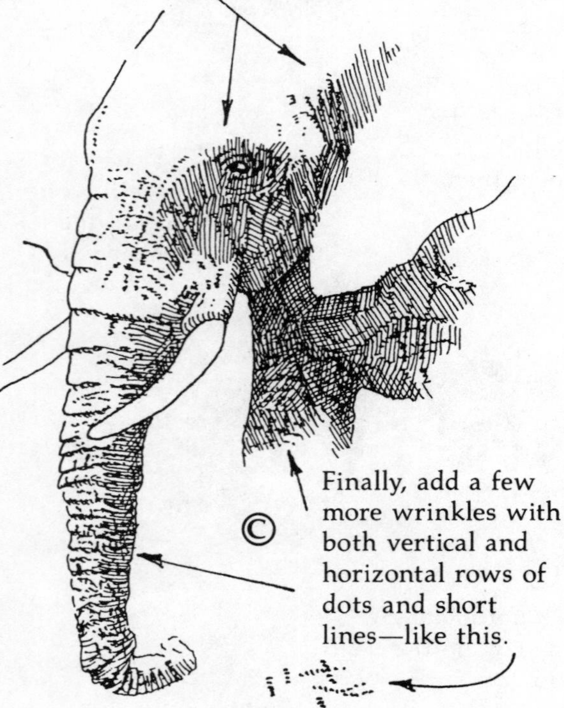
Ⓑ
Then add the tone by
hatching and crosshatching.
Ⓒ
Finally, add a few
more wrinkles with
both vertical and
horizontal rows of
dots and short
lines—like this.

F. Lohan

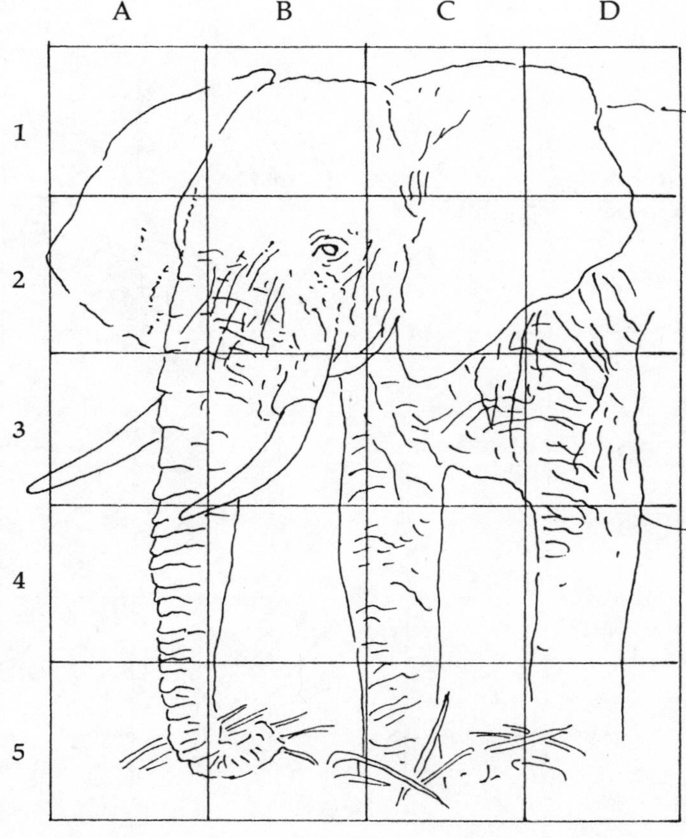
A
B
C
D
1
2
3
4
5

Figure 10-5
Use a sharp pen for this exercise.
I used a 3×0 technical pen.

11 Flowers

White Lilies

Wild Strawberry

Water Lily

Smooth Rose

Common Violet

In general, ink flower drawings should be done with a fine pen point. This allows you to better indicate the delicacy of white or light-colored petals and the play of highlights on the darker leaves.

A loose interpretation of a floral drawing is demonstrated in figure 11-1, White Lilies. In this drawing there is no attempt to carefully draw a thin, single-line outline of the leaves and flowers. Rather, these outlines are deliberately done with shorter, overlapping strokes to create a multiline outline with a looser, less formal feeling. In this exercise the background is made dark to show off the white petals. Water Lily, in figure 11-3, also has a dark background, this time dark water, to show the whiteness of the flower. The remainder of the exercises in this chapter are simple vignettes with no toned background. You must be careful whenever you tone white or light flowers; it is easy to add too much ink and darken them excessively.

White Lilies

Ⓐ Deliberately make the outlines loose, showing several lines in each outline.

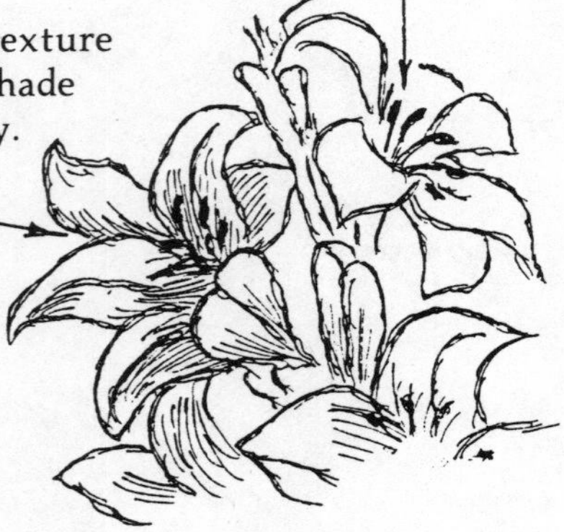

Ⓑ Add the anthers.

Ⓒ Add texture and shade lightly.

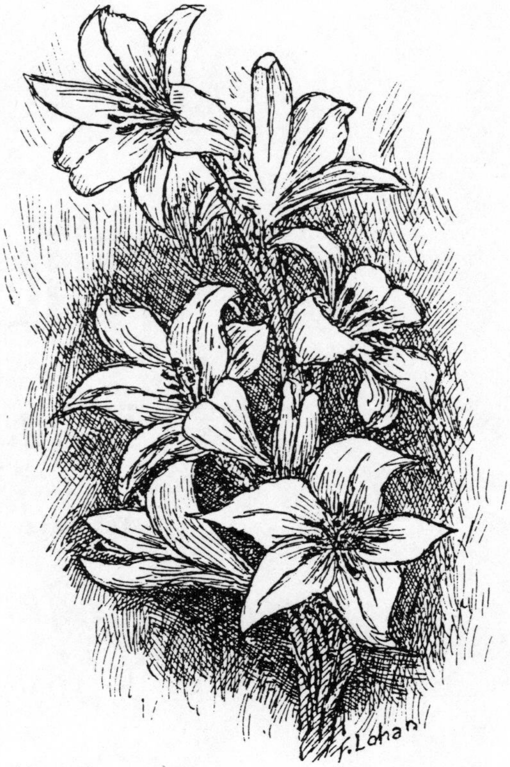

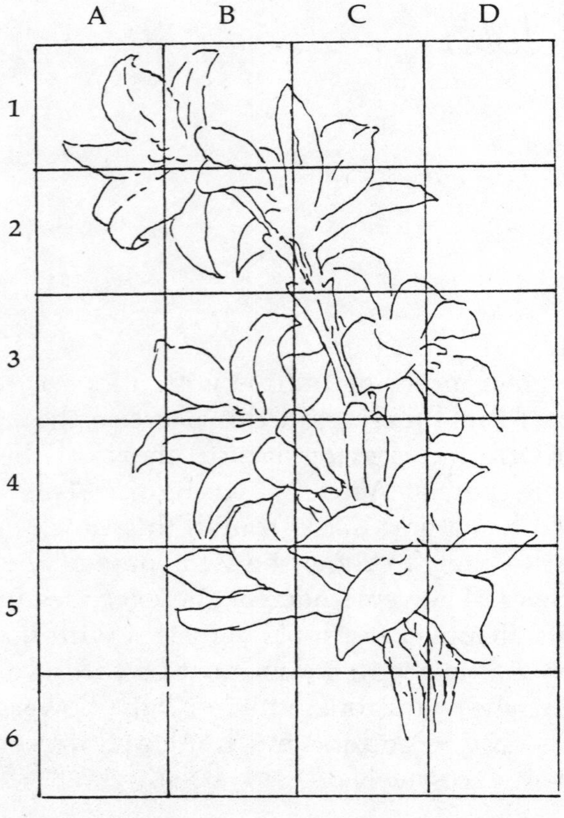

A B C D

1

2

3

4

5

6

Ⓓ Hatch and crosshatch the background.

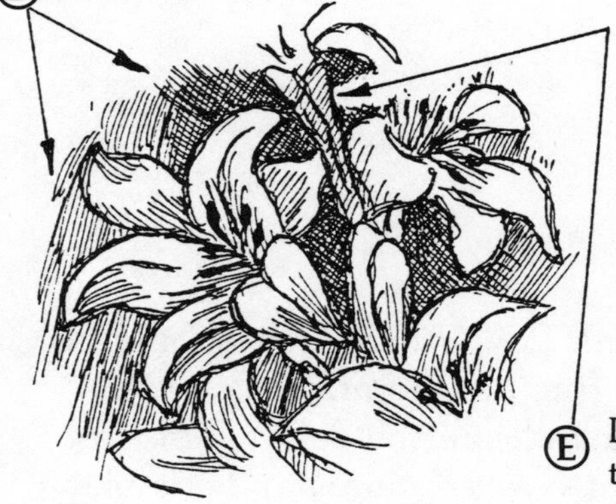

Ⓔ Lightly hatch the stems as the last step.

Figure 11-1
I used a 3×0 technical pen for this exercise. Use the pen lightly when you texture the flowers. They are white; the right amount of pen work will give that impression, but too much will destroy that impression.

Wild Strawberry

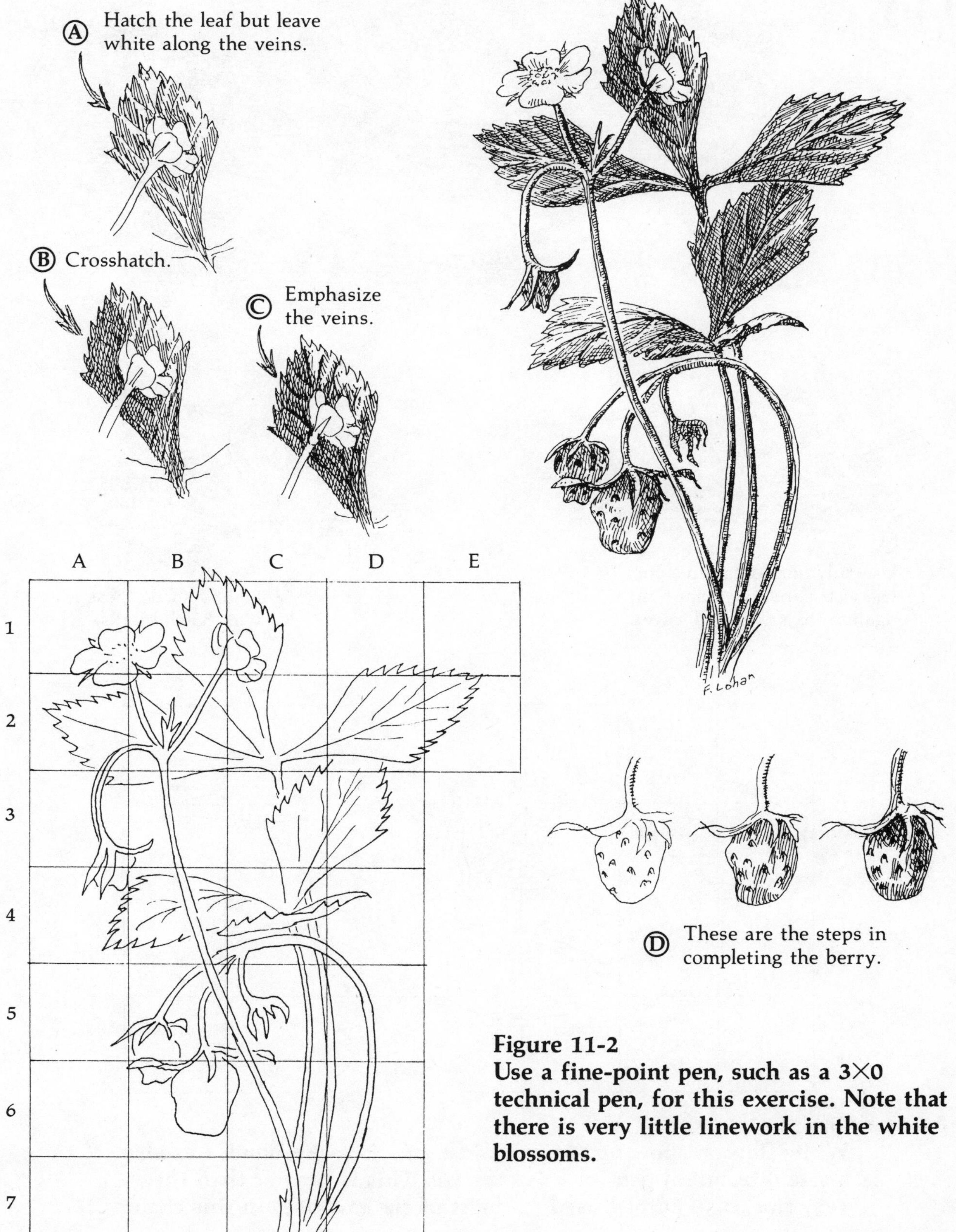
Ⓐ Hatch the leaf but leave white along the veins.
Ⓑ Crosshatch.
Ⓒ Emphasize the veins.
A
B
C
D
E
1
2
3
4
5
6
7
F. Lohan
Ⓓ These are the steps in completing the berry.

Figure 11-2
Use a fine-point pen, such as a 3×0 technical pen, for this exercise. Note that there is very little linework in the white blossoms.

Water Lily

Ⓐ Use only horizontal lines for the water and put them tight against the petals and leaves.

Ⓑ Lightly shade these leaves with hatch marks.

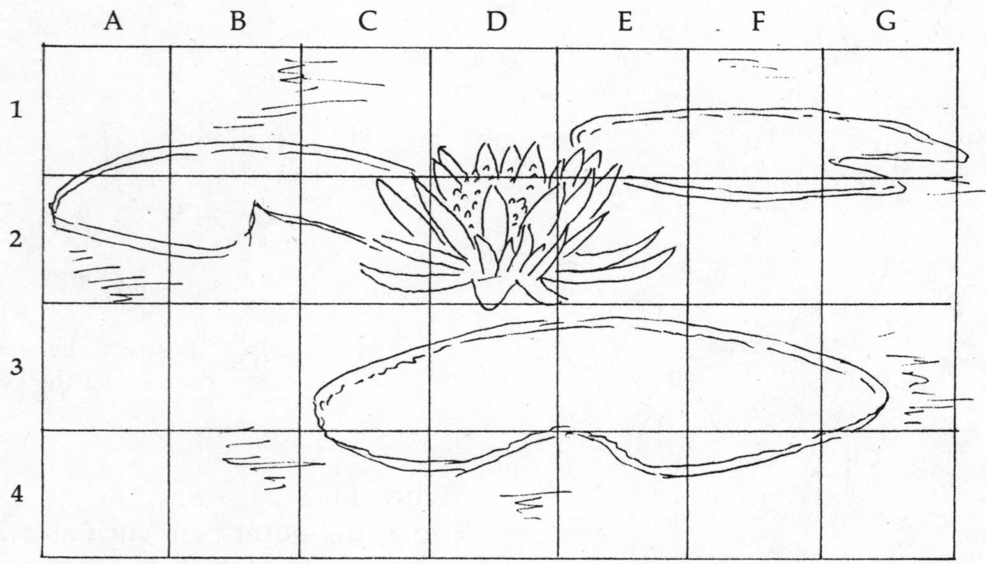
A B C D E F G
1
2
3
4

Figure 11-3
White flowers show up nicely against a dark background. I used a size 0 technical pen for this exercise. This is heavier than the very fine, 3×0 point I used for most of the exercises in this chapter.

Smooth Rose

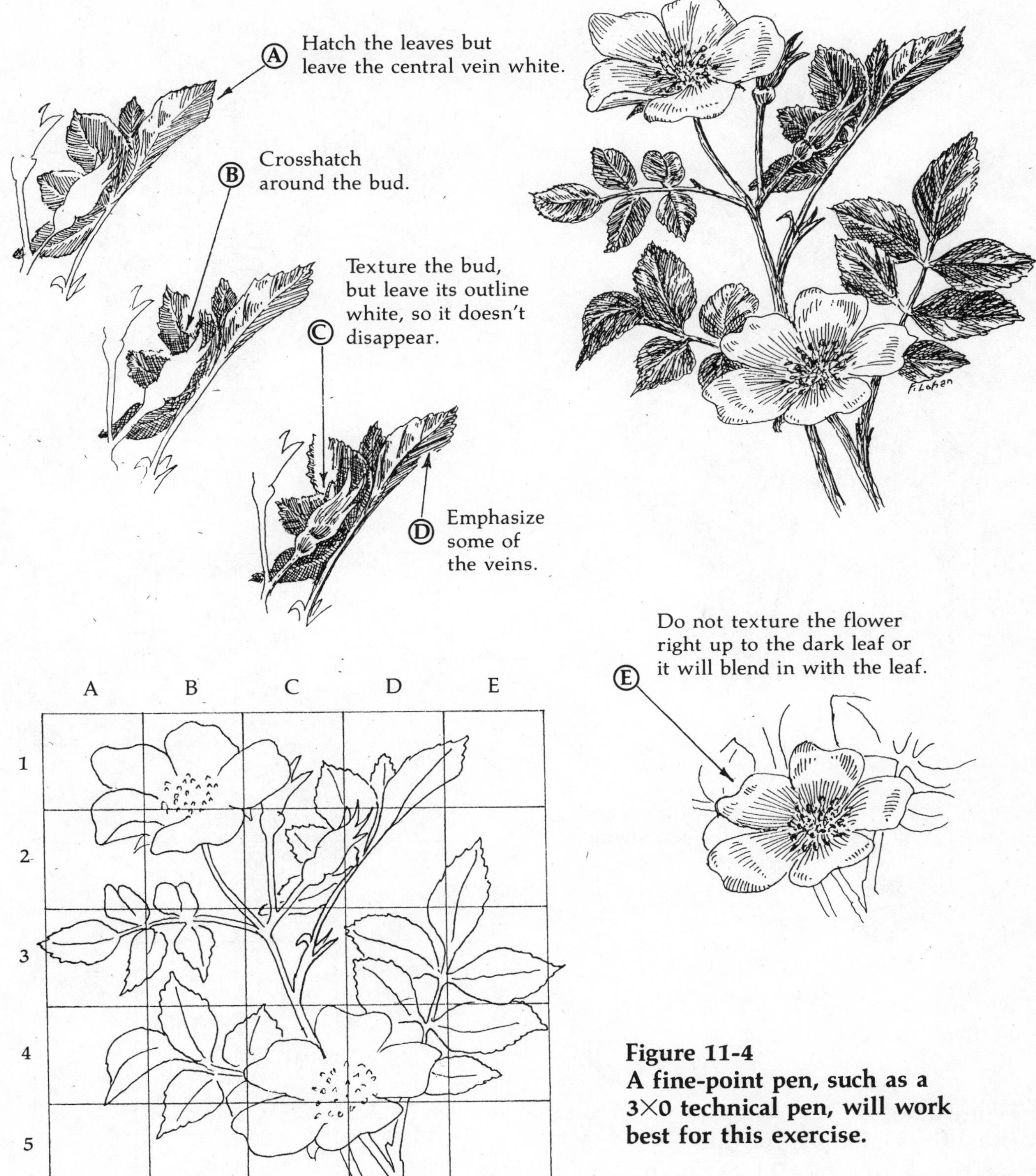
Ⓐ Hatch the leaves but leave the central vein white.
Ⓑ Crosshatch around the bud.
Ⓒ Texture the bud, but leave its outline white, so it doesn't disappear.
Ⓓ Emphasize some of the veins.
Ⓔ Do not texture the flower right up to the dark leaf or it will blend in with the leaf.
A
B
C
D
E
1
2
3
4
5
F. Lohan

Figure 11-4
A fine-point pen, such as a 3×0 technical pen, will work best for this exercise.

Common Violet

F. Cohen

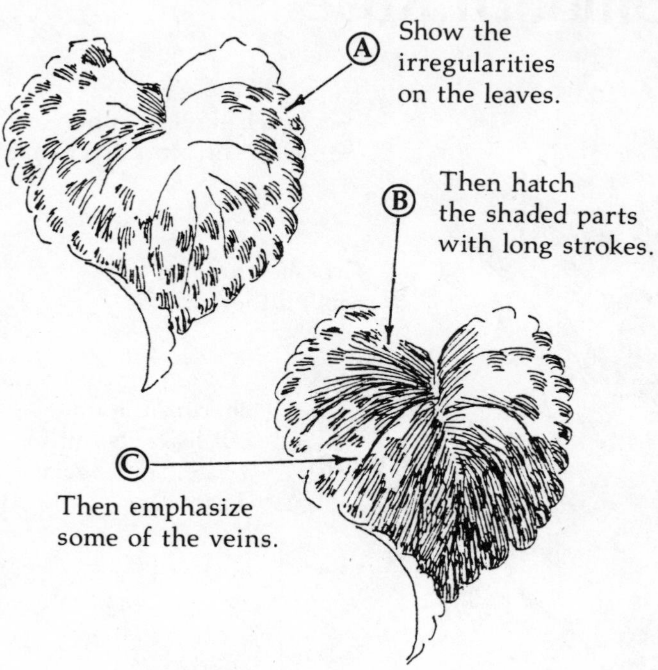
Ⓐ Show the irregularities on the leaves.
Ⓑ Then hatch the shaded parts with long strokes.
Ⓒ Then emphasize some of the veins.

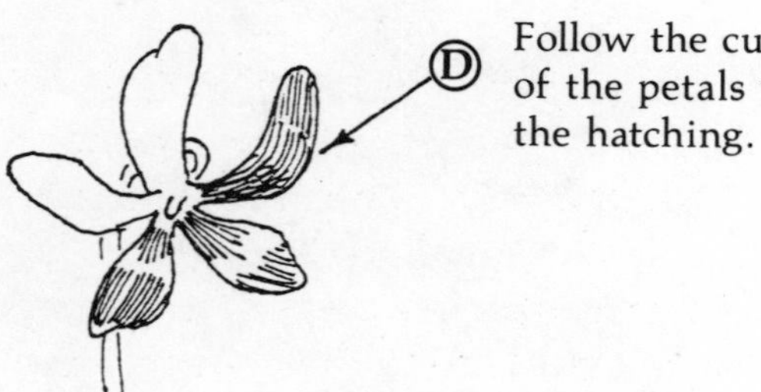
Ⓓ Follow the curve of the petals with the hatching.

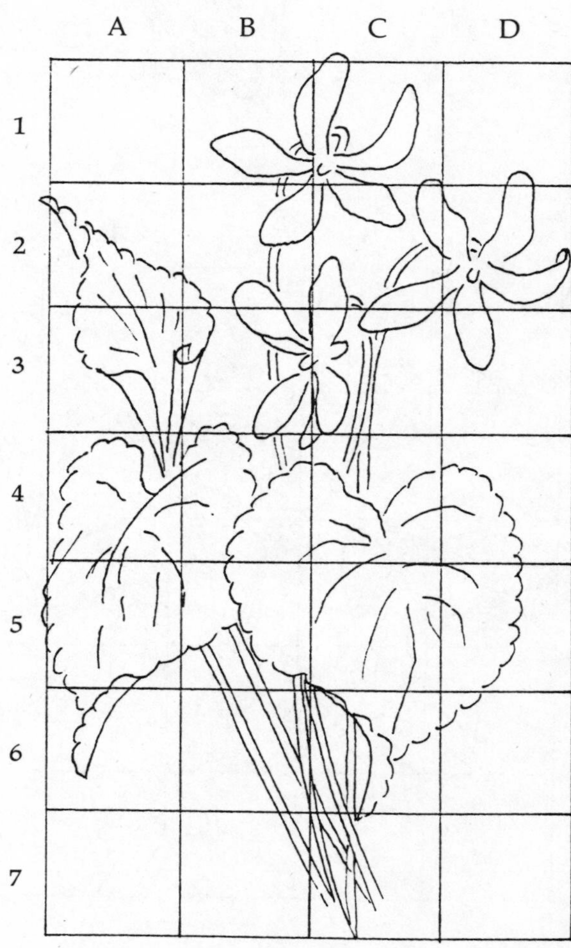
A
B
C
D
1
2
3
4
5
6
7

Figure 11-5
Use a fine-point pen for this exercise. I used a 3×0 technical pen.

12
Faces and Clothing

Facial Asymmetry
Facial Proportions
Rendering Faces
Wrinkles, Folds, and Creases in Clothing
Some Faces for Practice

The human face has few lines. The face's tonal variations are delicate and difficult, if not impossible, to fully capture with the pen. Usually line is necessary to help delineate the eyes, nose, and mouth, whereas pure tone would be used for this if you were dealing with any of the colored media or the pencil. There is a lot that you *can* accomplish with the pen, however, and the suggestions in this chapter will assist you in getting started on your own experimentation.

No face is completely symmetrical. There are slight differences in the size of each eye, in the cant of the nose, in the angle of the mouth in relation to the centerline of the face. Large deviations from symmetry lead to grotesque images; slight ones lead to realistic likenesses. If you are after capturing a specific likeness you must try to discern these deviations from symmetry, for they are the heart and soul of the subject's likeness. Caricaturists have learned to spot these deviations immediately, and they can almost magically capture a likeness by exaggerating these deviations.

Perhaps more than with any other subject matter, capturing a facial likeness requires the development of a sharp eye.

Facial Asymmetry

A
B
C

Figure 12-1
Very few human faces are truly symmetrical. There are differences between the left and right side of just about every face. Drawing A shows a pretty, symmetrical face, and B shows the same face with the eye opening on your right a little smaller than the other, and the half of the mouth on your right a little smaller than the other half.

When you are trying to capture a likeness, paying attention to small differences in facial symmetry is quite important. C shows a smile in which the mouth is slightly askew, a common feature.

Facial Proportions

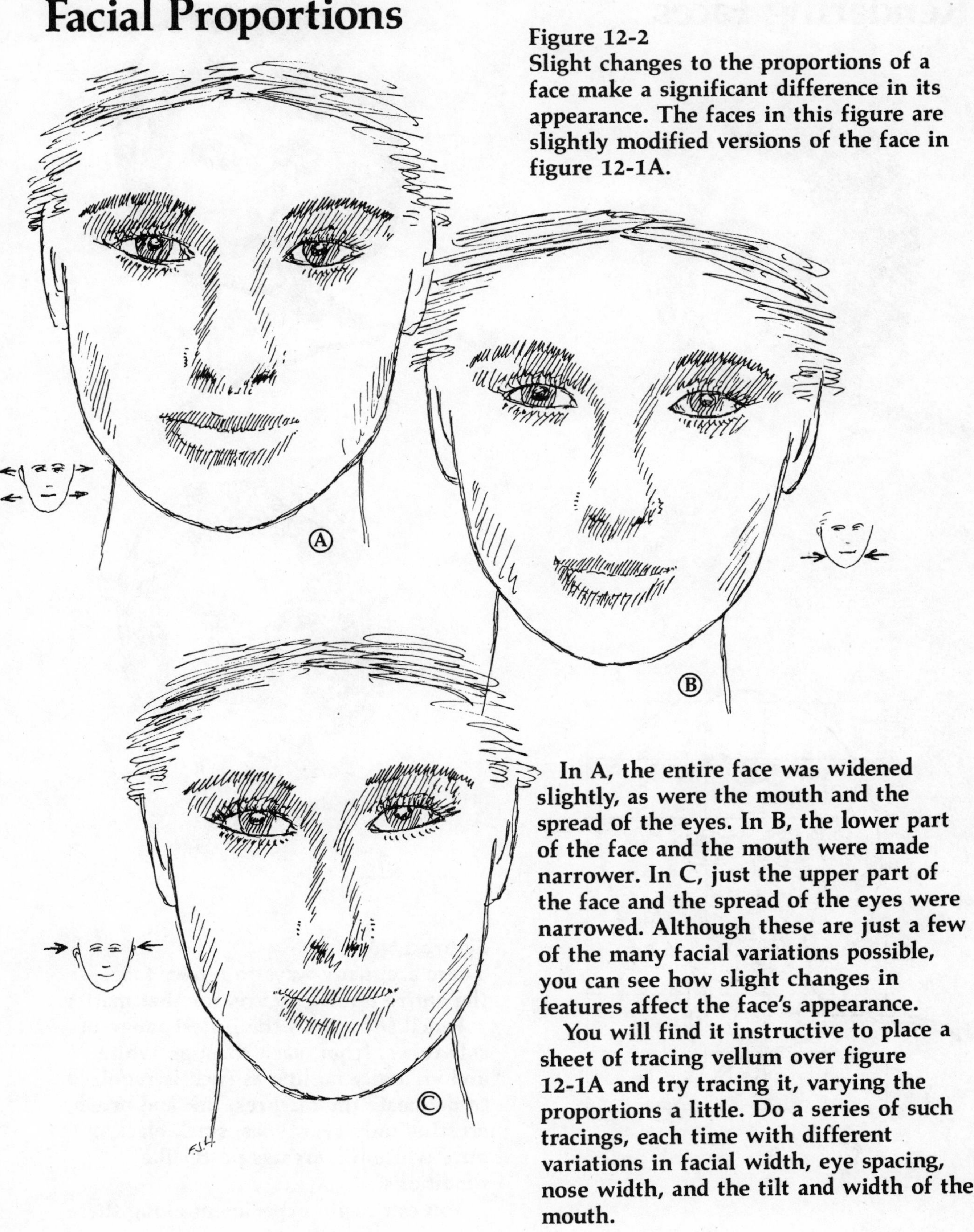
A
B
C

Figure 12-2
Slight changes to the proportions of a face make a significant difference in its appearance. The faces in this figure are slightly modified versions of the face in figure 12-1A.

In A, the entire face was widened slightly, as were the mouth and the spread of the eyes. In B, the lower part of the face and the mouth were made narrower. In C, just the upper part of the face and the spread of the eyes were narrowed. Although these are just a few of the many facial variations possible, you can see how slight changes in features affect the face's appearance.

You will find it instructive to place a sheet of tracing vellum over figure 12-1A and try tracing it, varying the proportions a little. Do a series of such tracings, each time with different variations in facial width, eye spacing, nose width, and the tilt and width of the mouth.

Rendering Faces

(A)

(B)
(D)

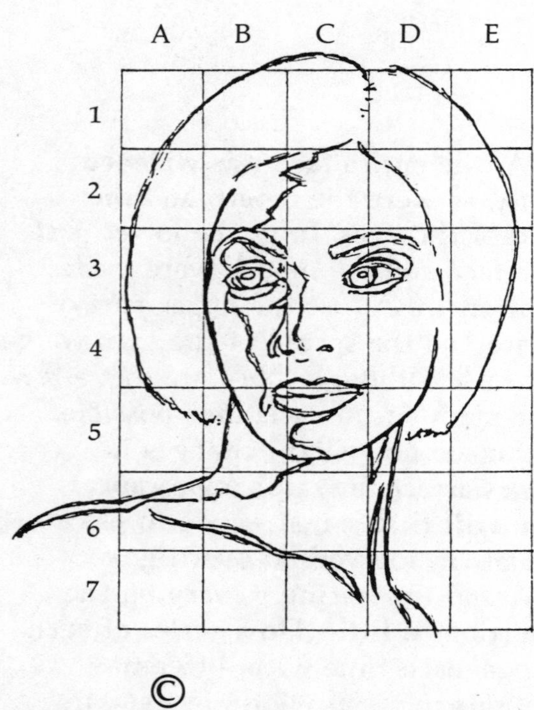
A B C D E
1
2
3
4
5
6
7
(C)

Figure 12-3
There are many ways to render faces—the entire human figure, for that matter.

Pencil (A) allows the fullest range of soft tones, from black through white, and virtually no line as such is required to delineate the features. Ink and brush, creating only two tones, stark black or pure white (B), creates posterlike renditions.

You can easily experiment along these

E
F
G
H

lines by using the gridded outline in C to create your own working outlines at whatever size pleases you. Place tracing vellum over your outline and try for yourself some of the variations shown in this figure.

D shows a medium-point pen rendering. E shows a rendering drawn with a fairly heavy pen. F and G show two additional approaches—drawn with a fine-point and a medium-point pen. In G, note the use of just vertical and horizontal lines in the crosshatching.

Small busts are good models to use for practice in sketching faces. Use a strong sidelight to create deep shadows on the face to help form the features (H). Another excellent source for models are the Sunday supplement clothing ads in your weekly newspaper.

Wrinkles, Folds, and Creases in Clothing

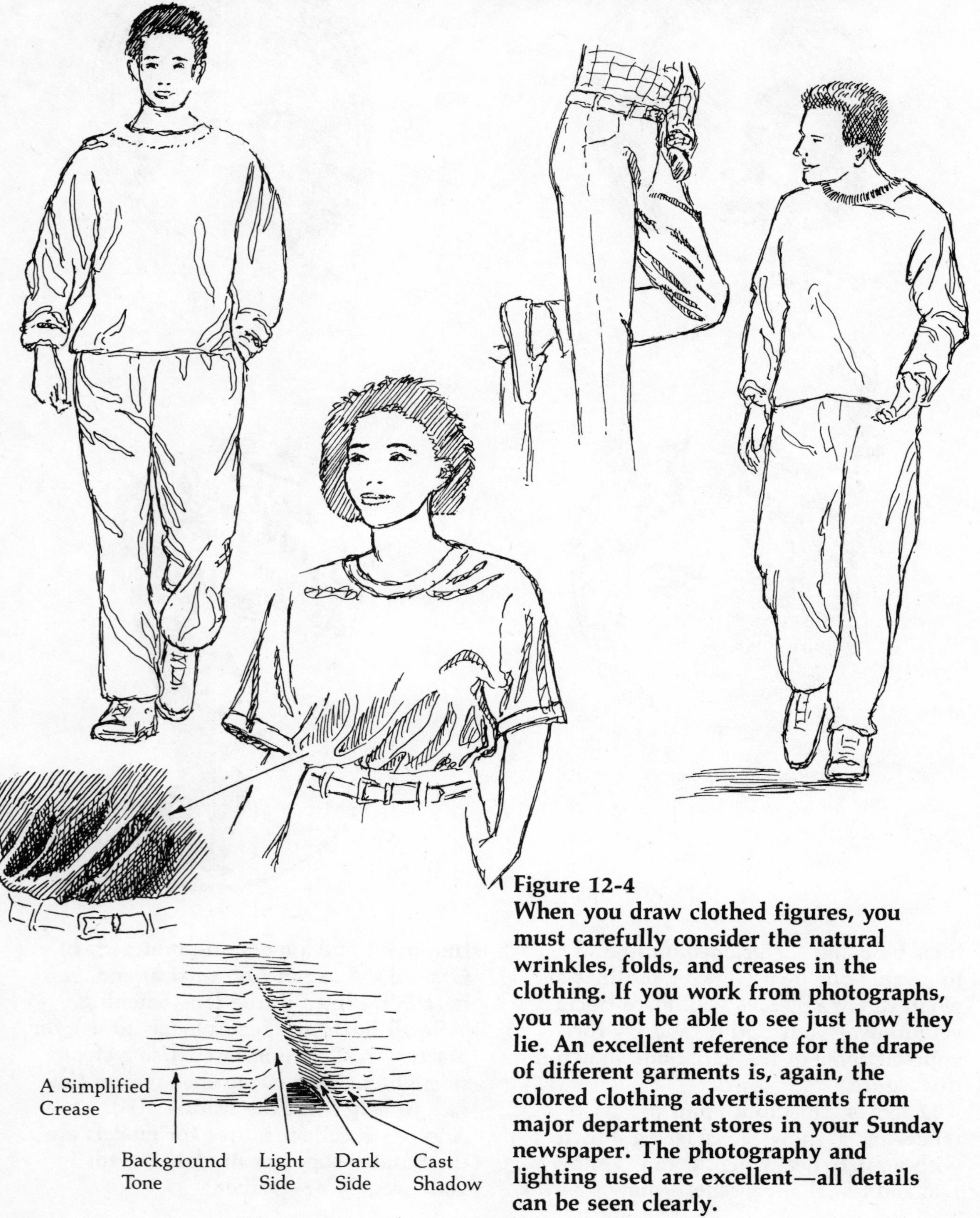
A Simplified Crease
Background Tone
Light Side
Dark Side
Cast Shadow

Figure 12-4
When you draw clothed figures, you must carefully consider the natural wrinkles, folds, and creases in the clothing. If you work from photographs, you may not be able to see just how they lie. An excellent reference for the drape of different garments is, again, the colored clothing advertisements from major department stores in your Sunday newspaper. The photography and lighting used are excellent—all details can be seen clearly.

Some Faces for Practice

A B C D E F G H
1 2 3 4 5 6 7 8
A B C D E
1 2 3 4 5 6 7
A B C D E
1 2 3 4 5 6 7
A B C D E F
1 2 3 4 5 6 7

Figure 12-5
Use these gridded outlines of faces to make copies for your practice of some of the things discussed in this chapter. Make the face a little narrower, then make one a little wider or more pointed, and so on. You will see the difference that small changes bring about.

13
On Your Own

No one can teach you to draw. You must learn to draw, perhaps assisted by the advice and suggestions of others like me, but nevertheless entirely on your own, through practice.

If you have a keen and solid interest in drawing, the necessary practice will not seem onerous, but rather delightful and rewarding in itself. The only path to proficiency in drawing lies through the thorny thicket of practice, practice, and more practice.

I hope this book has boosted the interest you must already have in drawing by providing you with some hints, suggestions, and shortcuts that will help you gain proficiency a little more quickly than you might have if you were completely on your own.

Draw whenever you have the urge to draw. Draw anything that appeals to you. Copy parts of the work of others to try to determine how they achieved a particular effect that appeals to you. The pen and the pencil are media easy to work with at a moment's notice—there is no time-consuming setup before you get going or cleanup after you finish a session the way there is with paints. Travel with your pens or pencils and a few three-by-five-inch, plain index cards, and you will be ready in seconds to sketch something that attracts your attention. Or use your photographs to draw scenes from places you have known and loved. If you have the interest in drawing you will improve with time simply by drawing. It is all up to you.

Bibliography

Blake, Wendon. *The Drawing Book*. New York: Watson Guptil, 1980.

Blake, Wendon, and Ferdinand Petrie. *Landscape Drawing*. New York: Watson Guptil, 1981.

Cole, Rex Vicat. *The Artistic Anatomy of Trees*. New York: Dover Publications Inc., 1965.

Hamm, Jack. *How to Draw Animals*. New York: Putnam Publishing Group, 1969.

Leslie, Clare Walker. *Nature Drawing: A Tool for Learning*. New Jersey: Prentice Hall, 1980.

Loomis, Andrew. *Drawing the Head and Hands*. New York: Viking Press, 1956.

Loomis, Andrew. *Creative Illustration*. New York: Viking Press, 1947.

Peck, Stephen Rogers. *Atlas of Human Anatomy for the Artist*. New York: Oxford University Press, 1951.

Pitz, Henry C. *How to Draw Trees*. New York: Watson Guptil, 1972.

Poore, Henry Rankin. *Composition in Art*. New York: Dover Publications, Inc., 1967.

Ruskin, John. *The Elements of Drawing and the Elements of Perspective*. New York: E. P. Dutton, 1907.

Additionally, there are hundreds of contemporary books on every aspect of drawing at your library and bookstores. Many are worth your perusal. Browse through them and spend some time with those that catch your fancy.

Other Books by Frank J. Lohan

Pen & Ink Techniques, Contemporary Books, Inc., Chicago, 1978.

This pen-and-ink sketching book for the beginner describes the materials required and gives ten basic step-by-step demonstrations as well as reference sketches covering a wide variety of subjects.

Pen & Ink Themes, Contemporary Books, Inc., Chicago, 1981.

This sketch-filled idea book shows artists how to look around themselves to find sources of subject matter to sketch.

Pen & Ink Sketching, Contemporary Books, Inc., Chicago, 1983, indexed.

Thirty-six step-by-step pen-and-ink demonstrations are included in this book. The subject matter covers barns, owls, raccoons, mountain lions, deer, ducks, songbirds, toads, stone lanterns, boats, and more.

Wildlife Sketching, Contemporary Books, Inc., Chicago, 1986, indexed.

Chapters on materials, drawing techniques, and basics of perspective introduce this book on how to sketch songbirds, trees, animals, flowers, mushrooms, water birds, reptiles, amphibians, and more. More than six hundred individual drawings are included to show the artist how to draw each subject in pencil and in pen.

Countryside Sketching, Contemporary Books, Inc., Chicago, 1989, indexed.

How to sketch American and British countryside landscapes, mountain scenes, rural structures, and much more with the pen and the pencil. Fundamentals are included for sketching trees, rocks, buildings, lakes, waterfalls, mountains, ruined castles, ancient stone circles, homesteads, and more. More than four hundred explanatory drawings show how you can draw such subjects.

Sketching Birds, Contemporary Books, Inc., Chicago, 1990, indexed.

After sections on tools and materials and drawing techniques, fifty-nine step-by-step lessons show the artist how to draw sparrows, baby robins, herons, ducks, geese, orioles, woodpeckers, sandpipers, ospreys, owls, hawks, and more with the pen and the pencil. A section on making your own notepaper from your drawings is included.

Sketching Cats, Contemporary Books, Inc., Chicago, 1991, indexed.

From kittens to Siberian tigers, ways to sketch many different felines with the pen and with the pencil are presented in sixty-three step-by-step lessons. Sections on tools and materials for sketching as well as on techniques for using them are included.

Index